LOST CLEOPATRA:
A TALE OF ANCIENT HOLLYWOOD

BY PHILLIP DYE

LOST CLEOPATRA: A TALE OF ANCIENT HOLLYWOOD
By Phillip Dye
Copyright © 2020 Phillip Dye
No part of this book may be reproduced in any form or by any means, electronic, mechanical, digital, photocopying, or recording, except for inclusion of a review, without permission in writing from the publisher or Author.

Published in the USA by:
BearManor Media
4700 Millenia Blvd.
Suite 175 PMB 90497
Orlando, FL 32839
www.bearmanormedia.com

Paperback ISBN: 978-1-62933-595-7
Case ISBN: 978-1-62933-596-4
BearManor Media, Orlando, Florida
Printed in the United States of America
Book design by Robbie Adkins, www.adkinsconsult.com

DEDICATION

To Liz, the vamp who stole my heart.

Acknowledgements

This book would not have been possible without the assistance, suggestions and input of many individuals and organizations. Kevin Brownlow, Hugh Munro Neely and the late Robert S. Birchard actively supported this project from the beginning. Valuable support also came from Andi Hicks of Timeline Films, film historians Roy Liebman, Anthony Slide and many others.

In writing this book, I depended heavily on those who researched the maze of information surrounding Theda Bara and William Fox before me. I am most grateful to Eve Golden and Ron Genini who cut through the tangles of misinformation for their biographies of Theda Bara. After much neglect from film historians, the story of William Fox was given just due by Vanda Krefft for her biography of Fox. I am also indebted to Merrill T. McCord and Aubrey Solomon for their books on the Fox Film Corporation, as well as others who researched and wrote on early Hollywood history.

I also thank Justin Leiber and the late F. Gwynplaine MacIntyre for the information they shared about actor Fritz Leiber; Mark Shoemaker of the Art Deco Society of Los Angeles for his article and additional information on Adolph Feil, who created jewelry for Theda Bara's Cleopatra; the late William Mann who granted me permission to use quotes from George James Hopkins's unpublished autobiography; Marc Wanamaker of Bison Archives for sharing his collection of stills with me; Jim Sleeper, who shared information about the filming in Balboa Bay; Eve Golden, whom I interviewed in part for this project; Alan Adler, formerly archivist at Twentieth Century Fox; Randy Bryan Bigham and Leslie DeBauche for information on Theda Bara working with Albert M. Lythgoe at the Metropolitan Museum of Art, Ned Comstock of the Cinematic Arts Library Archives at the USC Cinematic Arts Library and Archives, and Joan Craig Birdsall for sharing her reminisces and additional information on Theda Bara.

I am thankful for the additional support from my former film professor, Dr. Milton Timmons, Dorin Schumacher, Mary Ann Cade, Brinke Stevens, Ted Newsom, Byrone Caloz, Oliver Sheppard, Sophia Yoshida, Kevin Jordan, Susan Kurtz, Marina Loos, Jeff Lawson, Marjorie Margel, Sandy Lucas, Rosemary C. Harne, Kevin Jordan, Marilyn Slater, Dave Pleger, Glenn Andreiev, Jorge Finkielman, Eliza Leigh Vincz, Michael D. Mortilla, Bill Piper, and Frank Thompson.

I wish to thank Liz Standard for proofreading my manuscript with its uncounted typos and inexplicable grammatical errors, until she was taxed beyond human endurance.

I want to thank all the fine folks who assisted me at the Wisconsin Center for Film and Theater Research, the Library of Congress, the George Eastman

House, the UCLA Special Collections Library, the USC Special Collections Library, Cincinnati Public Library, Cleveland Public Library, the Newport Beach Library, the Billy Rose Collection at the New York Public Library, the Museum of Modern Art, the Kobal Collection, the Hollywood Heritage Museum, the National Film Information Service, Eddie Brandt's Saturday Matinee, and especially the Margaret Herrick Library at the Academy of Motion Pictures Arts and Sciences.

Unfortunately, in the course of working on this book, I suffered computer difficulties that wiped out many records of those with whom I communicated in regards to this project. As I am unable to express proper appreciation by naming them here, perhaps my profuse apologies and eternal gratitude can assuage their undying hatred and thirst for revenge for the omission.

Table of Contents

INTRODUCTION 1

CHAPTER ONE: A FOX THERE WAS 10

CHAPTER TWO: DESTINY'S DARK ANGEL 34

CHAPTER THREE: 'THE FLAMING COMET IN THE CINEMA . .66
FIRMAMENT'

CHAPTER FOUR: 'SHAKESPEARE—MODIFIED SLIGHTLY'. . . .102

CHAPTER FIVE: 'INTO A NEW WORLD'. .139

CHAPTER SIX: 'IN SUPPORT OF THE DIVINE THEDA'. 164

CHAPTER SEVEN: A DAY IN THE LIFE OF CLEOPATRA 190

CHAPTER EIGHT: 'WE CAN GET AWAY WITH MURDER HERE' . .222

CHAPTER NINE: 'DRESS YOUR USHERS IN ROMAN TOGAS'. . .247

CHAPTER TEN: 'IT'LL NEVER SHOW IN PENNSYLVANIA!'. 284

CHAPTER ELEVEN: 'TIE A CAN ON HER' 327

CHAPTER TWELVE: 'THE GRAND ILLUSION'. 358

CHAPTER THIRTEEN: THE END 390

NOTES 420

BIBLIOGRAPHY 456

INDEX 463

INTRODUCTION

Theda Bara as Cleopatra as the Sphinx. (Courtesy of Marc Wanamaker / Bison Archives)

THIS IS THE STORY OF *Cleopatra*, a motion picture made in 1917; how it was made, how it was received, how it was lost, and why its absence is such a tragedy. This is a true story, except for the parts that are not true.

The tale involves different personalities who became involved in the production, including Ruth St. Denis, one of the founders of modern dance; Anne Haviland, the 'famous psychic perfumist;' Edward Bernays, 'the father of public relations;' Major Funkhouser, the powerful Chicago censor; and

The guiding spirits behind Cleopatra. *J. Gordon Edwards, Theda Bara, and William Fox. Not pictured; the rarely photographed Adrian Johnson. (Author's collection)*

Topsy, the Army camel. However, the two dominant figures in the story of *Cleopatra* were its producer, William Fox, and its star, Theda Bara.

Both had similar backgrounds as the offspring of Jewish immigrants arriving in America during the great migration from Europe in the latter half of the Nineteenth Century. Yet they grew up in entirely different worlds. When they met, they would make some forty films together. Theirs was not a close collaboration; the two hardly ever spoke to one another, but they were instrumental in the rise of Fox Film Company. This would not have existed without William Fox, but would Fox have prospered as fast without Theda Bara? Her popularity as a man-devouring vamp bankrolled the company's expansion to California and the epic that would be *Cleopatra*. This is also the story of the spectacular rise and downfall of the careers of both Fox and Bara.

Two important figures will seem to get short shrift. Although not absent from the story, there will be little information on the screenwriter, Adrian Johnson, and the director, J. Gordon Edwards, because so little information is available. Even before the auteur theory that claimed directors were the 'authors' of the films they made, leading directors were names with which to be reckoned. They actively promoted themselves as great artists, such as D. W. Griffith, Cecil B. DeMille and Herbert Brenon. In contrast, Edwards' press statements followed the party line of Fox promotional material. He rarely talked about himself, preferring to dwell in the shadow of William Fox and the stars of his pictures. He gave few interviews and wrote no autobiography. His early death and the loss of most of his films have relegated him to footnotes of film history, instead of crediting him as one of the leading filmmakers of the era. Consequently, almost all information about his moviemaking techniques come second hand, filtered through articles about his productions or reminisces of those he with whom he worked.

There's even less information about Adrian Johnson, who had been one of the top writers of early Fox films, but who generated hardly any press attention. Fortunately, as reticent as he was with the press, he was quite verbose in writing notes in the *Cleopatra* scenario and other scenarios, giving marvelous insights into the pre-production preparations of *Cleopatra*.

As a student filmmaker, I had learned film history, and as a history buff, I had become fascinated by old movies, especially silent films. Having read in Daniel Blum's *A Pictorial History of the Silent Screen* (1974) about the fabled temptress Theda Bara, bestowed with an imaginative and imaginary biography, I naturally wanted to see some of her films. At the Silent Movie Theater in Los Angeles, I would write in the request book asking for *Cleopatra*, *Salome* (1918), and other of her movies to be shown. One evening, the theater manager Laurence Austin, who introduced each show, responded to my requests by reporting to the audience that someone had been pestering for *Cleopatra* to be shown. He regretted he could not show the film; no one could. Every print of it had been lost, along with almost every other film Bara had made. There was an audible gasp, or rather a collective sigh of sadness from the audience as if he had announced the death of the star herself. In a way, he had.

I was saddened but also stunned. I knew that many silent movies had been lost over the years. Until then, I had not thought that such major films as *Cleopatra* were gone. When I started research for an article on Bara, I discovered it was true. Although she had been one of the leading movie stars of her era, hardly any of her films survive.

It might have ended there, but while doing research at the Academy of Motion Pictures Arts and Sciences Margaret Herrick Library, I found in

Before the Roaring Twenties, Theda Bara created a sensation with her risqué screen behavior, such as wearing this infamous outfit in Cleopatra. *(Author's collection)*

their collection more than one hundred production still photos from the lost *Cleopatra*, hinting at the glorious film that once had been. These gave, I thought, a good impression of what the movie must have looked like. That's how this book came about.

The glamorous era of silent cinema was the 1920s. Arthur Knight, in his book *The Liveliest Art* (1957), dismissed the entire period from 1914 to 1919 as best forgotten, with the exception of D.W. Griffith's first epics and 'Charlie' Chaplin's comedies. Many of the surviving films of the period seem clunky and poorly made compared to their successors of the 1920s. Yet it was actually a critical era in the history of cinema. This period of time saw the displacement of the film pioneers. It saw the rise of both the studio system and the star system, which would dominate the motion picture industry for decades. It saw feature films dominate movie screens. It saw the choosing of southern California as the center for film production when it could have easily ended up elsewhere. It saw the changing of 'Hollywood' from the name of a small town to the name of the American film industry.

Although it was the top box office release of 1918, one might hesitate to call *Cleopatra* a landmark film, following so close on the heels of D.W. Griffith's *The Birth of a Nation* (1915) and *Intolerance* (1916). Even so, *Cleopatra* was hardly a typical picture, nor was the lead player a typical star. Yet through the merging of star power and industrialization of filmmaking, the epic thus created symbolized the glitz and hoopla of Hollywood. Through the story of the making of this picture, one can see the formation of the idea of 'Hollywood'; not just as a center of American motion picture production, but as the glamor capital of the world. I propose to tell this story by highlighting one movie, one production company, one movie mogul, and one movie star.

Necessarily, I am obliged to pass over the influence of foreign cinema and the other major American studios. I will briefly describe other production activities at Fox. I will mention major figures such as D.W. Griffith, Charles Chaplin, William S. Hart, and Mary Pickford as touchstones to tell the story, ignoring the countless other filmmakers, actors, and technicians who deserve mention, but this book is too damn long already.

Sometimes, the era in which *Cleopatra* was made is referred to as a bucolic time of innocence. Yet the end of the Gilded Age in America was tarnished and peeling, revealing a much crueler world beneath. Race relations were at their nadir. African-Americans had been stripped of their civil rights. Race riots and lynchings were not uncommon. There was a tremendous gap between the rich and the poor. Child labor and abysmal working conditions were normal. Labor disputes were frequently violent. Women were denied many rights, and suffragettes campaigned for women's right to vote. Across the border, the Mexican Revolution was claiming hundreds of thousands of lives.

Over everything hovered the First World War, which looked like Armageddon, as the wonderful inventions of the past decades became weapons of destruction. Some wondered whether civilization itself would survive the bitter fruits of the modern age.

Some filmmakers tackled heavy social issues such as racism, venereal disease, abortion, forced prostitution, alcoholism, drug abuse, graft, and corruption. Most others preferred to make—and many moviegoers preferred to watch—prosaic movies made with sweet ingénues and handsome heroes, with love triumphant, good defeating caricatured evil, and con-

For Cleopatra, *Theda Bara actively participated in the writing of the script, did research for her role, helped designed her costumes, and even personally commissioned a jeweler to make jewelry for the part. (Courtesy of the UCLA Special Collections Library)*

trived happy endings. No wonder W.C. Fields called Hollywood a gold cap on a rotten tooth.

When Bara's film career ended, she wanted everyone to know that she was not the Theda Bara of film fantasy, but just a nice Jewish girl from Cincinnati. Many Bara biographers fell for this trap, blaming the Fox press agents' hyperbole for painting her as 'the most mysterious woman living.' Even as a child, Bara was a strange little girl, and things got weirder as she became an adult. The 'nice girl from Cincinnati' may have been just another of the facades she put up, concealing the enigma that was and is Theda Bara.

As a consequence of the Fox publicity campaign, Bara has been long regarded as a fraud and as a joke. Worse, several film historians have concluded she was a lousy actress who only lasted as long as she did thanks to the Fox publicity campaign. While whether she was a good or bad actress is purely subjective, the absence of most of her films prevents mod-

A reviewer said, "Theda Bara's conception of the role of Cleopatra is daring, vivid and picturesque." (Author's collection)

ern viewers from reaching their own conclusions. One is stuck with the reviews of her films, which are all over the map regarding her acting abilities. Some reviewers absolutely loathed her, while others praised her to the skies. Take your pick.

Similarly, William Fox has been neglected for his leading roles in the battle with the monopolistic Motion Picture Patents Company and in the building of the American film industry. After he was sidelined from the business, Hollywood insiders and then film historians dismissed him as a crass, uncouth, and uneducated 'pants presser.' Fortunately, recent scholarly books on Fox portray him as a driven, if flawed, entrepreneur who helped shape the Hollywood studio system, leading American cinema to dominate the world market.

A word of caution. Just as the historical Cleopatra was subject to a misinformation campaign blackening her reputation (causing the infamy unintentionally which made her famous today), practically all the information about Fox, Bara, and the movie *Cleopatra* is suspect.

Even Theda Bara, in her unpublished autobiography, and William Fox, in the biography he never intended to be published, distorted the truth and frequently engaged in bald-faced lies. Doubt is even cast on some accounts readily accepted as authentic. Going past the falsehoods of Fox press releases, journalistic integrity was not particularly strong in newspapers of the 'teens, and in entertainment reporting, it was practically nil.

Other sources are just as suspect. Raoul Walsh, in his autobiography and in interviews, turned out to be a frequent liar. He probably assumed (or didn't care) that many of his statements would easily be proven false with very little research. Consequently, many of the statements made by nearly everyone involved in this story must be taken with a grain of salt. One must guardedly sift through the gravel of falsehoods to find nuggets of truth. Instead of considering the possibility that a statement is untrue, I urge the reader to consider the likelihood it is untrue. It's hard to fact check when everyone is lying.

This is not to say everyone is lying all of the time. Some lapses are from faulty memory, especially of those reminiscences about events decades earlier, possibly the case with Raoul Walsh. When Robert Hamilton Ball interviewed Theda Bara in 1949 on her work in *Cleopatra* as well as *Romeo and Juliet* (1916), he referenced magazine articles, purportedly written by her for *The Forum*, such as 'How I Became a Film Vampire.' Bara could not recollect writing these articles, leading Ball to "suspect they were ghosted or the effusions of the publicity department." Yet these articles have served as the primary sources on Bara for her biographers.

"Almost everything in print on the Bara name is wrong," concluded Ball.

However, the articles in question were published after Bara left Fox when she was no longer serving under his publicity machine. It is likely she wrote them herself or at least approved of them, and in the decades since, she had merely forgotten about it. Not that everything she wrote in the articles was true.

Then again, some of the more dubious claims have also been revealed to be true. Most biographers of Bara concluded that her pre-WW1 European travels were just invented embellishments to liven up a lackluster theatrical career. Researchers for Timeline Films discovered a document proving she indeed returned from Europe in 1910. Newspaper columnist Louella Parsons in her 1944 memoir, *The Gay Illiterate*, describes one notorious interview conducted with Bara in a Chicago hotel room. Several Bara biographers concluded it never happened, partly because Bara herself denied it. However, Bara describes the interview almost exactly the same way, but from a different perspective, in her unpublished memoir.

For decades, there was little reliable material on William Fox, Theda Bara, and the films they made, obscured by their lies and the lies issued by the Fox publicity department. In recent years, much material has come to light, including the memoir attributed to Bara (film historian Robert S. Birchard thought it was ghostwritten—but I wonder if anyone would hire a ghostwriter who would make so many typos). Whether the new information is reliable is anyone's guess. So amid the hoopla, ballyhoo, tommyrot, and balderdash, keep a slightly open mind.

For example, I can't prove Theda Bara was or wasn't the reincarnation of the original Cleopatra. I can only quote press reports that said she claimed she was. The reader will have to conclude whether it was something a reporter made up, or it was a press release for Fox publicity which Bara had no part in, or that she made the statement under instructions from her press agents, or that she made the claim herself and was pulling everyone's leg, or she actually believed she was the reincarnation of Cleopatra, or she actually was Cleopatra reborn. Who can say for certain?

If I can't completely sort the wheat from the chaff, I can assure you that it is quite tasty chaff, and if not entirely nutritious, makes for excellent roughage.

So let us go back to a time in ancient history, an era of ruthless empire builders, loyal and industrious lieutenants, conniving cohorts, and a beautiful, ambitious queen, and the movie they made about old-timers with similar pursuits.

Most of all, I want you to want to imagine the fabulous epic that was *Cleopatra*, the biggest blockbuster release of 1918. It remains a symbol of the glamor of early Hollywood that still beguiles and fascinates a century later.

You'll have to imagine it, for the movie no longer exists.

CHAPTER ONE: A FOX THERE WAS

William Fox (Author's collection)

Thomas Alva Edison is often credited with the invention of the motion picture. The origins of motion picture are actually more complex than that. No matter: Edison owned the important patents.

Even as the novelty of moving pictures delighted the public, the Wizard of Menlo Park failed to grasp the potentials of this new form of media. He regarded motion pictures as no more than a toy—that his peepshow machines called kinetoscopes would be like his phonograph, that it would grace a few parlors and penny arcades showing minute-long films, and nothing more. However, kinetoscopes and their one-minute movies became obsolete with the introduction of the movie projector, which allowed many people to see a film at the same time. To Edison's chagrin, rival producers capitalized on the growing public fascination with the new gizmo. Initially, he tried to stamp out the competition with a storm of litigation. That took time and money, and the Patents War, as it became known, quickly turned ugly. Hired thugs assaulted film crews, cameras were smashed, and there were even shoot-outs behind the cameras instead of in front of them. The beginning of the American film industry was marked with violence.

Edison realized the ineffectiveness of court action against rogue producers, and violence just made things worse. Changing tactics, he united his Edison Films with the other biggest film competitors (Kleine, American Pathé, Vitagraph, Essanay, American Biograph, Kalem, Lubin, Selig Polyscope, and Méliès's Star Film Paris) and formed the Motion Pictures Patents Company in 1908. This Trust announced it had the sole right to make and distribute motion pictures in the United States.

The Trust not only produced the majority of films made, but it also controlled the patents for projectors. Movie theater operators had to pay a weekly license fee of two dollars to show Trust films—and only Trust films—or they would be shut out of the market and forced out of business. The plan was to cut off independent producers from the exhibitors. The Patents Company also had an exclusive agreement with the largest manufacturer of raw stock, Eastman Kodak. This denied unlicensed producers the film they needed to make their movies, forcing them to buy more expensive foreign stock. The Trust had the motion picture business sewn up tight. Or so they thought.

After the general mechanics of motion pictures had been developed, the forefront of cinema moved to exhibition, where theater owners saw first-hand what the public enjoyed most in their film fare. Vaudeville theaters screened short films to supplement the live performances, though some managers regarded movies as 'chasers.' These were bland 'flickers' used to bore the audience into leaving after the main show, making room for a new paying audience.

By the turn of the century, there were theaters that showed only motion pictures. Called 'nickelodeons' or 'nickelettes' in the United States, because the admission was 5¢, these were usually storefront shops or business offices converted into small theaters. All that was needed was a projector on one end of the room, a screen—sometimes a mere sheet—hung at the other, and chairs or benches in between. Musical accompaniment might come in the form of someone playing a piano, or movies were just run in silence.

These makeshift theaters showed a variety of films in one sitting, each film rarely longer than a dozen minutes. Thousands of short movies were literally cranked out to meet the demand. Some nickelodeons advertised 'Shows changed daily.'

Even though created under the auspices of American inventor-hero Edison, the motion picture industry itself was not considered respectable, since much of the product had mostly lowbrow appeal. Moreover, to battle the Trust, it required a lot of moxie and *chutzpah*; words used in urban ghettos where the latest wave of immigrants and their offspring, fighting in the hardscrabble of slum life, seized the initiative in the vacuum that respectable businessmen disdained.

"Every section of the city was represented," reported *The New York Daily Tribune* on the first meeting of the Motion Picture Association of Theater Owners in 1908 "Chubby-faced Irishmen with clay pipes between their teeth were there, as well as Hungarians, Italians, Greeks, and just a handful of Germans, but the greater portion of the assembly were Jewish-Americans, who practically control the enterprise."

Most proprietors have been forgotten, but a few of the Jewish immigrant entrepreneurs became legendary. Ben Warner of Poland settled in Youngstown, Ohio, and gambled the family's meager savings to buy a nickelodeon in 1903. He let his sons run the business. In 1918, the Warner brothers ventured into production. In 1906, Carl Laemmle from Germany quit his job as a bookkeeper and started one of the first movie theaters in Chicago. He went into distribution and production, founding Universal Pictures. Lazar Mayer from Russia gave up his profitable junk and scrap business to buy and renovate a run-down nickelodeon in 1907. After building up the largest movie theater chain in New England, he moved first into distribution (making a fortune with *The Birth of a Nation*), and then into production. He changed his name to Louis B. Mayer. Marcus Loew, son of Austrian immigrants, partnered with Hungarian immigrant Adolph Zukor in owning a chain of peepshow penny arcades. They expanded into owning nickelodeons, and then they went their separate ways. Zukor founded the Famous Players film company, which later became Paramount Pictures. In the 1920s, Loew bought and unified the production companies of Metro, Goldwyn and Louis B. Mayer, creating MGM.

Technically, William Fox was an immigrant. He had been born in Tulcheva, Hungary, around 1878. His parents, Michael Fuchs and wife Anna Fried, brought him to America when he was an infant. William Fox knew the immigrant ghetto New York's Lower East Side as his childhood home. It was a hard life. He was the first of thirteen children, of whom only six survived to adulthood. Although the family had taken the Fox name (possibly assigned them by immigration authorities to 'Americanize' them; William had been re-named from Wilhelm or Vilmos or even Melech: 'King') they remained devoutly Orthodox German-Jews. William was expected to attend Hebrew school.

As a young child, William fell off an ice truck and broke his left arm in three places. Since his family was unable to afford proper medical care, he was taken to a local doctor who removed the elbow joint. Fox's arm remained stiff and useless for the rest of his life. Yet he was so driven to excel in spite of it that he played stickball with greater determination with his remaining good arm, and after becoming an adult, played one-armed golf better than his unimpaired opponents.

At nine years old, William Fox operated a pushcart, peddling candy, newspapers, umbrellas, and his father's homemade shoe polish. By age eleven, he dropped out of school, lying about his age so he could work twelve hour days in a garment factory alongside his father. Lacking labor unions or any government oversight, garment sweatshops were hellish workplaces of long hours, minuscule wages, and abominable conditions. Yet a man with drive could get ahead. William Fox started as a cloth sponger. Soon, he was a foreman over a dozen garment cutters, taking home seventeen dollars a week and becoming the main wage earner for his family. He paused only on his thirteenth birthday, faking illness so he could take time off work to attend his own Bar Mitzvah. Aside from that, he drove himself furiously. He worked six days a week, putting in an additional five hours on Sunday. His father did not share William's zeal for work and advancement.

"My father . . . was just as happy when he worked as when he didn't work. He never worried," William recalled bitterly. "I did the worrying, I did the bargaining for food."

His bitterness against his father was so great that after his father's death in 1936, he reportedly spat on the coffin and muttered, "You son of a bitch."

William Fox was a man driven by inner demons. As a film producer, he frequently approved of screenplays, then called scenarios, that depicted fathers as shiftless, lazy, corrupt, or criminal.

"Every penny was something I denied myself," Fox remembered, "with the thought in mind that if I was going forward, I had to have money. Capital was what I needed."

"Long years of poverty made him join the Socialist Party," noted one writer in 1951 when reviewing Fox's career. "He left it as soon as he accumulated his first hundred dollars which ranked him among the capitalists."

Fox had other aspirations than just being in the rag trade. As a teenager, he teamed with comedian Cliff Gordon in a vaudeville act, the Schmaltz Brothers, but without success. However, his experience on stage, and more importantly, backstage, as the Schmaltz Brothers' manager and agent, may have guided his sudden career shift.

Amid the cutthroat competition and appalling conditions of the sweatshops, William Fox clawed his way up. He took another pause to get married at the claimed age of twenty-one to Eva Leo, sixteen, to whom he had proposed on their second date. Fox was a young man in a hurry. When he asked his boss for a $3 raise, as he had a wife to support and was only earning $20 a week, his boss told him that $20 was $2 more a week than he was worth. So Fox quit.

His hard work and penny-pinching had paid off, as he amassed enough money to invest in a business. Some sources claim Fox opened his own garment factory, the Knickerbocker Cloth Examining and Shrinking Company, but according to film historian Merrill T. McCord, Fox never owned his own garment business.

Having seen Edwin Porter's exciting and then groundbreaking film, *The Great Train Robbery* (Edison, 1903), Fox wanted to become involved in motion pictures in some way. It is a matter of speculation whether he was more inspired by the artistry of the film or by the long lines of moviegoers eagerly paying to see it. In 1904, he combined with two partners, each contributing $1,666, to pay $5,000 for a Brooklyn penny arcade that included kinetoscopes, with a 146-seat nickelodeon on the third floor. They supposedly bought it from J. Stuart Blackton, a film pioneer of the Vitagraph Company.

"It was a strictly commercial proposition," Fox recalled years later, "I was looking for an outlet for my business acumen which hadn't found sufficient expression in the cloth examining and shrinking business."

For all of his business acumen, Fox soon found out he had been hoodwinked. Blackton had hired people to pack the house, to give the impression of a profitable establishment. The next day, Fox had only two customers. Realizing he was in danger of going broke, and galled at being conned by a 'goy,' Fox was undeterred. At the suggestion of a friend, he hired carnival performers to perform magic tricks outside the theater to attract attention.

"The sword swallower did swallow a sword. I do not know how he did it. I suppose it was one of those collapsible things. I thought it was going right through. Soon a crowd gathered, and then he said he was concluding his performance upstairs. It was two flights up, and the crowd followed him up."

When the performers finished their acts, Fox showed some 'meaningless' film footage, but even with that, the audience was hooked.

"I remember distinctly, when in the first picture the wind blew through the leaves of the trees, hearing an old fellow say, 'They can't fool me, gol dern 'em; I know someone is shaking the screen.'"

Fox charged no admission for a week, building up a clientele. After he started charging, the audiences kept coming. Fox increased profits by giving change to customers in pennies—then had coin-operated vending machines and kinetoscopes lined up at the exits to encourage patrons to spend a little more money on their way out. Turning an unprofitable theater into a profitable one, Fox went on to buy nickelodeons and vaudeville theaters until he had twenty-five theaters in Brooklyn and Manhattan. These were all small theaters with under 299 seats to avoid pesky fire regulations required of larger theaters. When he did acquire bigger theaters, it required connections with Tammany Hall politicians as business partners to clear the proper permits with the fire commissioner.

According to Fox, he bought an old burlesque theater in the Williamsburg section of Brooklyn. It was miserably run down, with gaping holes in the roof and an orchestra pit full of water. Fox had to bargain with the authorities to get permits for renovation, but he knew the biggest renovation had to be in the minds of local residents, who called the theater 'The Bum.' By circulating handbills throughout the neighborhood, he convinced the locals that it was Williamsburg residents themselves being insulted by the appellation, rallying them to defend the honor of their community. He recalled on opening night "ten thousand people marched down Grand Street with ten bands playing. Yes, sir! And the people carried banners. One of 'em read, 'We are the Respectable People of Williamsburg.' That was the last ever heard of 'The Bum.' It has been a family theatre ever since."

Fox was determined not to just clean up one theater, but keep all his theaters clean and friendly to the family trade, and safe for mothers bringing their children. That did not just include the theaters themselves but the content of the shows.

"I would not allow anything on the stage and screen that I was unwilling to have my wife and daughters see."

"I catered to the family trade and made the discovery that the greatest existing enemy of the saloon and the dive is the motion picture theatre. As proof positive of this, the many saloons in the vicinity of my movie theatres found business so unprofitable that they closed their doors, so that, unwittingly, I became a reformer."

For ten weeks, Fox hired a genuine reformer, Carrie Nation, the champion of temperance, to lecture about the hazards of demon rum and talk about her exploits. She made a little money on the side selling souvenir toy hatchets, reminders of her well-publicized attacks on saloons. Also against tobacco, Nation flew into a rage when she once caught Fox smoking a cigar. To mollify her, Fox gave up tobacco while she made a very profitable tour of his theaters, but returned to the demon weed when she was gone—in fact, he was rarely seen in public without a cigar.

If not quite a reformer, Fox was certainly open to innovation. He himself was not an idea man, but he knew a good idea when he heard it. The songwriters of 'Tin Pan Alley' sent singers called 'pluggers' to sing their new songs at vaudeville theaters and nickelodeons. They hoped to coax audiences into buying their sheet music. One of the more enterprising of them came up with photo slides that projected the lyrics on the movie screen, so audiences could sing along with the plugger. Out of all the exhibitors in New York, only William Fox took a chance on the concept. The plugger arrived with the slides and sheet music for the song *The Little Lost Child* at Fox's Union Square Theater. The sing-along program proved such a hit with the audience that Fox immediately expanded the practice to his other theaters. Soon others followed his example, and the slide sing-along became the standard part of the program in theaters across the country.

From exhibition, Fox took the next step of getting into movie distribution, founding his own film exchange company, the Greater New York Rental Company, in 1907.

Despite the burdens imposed on them by the Trust, nickelodeon owners often found the business quite lucrative, inspiring others to open their own theaters to get in on the action. One press agent compared it to the Klondike gold rush. Naturally, such freewheeling free enterprise attracted the attention of social reformers. Some of their concerns were justified. Many nickelodeons were deathtraps. Fire was the paramount fear, especially in second and third-floor operations. Many nickelodeons had blocked or inadequate exits, and rampant overcrowding of theaters was the norm. Add to the mix hot projectors and highly flammable films, and the recipe for disaster was complete.

Another worry was that the small, over-crowded theaters were breeding grounds of disease. The improvised theaters rarely had proper ventilation, and moviegoers from tenement slums rarely had proper hygiene. Fans were sometimes installed to stir the stale air. Other theaters tried to mask the bad smells with more pleasing ones. Actor-director Raoul Walsh and actress Mabel Normand visited one such theater.

"By the afternoon the place smelt like a menagerie," Walsh recalled, "so the management would walk up and down the aisles spraying a pump gun filled with the odor of magnolia or rose blossoms."

The irrepressible Normand, apparently acting as a music critic, grabbed the atomizer and sprayed down the pianist.

Neither scents nor fans were effective against the "foul air laden with death-dealing germs," as one reformer speculated. A newspaper declared "moving picture places" were "foci for the dissemination of the tubercle bacilli."

It wasn't just the physical health of movie patrons at risk, according to the reformers. From the very beginning, the subject matter in films lent to the accusation movies was lowering morality, despite Fox's claim the movie houses drew customers away from saloons. Then, as now, filmmakers were accused of causing crime by inspiring miscreants in their deeds. In 1910, Reverend Wilbur Crafts of Cleveland, Ohio, declared, "Movies are schools of vice and crime offering trips to hell for a nickel."

Sex caused much alarm in protectors of public morality. Pornography, of course, existed in one form or another, but there were also films in general release that shocked decent folk.

Whether they feared audiences would be burned alive, catch contagious diseases, or suffer moral decay, social reformers clamored for government action against the nickelodeons. In Chicago, a censorship ordinance was passed in 1907 requiring nickelodeons and larger theaters to obtain police permits in order to show films. Movie theaters there were also restricted to the first floor of any building. In a crackdown on supposed smut, the police raided New York nickelodeons on midnight, Christmas Eve, 1908. Those that were genuine safety hazards were shut down permanently.

In order to re-open the others, exhibitors had to promise to show no more questionable material. To back up their promise, the exhibitors formed an alliance and elected as their leader William Fox, known for showing only decent family fare. They also recognized in him a forceful leader for dealing with city officials and the Trust. As one of them put it, "We elected Bill Fox because he could holler the loudest." The alliance successfully defeated an effort to ban the showing of films on Sunday, another bugaboo of reformers.

Fox continued building his empire, buying up both vaudeville theaters and nickelodeons. He even rented the prestigious New York Academy of Music on 14th Street for stage shows and movies. Part of his formula for success was combining vaudeville acts with movies at prices working-class families could easily afford. Vaudeville remained the chief form of popular entertainment. However, Fox realized that movies were becoming more popular.

"Everywhere it is the pictures, more than the vaudeville acts, that hold the audiences. The only explanation I can find is that motion pictures, perhaps, realize the American idea of speed and activity."

Fox himself embodied the American idea of speed and activity when he concluded his future was in motion pictures.

"My one task," he recalled later, "was to get there ahead of the others."

By 1910, crude storefront nickelodeons were giving way to theaters specially built to show movies. These cleaner, better-ventilated theaters were able to draw more middle-class customers. Yet Fox became dissatisfied with the quality of most movies available. He believed that audiences wanted longer and better movies, and would be willing to pay more to see them.

Movie production was still dominated by an iron-fisted Motion Picture Patents Company. The Trust was determined to keep wages and rental fees low, and as a result, kept the quality of pictures down as well. They refused to permit films longer than one or two reels in length—ten to twenty minutes. The price of movies was fixed at twelve cents a foot, which the exhibitor had to buy, not rent. Price ceilings were placed on every aspect of film production.

"They regulated the wages paid in every branch of the industry," Fox recalled. "In their judgment, no man who wrote a story and gave his brains to create material for motion pictures was entitled to more than $25 for the finest story that he could write . . ." The Trust established a salary of $50 a week for directors, and "The highest salary they agreed to pay a performer was $60 a week. They made up their minds that this was not an industry or art but it was a mechanical occupation and that it required no brains."

Incredibly, under threat of legal action, no actor, director, or writer could be mentioned by name in a movie company's advertising. The Trust thought if the names of this personnel became known, they would become celebrities—and demand higher pay. Florence Lawrence, one of America's first movie stars, could only be advertised as 'The Biograph Girl' after the film company for which she worked. Mary Fuller was 'The Edison Girl' and Florence Turner (whose duties included both acting in lead roles and being wardrobe mistress) was 'The Vitagraph Girl.' Lead actress and screenwriter Gene Gauntier and then-comedienne Ruth Roland were both advertised as 'The Kalem Girl.' Mary Pickford became known for her role of 'Little Mary,' fans not learning of her surname until later. When stymied in their efforts to learn the names of American lead players, British exhibitors sometimes invented names for them; Mabel Normand was known in Britain as 'Muriel Fortesque.' Obsessed with keeping costs down, the Trust could not fathom that 'stars' could draw audiences and increase profits.

Required by the Trust to buy copies of their films outright, theater owners resold the movies to exchanges that would rent them to other exhibitors. Exhibitors, fed up with poor quality Trust films, rented films of independent producers. When the Trust found it could not stop exhibitors from obtaining films from the independents through the rental exchanges, it formed its own exchange. Created in April 1910, the General Film

Company bought up film exchanges as part of the Trust's stranglehold on the industry. The Warner brothers were among those forced to sell their rental exchange to General Film Company.

"They controlled the majority of the theatres of the country," Fox remembered, "They had driven out of business, legally or illegally, every man who had started in this business ten years prior. They either bought him out or drove him out."

In a year, they had nearly accomplished their mission. One important exchange they did not own was the Greater New York Rental Company belonging to William Fox.

The lords of the Trust had always ignored his requests for better films; instead, they offered to buy his exchange. General Film Company general manager Percival L. Waters warned Fox, "We are a great, gigantic wheel and you are a little splinter. Every time we meet you, we have to run over and crush you, because you are a stumbling block."

So Fox demanded the outrageous sum of $150,000. They refused, and they canceled his license to exhibit movies on the trumped-up charge that he had shown Trust films in a brothel. Hat in hand, Fox went to the Trust and offered to reduce the price to $90,000. They accepted, and they reinstated his license. Then Fox said that he changed his mind and wouldn't sell. They again revoked his license—and walked right into his trap.

Using his Tammany Hall connections, Fox sued the General Film Company for common law conspiracy for triple damages, and he got an injunction against the Trust denying him films. Fox pressured the federal government to break the patents trust under the Sherman Anti-Trust Laws. Fox hung tough during the years of litigation that followed. Others, following suit, also filed suit.

During his battle with the Trust, Fox hired 'Short, plump, blue-eyed' Winfield Sheehan. The son of Irish-American Catholics, he began as a cub reporter in Buffalo, and then he moved to New York City in 1902 as a crime reporter for the New York World. In 1910, he became secretary first to the New York fire commissioner, then to police commissioner Rhinelander Waldo. Sheehan was suspected of involvement in several police graft cases and one murder case, that of bookmaker Herman Rosenthal, killed in 1912 after exposing police corruption and extortion racket. Sheehan was never indicted. During the Motion Picture Trust struggle, he lent William Fox strong-arm muscle and political influence.

Anti-Motion Picture Trust ad in a trade magazine. (Author's collection)

"Bill Fox needed a standing army and he came to me to raise it," Sheehan remembered. He arranged for a bunch of burly ex-cops to guard Fox's office against Trust thugs. Soon he was working for Fox himself as a private secretary, then as General Manager at Fox.

The Trust was assailed on all fronts. There was legal action from Fox and others. There was shouting and open defiance by Carl Laemmle, who rallied the independent producers, and in the process, he founded Universal Pictures. Learning of Fox's lawsuit, Eastman Kodak ignored its agreement with the Trust and resumed selling raw stock to the independents. There were filmmakers, such as Biograph's D.W. Griffith, who wanted to make longer, better films, and chafed under the restrictions imposed by the Trust. There were performers deserting the Trust's wage ceilings for the better pay of the independents. There was the competition of quality foreign films that the public demanded to see, such as legendary stage star Sarah Bernhardt in the four-reel versions of *Queen Elizabeth* and *Camille* (both France 1912). These made motion pictures 'respectable' enough for upper and middle-class folk to patronize. Yet it was Fox who led the charge with his legal action.

W. Stephen Bush in the exhibitors' trade magazine *Moving Picture World* described him like "a warrior who had stepped out of the pages of Homer he stood defying incredible odds, matching his wit and strength against the combined resources of a combination eager to destroy him, and not too scrupulous about its means and methods. The bravery of the man called forth the unanimous but whispered admiration of every man outside the monopolistic circle. But even the most optimistic feared for the final fate of Fox."

Writing in 1916, *The New York Times* recalled how Fox "refused to accede to the demands of the Film Trust. The fight resembled that of a bulldog yapping at the heels of an elephant. But in the end, the bulldog won."

By the time the case reached appeals court, the General Film Company paid William Fox $350,000 to drop all charges. It was too late for the Trust. President William Howard Taft was running for re-election. Trying to prove he was as much of a trustbuster as his opponents, Democrat Woodrow Wilson and Bull Moose candidate Teddy Roosevelt, Taft nudged the Justice Department into filing an anti-trust suit against the Trust on August 15, 1912. The expiring Patents Company was finally clubbed over the head, although it didn't stop twitching until 1918 when its last appeal was exhausted.

The dam had burst, and the Trust companies struggled to compete with the flood of independents making better quality films and taking advantage of the public's desire to see 'stars.' Within a few years, most of the Trust companies went belly-up or were absorbed. Instead of trying to stay ahead of the pack, they had tried to restrain it, with the result they had been stampeded over and left in the dust. From then on, market forces dictated who would fail and who would thrive; who would provide the movies the public wanted to see (or what censors would let them see, anyway).

Meanwhile, Fox had decided to make his own films. In late 1913, he established the Box Office Attraction Film Rental Company–later changed to Box Office Attraction Company of America–as a parent company to his exchange company and other exchanges he was forming. It was to buy or rent 'the best of foreign and American photoplays' for distribution to other exchanges or distributors. Fox would buy or distribute most of the films for the Balboa Amusement Producing Company, based in Long Beach, California. These included *Will o' the Wisp*, *The Criminal Code* (four-reels), and *St. Elmo*, a six-reeler based on the very popular novel. Fox also organized other independents into the National Independent Motion Picture Board of Trade, with himself elected as president. His wife, Eva, became his story department; culling possible movie plots from stories in women's magazines. For his first productions, Fox relied on tested material, short stories, novels and plays, rather than original screenplays.

Along with owning movie and vaudeville theaters, Fox had been producing stage plays at the Academy of Music. With his stock company of actors and directors, Fox had the means of entering into film production. Fox sent his top stage director, J. Gordon Edwards, to Europe to study filmmaking.

John 'Jack' Gordon Edwards was born in Montreal in 1867. He received education at a military academy, pursuing a career as a British Army officer, until the siren call of the stage led him to a theatrical career, first as an actor. The Canadian stage was limited to repertory theater, so like many other aspiring Canadian actors, he went to the United States. Turning to producing and directing, he put on plays at the Suburban Garden Theatre in St. Louis, Missouri. Later, in New York, he met William Fox, who hired him in 1910 to direct plays at the Academy of Music. After he returned from Europe, Edwards became head of film production for Box Office Attraction.

The first feature they produced was *Life's Shop Window*, made on Staten Island at a cost of $4,500, Fox paying $100 for the story rights. Directed by Henry Behlmer, it featured Claire Whitney and Vitagraph star Stuart Holmes; both of whom would be major leads in a number of early Fox films.

Fox and Edwards tensely waited for the response as the film was run in front of its first audience. When it was received in silence, Fox momentarily lost his nerve.

"Burn the damn thing," ordered Fox.

"No, let's run it," urged Edwards.

Released in 1914, *Life's Shop Window* earned some money and devastating reviews, but it got the ball rolling. By the end of the year, Box Office

Attraction had released four more features. William Fox, former cloth sponger, was on his way to becoming a movie mogul.

One of the most profound influences in the history of cinema was the First World War. With its outbreak, much of the flourishing European film industry was shut down virtually overnight. Hordes of production personnel enlisted or were conscripted to be thrown into the maw of war, some never to return. Among the French casualties were comic genius Max Linder and director Abel Gance, both wounded. Maurice Chevalier was wounded and taken prisoner (he used his time in a POW camp to learn English). Austrian Fritz Lang was wounded three times. What is not known is how many possible directors, writers, cinematographers, and actors who might have revolutionized European cinema instead died at Verdun, the Somme, or countless other battlefields.

France, the preeminent filmmaking country in the world, lost its dominance to the upstarts across the Atlantic. For while the war curtailed European film production, it also popularized cinema. Eager to see newsreel footage of the war, the number of movie patrons increased worldwide, and they saw American dramas and comedies along with them. The American film industry, which later became known as Hollywood, gained ascendancy, which despite the travails it was to go through, it would never relinquish.

By 1914, the wooden benches and stretched sheets hung for screens of early nickelodeons had disappeared. Larger and more luxurious movie theaters arose in their place. Films were also becoming larger and more luxurious as well. Feature length movies, of an hour or more, became more common in America. Refining the art of film, D.W. Griffith made his own landmark epic, *The Birth Of A Nation*. Thomas Ince was becoming a creative force in cinema, aided by such talents as director Reginald Barker, screenwriter C. Gardner Sullivan, and actors William S. Hart and Sessue Hayakawa. The fledging 'star system' began making actors like Francis X. Bushman, Mary Pickford, Blanche Sweet, and Clara Kimball Young rich and famous. Producer-director and sometime actor Mack Sennett cranked out comedy shorts with his Keystone Kops, creating comic stars such as Ford Sterling, Charles 'Charlie' Chaplin, Mabel Normand, and Roscoe 'Fatty' Arbuckle. The 'Peerless Fearless Girl' Pearl White was doing her own stunts in the serial *Perils of Pauline* at Pathé. Actor-turned-director Cecil B. DeMille completed his first feature film, *The Squaw Man*, in a sleepy town called Hollywood.

Into this burgeoning industry came William Fox.

Deeply affected by the tough childhood that left him the main breadwinner for his family, Fox became very controlling, a tyrant at the home and the office. Often he saw the same faces at both. He put to work his two brothers, Aaron as treasurer, and Maurice in a lowly clerical position in the print department. His two brothers-in-law, Jack and Joe Leo, were also put on the payroll. Jack was put in charge of distribution, and Joe commanded the expanding chain of movie theaters. Even his father Michael served as the secretary of William Fox Amusement Co. Fox had them all securely under his thumb. One sister attempted to escape his control by becoming a writer at another studio, but rumor had it that nevertheless her salary was paid by Fox himself.

Fox was always self-conscious about his looks—about his increasing baldness, which he tried to hide by combing his remaining hair over, and about his crippled arm, always keeping his left hand stuffed in his pocket when in public. There are few publicity photos of Fox.

"This mug of mine won't sell tickets so just forget about me," Fox told Glendon Allvine, his chief publicist in the late 1920s.

"In his heyday he let his dark mustache grow thick," notes Norman Zierold, "ordered himself photographed in a cold forbidding pose which he decreed was official, and then shaved off the mustache."

Photos of Fox are harder to locate than those of the far uglier Carl Laemmle.

Fox also was painfully aware of his lack of education. He dreaded falling into grammatical flubs and misusing words, such as saying 'insipid' when he meant 'insignificant' and pronouncing 'film' as 'fil-um.'

In the early days of being an exhibitor, he was also self-conscious about the movie business, which was not considered a reputable trade. Bankers and financiers were slow to support cinema until long after it became a flourishing business. Fox cautioned his two young daughters, "Don't tell your friends your father is in the cinema business. It isn't quite respectable."

Nevertheless, he eventually consolidated his interests in 1915 under the Fox name. Box Office Attraction became the Fox Film Company, alongside the William Fox Circuit of Theatres Corporation, William Fox Theatrical Enterprises, William Fox Theatre, Inc., Fox Theatres, Fox Varieties Company, William Fox Entertainment Company, William Fox Productions Company, William Fox Dramatic Displays, Inc., William Fox Exhibitions, Inc.,

William Fox Playhouse Corporation, William Fox Inc. and, oddly using his father's name, the Michael Fox Amusement Company.

"Mr. Fox is one of our notorious offenders in the matter of plastering his name all over the titles and advertising matter in connection with all of his pictures," complained *Wid's Daily*, a motion picture trade magazine.

Quizzed along with other 'leading film men' by *Motography*, another trade journal, regarding his new year's resolutions for 1915, Fox declared, "To be regarded as the 'Tiffany' of the moving pictures business. To get the best and give the best. To make money—and I appreciate that the way to do it is to produce the pictures that get the money. To have the support of the leading theatre owners in the country."

Whatever else may be said of him, Fox had *chutzpah*; he aspired to be top of the industry when he had been a movie producer for only a couple of months.

"FOX USES EVERY HOUR" was a headline in *Motography* a year later, "head of Big Picture Corporation has tasks arranged for every moment of the day and even works far into the night.

"William Fox, head of the Fox Film Corporation is a busy man. His schedule for the day's work is usually as follows: He arrives at the office about 9:30. By 10 o'clock he has seen the financial reports and the box office sheets for the preceding 24 hours of his twenty odd motion picture and vaudeville theaters in and outside of New York City. At 10:30 he is actively working with one or more scenario writers to make practical alterations in a story he intends to make into a picture. By noon he has effected, in many cases, a complete alteration of a story. Between noon and 12:30 a boy has brought him coffee and sandwiches from a Broadway restaurant and in twenty minutes lunch is over. By 1 o'clock he knows every detail from tabulated reports of what his organization has done, from New England to New Orleans and Los Angeles. By 5 o'clock in the afternoon he has spent two hours or more in a locked projection room with a stenographer, a film cutter and a technical expert watching portions of a picture in the course of making, or full run of a complete five reel-production.

"At 6:30 he has dinner, during which he has had his contract man tell him about the financial arrangements with the players made during the day. At 8 o'clock he is back for the night session in the projection room, which begins with a running of every foot of film which has been developed during the day at the laboratories.

Fox's top directors of early 1915: J. Gordon Edwards, Herbert Brenon, Frank Powell, and Edgar Lewis. (Courtesy of Vanda Krefft)

"When that is ended there begins the nightly fight with the three weeks ahead release that must be whipped into just the shape he wants before shipment out to the branch offices. This over, usually about 1:15 in the morning, William Fox has finished his day's task."

The Motion Picture News commented, perhaps sarcastically, "A careful computation, in which an expert statistician assisted, proves conclusively that William Fox works twenty-six hours out of every twenty-four."

"It has always been a charge that the Fox Film organization was a one-man organization," Fox told Upton Sinclair in 1933. "That was never said as a compliment to me, but as a criticism. They were right when they said that."

In early 1915, a press release claimed that Fox viewed more than 50,000 feet of film a week, and called him "his own most exacting critic."

"Time and time again he orders changes and cuts made that drive his directors to the verge of despair," the statement said, "but he insists rigidly that product must be 'better than the best' before he will permit it to be released."

Fox had more than his share of eccentricities. He always wore white socks, even at board meetings, because of his fear of 'impure dye.' A believer in numerology, he thought the number 'three' had significant meaning in his life. He had arranged to be married the first hour of January 1, 1900, so his twenty-first birthday, wedding, and start of a new century all coincided as three propitious events on one day. Maybe that was the reason for the rush to propose—to get married on as auspicious day. How he arranged to be born on January 1st is unknown. He said he discovered his 'personal God' when he was thirteen, one who personally intervened on his behalf in the form of Providence. Fox also believed he could read the thoughts of others by mentally entering their minds.

He must have experienced rabid antisemitism in his youth, for he always believed gentile businessmen and financiers conspired against him for being a Jew who was both aggressive and successful in business. The fight with the Trust only seemed to confirm that for him.

Rivals and employees often loathed him, referring to him with contempt as the 'pants presser' in sneering reference to his earlier career—and quite possibly an antisemitic jibe. Even those who admired him didn't necessarily like him. Allvine commented, "Among the early pioneers, William Fox was not a lovable character, like Uncle Carl Laemmle or Joe Schenck."

"William Fox was a tough man," actor George Walsh simply remembered. "He was strictly business."

"Although William Fox was relentless, heavy-handed, and nearly merciless in his dealings with many employees, competitors, and exhibitors," observed McCord, "he was thoughtful and considerate at times, continued to be charitable and strongly patriotic, and spearheaded efforts in behalf of the industry. He had a good word for some, and some had a good word for him."

Hiring talent was one thing Fox was willing to spend bundles of money on. Fox began signing up anyone he thought would become 'stars,' such as former showgirl Evelyn Nesbit, famous for being the woman over whom husband Harry Thaw shot distinguished architect Stanford White. Being involved with a celebrity scandal did not always result in acting ability, and her films were poorly received. Fox also contracted Danish stage and film star Betty Nansen, whom Fox publicity declared the 'Greatest Tragedienne in the World.'

J. Gordon Edwards directed her in *Anna Karenina, The Song of Hate, Should a Mother Tell, A Woman's Resurrection*, and *The Celebrated Scandal* (all 1915). However, foreign stage fame did not translate into American movie success, and Nansen soon returned to Denmark.

Fox made film history distributing cartoonist Windsor McCay's experimental animated shorts, including *Gertie* AKA *Gertie the Dinosaur* (1914). However, McCay was under contract to William Randolph Hearst, who insisted he leave off the animating and return to drawing comics for Hearst newspapers.

William Farnum (Author's collection)

Fox had more lasting success with William Farnum, who gained stardom with his first film, *The Spoilers* (Selig, 1914), the first of five film versions of Rex Beach's novel. Hired on J. Gordon Edwards' recommendation, Farnum became the top male lead at the Fox studios, often in prestigious dramas.

Life's Shop Window had been filmed on Staten Island, but Fox followed the example of other film companies and set up more permanent production facilities across the Hudson from New York in Fort Lee, New Jersey. Before California became associated with motion pictures, Fort Lee was the major center of movie production in the United States. Sixteen production companies had studios there, taking advantage of the then-undeveloped rural locales that included cliffs of the Palisades and wooded areas. Many early Westerns were filmed in Fort Lee, far from the Wild West, as film historians delight to report.

"Cameras were everywhere, grinding out dramas," *Photoplay* magazine reported. "Burglaries and dynamite and fat men rolling down hills, and nobody even turned to look at them. Kindly old ladies didn't blink an eyelid when three galloping Mexicans were shot and killed at their very door."

With his wife reading novels and magazines for suitable stories, Fox searched for stage properties to turn into movies.

In 1933, Fox told Upton Sinclair that when he started producing, he wanted to make only morally uplifting movies, and "that any clergyman may have any Fox film free of charge at any time for showing in any synagogue, church or Sunday school, any hospital, orphan asylum, or home for the aged."

Yet in 1914, amid the dog-eat-dog competition of dozens of movie companies cranking hundreds of films, all vying for the dimes of movie-goers, Fox wanted stories that sold tickets. Nothing draws audiences like sex.

White slavery films had become very popular. It gained prominence with Universal's *Traffic in Souls* (1913), a drama about young immigrant women being forced into prostitution. To counter charges of offering salacious material, screenings were combined with a lecture about the evils of the white slave trade. It proved a tremendous box office success, generating some imitators, but the 'white slave' film fad quickly ran its course. In its place rose another subject of sexual titillation: the vampire.

In the Victorian era, there was a popular 'scientific' belief that loss of semen through sex actually sapped the life force from a man—that when a man wasted his sperm in sexual intercourse for other than procreation, it weakened him not only morally but also physically. Loss of 'precious bodily fluid' was said to cause dementia and disease, along with moral and neurological disintegration. Fortunately, according to 'leading scientific' opinion of the time, good women were completely immune from sexual desire, helping save men from the dire consequences of lust. Yet every now and then, it was a woman's odious duty to 'lie back and think of England.'

Which is one reason why loose women were considered so wicked. They not only led men astray, they also literally destroyed men with their unnatural desires. Thus a *femme fatale* was considered literally vampiric, draining a man financially, mentally, physically, and spiritually. Following this theme, Pre-Raphaelite artist Sir Philip Burne-Jones produced a painting,

The Vampire (1897), in which he tried to show a woman without a soul; a sexual, devouring being that seduced and thereby destroyed men, leaving them drained husks. Some think Burne-Jones painted a younger, thinner version of himself into the picture as the male victim. The 'vampire' resembled a famous actress with whom he had an affair, Mrs. Patrick Campbell. The flamboyant and free-spirited Campbell is alleged to have commented about her indifference regarding the sexual practices of others, "so long as they don't do it in the streets and frighten the horses."

Inspired by the painting, Rudyard Kipling, the man who later called the female 'the more deadly of the species,' wrote the cynical and misogynistic poem, *The Vampire*, its opening lines:
A fool there was and he made his prayer—
(Even as you and I)
To a rag and a bone and a hank of hair—
(We called her the woman who did not care),
But the fool he called her his lady fair—
(Even as you and I)

In 1909, Porter Emerson Browne turned the poem into a play, *A Fool There Was*. Kipling's 'woman who did not care' was transformed into a *femme fatale* who deliberately set out to ruin her lover for the sheer pleasure of ruining him. The melodrama, produced by Robert Hilliard, who also played the 'fool,' with Katharine Kaelred as the Vampire, enjoyed a successful run on stage.

In writing film history, one must be careful in identifying anything as 'the first.' A candidate for the first film vampire (of the *femme fatale* variety) is the Selig Polyscope's one-reeler, *The Vampire* (1910). *Moving Picture World* magazine described it as a "picture dramatization from Sir Ed Burne-Jones' famous painting, with suggestions from that world famous poem by Rudyard Kipling, each conceded a peer in the literary and world of art. This great subject handles deftly the realms of the imaginary inner circle of society." Not credited at the time, Margarita Fischer has been identified as 'Loie - the Vampire.'

Kalem made *The Vampire* (1913) starring Alice Hollister and followed a similar theme of the man-destroying *femme fatale*. It featured vaudeville dancers Alice Elis and Bert French performing their 'vampire dance,' which re-enacted the Byrne-Jones painting. 'Vampire' had already become synonymous with *femme fatale*, and sometimes was applied to seducers as

Virginia Pearson (Author's collection)

well as seductresses. *Saved From The Vampire* (Biograph, 1915) featured what was called a 'he vampire' as the villain.

How influential these earlier versions of *The Vampire* were on William Fox is unknown, but he was adept at sensing a trend. In 1914, he bought the filming rights to the play *A Fool There Was* and hired Frank Powell to turn it into a movie.

Powell had started as an actor and a director on stage. He had moved into the film industry during the pioneer days at Biograph, working under D.W. Griffith, cinema's master craftsman. He had been one of Griffith's protégés and was an assistant on his early films. Powell was shooting *The Stain* (1914) for Pathé when he was signed by Fox to direct *A Fool There Was*. Powell cast Edward José, star of his current picture, to play 'the fool.' Powell considered using the other star of *The Stain*, Virginia Pearson, in the role of 'The Vampire,' since she had played the part on Broadway in 1910. Stage star Valeska Suratt was also considered for the role; both would later appear in Fox films.

Fox had reasons to pass on these established actresses. He later claimed he had consulted with Robert Hilliard, who told Fox, "In my experience, I have had to change my leading lady six times. As soon as one scored a tremendous hit in the part, she believed herself to be a Sarah Bernhardt and became unmanageable, and I had to let her go. My advice would be to put the girl you choose under contract, and the part will make her."

An actress who wasn't a star was cheap, pliable, and disposable.

Additionally, Edward José, who had played on stage opposite Sarah Bernhardt, was already cast as the male lead. Fox might have balked at the idea of paying extra money for a 'name' actress, especially since the movie had the added expense of filming exteriors in Florida. So he was willing to consider a non-star in the role of 'The Vampire' when Powell showed up at his office with a stage actress who was a complete unknown. This unknown would become the first American movie sex goddess.

CHAPTER TWO: DESTINY'S DARK ANGEL

Theda Bara, Vampire (Author's collection)

In 1915, massive armies clashed in Europe on multiple fronts, causing tremendous casualties, but the deadlock remained. Italy declared war on Austro-Hungary and expected to march into Vienna to dictate terms. Blocking the way were the Alps, and armies experienced the frozen hell of stalemate in the mountains. In April, the Allies attempted to force their way through the Dardanelles to compel the Ottoman Empire's surrender. The Allies eventually withdrew, leaving behind nearly 60,000 killed.

In 1915, Charles Chaplin wriggled out from under the thumb of Mack Sennett at Keystone to seize the greater freedom and more money offered by Essanay, one of the Trust film companies struggling to survive. Chaplin continued to refine both his 'Little Tramp' character and his filmmaking techniques in a series of short comedies that became classics. They also helped Essanay keep afloat for a couple more years. Also in 1915, another Trust company, American Biograph, which launched the careers of D.W. Griffith, Mack Sennett, the Gish sisters, Mary Pickford, and a score of other major movie talents and helped make cinema a recognized art form, went out of business. That same year Triangle came into being, combining the talents of three of the most important creative producers in American film, Griffith, Sennett, and Thomas Ince, whose names alone gave the added prestige to charge higher than average ticket rates for their movies. Nickel tickets disappeared; now admission cost 10¢ or even 25¢. Originally a distributor for several movie companies, Metro released its first production in March 1915. It soon became one of the top movie companies, making sixty features a year. These starred such screen idols as Francis X. Bushman, Beverly Bayne, Mary Miles Minter, and Olga Petrova.

Also in 1915, as Americans uneasily watched empires battling in Europe and feared being drawn into the foreign war that seemed to be tearing civilization apart, another shadow started looming across America on its movie screens. Movie heroines were often depicted as virginal ingénues, naïve and innocent. While audiences still mooned over Mary Pickford, 'America's Sweetheart,' another actress began evoking completely different emotions. Called the 'Wickedest Woman in the World,' Theda Bara was nobody's sweetheart.

One of the first American movie actresses promoted as a sex symbol, Bara became the silver screen's original love goddess.

"She has the science of silent seduction worked out to the nth power," observed the *New York Evening Mail*. "By the twinkle of an eyelid and a squirm of the body she has all the gallants in the neighborhood trotting Bara-ward."

The promotion went further than that. Bara was ballyhooed in newspapers across the country as 'Destiny's Dark Angel,' 'Hell's Handmaiden,' a 'Love Pirate,' and the 'High Priestess of Sin.' Legend told how she was the illegitimate daughter of a French artist and an Arab princess. As a child, she was reportedly weaned on serpent's blood. She was fought over by

Bedouins, and she was given in mystical marriage to the Sphinx. She was reputed to be an Egyptian seeress with supernatural powers. In Europe, she became a famous actress in the Grand Guignol. Wreaking havoc on European males, she left a trail of broken hearts and ruined lives before turning her predatory talents to American movies. No wonder the sultry siren of the silent screen was dubbed 'The most mysterious woman living.'

For years, the only mystery was the year of her birth. She claimed it was 1890. Recent biographers state that she was actually born in 1885, making her neither the first nor the last actress to lie about her age. Other facts were not in dispute: She was born Theodosia Goodman in Cincinnati, Ohio. Both her parents were immigrants; her father was a Polish Jew named Bernard Goodman and her mother, Pauline Louise Françoise Bara de Coppet, was Swiss of mixed Italian and French descent (another source says French-German). Her father was a partner in the firm of Ochs, Weil, and Goodman. Some sources say that this was a wholesale clothing firm, others that Goodman was a tailor, but apparently a very successful tailor. An intelligent and well-bred woman, Pauline partnered with another woman in their own business in wig-making and hair care products, Dunkelmyer and De Coppet. Bernard wooed and won the reluctant Pauline, who nonetheless kept her business. The Goodmans catered to the middle-class so successfully that they became a part of it. They had two servants, easily affordable at the time by middle-class families when labor was cheap. The fact that they were immigrants and their servants were American-born was an interesting twist on the usual situation of Americans having immigrant servants; the Goodmans, like William Fox, embraced the American Dream and were completely assimilated.

They were so Americanized, that they named their firstborn Theodosia, after maverick politician Aaron Burr's beautiful but tragically fated daughter, whose disappearance at sea became a part of American myth and folklore. One tale told how the pirate captain Dominique Youx, after capturing her ship which had been dismasted in a storm, made her walk the plank, and she "descended into the sea with graceful composure, as if she had been alighting from a carriage." More likely her ship sank in a storm off Cape Hatteras, 'the graveyard of ships.' Even at the time of her birth, Theodosia Goodman with linked to mystery, not least of which is why two immigrants would name their daughter after the ill-fated daughter of a disgraced American politician.

In contrast with William Fox's hard childhood in the New York ghetto, Theodosia grew up in a thoroughly Midwestern middle-class family. She was rambunctious and always getting into trouble.

"And you could not remain angry with her very long—she would be so contrite and sorrowful and would say such sweet 'blarney' to you that it was impossible to be serious," her mother said, "I remember once having her gaze at me adoringly for a long, long time after a scolding, and then say, 'Mamma Dearest, you are so beautiful and I love you so very much—when you die, I'm going to have you stuffed.'"

A brunette with big dark eyes (although she did claim she was blonde and her eyes were blue when she was young), Theodosia Goodman had the dramatic urge early on. At school, she recited maudlin oratorical pieces as *The Dirty-Faced Brat*, about a starving boy who shovels snow in the bitter winter cold to earn money for food, and *Which Shall It Be?* which her school principal found moving enough to cause him to wipe tears from his eyes.

"I always had the instincts of an actress." she remembered "The difficulty sometimes in my childhood ambition was to get an audience. I needed advertising, no one knew what an actress I was."

Her first public performance was at the age of seven in Avondale, a largely Jewish neighborhood of Cincinnati where Theodosia grew up. An audience of friends and neighbors assembled in a barn with promises of lemonade and cookies.

Comparing it with later nickelodeons, she said the barn had ventilation that "was almost as good as the average motion-picture theater. It was almost about as decorative."

Her little brother, named Marque, rounded up the audience, then barred the way out against anyone leaving before the performance was concluded, the grateful sister recalling him to be "the most determined manager I ever had."

"I gave the entire entertainment alone. I sang, I danced, I recited, and how happy I was to make an exhibition of myself. No star has ever enjoyed such absolute dominion as I had that day. It was the dawn of my career. Even then, I knew that hundreds of thousands of people would someday come to see me as an actress."

Although she otherwise had a modest, even shy, demeanor, Theodosia, nicknamed 'Theo,' 'Teddy,' and 'Theda' (pronounced 'THAY-da'), was intelligent, imaginative, and highly ambitious. She sought more ways of getting attention. In 1897, at the age of 12, she was scheduled to tell the story of the Biblical Queen Esther at her Bat Mitzvah. When introduced, she came out barefoot, wearing only a sheer gossamer wrap that she claimed was an appropriate costume from Old Testament days. The crowd of guests was shocked. The rabbi told her she must change back into the nice clothes she had arrived in. Teddy refused, citing she needed historical accuracy for her presentation (or her interpretation of historical accuracy, anyway). Her mother was so overcome with embarrassment she went into labor. Soon Teddy had a little sister, named, appropriately enough, Esther, although she would mostly be known as Lori. Teddy's Bat Mitzvah was re-scheduled, and she was allowed to present the story of Esther in costume, which she repeated for the Women's Improvement Club of Cincinnati at their intrigued invitation.

"Through all the usual little obligations and home duties of an average school girl, I was dreaming about fairies," Theodosia remembered. "I knew that whatever you wanted, whatever you wished hard enough for, the fairies would give it to you . . . . The big trees in our garden were filled with gnomes and I used to talk to them just as if they were really there. Like many children, I lived in a world of incomprehensible imagination."

Theodosia and her sister Lori collaborated on writing fairy stories, fairly typical little girl behavior, but something about fairies stuck with her, for as she wrote in 1919, "I believed in fairies, I still believe in them."

"Often I did not understand her, often now I do not understand her," her mother remembered, "At times she is as simple and direct as a child, full of fun and mischief and laughter as a child of ten. At other times, she is so remote and even to me, her mother, strange."

Theodosia attended Walnut Hills High School, a college prep school, where she was a member of the Dramatic Club and served on the literary staff of *The Gleam*, the school paper. She demonstrated talent as a writer, but acting remained her calling. Wrote one of her classmates, "Theo excels in the literary art, and her work bears the stamp of true genius. Her literary ability, however, is not her only claim she has to fame— her histrionic (acting) talent is a characteristic well known to those who have witnessed a performance of the Senior Dramatic Club. She is an entertaining conversationalist."

"She loved to act, she made up her mind to be an actress when she was six and nothing ever changed or influenced her resolution," her mother recalled. "We tried everything to divert her; music, drawing, dancing, riding. These only served to make her more keenly desire the very thing we were trying to avoid."

Every night, Theodosia prayed she would grow up to be tall, have black hair, and be a famous actress. The black hair would later be accomplished by a bottle of hair dye, genes provided her with the claimed height of 5'6" (although she

Theodosia Goodman, 1903: Proper Edwardian lady. (Author's collection)

would gain more height in a technique to be described later), and while becoming a famous actress proved trickier, she was determined. The quote she selected to symbolize her ambitions was from 'The Pupil of Cimabue' by E. Cavazza: "With heart and fancy all on fire, To climb the hill of fame."

Although one Cincinnati resident claimed that Theodosia wanted to become a movie actress, this is unlikely, as no one at this period considered movies a legitimate venue for thespians. For Theodosia, acting meant the stage, and her goal was Broadway. The vague story about Theodosia's theatrical career turns vaguer, with publicity agents and the actress herself muddying the waters with false information, although Joan Craig, who as a little girl befriended her late in her life, fills some of the gaps in her book, *Theda Bara, My Mentor* (2016).

Graduating high school, Theodosia attended the University of Cincinnati, still an unusual move for a woman, completing two years.

When her father suffered an injury to his hand, rendering him unable to work, Theodosia filled in as a fabric cutter under his supervision. After he recovered enough to resume working, she helped her mother at her shop. Wig making bored Theodosia, who found more interest in concocting face powder to cover blemishes, perfumes and scented bath powder, which she sold at her mother's shop. Make-up was only starting to become respectable for decent women to wear, and Teddy was much in demand to apply make-up to Pauline's wealthy clientele. Theodosia seemed poised to follow her parents' careers, to become a businesswoman until some man came courting her.

In 1906, Sarah Bernhardt came to America on one of her many farewell tours. Teddy saw her at Cincinnati's Grand Opera House in a performance of *Camille*, reviving her interest in performing. Enrolling as Theo Goodman in an acting school in Chicago, she found work as a stagehand. She stayed at the exclusive Schlitz Hotel in neighboring Milwaukee, even though she couldn't afford to pay the rent there. Instead, she approached the management with a scheme in which she would serve as hostess to a singles club at the hotel. Respectable men and women could not speak to one another unless they were properly introduced. At the hotel's 'Social Singles Hour,' she could make the introductions, then lead the couples in a promenade around the hall. In exchange, Schlitz provided her room and board. The Singles Social Hour was very successful, and one can see how it would appeal to Theo, who remained a shy, retiring type. Playing hostess forced her to socialize. Another woman might have used the situation to browse for a beau, but romance wasn't on her mind.

Across the street from the Schlitz Hotel was the Davidson Theater, where Theodosia attended every performance of Sarah Bernhardt when her tour took her to Milwaukee. She may have even visited Bernhardt at the hotel. Perhaps it was not just Bernhardt's acting skill that impressed Theo.

Stephen Gundie in *Glamour: A History*, called Bernhardt "a modern celebrity who practiced conspicuous self-display and deliberately sought sensation. She was self-consciously artificial and made ample use of cosmetics and jewelry. Exoticism and eccentricity were her hallmarks...."

Newspapers reported every facet of the diva's life to scandalized and entranced readers, from the Asian-inspired robes and hats she wore in public; her menagerie of exotic pets including monkeys, a cheetah, and 'jewel-encrusted snakes,' to her habit of sleeping in a pink silk-lined coffin.

"Her performances and offstage publicity stunts blended seamlessly in a continuous effort at startling and dazzling her audiences," observed Gundie "She was seen as the Sphinx of Paris, a symbol and ideal more than a woman."

While Bernhardt essayed such roles as Camille and even cross-dressed to play Hamlet, it was as Cleopatra, Phèdre, and Empress Theodora of Byzantium that sparked and fed into the Western fascination with the Orient.

It was too much for some Victorians, and clergy denounced her from the pulpit for her immorality Gundie notes, "in so doing they only increased the public's fascination. She was the exact antithesis of Victorian puritanism and bourgeoisie gender values and was seen as a real-life femme fatale. As such, she was irresistibly glamorous. The glamour of the actress derived from her fame and her lifestyle but also from her capacity to merge her personality with the roles she played."

As film scholar Gaylyn Studlar points out, "Bernhardt's performances, like Bara's, violated the dearly held Victorian belief that women were primarily spiritual rather than sexual or physical beings."

At last, Theodosia set out for the Great White Way to fulfill her dream, with her father reluctantly paying her way to New York. Living in a small hotel near Washington Square, she entered the stage under her mother's maiden name de Coppet. It is known she had a small role in a 1908 Broadway production of Ferenc Molnár's *The Devil*, and probably went on tour with the rest of the company. According to some sources, Theodosia de Coppet became known in theater circles for being adept at *femme fatale* roles and her interest in spiritualism.

Spiritualism had become very popular in the mid 19th Century, especially with the middle and upper classes, and had many followers in the intellectual and scientific community. Significantly, it was a field in which women, barred from male-dominated professions, could become prominent. The beliefs vary, but much of it centered on the ability of the living to communicate with the dead, and these 'spirits' could offer guidance to the living. There were fraudulent mediums who fleeced some victims, but there were also 'white mediums' who sincerely believed in life beyond the grave, and that they could communicate with spirits.

"Nothing happens without a cause," Theo stated in the notes for her autobiography "I believe that in all things we are guided by a power beyond ourselves."

It was through yielding to that beneficent power that one could be guided by the spirits, but when people force their desires or will against that directing wisdom 'which knows better what is best for us,' that they are led astray "into strange channels and dangerous harbors, and oft go far, far adrift."

"Call them good fairies, call them guardian angels, call it as did Socrates 'a divine sign,' there is that power of guidance beyond and back of life for all to implore, for all to conjure, for all, if they will, to rely upon. And as I have found, when our purposes are unselfish and not base, when we submit our own will to a greater will, that power never fails."

Even with spirit guidance, theatrical success proved elusive. There were years of disappointment. Details of this period are sketchy, and sources vary in their accounts of her activities. She may have played supporting roles in a Yiddish theater on the Lower East Side. She supposedly got a small role in a road company at $25 a week. When that was cut to $18, she quit and returned to New York.

"I absolutely declined to have my salary cut," she remembered, "In this respect, I was a real actress."

She jumped at a chance to travel to Europe to perform in Greek drama. When that prospect collapsed, she joined an open-air company giving 'very poor Shakespearean performances' around England, although she was in ill health. "However, my fairies stayed with me, retained by their hopeful impulses, and sustained me."

Biographers long believed these foreign travels may have existed only as invented embellishments to her lackluster stage career; a tactic still honored by struggling actors to this day. Evidence exists she did indeed travel to Europe. What she did abroad is a topic of speculation, but a tantalizing and startling story emerges from the pens of Preston Sturges, later the director, and his mother, Mary Desti, friend and confident of the legendary modern dancer, Isadora Duncan.

According to Mary Desti's book *Isadora Duncan's End* (1929) and an article in the *Brooklyn Daily Eagle*, 'a very famous film vamp' put a curse on Isadora Duncan. Around 1910, the 'vamp' had become involved with an equally unnamed 'young man,' who had become highly agitated by her delving into spiritualist practices and felt "his only salvation was in getting away" from her. While driving in Paris one day, Desti, Isadora, and the vamp were riding in the car when Isadora informed the vamp that the young man was being 'packed off' out of the country. Upset, the 'vamp' rose to her feet and screamed, "You have taken my mate from me. What about my child?"

Isadora assured her she would take care of her and her child, although there was no child. The 'vamp' was not assuaged, and declared wrathfully in a trembling voice, "I curse you. The gods of my fathers curse you and your children forever."

That might have put the kibosh at 'the vamp' remaining as a guest of Isadora. It seems Desti agreed to take her in. Her son, Preston Sturges, then aged about 12 and called Edmund, recalled in his autobiography, his 'first adventure with a movie star.'

"She was, as a matter of fact, the only movie star I ever slept with, practically. Mother had run into her at Isadora's and, discovering that the girl was temporarily hard-up because she was waiting for her father to forward money for her passage back to New York, Mother invited her over to our place."

Identifying her as Theodosia de Coppet, Sturges described her as being, "about seventeen, very dark and snakey, and just at the end of some kind of adventure with a member of the Duncan family ...."

"She was a mysterious girl who used to receive messages from the spirits, which she would write down with her right hand while holding her left hand over her eyes and be absolutely astonished when she looked and read what the spirits had written to her."

Theodosia shared young Edmund's bedroom with him, she sleeping in his bed while he slept on a cot.

"We used to talk practically all night. She explained to me that she was not like other women, but much more primeval."

Telling him she could smell him, she purred, "Oh, I don't mean anything unpleasant, you understand, I mean as a tigress, for instance, might smell her prey before leaping on him.' Across the dark came the sound of Theodosia inhaling deeply."

Sturges regretted, "this passionate affair never went beyond the conversational. I was never leaped upon, and Mother and I put her on the boat train." He didn't hear of her again until after she gained stardom.

Although the evidence is indeed scanty, how unlikely is it that Theodosia was a houseguest of Isadora Duncan and Mary Desti? From these women, certainly, the Midwestern, middle-class American would have witnessed the 'wild bohemian life' of these women and others, who smoked, drank and had casual sex, with men and each other, and otherwise did not conform to the norm. How much did Theodosia want to emulate the women she saw in Paris, especially Duncan?

"Isadora Duncan could have been known as *La Grande Horizontale*," noted Valerie Lawson in her review of a Duncan biography, "Her life was defined by sensations and appetites—for sex, food, wine, freedom from all restrictions, living life to the hilt."

Desti's account suggests the vamp star may have been with child by the 'young man' she also doesn't name. Film historian Hugh Neely thinks this could have been Raymond Duncan, Isadora's brother, who was sent to Moscow around this time to open a school for her, with the possible additional motive of getting him away from Theodosia's alarming spiritualism. What happened to the child (if there was a child, born or unborn) remains a mystery.

As for the 'vamp star's curse,' a few years later, in 1913, there was a tragic accident in which an automobile carrying Isadora Duncan's two young children stalled. The chauffeur got out of the car to crank the engine. The car leaped to life and drove into the Seine, drowning the two children with their nanny. Desti wrote that this happened on the exact same spot the vamp star uttered her curse. Fifteen years later, in 1927, another freak accident killed Isadora. Wearing a long scarf, she got in a convertible car being driven by her latest lover, calling out to Desti, "I go to love!" which Desti chose to remember as "I go to glory!" The trailing scarf got caught in a rear wheel, quickly winding to snap Duncan's neck.

Desti's relaying the tale of the 'vamp's curse' might have an attempt to displace her own feelings of guilt; after all, she had given Isadora the fatal scarf. There is the eerie coincidence of the curse being uttered in a car, and the deaths occurring in cars, but there's no indication of Theodosia ever cursing anyone else. Probably not wanting to be sued, Desti doesn't name Theodosia, just identifying her as a 'vamp star' not even as a 'future vamp star.' Preston Surges had no qualms of identifying Theodosia de Coppet as she was already dead when he wrote his autobiography, although he gets her age and the dates wrong.

Perhaps not wanting to remember her years of struggle, Bara was very vague about her pre-stardom days, but in 1919 she recalled "a year or two of weird incomprehensible experiences which are too intimate for the public eye. They concerned the usual emotional surprises that are the mystery of youth. They were perhaps romantic. They flourished for a time in that beautiful twilight called love."

After her indulgent father provided funds for passage, she re-entered the country at Ellis Island on October 20, 1910, disembarking from the RMS *Teutonic*, traveling under her stage name of Theodosia de Coppet, and giving her age as 24.

"I returned to New York a slender, pale, sad-eyed girl. If I had had any ambition to interpret the vampire character I couldn't have looked it by any stretch of the imagination."

Theodosia de Coppett, March 1912: Greenwich Village actress and playwright. (Author's collection)

She lived in Greenwich Village, already gaining a reputation as a Bohemian haven of struggling artists, writers and theater folk. In 1911, she joined a company touring the popular musical *The Quaker Girl*. Famed actor DeWolf Hopper was the star. His wife Hedda Hopper, later the gossip columnist, remembered, "Theodosia played a Frenchwoman with an accent that wouldn't fool a five-year-old. Oh, brother!"

Hedda also recalled, "Theodosia then was a believer in spiritualism and read about it constantly. In a traveling troupe, when you have time on your hands, those things are contagious. Theo's spirits got me to the point where I began to hear tappings on the wall behind my bed."

In 1912, Theodosia was on the road appearing in a three-act comedy, *Just Like John*. She tried her hand as a playwright, as the US Catalogue of Copyright Entries lists in name of 'Theodosia de Coppet, New York,' as having copyrighted, *The Bubble*, 'a play in four acts' on June 24, 1912, with T. de Coppet and Norman Rose sharing writing credits. Records also show 'Theodosia B. De Coppet, New York,' as having copyrighted on July 29, 1913, *Mammy Chloe, or, The Pendletons of Virginia*, 'a drama in four acts with a prologue,' under the pen name of T.B. De Coppet. Other plays by De Coppet were *Norah's Chance*, and *A Russian Tragedy* with Loys Norton in April 1914. The 'B' may have stood for Baranger or Bara, as she later claimed to have used the latter name as a pen name for writing plays. There is no evidence of any of these plays being produced. Her mother and sister moved to New York to help her, but Theodosia continued to struggle.

"The theatrical engagement that I expected to last a whole season collapsed after a few weeks, and try as I might, I couldn't find anything to do. One day I was asked by a director of movie pictures if I would like a part in a screenplay he was about to produce. I didn't know anything about moving pictures in those days, so I went over to the studio to find out what it was all about."

Theodosia was appalled at what she saw during the filming of a comedy.

"Being accustomed to the more or less orderly procedure of the theater, I couldn't see how any form could come out of such chaos. A perfect pandemonium was going on, and, from what I could see, a knowledge of acting was the last thing that troubled either the director or the actors. I slipped out and went home. I needed money, but not badly enough yet to get it in that way."

She was nearly broke when an agent for a motion picture company approached her. Struck by her big brown eyes and thinking she would photograph well, he offered her the enormous sum of $175 a week to appear in movies. Regarding motion pictures as inferior to legitimate theater, as most actors believed then (and some still do), she turned him down, and haughtily declared she would not appear in movies 'even for a million.' Saying she despised movies, "nothing would induce me to become a moving picture actress."

Then disaster struck in the form of a fire in her apartment. She later thought, "It seemed to me that the fairies interfered in my favor again" although "My mother and sister and I barely escaped our lives." There followed a run-around with her insurance company, which grudgingly paid $900 on a $2,000 policy. Living on this amount, Theodosia was desperate for money.

"I put my pride in one pocket and my ideals in the other and, with a heavy heart, set out once again for the picture studio."

She later claimed that her 'spirit contact' advised her to try movies. She may have encountered Cecil B. DeMille, who later regretted "failing to take much notice of Theodosia Goodman although she used to come to our office hopefully when she heard we might be casting."

On the verge of turning 30, Theodosia was nearly twice the age of many popular actresses when they entered film. Mary Pickford started at the age of 16, Lillian and Dorothy Gish were 16 and 14 respectively, Norma and Constance Talmadge were 17 and 16, Bessie Love was 17, Mabel Normand, Beverly Bayne and Florence LaBadie were all 16, and Blanche Sweet was 14. More commonly, women were in their late teens and early twenties when they got their big break. With the exception of established stage stars who carried their fame over into films, actresses as long in the tooth as Theodosia didn't stand much chance of landing lead roles in movies.

Glancing at the competition, Mary Pickford and Lillian Gish wannabes, she shrewdly decided to concentrate on looking exotic. At some point in her stage life, she dyed her waist-length hair black and accented her large dark eyes with make-up, hoping to get noticed. She was to succeed beyond her wildest dreams.

Theodosia went to the director who had approached her earlier and told him, "I'll be very glad to go into pictures if you can use me. I watched you the other day, and it all looks dreadfully complicated to me, but I'll do my best. Of course, I don't know anything at all about picture acting, but—"

"Oh, that's all right,' he said, genially, 'that doesn't matter. How do you look in a one-piece bathing suit?'

"Now I suppose I ought to have gone home again and starved, nobly or ignobly, but I didn't," recalled Bara "Next day I reported with the one-piece bathing suit."

The years of struggle had taken its toll on the girl with artistic aspirations, who regarded making movies, appearing in a one-piece bathing suit yet, as 'prostituting' herself.

"It's all well to say noble things about rather starving than debase one's art, but the butcher and the baker and the candlestick maker are not going to supply you with their commodities unless you are able to pay for them in cold, hard cash. Your flights of fancy won't bring you three meals a day."

The director was Frank Powell, who was at Pathé shooting *The Stain* when Theodosia approached him looking for work. He knew Theodosia from the stage and was struck by her exotic appeal, thinking she would be perfect in the role of 'The Vampire.'

To keep her on hand and not starving, Powell put her in *The Stain* as an extra. This later started a controversy, when some disputed her claim that she 'started as a star,' saying she had worked as an extra before becoming a star.

"I was never an extra player, as many writers have said," she declared, "but I do not want the wrong impression to get out that I would not have liked to have been one, for there is nothing so important as being with an organization and climbing up from the ranks."

Her role in *The Stain* was more of a holding pattern for her debut in *A Fool There Was* than how she made a living. Her assigned role was that of a nun. The costume department had only two nun's habits already assigned to other extras, so Theo went home and made her own costume, determined to get in the film.

Wanting her to play the Vampire, Powell brought Theodosia to Fox and convinced him to sign her to a contract. Some sources say it was for $100 a week, but Fox biographer Vanda Krefft says it was $75 a week and for only three months. Even though she was 'dead set' against playing a villainess, Theodosia grudgingly accepted the role of the Vampire (or so she claimed, but given her financial problems, hard to believe). Still, she had ideas of her own, especially when it came to publicity, and asked Fox for a press agent. "You don't need one," he replied, but eventually he relented. She was also able to wheedle out of Fox an extra $50 a week to buy the lavish gowns she needed for her character, since in this era actors provided their own costumes in movies with modern settings. That a struggling actress managed to wring these expenses out of the penny-pinching Fox suggests her powers of persuasion, or maybe he was simply impressed by her *chutzpah*.

Because the leading woman was an unknown, the advance publicity concentrated on the male star, Edward José, but some attention was given to this new player. Press releases to newspapers and movie magazines were issued to keep stars in the public eye between movies or to build up publicity during production or before a movie was released.

Lobby card featuring Theda Bara. (Author's collection)

Ballyhoo, hucksterism, humbug and outright fraud have always been a part of show business, even before P.T. Barnum allegedly declared, "There's a sucker born every minute." Barnum took the desiccated upper body of a monkey, stitched onto an equally dried-up fishtail, and he displayed it in his museum as a 'mermaid.' One of the most famous publicity stunts in the movies occurred in 1910, when Carl Laemmle of the Independent Motion Picture Company (IMP), hired 'The Biograph Girl' Florence Lawrence away from Biograph. Laemmle concocted a newspaper story claiming Lawrence had been killed in a streetcar accident. Then he published an advertisement saying that 'enemies' of IMP had created the story about the fatal accident. 'The Imp Girl' Florence Lawrence was alive and appearing in his next production, *The Broken Oath*. Lawrence became the first American movie star widely known by name.

For the release of *A Fool There Was*, Fox launched the first known movie studio re-write of an actor's biography for promotional purposes. Capitalizing on xenophobic attitudes in America at the time, the actress playing the 'Vampire' was made as exotically foreign as possible. After all, foreigners were thought to be capable of all sorts of evil.

First came a name change, to distance her from the failed actress Theodosia de Coppet. Nor could Fox have a bad woman named Goodman. Theda Bara emerged, which the publicity department, concentrating on her exotic appeal, insisted was an anagram for 'Arab Death.' So it was, but 'Bara' came from her mother's Italian side of the family name, which sources list variously as Bara or di Barra, and that her maternal grandfather's name was François Baranger de Coppet. She may have already used Bara as a pen name. 'Bara' is also Italian for 'coffin.' 'Theda' had long been a nickname for Theodosia, all of which suggests she came up with the stage name herself, rather than having it imposed on her by press agents. They still managed to get the name wrong in their early advertising, listing her as Thedda Barra.

The press agents were Johnny Goldfrap and Al Selig. Both were former newspapermen. John Henry Goldfrap, according to *Motography*, had been "a rancher, an advance man, a reporter, a rewrite man on the *Morning World* and the *Evening World*, and for a long time devoted his talents to juvenile fiction, scenario writing and magazine work before beginning his career as a publicity man.... While with the Fox Company he launched the big advertising campaigns for Betty Nanson, William Farnum, Theda Bara, Nance O'Neil and Annette Kellermann."

Not much is known about Al Selig (sometimes identified as A.L. Selig), except he remained as Bara's press agent during her entire tenure at Fox, then performed the same job for William Farnum. For the publicity campaign, Goldfrap and Selig hammered out what Bara may have herself suggested.

"Prominent actress imported from Paris," it was announced by Box Office Attraction in a press release, "Director Frank Powell was confronted by a problem. He needed an actress of scope and ability to play a woman who lures a man to dissipation and finally to a degrading death in her arms.... Powell recalled a girl he had seen at the Théâtre Antoine, an actress who fulfilled absolutely the type he required."

"Theda Bara is the daughter of Giuseppe Bara, one of the foremost sculptors of the modern school. Her mother is Theda de Lysie, one of the best-known of the French emotional actresses. As a young girl Mlle. Bara studied painting with her father as a preceptor. Later she joined her mother in classic drama, playing vampire roles at the Théâtre Antoine, where she was seen by director Frank Powell, who remembered her when casting *A Fool There Was*."

Theda Bara as The Vampire in A Fool There Was *(Author's collection)*

Bara barely made it to Florida for the initial shooting. The cast and crew set sail for St. Augustine on the German steam yacht *Essen*, which was immediately stopped outside New York harbor by a boarding party from two British cruisers searching for contraband and German agents. The company nearly lost its male lead when a British officer addressed Edward José in German to trip up the possible German national, and the Belgium-born actor replied in kind, resulting in his arrest. Only hurried cables with assurances of José's true nationality from Winfield Sheehan to the British government resolved the crisis and the steam yacht was allowed on its way with the movie's titular fool on board.

More harrowing for Bara was her first day before the cameras in St. Augustine at the steamship pier.

"I shall never forget the terrible experience of my first scene. I had to wear a makeup in the public street and I felt like a lost soul.... There must have been 2,000 people standing around looking at me .... The whole world seemed to have turned into human eyes. I trembled, I shook, and I all but died right there on the dock."

Apparently, Bara sought counsel from her spirit guides. Some of the crew nervously noticed she would sometimes face a corner of the set, quietly talking to herself. When this was reported to William Fox, he was unfazed, replying, "Well, any girl who does that is ambitious."

In *A Fool There Was*, a distinguished businessman, 'The Husband,' John Schuyler, happily married and with a family, accepts a diplomatic assignment overseas. 'The Vampire' reads about his appointment in the newspaper. She is a serial seductress; she seduces wealthy men, becomes their mistress until they are destitute and broken in wealth, health and spirit. Then she abandons them for her next conquest. Snubbed earlier in the film by Kate, 'The Wife,' the Vampire sets her sights on the Husband. She deserts her last lover, having squeezed him for all he is worth. He pursues her to the ocean liner on which the Husband is departing. On the way, she encounters another of her cast-off victims; the dilapidated remnant of what had once been a respectable gentleman, now a skid-row bum.

"See what you have done to me, and still you prosper, you hellcat!" he snarls at her. She smiles mockingly in response. The bum sees the lover in pursuit, but his warning to the desperate man is unheeded. When the cast-off lover, gun in hand, confronts the Vampire, she gives him the kiss off with the immortal line, "Kiss me, my fool!" Still under her sway, he does not shoot her. Instead, he puts the bullet into his own head. The Husband, having boarded the ship, is unaware of the commotion as the Vampire arranges for his deck chair to be placed next to hers.

Soon the Husband falls under the Vampire's spell, losing his will and self-esteem as she lures him into the world of sex, alcohol and drugs. His conduct gets him fired from the diplomatic mission, and rumors of his affair filter back to his distraught Wife. Intercut with scenes of the Husband's dissolution are shots of the family he deserted, homey scenes he may no longer witness, and the Wife pining for her lost husband. She makes a determined effort to free him from the Vampire, finding him reduced to a shell of his former self. Before she can hustle him out the door, the Vampire returns and exerts her indomitable will over him again. Defeated, the wife leaves without him. The film ends with the triumphant Vampire clutching a rose in her teeth over the prostrate and expiring husband.

"In playing this fascinating but despicable character the actress must make her ability to charm men seem plausible," Bara said of her role. "She must not be merely flirtatious. Her creation must manifest mental as well

The Vampire triumphant over the body of 'the Fool' (Edward José) in A Fool There Was *(Author's collection)*

as physical charm. It must show traces of kleptomania. Every vampire in real life steals the affections of men partly because she cannot help stealing. The vampire is rarely the oversexed 'rag and bone and hank of hair' which Burne-Jones and Kipling painted and described. Far more likely is she to be the woman who gains amusement and a gratification of power-love out of conquering masculine hearts.

"It is sport for her. It entertains her, and in the end it becomes her occupation. She practices the art studying how she can gain more skill, just as a yeggman schools his fingers in opening safes or just as a pickpocket trains himself in the business of the deft extraction of purses."

Press releases claimed Isadora Duncan taught Bara how to make the lithe, sensual movements of the vampire: possibly an invention of Selig and Goldfrap, but then again, if she had been a guest of Duncan in Paris . . .

Released in January 1915, *A Fool There Was* is unspeakably crude by modern standards. (D.W. Griffith's groundbreaking epic *The Birth Of A Nation* was released a month later.) It was filmed almost entirely in long static shots, with only a few close-ups. Lines from Kipling's poem were inserted to the effect of slowing down an already slow-paced film. Nevertheless, *A Fool There Was* proved a sensation. Edward José was praised for his performance, but the spotlight was on Bara. The American movie public had never seen anything quite like this, and Bara's performance caused an uproar.

"As the Vampire, Theda Bara gives the woman not one redeeming feature, her only appeal being purely animal," stated the *New York Morning Telegraph*.

"She is imperious, a fury, a perfect volcano of conflicting emotions. The only pleasure she gets out of life seems to be in inflicting pain and anguish upon foe and friend alike. It is quite the most revolting but fascinating character that has appeared upon the screen for some time. Magnificent gowns—and an occasional lack of them—add greatly to the forcefulness of Miss Bara's work."

"Miss Bara misses no chance for sensuous appeal in her portrayal of the Vampire," wrote *The New York Dramatic Mirror*, "She is a horribly fascinating woman, vicious to the core, and cruel. When she says, 'Kiss me, my fool,' the fool is generally ready to obey and enjoy a prolonged moment, irrespective of less enjoyable ones to follow."

For a generation, 'vampire' did not refer to the blood-drinking undead but, instead, an unscrupulous woman who used her sexuality to manipulate and destroy men. Because of this film, the slang word 'vamp' entered the dictionary as both a noun and a verb. 'Kiss me, my fool!' was the catchphrase of the decade, and was as familiar to the moviegoers of the time as 'May the force be with you' is to modern audiences.

The actual star of the film, Edward José, found himself being ignored as everyone marveled about Bara, much as Marlene Dietrich stole the movie *The Blue Angel* (Paramount, 1930) out from acclaimed Oscar-winning actor Emil Jannings. Shortly after the completion of *A Fool There Was*, José had a falling out with Fox and left the company. He later became a film director. He also claimed credit for 'discovering' Theda Bara and that he directed much of *A Fool There Was*.

Her actual discoverer, however, did not flourish after Bara's success. Frank Powell directed her in one more film, but he later broke with Fox. He fell on hard times and ended up begging for a job from his former mentor, D.W. Griffith.

In The Kreutzer Sonata, *Nance O'Neil as Miriam discovers her sister (Theda Bara) has stolen her husband, while O'Neil, 'The American Bernhardt,' discovers that Theda Bara has stolen the whole movie from her. (Author's collection)*

Before the release of *A Fool There Was*, Bara shot two more Fox pictures. Still an unknown, she was cast in a supporting role, albeit as the *femme fatale*, in a film based on Tolstoy's story *The Kreutzer Sonata*. The director, Hebert Brenon, had already built a name for himself as a director at Universal when hired by Fox. Star billing went to the famed stage actress Nance O'Neil, dubbed 'The American Bernhardt,' in the role of Miriam. Bara played her beautiful but ruthless sister who connives to steal Miriam's husband, a brilliant violinist. Losing her mind, Miriam kills her sister, her husband and herself.

"I was assigned to support of a well known star," Bara recalled. "Again I was a 'vampire,' and I was not particularly happy in the role."

Eve Golden, who wrote a biography of Bara, suggests that Fox assigned her the supporting role to keep Bara in line. If so, the ploy backfired.

"When I found myself cast in my second picture in support of an artist," Bara remembered, "I felt only an ambition to do as well as she did."

Bara and William E. Shay in The Clemenceau Case *(Author's collection)*

One reviewer thought she succeeded when he compared her with O'Neil. "Startling and remarkable, their acting is splendidly realistic and emotionally powerful."

"When the picture was released there were indications that I had done well." Theda recalled, "Exhibitors wrote to me that my name had been the drawing feature. It is a name, therefore, that has some emotional value in a world in which romance is a food all hearts crave."

Winfield Sheehan reported to his boss that exhibitors were ignoring O'Neil and advertising Bara's presence in *The Kreutzer Sonata*—and filling their theater seats. Fox realized he had a major box office star in his hands and under contract—which was about to expire. When her next film, *The Clemenceau Case*, also directed by Herbert Brenon, was released in April of 1915, Bara got top billing—in fact, she never again shared star billing with any other actor.

It was another *femme fatale* role—now called 'vampire' role—as Iza, an evil and exotic Parisian determines to avenge the wrongs men had done to women. She lures Pierre Clemenceau into marriage, then seduces and destroys the men around him, including his best friend. In the final scene,

Pierre, having learned of her crimes, stabs Iza to death in her luxurious boudoir to prevent her from destroying any other lives, then calmly goes to the telephone and calls the police. "Sergeant, send up your man. I have just killed my wife."

Bara claimed her scream when being stabbed was so realistic that the actor, director and even the cameraman thought she had actually been stabbed and filming stopped as they rushed to her aid. Fox publicity promoted *The Clemenceau Case* with more absurdities than they had ballyhooed for *A Fool There Was*. Reportedly, Iza's pet snake, played by "giant king python— the largest of his kind in captivity" was on loan from the Bronx Zoo. People cowered in terror as the reptile was transported to the movie set by taxi with a 'Hindu keeper' playing a flute to keep the snake mesmerized. Also mesmerized was the film crew as Bara coiled the serpent about her for the scenes in which Iza petted and played with the snake.

The movie no longer exists, but still photos of Bara and the snake do survive, and with them, Eve Golden puts the lie to this particular fable.

"The king python, of course, was about a dangerous as a wet sock. Stills reveal it to be the most unconvincing stuffed snake ever to appear before a professional camera. Theda seems barely able to keep a straight face as she clutches the toy to her in an attempt to keep it from falling to the ground with a thud."

The reviewer for *Dramatic Mirror* did not care much for *The Clemenceau Case*.

"Were the National Board of Censorship possessed of any judgment whatsoever, this is the kind of picture it should place the ban of disapproval upon .... no wholly pure minded man or woman could take a great deal of pleasure in witnessing such an exposition of female depravity."

The reviewer added that both Bara and director Brenon "were too good to be engaged in a picture production of this kind."

William Fox formally incorporated the Fox Film Company in February 1915. Knowing he had hit pay dirt with Theda Bara, he began to produce more 'vampire' movies. The first of these, specifically made to capitalize on Bara's increasing fame, was *The Devil's Daughter*, a film version of Gabriele D'Annunzio's stage play *La Gioconda*. The eccentric Italian playwright had written this melodrama for famed stage actress Eleanora Duse, who had toured America with it. Fox publicity wanted people to forget about that:

La Gioconda could only have been written for the famous Parisian actress Theda Bara.

"I first met D'Annunzio when he came to Paris to put on a playlet of his at the Théâtre Antoine," Bara recounted for reporters, "I shall never forget my first impression of him. Dark, piercing eyes, a high-pitched screaming voice, and an air of overwhelming conceit. He carried a small dog and shaded himself from the sun on the boulevard with a rose-colored parasol. His clothes were all pure white, but a scarlet sash about his waist made a vivid splash of color. The playlet he was putting on was a mystic sort of thing with a wicked woman of the world as heroine. Another actress was cast for this character. But as soon as she came on the stage, D'Annunzio shrieked out in his shrill voice that she would not do at all. The actress was furious. She stepped up to the author and gave his face a ringing slap. D'Annunzio merely laughed. Then his eyes fell on me. D'Annunzio insisted that I should play the leading part in his sketch .... He declared that if I did not take the part, he would not put on the playlet ..."

From Italy, Gabriele D'Annunzio proclaimed, via the Fox publicity department, "There is no one else on earth who is half serpent and half woman like my Gioconda, except Mlle. Bara."

The real D'Annunzio was probably too busy laying the foundations of Italian Fascism to pay attention to the American nonsense.

In *The Devil's Daughter*, Bara's character, La Gioconda, discovers the man she loved and trusted has betrayed her.

"As this man has done to me, so will I do henceforth to all men," she declares in the dialogue title, "My heart is ice, my passion consuming fire. Let all men beware."

One reviewer said of her performance in *The Devil's Daughter*, "Mlle. Bara's facial expression is wonderfully brutal and fiendish, but every movement shows grace and charm."

Bara next appeared in *Lady Audley's Secret*, based on the sensational 1862 novel by Mary Elizabeth Braddon, which had already been filmed several times. The lead character commits bigamy, deserts her child, pushes one husband down into a well, considers poisoning the other husband and sets fire to a hotel to dispose of some other men. Not at all the proper Victorian lady—but not a true vampire, as Bara's character was mentally ill. Although her performance got good reviews, this old Victorian melodrama didn't click with audiences. They wanted a vampire.

Herbert Brenon directed her next film, *The Two Orphans*, based on the 1872 French play *Les deux orphelines*, later adapted by D.W. Griffith as *Orphans of the Storm* (1921).

The Fox production shot in part on location in Québec, Canada, to take advantage of the European style architecture; an additional expense, but Fox thought it worth the additional investment. Besides, building exterior sets also cost money. Bara played Henriette, searching 18th Century Paris for her lost, blind and kidnapped sister. Reviewers especially praised Bara's performance.

Bara in The Two Orphans. *(Author's collection)*

"To turn from a sinuous vampire ... and become a gentle innocent young girl, would seem a hard thing to accomplish," noted the *Detroit Free Press*, "The result shows what a powerful versatile actress can accomplish."

Said one reviewer, "Tender, bewitching and passionate in turn, her work touched the high-water mark of artistry and furnishes undeniable proof of her extraordinary versatility."

The reviewers liked it, but Bara fans wanted to see her vamp. When word got out she was playing a good girl, they ignored the picture. Looking at the disappointing receipts, Fox wondered how Bara's next picture would do. It was a vampire picture, but after the lackluster business on the last two films, perhaps it was time to rev up the publicity to focus on that.

Sin, directed by Brenon, found Bara as an Italian vamp who coerces her fiancé into stealing the 'sacred jewels of the Madonna,' but the enormity of the crime drives him to suicide and her to insanity.

Theda Bara and Warner Oland in Sin *(Author's collection)*

A press release for *Sin* told of Bara personally searching for authentic period jewelry for the part. She discovered a locket her father had given her mother as a wedding gift, which had been stolen as they traveled through Italy. Theda telegraphed the news that the heirloom had been recovered to her mother, who was doing Red Cross work in Paris—a touching finish to a completely bogus story.

However, the publicity campaign was about to switch to overdrive.

"*SIN* with Theda Bara!" beckoned the movie's ads with a very salacious tagline.

Publicity photos of 'Our Mary' Pickford often showed her smiling in girlish curls, wearing pretty dresses and perhaps holding cute, cuddly rabbits or ducklings. The antithesis of these were Theda Bara's bizarre publicity photos, shot by Jacob 'Jack' Freulich at Underwood and Underwood studios in New York. These depicted her wearing slinky or shapeless black gowns, her long black hair cascading over shockingly bare shoulders and arms, or, apparently naked, wrapped in some kind of white sheet. She posed with ravens and skeletons. The photos showed her with her complexion pallid and the rims of her eyes darkly kohled, revealing 'the wickedest face in the world, dark, brooding, beautiful and heartless,' as if to drive home the point that, 'The wages of sin is death.' Initially made to promote her movie *Sin*, these photos were used again and again in Fox publicity for a variety of her films, and became iconic of Bara, especially in the absence of her movies. These still photos represent much of how Theda Bara is regarded today.

Theda Bara with raven (Author's collection)

It is important to remember that it was Bara's performance in *A Fool There Was* and other early films that won over audiences; the Fox publicity campaign had merely mentioned her as a 'French actress imported from the Parisian stage.' Later on, it would be claimed that it was Fox publicity, calling her 'Hell's Handmaiden' and photographing her with skeletons and ravens, that caught the public's imagination.

Up to this point, Fox publicity had maintained the original press release of Bara being a Parisian actress with an Italian sculptor father and a French actress mother. Something a little more exotic was now desired to tantalize the movie-going public. She still wanted to be thought of as a sophisticated French actress, but that wasn't exotic enough.

"I sat up all night deciding what pin-point on the globe to select as my birthplace," she admitted later, "Because of that country's romantic mystery I chose to make myself a daughter of Egypt."

"Suppose we say I was born in Egypt," she suggested to the Fox publicity men. When Bara was asked to be more specific, she replied, "Oh, very well, make it two blocks from the Sphinx."

A variety of stories were released, inconsistencies be damned. One press release read: "Theda Bara was born in 1891 in Egypt— in the shadow of the Sphinx. She was the daughter of a French painter and an Arabian princess, who had eloped to an oasis in the Sahara."

According to Goldfrap and Selig, the princess-mother died soon after giving birth and her father sent this "Half-Arabian embodiment of wicked delight" to Europe to study acting, where she made her debut in England playing classic drama. Next, she "joined Jane Hading's company in Paris, the Grand Guignol Theatre, the Gymnase, and the Théâtre Antoine" before crossing the Atlantic to make her American debut in the movies.

Along with the release of her movies came an increasingly wild publicity campaign. What Bara had suggested, Goldfrap and Selig took to extremes. Stories concocted by them were sent out to newspapers across the country, with Bara vamp photos, and newspapers simply printed them with the photos, because they were free, they were entertaining, and they filled up space in the papers whenever they were short on copy. That they were audacious lies apparently didn't trouble some editors.

The Seattle Star ('The Only Paper in Seattle That Dares to Print the News') printed that, "a young man killed himself in her dressing room because she had spurned his love. He was furiously jealous of an East Indian Gaekwar then in Paris who had given the actress a wonderfully wrought snake bracelet containing an Indian poison. Mlle. Bara was showing the young man the secret spring by which the poison was released from the mouth of the hollow gold snake when he suddenly seized it from her and, placing the snake to his lips, died at her feet!"

Bara had the option of reading press releases before they sent out, but with her busy schedule, she did not inspect them all.

"Anyway, some of them were so wild that we didn't think they would be printed, or that if they were printed, they wouldn't be believed," Bara remembered, "But they were printed, and they were believed, too, I suppose. The wildest press stories are the most successful ones. A lot of young ex-newspapermen wrote them. I think I kept a whole publicity staff working nights."

The Fox publicity department produced even articles and letters purportedly written by her, so that today it is difficult to tell where the real Theda Bara ended and the publicity campaign began.

"My conception of the vampire character is not so much of a woman as it is of a youthful symbol of sin," Bara reportedly said "She afraid of nothing except old age and death. Her heart is a charnel house of men's dead hopes and withered ambitions. She thrives on the deaths. This vampire of mine possesses only one good or decent quality, her courage. Some night when she faces old age and her mirror shows her wrinkles, she will pass out. Gas or poison, I should think. But nothing that would disfigure her. Such is my conception of the woman who wrought the fool's undoing."

The tall tales varied to match whatever new role she filled. For the role of a vengeful Russian peasant, reports had her descended from a Russian grandmother whose seductions devastated most of Europe. When she had the part of a Frenchwoman, her 'Bourbon nose' supposedly showed her to be of French royal ancestry. Her Italian background was emphasized when she played an Italian. Since the heroism of the Belgians fighting against the invading German armies excited the admiration of Americans, the press was told of her 'proud trace of Belgian blood.'

Theda Bara, it was reported, had "deceived fifty men with her wiles, made one hundred families suffer, caused fifty children and one hundred wives to beg her to give back to them their daddies and their husbands."

Exactly who was keeping score on this account was not revealed, nor how Bara managed to keep the number of suffering people in such round figures, but much of the public believed it all. As put by *Photoplay*, a movie fan magazine, "shop girls read it and swallowed their gum with excitement."

Along with using the fear of exotic foreigners, the Vampire preyed on middle-class dread of the 'loose woman'; the mistress-whore who threatened the 'family values' as perceived by post-Victorian society. Mothers and wives fretted that some wanton woman might lead their husbands and sons astray—ignoring the fact that men often led themselves astray without the guidance of *femmes fatales*.

Columnist Wallace Franklin may have jokingly asked, "What midcountry wife, seeing her susceptible and cantaloupe-headed spouse off to New York, would be willing to venture his integrity and affection against an assault by Theda Bara, the arch-torpedo of domesticity?"

This was just a few months after the sinking of the ocean liner, RMS *Lusitania* by a German U-boat, with an enormous loss of innocent lives. It had caused shock and outrage even in neutral America. Comparing Theda Bara to a torpedo was a potent metaphor about how the Vampire threatened marriage and family, therefore society. Even so, Bara's Vampire was a character of fantasy, or as Marjorie Rosen described her, "she was *sex*, blatant and overt and so far removed from reality that she could not possibly be a threat to audiences newly probing their own sexuality. For sexual repression usually breeds extremism, her vamp had its roots firmly founded in Victorian denial. She was an absurd sexual distortion. She was unnatural; therefore, she was *safe*. The movie-going public could ogle without feeling guilt and discomfort—and most of all, without feeling desire.

"For there was no confusing Theda Bara with the girl next door. Not even with the *bad* girl next door. No woman at the time could have looked like her without being locked up or laughed off the street."

Rosen argued that Lillian Gish and Mary Pickford "could not have gotten away with" wearing "such outrageously flimsy costumes . . . . But Theda's exaggeration gave her amazing license."

Yet the Fox press releases went even further and even darker.

"Is this the wickedest face in the world? Its owner does not deny that it may be, since scientists have said that she is the reincarnation of the world's wickedest women and that their crimes have been chiseled in the lines of her features. Have the physical attributes of the scheming Delilah, of cruel Lucrezia Borgia, of diabolical Elizabeth Bathory— who slew 600 girls and young women so she could bathe daily in their blood and so retain her beauty— fatefully found reincarnation so that the women of this age may see face to face the loathsome depths to which the worst of their sex have descended? Are the souls of these monsters of ancient and medieval times welded with others to form the soul of Mlle. Theda Bara?"

In the entertainment business, balderdash was regularly mixed with the ballyhoo, but rarely was the fraud so blatant regarding a star's identity. As Anne Helen Petersen observed, "Fox didn't just give Bara a new name or a new ethnicity, it made her a *creature of the underworld*. Sure, part of this was just good, old-fashioned publicity playfulness, with the majority of the American public in on the joke. But part of it—namely, the conflation of ethnicity with sexuality and 'otherness'—was a manifestation of the Western obsession with 'Orientalism,' sometimes known as 'white people fetishizing Eastern cultures to reaffirm their own whiteness.' Her success, in other words, was part of a large-scale desire to look at otherness while simultaneously disavowing it in oneself . . ."

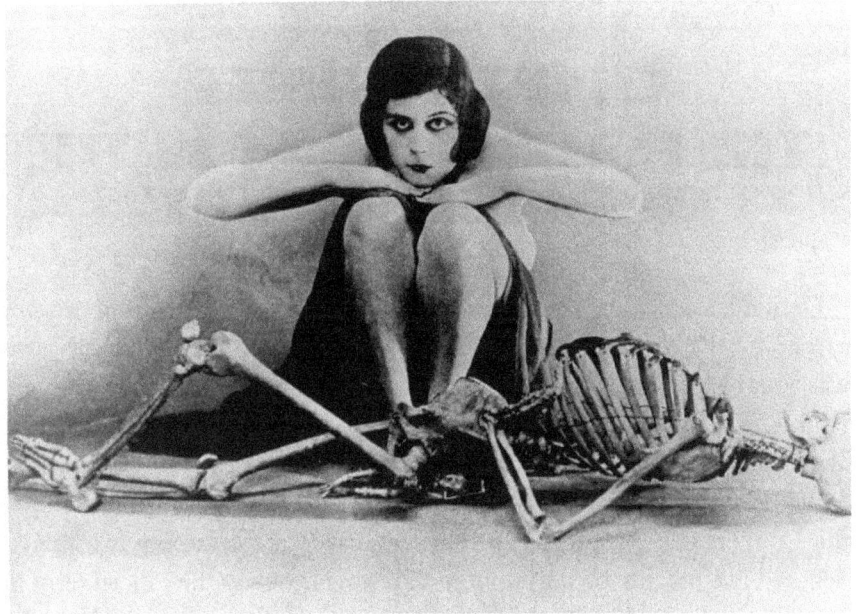

Theda Bara with skeleton, possibly of her freshly devoured victim. (Author's collection)

Americans had long regarded the influx of immigrants as a menace to their way of life. Not only American culture was endangered. According to the followers of the pseudo-science of eugenics with ideas about racial hygiene, the recent wave of immigration allowed in 'inferior races'—Jews, Gypsies, Irish, Italians, Slavs, Greeks—which would ultimately contaminate the gene pool. Much of the imagery of the Vampire, both in the movies and the publicity campaign, preyed upon these fears.

What was it like in this room full of Jews, immigrants and offspring of immigrants; Goodman, Fox, Selig and Goldfrap, who were well aware of the antisemitism and xenophobic attitudes of America? Were they selling out their own people with this strange creation of the evil foreign woman, or rubbing America's face in its own irrational fear of foreigners?

For Bara, at least, it may have been the fulfillment of a childhood fantasy, to be foreign and exotic; but the fantasy took on a bizarre life of its own.

CHAPTER THREE: 'THE FLAMING COMET IN THE CINEMA FIRMAMENT'

Derided as 'flickers' by sore-eyed patrons for the flickering images caused by the slow cranking of lazy projectionists, a more suitable term was sought by those trying to describe the new art form—or new entertainment medium anyway. Edison's Kinetoscope had fallen into disuse along with the machine itself. 'Nickel shows' went out with nickelodeons. 'Cinema' was derived from the French *cinematographe*, after the name of the Lumière camera-projector. 'Film' was used, in the same way as 'stage' denoted live theater. In 1910, 'photoplay' was chosen as the official term in a contest sponsored by the Essanay film company. Some preferred 'photodrama.' It was also called 'motion pictures,' 'moving pictures,' 'picture plays' or 'picture shows.' There was also the prosaic 'shadow play,' 'shadow stage' and 'silver screen.'

However, a slang term began to be more commonly used, much to the protests of purist grammarians. Early in 1915, *Photoplay* sent out the following question to newspaper editors across the United States: "Do you consider the word 'movie,' as applied to a moving picture theatre or film, a good word, and do you approve its use in your newspaper?"

Of one thousand inquiries sent out, the responses came back 511 in favor and 222 against. Those against were very vocal about their objections.

"Most certainly not!" *The New York Dramatic Mirror* replied to the question, "We have inveighed against the barbarism frequently in our columns."

The editor of the *San Antonio Light* said, "We use it sometimes but we don't like it."

"It is a corruption," wrote the editor of the *Macon Telegraph*, "and we have enough corruption now."

"Yes, popularly," replied the *Louisville Times*, "no, academically."

The editor of the *Sacramento Union* called it "a cheap slang term adopted into the language largely through careless newspaper use. It is a crude diminutive utterly unworthy [of] the great invention it represents. Motion pictures are destined to play a most important part in the education of the future, and they should not be belittled by such a title."

"It humanizes the motion picture," argued the *St. Paul Daily News*, "it gives it a friendly touch that a dignified name couldn't bring."

"There is no possibility of killing the word for a few years," the *Chicago Evening Post* commented, "but its slow death can and should be caused the mobilization of the photoplay editors of all newspapers and magazines throughout the country. The issue can be forced only by the absolute obliteration of the word from the vocabulary of journalism. *The Post* recommends the operation of this ruling at once."

One editor deemed it "the most expressive term possible!" Another editor declared, "I think 'movie' is one of the most rottenest counterfeits ever coined," and the *Cleveland Plain Dealer* simply barred the word from its columns.

"Yes, until an acceptable substitute is provided," said the *Toledo Blade*. "We spell it 'movy.'"

Ultimately, it was the *El Paso Herald* verdict which stood, "Not a good word, but it's here to stay; it is short and popular."

By 1915, movies were both popular and longer. Having embraced the feature film as the main fare attracting moviegoers, new companies sprang up to meet the demand. Those who couldn't compete fell by the wayside. Short films remained drawing cards too, but increasingly, shorts meant comedies.

William Fox preferred manly man William Farnum as the main star on his lot. Fox once said, "I have frequently expressed my profound admiration for his art and his manliness, so that it is no secret that I consider him the greatest living motion picture actor . . ."

That Theda Bara had become a bigger star virtually overnight bewildered Fox. He had contracted established stage stars with loads of credentials, but they failed to click with audiences. This strange Bara woman, this nobody, was getting rave reviews, tons of fan mail and, most importantly of all, packing the movie theaters. Having paid little attention to her when she was a short-term contract player in supporting roles, he now invited her to his office.

For all of their differences, the similarities were striking. The children of Jewish immigrants, both had worked in the garment industry, albeit briefly in Bara's case. Both were highly ambitious and slightly eccentric;

his magic number was 'three' while hers was 'four.' If Fox was poorly educated to Bara's educated and literary bent, both admired the classics and both strove for excellence in their work.

Bara admired Fox, saying his enthusiasm was "like an electric current" and he had a "natural, assertive, vehement swaying eloquence."

"After hearing Mr. Fox say 'fillums,' you leave him with the firm impression that Mr. Webster's latest edition is wrong in the given orthodox pronunciation of the word."

At the same time, she found him reserved and inscrutable, "as enigmatic as the proverbial noncommittal demeanor of the Sphinx."

They had actually met before; in the summer of 1914. She had been acting in a comedy sketch, 'Bought But Not Paid For,' at one of his vaudeville theaters, but as Bara noted, "The 'comedy' certainly did not seem funny to me." The audience agreed, as during the opening performance, "the tomb could not be more silent."

Trying to liven up things a bit, Theda started shouting her lines, and "finished the act with a voice like a whiskey tenor." Fox had wanted to fire the act, but he allowed them to perform for "three more days. Then his patience gave out."

Bara had hesitated to remind Fox about this act, but after she told him, he remembered it, for "it had been doubtlessly so flagrantly bad he could not forget it ..... We had a good laugh."

It was something with which the failed vaudeville comedian could sympathize. A few biographers raised the possibility of a romance between Fox and Bara, as they were close to the same age.

"No rumor would ever surface about any flirtation between them," states Vanda Krefft "An affair would not have been out of the question."

Krefft insists Fox was a good family man who never strayed—but more than that, he was driven to expand his empire, and an affair with an actress would be a complication and a distraction.

Bara biographer Ronald Genini suggested a darker possibility, "Was Bara sexually exploited by William Fox? The road to screen success via the casting couch is an old cliché that probably has a strong factual basis, though we may never know how many of the old stars were sexually involved with a studio chief."

If not Fox, there was Winfield Sheehan, Fox's General Manager. Glendon Allvine described him as "a complex character: affable, sentimental, suspicious, cynical, ruthless, and a squat dynamo of energy." He was also a notorious womanizer who had no qualms about cheating on his wife whenever he had one. He might have gone after Bara, but would Fox have let him? Or cared?

Still, Fox couldn't see the appeal of Theda Bara. His feminine ideal was his mother, whom he idolized, and his wife, who idolized him. They represented the matron, the woman serving as the foundation of the home, family, and society as a whole. He relied on them for maintaining his household while he conquered the world of film and theater. Mothers and wives served as the bulwarks of civilization, safeguarding the family from temptations and moral decay. Yet these same women, who were the majority of his movie audience, were flocking to see this weird creature before him, whom critics claimed threatened the moral fabric of society. Why?

Theda Bara at the studio (Courtesy of Robert S. Birchard)

It wasn't as if Bara was exceptionally beautiful. Eve Golden said, "her looks are considered rather plain and bovine. She had a heavy jawline and rather cumbersome nose . . . . Even in her day she was thought a few pounds overweight." Vanda Krefft described her as having "a broad, flat face, asymmetrical features, strong jawline, and thick-waisted, chubby-legged figure, she looked mostly like she was: a middle-class, Jewish tailor's daughter from Cincinnati, Ohio."

It may seem odd to modern eyes that Bara could have been considered a great beauty in her day. Although young ingénues were pretty and had their appeal, popular standards of beauty included older women whose looks were described as 'matronly' as a compliment. The more full-bodied physique was the aesthetic for both women and men, the stolid William Farnum being an example. When Frank Powell wanted Bara to wear a one-piece swimsuit in *A Fool There Was*, Bara demurred plaintively she was 'too thin' to be considered sexy. Yet it was her face that enraptured audiences.

"The lustrous beauty of the screen apparition glowed brighter in this living presence," a reporter wrote. "It was the rich dark beauty of the Gallic and Oriental races—large dark eyes, black hair, white, evenly matched teeth set in a mouth whose frequent smiles belied the tragedy that lurked in its drooping corners. The head was well-shaped and the profile good, so that ... the merciless camera would have the utmost difficulty in catching Miss Bara in an unbecoming pose."

Still, one can't help but wonder whether some reviewers became overgenerous with their praise of the beauty of actresses, especially of distinguished stage stars appearing in films. In *The New York Times* review of *The White Raven* (1917), the critic described the star Ethel Barrymore in the role of a saloon singer as "lovely to look upon, never more so than in the sketchy costume of the dance hall, and she has adapted her fine skill to the new medium."

Even a young Ethel Barrymore looked like Ethel Barrymore.

What was it about Bara? Those who met her called her 'timid' and 'intellectual.' How could she play a *femme fatale*? As is often the case, the nicest people play the best villains, because they are allowed to release some of their inner inhibitions and go wild. Something happened when Theodosia appeared before a camera and became Theda Bara, with a special fire that captivated audiences. She had an almost mystical power, only hinted at in still photos, which caused more than a few journalists and many adoring fans to describe her as not just beautiful but as a 'raving beauty.'

"From this naïve kindly girl," recalled Fox screenwriter Rex Ingram, "what Hollywood today calls a sex-menace, fairly radiated. Very shortsighted, her eyes suggested eyes of a sleepwalker, and when she appeared you somehow felt that the shades of Baudelaire, Edgar Allan Poe and Bram Stoker were hovering around."

To keep Bara happy, Fox raised her salary and renewed her contract. However, still unsure whether her success was a fluke, he did not sign her to a long-term contract. She was still cheap, disposable—and pliable.

June Caprice, Fox's ingénue in competition with Mary Pickford. (Author's collection)

Krefft called "Theda a docile mannequin whom he could dress up to convey his idea of sexual allure," and she was easily manipulated. When Bara protested she didn't want to do a movie she thought inferior, "Mr. Fox urged me, saying there was no other script ready and promising that if I didn't like the picture upon completion, he would burn the film," Theda recalled. Even when she thought the movie was bad, she felt she couldn't ask Fox to destroy it, as it would mean "a loss of $30,000 to $40,000."

Critics often accused William Fox of being tight-fisted and cheap; part of this might have been antisemitism, picturing him as a grasping Jew. A pragmatic businessman who drove a hard bargain, he could be quite ruthless when he chose to be. Yet the evidence points to a businessman who was willing to lavish enormous sums on stories, talent and productions when he thought there could be a return on the investment.

Bankrolled by the success of his Bara movies and other films, Fox expanded production and hired additional talent. He searched for new stars to add to his roster. Pretty June Caprice (birth name Helen Elizabeth Lawson) became the Fox rival of Mary Pickford. Fox may have been hedging his bets in signing Caprice, as she reportedly had won a Mary Pickford lookalike contest, and Fox renamed her 'Caprice' after the Pickford film of that name. Yet, looking like Mary Pickford is not the same as being Mary Pickford. Caprice never enjoyed the success of Pickford, or for that matter, Pickford's closest rivals, Mary Miles Minter at Metro and Marguerite Clark at Famous Players-Lasky. Nobody successfully challenged America's Sweetheart, though Clark came closest to overtaking 'Our Mary'.

Fox also contracted Gladys Brockwell, who played fallen women and long-suffering heroines in weepy melodramas in competition with Clara Kimball Young, Norma Talmadge and Pauline Frederick.

Fox was hiring other talents as well. Actor-writer-director Raoul Walsh, who had been working under D.W. Griffith, directed a two-reeler that impressed Fox. He sent Winfield Sheehan to California to hire the 23-year-old director away from Griffith's Fine Arts Studio. Sheehan asked Walsh what he earned at Fine Arts, which for all the critical praise, operated on a shoestring. Walsh, only making $40 a week, got cagey. Sheehan boasted he already knew what everyone's salary was at Fine Arts, but told Walsh to name his price. Wanting to stay at Fine Arts, Walsh demanded the 'outrageous' sum of $400 a week. Instead of flatly refusing him, Sheehan said he would have to check with William Fox. The next day, Sheehan handed Walsh the contract for $400 a week, which a stunned Walsh signed. Walsh asked the Fine Arts studio manager, Frank Woods, what he should do.

"Mr. Griffith told me to hold onto you, Wally Reid and Henry Walthall," Woods said, but admitted that Walsh would make more money at Fox than he would at Fine Arts, adding that Fox would "fold in a year."

"Because of my picture?" Walsh asked.

"No, but you know these fly by night companies."

As he left Woods' office, Walsh heard him mutter, "Who's backing them—God?"

Returning with Sheehan to New York, Walsh met William Fox.

"He was a dynamic character. He was the first one to really set the big salaries for directors, actors and actresses. He believed in getting the best of everything."

Fox announced what he planned to do with all these stars, directors and scenario writers he had rounded up: he would release a major production every week. Walsh's first directing assignment at Fox was *Regeneration* (1915), one of the earliest gangster pictures. Walsh's next picture after that was with Theda Bara, to be set in Mexico or Spain.

Production could be haphazard and freewheeling in the early days of film, but it allowed for rapid shifts in direction, something which modern production companies are incapable of doing. This was an asset when disaster struck, as when a severe winter storm dumped a heavy blanket of snow on Walsh's exterior sets built at Fort Lee, New Jersey. Walsh recalled, "So I got an idea and I went down and I said, 'Mr. Fox, they can take this story, this *Siren Of Hell*, and lay it in Russia and use the snow.' He said, 'Boy, you're a genius.' So we got Russian costumes. Now he says, 'You will have to go and tell Miss Bara the change.' Those fellows always stayed away, you know—those money men. I said, 'You're the money man, why don't you go up and see her?' He said, 'I'm afraid she'd hit me.'"

"So I went up and saw Theda, she was a nice sort of girl, she was a wild vamp and lured men to their death on the screen, but she was a great girl off."

Walsh pitched the Russian picture, Bara agreed to it. Her Spanish costumes were replaced with Russian ones, and she found herself cast as a peasant woman seeking revenge against the noble who wronged her in *The Serpent*. A stroke of luck followed the unfortunate weather. A Russian troupe of about forty musicians, acrobats and equestrians had just finished a tour of America and were waiting in Jersey City for passage back to Russia. Walsh hired them to perform in his production, which he rushed to complete filming as the snow turned to slush.

"*The Serpent*, instead of being the dog I was afraid of, got a good press and made money," Walsh remembered. "And the picture turned out pretty good as a Russian picture."

"That it is a well made picture cannot be denied," said the review in *The Moving Picture World*, "but it is a unwholesome offering and a vulgar one."

There's a problem with this story. Walsh said the original title was either *The Siren of Seville*, with a Spanish setting, or *The Siren of Hell*, with a Mexican setting. Neither title was ever announced in the trade magazines,

Theda Bara as a Russian peasant in The Serpent. *(Author's collection)*

casting doubt on the veracity of this tale, which he told on various occasions and with various embellishments. Walsh managed to muddy the waters with his recollections so that these titles show up in some Walsh and Bara filmographies, despite their having never been announced, let alone made. Curiously enough, although Walsh supposedly authored the story, he completely forgot the details of the plot.

When Cecil B. DeMille announced the production of a screen version of *Carmen*, in the competitiveness of the period, Walsh (or so he claimed) convinced William Fox to rush into production with his own version. Walsh again directed, with Bara as the lustful gypsy Carmen, using the now-snow free Spanish sets to beat DeMille into the theaters.

Walsh found Bara to be "tractable, even humble, rare qualities in a rising star of her magnitude."

During shooting, the smuggler's boat Bara was on became swamped and sank. After the film crew rescued her from drowning, Walsh feared the worst.

"Sopping wet, with her make-up running down her face and her hair a sodden mess, I expected her to explode and walk off the set. Instead, she gave a watery grin and said, 'These things happen.'"

After drying off, Bara was ready for a second take in less than an hour with new costume and make-up.

"In all my directing career, I never met a more tolerant person . . ." Walsh recalled. "I had the luck and the pleasure to coach one of the nicest actresses I had ever met."

Nevertheless, Walsh gained the reputation at the studios as the director who 'tamed the wildcat Theda Bara.' The movie industry tended to believe its own press releases.

An alternate view of Bara came from Miriam Cooper, a movie actress who had worked under D.W. Griffith and was engaged to Walsh.

"I thought she was terrible," Cooper said of Bara "Her only expression was to duck her head and stare at the leading man or the camera with what appeared to be a searching look. And it was searching." Cooper claimed she was so near-sighted she would blunder into the camera and knock it over.

"She was overweight, coarse and unattractive, entirely different from the slender young Griffith girls. Mr. Griffith would never have hired her. But in stage makeup she looked exotic and sultry . . . . "

Cooper claimed that Bara had been excluded from a press screening of *Carmen*.

"Theda was furious. She had a case on Raoul and she thought I had arranged the whole thing to keep her away from him. The truth is that Raoul couldn't stand her . . .

"Raoul and I were very much in love, but even if he hadn't been, he'd have been glad to come home to me as a relief from Theda Bara," Cooper continued, "Between falling over the cameras and mooing at Raoul she was driving him nuts."

Walsh and Cooper married in 1916, but they divorced ten years later over Walsh's alleged infidelity. Sixty years passed before Cooper and Walsh wrote their reminisces of Bara. Walsh may have been responding to things said in Cooper's book. His autobiography was published a year after hers, and doesn't mention her by name, only calling her 'a mercenary witch.' Maybe Walsh liked Bara and fiancée Cooper was jealous. Perhaps Bara was something of a vamp after all.

Curiously, Cooper liked William Fox while nearly everybody else hated him; she quotes Walsh calling him 'pants presser.' She regarded Fox as "really a nice man, kind and considerate. But he was still primarily a businessman, and Raoul was an artist, like Mr. Griffith. We couldn't help wanting Mr. Fox to be like Mr. Griffith. Once you had worked for Griffith, you compared everybody with him."

At the press screening for *Carmen*, Cooper said it was the first time Fox had seen the picture. It ended with Don Jose stabbing and killing Carmen. Fox jumped up and blocked the projector.

"'Vhat are you trying to do, Raoul?" he shouted. 'Who vants to see such an ending? You vant the lovers should be happy. You don't vant the audience should valk out with a bad taste in their mouths.'

Walsh argued that that was the way the opera *Carmen* ended, and 'you can't change an opera.' The reporters who were present agreed with Walsh.

"Are we working for love or money?" Fox demanded to know, and without waiting for an answer, he stormed out of the projection room. Cooper remembered this as how movie moguls disregarded the original source material in their films.

"They'd have made Jesus Christ Greek if it would make money."

Eve Golden calls into question Cooper's assertion that Fox would have objected strenuously to Bara's death in *Carmen*. With the exception of *A Fool There Was* (scarcely a happy ending, with the villainess triumphant over the husband and family values), Bara died by one means or another in most of her subsequent films. In fact, Bara continued to suffer the consequences of her sins and died at the end in many of her films: stabbed in both *The Clemenceau Case* and *The Kreutzer Sonata*, burned to death in *Destruction*, stabbed again in *The Tiger Woman*, guillotined in *Madame Du Barry*, coughed to death in *Camille*, and executed in *Salome*. *Cleopatra* was no exception in that regard.

"Audiences loved to see her die in her films," said Golden in an interview, "and she did it very well."

However, from the beginning of cinema, moviemakers had compromised to turn literary works into motion pictures. At first, these were caused by budgetary and time restraints; some of the finer points of Mary

Theda Bara doesn't like the hand she's dealt herself in Carmen *(Author's collection)*

Shelley's *Frankenstein* were lost in Edison's ten-minute version of the story. Lew Wallace's epic novel *Ben-Hur* was less than epic in the equally short first movie version of the tale. That did not stop Wallace's heirs from suing the film company involved, Kalem, setting a legal precedent regarding literary rights and the cinema.

Producers had discovered that American audiences preferred happy endings to the grim ends suffered by characters in great literary works. *Deus ex machina* happy endings became the norm in Hollywood's renderings of the classic novels. *The Sea Beast* (Warner Brothers, 1926), a version of *Moby Dick*, contrived to have Captain Ahab kill the whale and return home safe, sound, and of course, happy. Herman Melville would have been horrified.

The Fox *Carmen*, however, had its own weird Hollywood twist to the ending, with Don Jose stabbing Carmen then riding his horse over a cliff to his death—which may have been Fox's actual objection—or how Walsh re-shot it to keep Fox happy; sources differ.

With the two productions racing to completion, publicity departments went into a frenzy to convince moviegoers which version of *Carmen* they should patronize. Newspapers called it the 'battle of the *Carmens*.' Both Bara and DeMille's star, famed opera diva Geraldine Farrar, weighed in with statements to reporters as the battle was joined. Instead of stealing customers from each other, the dueling Carmens provoked additional publicity and had audiences seeking both films out to compare.

"DeMille's production was marvelous, and everyone agreed that Miss Farrar was more beautiful than Theda Bara," Miriam Cooper recalled, getting in one last dig at Bara, "But this was a silent picture and Miss Farrar didn't sing a note. It was Raoul's version with Theda Bara, the sexy-looking vamp who had captured the country's imagination, that was the big moneymaker."

Carmen was a tremendous success, as was the DeMille version; Charlie Chaplin satirized both in his own version of *Carmen* AKA *Burlesque on Carmen* (Essanay, 1916). Bara's star shot further upward. More than three million people a week watched her movies. She received three to four thousand fan letters a week. Some fans, mostly housewives, but also a prison convict, wrote scenarios which they sent to her. Einar Linden, the Scandinavian opera singer who portrayed Don José to her Carmen, wrote a song dedicated to her entitled *Those Perilous Eyes*. Other songs from other composers followed, and her face, like that of other stars, graced numerous covers of sheet music. One newspaper reported, "Her picture on a poster outside is a guarantee of a crowd inside."

In *Carmen*, Bara had played a classic role and gone head to head with Geraldine Farrar, a top star, and proved her equal, at least at the box office. Afterward, Fox put her back into less prestigious vampire parts, but as Krefft asserts, "to suggest, as film historians tend to, that Fox merely tossed Theda into a series of cheap, tasteless potboilers misrepresents both the complexity of the situation and the character of the man. As he built up Theda's career during the first two years, Fox displayed considerable ambivalence."

He wanted to draw audiences with vampire films, but also had his story department search for *femmes fatales* in classic literature and theater to dignify the productions with the pretense of respectability.

Theda Bara in a tussle in Gold and the Woman. *(Author's collection)*

"All eighteen Theda movies that Fox released during 1915 and 1916 had pedigreed source material," notes Krefft. Of her 1915 films, *The Devil's Daughter* was based on Gabriele D'Annunzio's play, *Sin* came from Ermanno Wolf-Ferrari's opera *The Jewels of the Madonna*, *The Galley Slave* was a popular 1879 play by Bartley Campbell, and *Destruction* was based on the 1901 Émile Zola novel *Travail*.

Evil women were more 'safe' to audiences and censors if from a different age and country. Even though her characters were often motivated by revenge for wrongs done them by men, to further satisfy the censors, they would always suffer the consequences of their evil deeds. At the end of Bara's vamp films, she would die or go mad. The result that was her films were both exploitational and moralistic, a technique that Cecil B. DeMille would later master.

In *The Galley Slave*, Bara's character seeks vengeance on her husband who had sold her on the auction block. In *Gold And The Woman*, she was Juliet de Cordova, a Mexican adventuress using her feminine wiles to destroy an English colonel who cheated Indians out of their land. In *Destruction* ('The most famous vampire in her most daring role, bringing ruin and disaster to thousands,' proclaimed the press release), Bara's character seduces a wealthy manufacturer, tries but fails to seduce his son, and stirs up discontent among the factory laborers. An angry mob corners her in a mansion that catches on fire, burning her to death.

"It proves what her film friends have long feared," jibed the reviewer in the *New York Evening Mail*, "that she would one day suffer spontaneous combustion and go up in smoke."

Not all reviewers cared for the picture, however. Lynde Denig in *The Moving Picture World* observed:

"The horrors in this five-part melodrama are piled on so heavily, and the woman played by Theda Bara is so outrageously evil that an audience finds several of the scenes rather amusing. Here is an instance where the attempt to startle and terrify, because it is overdone, fails to carry conviction and the response of the spectator is far from that expected of the producer . . . the audience followed the first two reels patiently and after that revealed its good sense by laughing at the preposterous wickedness of the character portrayed by Miss Bara in her most forceful manner. For a time it appeared as if the melodrama were destined to become farce.

"There could be no better indication that the Fox Company has about reached the limit in the production of abnormal photoplays, likewise that Miss Bara is ceasing to touch the emotions by depictions of erotic women.

"Having provided a diet of horrors for many months, the Fox producers evidently thought the time had come to increase the dose and present in *Destruction* something more horrible than usual. But the public, instead of being stimulated, refused to swallow the new sensationalism and merely laughed."

Fox paid no attention to the critics' huffing; the vampire Bara still drew audiences in spite of the snickering. As the actress assigned such roles, Bara may have felt she had nowhere to go with the characterizations except over the top.

Even so, fighting the typecasting that was taking over her career, Bara begged for, and got to play, a sympathetic character in *East Lynne*, based on a popular Victorian play.

"Some critics pronounced Theda Bara a vampire and nothing else," said L.E. Eubanks in *Motion Picture Classic* magazine, "but they changed their minds when she appeared in *East Lynne* and almost forgot they had seen her in *A Fool There Was*."

The box office receipts for *East Lynne* and other 'good girl' movies were disappointing. Some sources list them as flops, others merely as not as big successes as her vamp movies. Either way, it convinced Fox to keep her in vampire pictures. Audiences simply would not accept her in 'good girl' roles, even if her picture were on the posters outside theaters.

Bara's performances were not limited to being before the camera. Goldfrap and Selig arranged press interviews that were shows in themselves. As carefully orchestrated as if on a movie set, Theda Bara played the role of Theda Bara.

"And the interviews," Bara later remembered. "They were staged. It took me hours to get ready for them. I had a special dress made that I never wore at other times."

Columnist Archie Bell interviewed Bara, armed with the knowledge that she was actually Theodosia Goodman of Cincinnati. However, she had him completely flummoxed by the bewildering things she told him. She convinced him that she had indeed acted in the Théâtre du Gymnase and the Théâtre Antoine in Paris, and before that:

"I can tell you of at least four times that I have been on earth," she told him, "yes, and I believe I could relate to you convincing incidents of those lives. I lived in ancient Egypt, probably Thebes. That city is as vivid in my recollection as the streets of New York today. I remember crossing the Nile on barges to Karnak and Luxor as plainly as I recall crossing the Hudson on the ferry today to come to the studio at Fort Lee. I do not expect other people to believe this. I know they will not, so usually I avoid mentioning the subject because people will think whether that I am seeking sensational and cheap publicity, or that I am a fool. And I am not a fool."

Then she reached into her generous cleavage to pull out two small clay models of the Egyptian god, Amen-Ra.

"He was my protector in the days of long ago, and he is my protector today," she explained, "When I was a little girl, my mother was walking me past a curio shop in Paris, where these were on view in the window. I wanted them because I recognized them in an instant. I went back each day and stood fascinated by them. One day my mother bought them for me, and they have never left me since. I sleep with them. They are always concealed about my clothing when I am acting."

The statuettes of Amen-Ra were set on either side of her plate as she dined on what Bell claimed was her traditional vampire feast of 'raw beef and lettuce leaves'— actually corned beef and cabbage.

She revealed other charms and amulets, including "an emerald ring given to me by a blind sheik, celebrated for his learning and wisdom . . . I was told that by keeping the ring, I would live long and that by praying to it I would get what I asked for. Have I tried? Yes, and I have always gotten what I prayed for.

"I also have a small crystal globe . . . I wear it suspended about my neck, waking and sleeping. It protects me from accidents. How do I know? Well, I never had an accident."

She also had, "A Maltese coral I keep to ward off attacks by animals— particularly dogs . . . A golden hand I wear to ward off the evil eye. I have had it since I was a child in Italy . . . A sailor gave me a shark's tooth to protect me from the dangers of the sea. My golden Inca god was given me by a Mexican, who promised that it would always protect me against fire and flood.

"While I wear many talismans, I do not think I am more superstitious than a lot of other persons. There are a lot of other things I believe in, but it would take too long to tell all of them."

Intrepid reporters duly informed readers that Theda Bara was actually Theodosia Goodman, or as Miss Curtis Pierce, writing to *Motion Picture Magazine*, quoted others as saying, "Theda Bara aint nothin' but a Cincinnati kike!" Some managed to muddle enough of the facts to add to the confusion. One magazine story had her born in a cyclone cellar in Kansas—as if she was carried in by a tornado instead of a traditional stork. She casually turned aside reporter's questions, often with the aid of either Goldfrap or Selig standing nearby.

"Were you born in Cincinnati, Miss Bara?"

"I wonder who circulated that story," Bara replied casually. "Where was I born, Mr. Goldfrap?"

"Egypt," Goldfrap answered his cue promptly.

"What does it matter who I am or whence I came?" Bara said to a reporter asking about her true origins. "Is it not enough that I am here, with a certain gift, perhaps, for expressing my feelings through the new pantomimic art of the cinema, without knowing my antecedents? . . . I

'V stands for Vampire' (Author's collection)

have the Bourbon nose. My mother was a descendant of the Bourbons ... Some say that Bara is Arab spelled backwards, but what's in a name?"

Bara herself lent to the hyperbole with her beliefs in the occult, spiritualism and reincarnation which she talked about in interviews. She read the palms of reporters interviewing her. Responding to reporters' questions, Bara either improvised or gave set answers.

"You ask me why men feel as they do about the vampire, what her power is. If I could tell you that, every woman would be a vampire, and the vampire business would be spoiled. Seriously, I do not know what gives certain women a strange, witch-like power over men. A vampire must never love. I have never loved, and if I ever fall under the spell of a man, I know that my power over men will be gone. Every woman must choose whether she will love or be loved. She cannot hope for both. You know we French people have a proverb that in love there is always one who kisses and one who merely turns the cheek. The vampire is content to turn the cheek. That is why she makes fools of men."

Even if Goldfrap came up with most of her speeches, it is easy to believe that a lot of Theda crept into her replies.

"But believe me, for every woman vampire, there are ten men of the same type, men who take everything from women— love, devotion, beauty, youth— and give nothing in return! V stands for Vampire, and it stands for Vengeance. The vampire that I play is the vengeance of my sex upon its exploiters. You see, I have the face of a vampire, perhaps, but the heart of a *feministe*."

Yet when questioned on her position on suffrage for women, she hemmed and hawed, trying to avoid answering until Goldfrap came to her rescue. Eve Golden pointed out this as proof Bara wasn't a feminist in the modern sense of the word. Bara wasn't, but she was likely under Fox instructions not to discuss politics with reporters, especially such divisive issues such as women's suffrage. However, in another sense, she was an unmarried woman who spurned having a husband and family to pursue a theatrical career; a very radical decision at the time. That she played very independent women—albeit, many of them vamps—had an influence on female moviegoers, even if she wasn't campaigning to get them the vote.

The same could be said for women who played heroines and battled villains in cliffhanger serials; they must have had some psychological impact on the women who made up the majority in movie audiences. If women demonstrated they were the physical, intellectual and moral equals of men on the screen—why not in real life?

In many respects, the 'vampire' in its crudest form was the female version of the stereotypical silent screen male villain, the oily, mustache-twirling devious seducer who tied heroines to railroad tracks. Bara disdained this caricature, saying, "My own idea of a vampire is the thoroughly human woman who is a blend of good and bad impulses.... There are such women, plenty of them. I have made an especial study of the type. It is a highly interesting one.

I am delighted to have this opportunity of displaying my work to American spectators and I hope I have succeeded in depicting the complex emotions of the panther woman as vividly as they have appealed to me."

These Bara interviews were spoofed in an article written by 'Theda Bearcat,' a pseudonym of some wag.

"I am not as black as I am painted. I was born beautiful. There is some ominous fate that stalked in my path when I was but a young girl trying to get along. It clutched me by the throat, dragged me aloft into its murky clouds, stifled my good resolutions and put me in pictures at a salary of $1,500 a week. I sincerely hope no other girl shall be preyed upon in this fashion."

Virginia Pearson poses with a rather alarming skull. (Author's collection)

Many didn't care about the truth. They loved the fantasy, and they loved Theda Bara. As columnist and ardent Bara fan, Wallace Franklin, wrote in *Photoplay*, "I wish to believe. I am going to believe. I do believe that Allah is Allah, and that Bara is Bara, that the ivory angel of purgatory is an Eastern Star, was born under the shadow of the Sphinx.... And I see no reason for disbelieving what it most pleases me to believe."

Even Archie Bell concluded Bara couldn't be from Cincinnati, "No, it is impossible. Theda Bara must have been born on Saturn, Mars ... or perhaps on Venus."

With the success of Theda Bara, a slew of competing 'vampires' sprang up at Fox and other studios. Man-eating vamps were everywhere in movies, grinding down men and rival women alike. Screen vamps tended to be tall and voluptuously full-figured, so they physically, as well as psychologically, dominated men. The sultry Nita Naldi, vamping Rudolph Valentino in *Blood And Sand* (Paramount, 1922) and other movies, weighed in at 180 pounds, which is why Theda Bara, at 135 pounds, could describe herself as 'a little thin.'

After losing out the lead role in *A Fool There Was*, Virginia Pearson, Valeska Suratt and later Madlaine Traverse formed the line of second-string vampires at Fox studios, but Bara also had rivals at other studios. Alice Hollister declared herself the 'Screen's First Vampire,' having starred in the 1913 film, *The Vampire*. Wanda Petit started out as a 'good girl,' then changed her name to Wanda Hawley and turned into a 'bad girl.' Louise Glaum also started out in 'good girl' roles at Ince studios, but she found herself cast as beguiling dancehall trollops leading men astray in William S. Hart westerns, such as in *Hell's Hinges* and *The Aryan* (both Triangle, 1916), then vamped in the leading roles in a number of vampire pictures. Ince publicity declared her 'The Vampire de Luxe.' Lillie Leslie was the chief vampire at the Lubin studio, while Cleo Ridgely's evil characters made 'good girl' star Blanche Sweet's life difficult in a number of films.

"Here comes the latest thing in Vampire Ladies! 'Ware, Theda!' announced *Motion Picture Classic* "Marie Wayne is the snaky, sinuous lady who has been hailed by critics as the newest surefire vampire. Her inequities are directed towards Pearl White in the Pathé serial, *Pearl of the Army*."

Signe Auen played the title role in *The Fox Woman* (Majestic, 1915), and *Motography* commented, "Usually, vampires are pictured as brunettes with

Vamping a stone wall. Louise Glaum works her wiles on distinctly uninterested William S. Hart in The Return of Draw Egan *(1916) (Author's collection)*

raving black hair, sensuous red lips, and sparkling eyes . . . . The idea of a blonde leading men on and taking their souls is a new one, but welcome."

Phony biographies also flourished. Olga Petrova played *femmes fatales* in such films as *The Vampire* (Solax, 1915) and *The Scarlet Woman* (Metro, 1916). Metro publicity claimed she was a Russian noblewoman born in Warsaw. She was actually English-born Muriel Harding. When Nita Naldi gained attention after her movie debut in *Dr. Jekyll and Mr. Hyde* (1920), the studio provided a phony biography that told of her exotic Spanish-Italian

Theda Bara as a vampire in her natural habitat. (Author's collection)

background. Her real name was Mary Dooley or Donna Dooley, or Anita Donna Dooley (sources differ) of Irish descent, and reporters interviewing her could not help noticing her thick New York accent.

The Vamp could be recognized by her trademark elongated cigarette holder, hoop earrings, bare shoulders and spit curls. In movies, vamps could often be seen in their natural habitat, the boudoir, lounging on leopard skin couches or tiger skin rugs. Most of all, what identified the vamps were their stunning gowns, dubbed 'vamping outfits.' Some of these were dazzling, many were ludicrous, with spider web motifs, trimmed with the fur of predatory cats, or magnificently outrageous headdresses of peacock feathers. Some were the fantastic creations of the studios, but in the case of Louise Glaum, she designed and made them herself with the assistance of her sister. Each vamp actress claimed, via publicity departments, to be the 'Queen of the Vampires.'

Yet it was Theda Bara of the half-lidded eyes, the curled lip, the emoting pout, the languid arm draped over her arched brow who became most famous. It was Theda Bara of the smoldering gaze, signifying predatory lust, who personified the public image of the Vampire. As George Walsh, an actor who appeared with her in several movies put it, "She doesn't steal the show. She *is* the show."

The vampire Theda Bara fascinated both men and women. Men lusted after her, despite the aura of evil, for the promise of sex laced with danger men found especially alluring. In *The New Yorker* in 1952, writer S.J. Perelman recalled the effect Bara had on him when he was in the sixth grade and overheard a couple of teachers excitedly discussing her.

"'If you rearrange the letters in her name, they spell "Arab Death,"' one of them was saying with a delicious shudder. 'I've never seen an actress kiss the way she does. She just sort of glues herself onto a man and drains the strength out of him.'

"'I know—isn't it revolting?' sighed the other rapturously. 'Let's go see her again tonight!'

Perelman raced to see the Bara movie, becoming spellbound.

"For a full month afterward, I gave myself up to fantasies in which I lay with my head pillowed in the seductress's lap, intoxicated by the coal-black eyes smoldering with belladonna....I saw myself oblivious to everything but the nectar of her lips . . ."

It was among women Bara had a special appeal. They regarded her with mixed loathing and awe. At a time when women had few rights and were forbidden most of the pleasures men took for granted, here was a woman who smoked, drank and used drugs—most of all, a woman who not only knew about sex, and was aware of her own sexuality, but used men's desire against them to utterly destroy them. Her victims were often middle-aged men of wealth and prominent status—the male professional elite who ran the world—and she, a woman, had the power to reduce them to literally groveling at her feet.

"There was Theda Bara," Olga Petrova observed condescendingly, "whose shadow typified the Circe, the vampire, the wrecker of hearts and homes that millions of drab women, living drab lives, longed in their secret hearts to resemble."

Victor Freeburg noted in 1917, "few are either daring enough or desirous enough of leading a vampire existence but through the medium of Theda Bara they can do her deeds and live her life."

No wonder they swallowed their gum in excitement.

***

In February 1916, the Germans began their offensive against the French at Verdun. The battle lasted eleven months and cost more than 300,000 lives. In July, a combined French and British force launched the Somme Offensive, resulting in well over a million casualties, with roughly 300,000 killed. The stalemate on the Western Front continued. In March 1916, the horrific Mexican Revolution spilled over onto American soil when guerrilla leader Pancho Villa raided Columbus, New Mexico, and was bloodily repulsed. Not satisfied with that, President Wilson sent an expeditionary force into Mexico in pursuit. The wily Villa evaded the Americans until they gave up and went home. In April, British troops crushed the Irish Nationalists' Easter Uprising in Dublin. In the United States, activist Emma Goldman was arrested for lecturing on birth control and Margaret Sanger was arrested for distributing information on contraception.

In 1916, Charles Chaplin signed a contract with Mutual, for $10,000 a week, with a signing bonus of $150,000 making him one of the highest paid people in the USA. Mary Pickford signed a contract for $10,000 a week plus profit participation, guaranteeing her over $1 million per year. Samuel Goldfish and Edgar Selwyn founded Goldwyn Pictures. Goldfish later changed his name to Goldwyn and became an independent producer. Adolph Zukor's Famous Players Film Company and Jesse L. Lasky's Feature Play Company merged to become Famous Players-Lasky, with Paramount Pictures as their distributor.

Determined to move away from the freewheeling early days of cinema to a rigidly organized studio system, William Fox strove to streamline the production process. Wanting to make movies the way Henry Ford made Model Ts, Fox turned his Fort Lee studio into a 'film factory,' a manufacturing center for the product to be sold at his theaters. He had made thirty features in 1915; in 1916, he intended to nearly double that. To speed up the creative process, he built 'companies' around a director, a writer and camera crew, often to make movies with an assigned star.

Up to this point, Fox had put Bara under a number of different directors: Frank Powell, Herbert Brenon, Raoul Walsh, Will S. Davis, James Vincent, Bertram Bracken and J. Gordon Edwards.

"Some directors are wonderful," Bara said in an interview "They give you such funny advice on manners and deportment. One time I asked my director about a certain scene. 'Do I repulse the advances of this man or do I lead him on?' I asked. The director was stumped. He hadn't an idea of

J. Gordon Edwards and Theda Bara outside her dressing room bungalow. (Courtesy of Robert S. Birchard)

what to do. Finally he hit upon a lively answer. 'Oh, just keep the audience guessing,' he said."

Sometimes she relied more on her cameraman than her director.

"My cameraman is my artistic speedometer," she stated. "If he likes a scene, I know it's good; if he shakes his head sometimes I cry a little because I am so tired, but I always do a re-take."

Fox decided to pair Bara with his top director, J. Gordon Edwards. They had worked together before in *The Galley Slave*, but now they would collaborate exclusively with each other on making movies for the next three years.

In 1915, Edwards had made *The Song of Hate*, "a modern society drama, based on Victorien Sardou's universally known *La Tosca*," starring Betty Nansen.

"As directed by J. Gordon Edwards," notes *Motography*, "it is a poignant exposition of the sins and follies of the twentieth century men and women. The production has screened massively and engages the services of hundreds of people. From the first scene flashed upon the screen to 'Passed by the National Board of Censors', there is said not to be a dull moment in the throbbing and thrilling action."

Edwards was less a creative artist to William Fox than a factory foreman, churning out product to a specific quota. Edwards later directed William Farnum (who would have preferred to make only four features a year), and it was only through Edwards' "bull dog insistency and systematic operations" that he delivered eight a year. William Fox observed that to replace Edwards it would require 'two first class directors,' one in pre-production and the other in production, to get the same result. In 1916, he would make eight features with Theda Bara.

Not that Edwards was a tyrant on the set. Sometimes, he was too much of a gentleman to be in the movie business. He asked to be removed from filming *The Blindness of Devotion* (1915) because he didn't know how to tell famed Shakespearean actor Robert Mantell his noticeable limp was ruining the picture. Fox instead had Edwards film an early scene in which Mantell's character is shot in the leg in a fight, justifying the limp.

Edwards worked briskly and efficiently, and he and Bara were to make an hour-long feature movie about every six weeks, called 'Theda Bara Superproductions.' Although she enjoyed working with Edwards, Bara was not pleased with the way these films were made.

"The studio became a factory, and I can think of no more applicable simile than to say we manufactured pictures in about the same way they make sausages. They were just turned out, one after another."

Fox had little patience for those trying to buck his system. Rex Ingram had been a writer and actor, contributing to *The Song of Hate*, *The Galley Slave*, and other of Edwards' films when Bara "reproachfully asked me why I had never written a story for her." Ingram replied he had. She wanted to know the title, as Ingram put it, "Titles seemed to mean more to her than yarns."

On being told the title was *Black Orchids*, she said she would do that next.

"I said it might be a good idea to read the script before making up her mind, but she said her mind was already made up, and she would talk to Mr. Fox."

After reading Ingram's outline, "Mr. Fox thought it was just the thing for Bara and told me to go ahead with a scenario and he would let me direct the picture. I tackled the job with a will, for I was fed up with writing for others to have fun producing what I wrote. I wanted to go out on the set and have fun myself."

Unfortunately for Ingram, Fox reneged on his promise to let him direct and assigned Edwards as director. Ingram insisted he direct, or he would take the scenario elsewhere. Without a word, Fox handed back the scenario. Ingram directed *Black Orchids* at Universal instead, starring that studio's vamp, Cleo Madison.

Throughout 1916, Edwards and Bara cranked out the 'Theda Bara superproductions,' which were mostly moneymaking vampire films. In *The Eternal Sapho*, she ruins men's lives while wearing a series of stunning gowns that, according to one critic, were designed to show off the agitated heaving of her bosom. In *The Tiger Woman*, she was the ruthless Princess Petrovich, who loves only pearls and destroys everyone around her to get them. *The Vixen*, 'The Story of a Woman Who Raised Havoc with a Dozen Lovers,' had Bara's character out to steal her good sister's boyfriend. One of her lines was "It is true I have no heart, but then I am more comfortable without one."

Bara still fought for 'good girl' roles that she would play in *Her Double Life* and *Her Greatest Love*, but still, no audience interest.

In something of a compromise, Bara was allowed to be both exotic and good as Cigarette, the tomboy heroine of Ouida's novel, *Under Two Flags*,

Theda Bara as Cigarette in Under Two Flags *(Author's collection)*

set in French Algeria. Its finale had Cigarette throwing herself in front of a firing squad to take the bullets intended for her lover. Fox publicity informed the press that as a child, Theda Bara would jump on one of her father's horses and ride out into the Sahara, visiting Bedouin tribes, eating dates and drinking camel's milk.

"It was just like getting home again," she told reporters during shooting on location in Florida sand dunes, which was substituting for the Sahara.

"I could feel the dryness of the desert air in my throat and the playing of desert sands about my bare feet. It's a strange coincidence. I was born at an oasis in the Sahara, and now in the Ouida story I am back again. There seems to be a strange fate which haunts my work in the picture and draws me back often to the scenes where I spent my childhood or my earlier years."

After a scene shot in a raging sandstorm (created by grain and chaff propelled by giant fans) Bara said, "One of my earliest recollections is linked with a simoom which swept across the desert and scattered destruction in its path. A heated, beating sand went before it and almost buried our tent. We crept close within it and afterward had to dig our way through to the air. It was almost stifling, and I remember how I cried as my mother and father lay close against the ground, pushing their way through the treacherous sand.

"Acting in this picture has aroused the call of the desert to me again, and I sometimes feel as if I'd like to return there and live again, for a short time, the wild, unruly life of the desert children."

One imagines there were very few desert sandstorms in and around Cincinnati. Nevertheless, *Under Two Flags* gave Bara one of her favorite roles. Another was when she played courtesan Marguerite Gauthier in the Fox version of Alexandre Dumas' *Camille*, updated to modern times.

When Metro announced it was casting its top stars Francis X. Bushman and Beverly Bayne in a screen version of *Romeo and Juliet*, William Fox immediately started his own competing production of Shakespeare's play, with Bara as Juliet. Some had trouble envisioning the buxom Bara in the role of a 14-year old girl, while others thought her Juliet was a bit sophisticated for her age. Bara responded to the latter criticism, "Juliet lived in a period of passionate abandon. Italy, in the days of Romeo and Juliet, was no place for a Sunday school girl."

Harry Hilliard and Theda Bara in Romeo and Juliet. *(Author's collection)*

Even her critics praised her performance for its 'usual intensity,' and 'a signal triumph of versatility.' One called her the 'Chief Treasure of the House of Capulet.' *Romeo And Juliet* received rave reviews in London, where a reviewer called it a "riot of action and a bounty of beauty" and high praise went to "Mlle Theda Bara, the famous Parisian actress," although what Parisians thought of her was unrecorded.

Bara played the dancing gypsy girl Esmeralda in *The Darling of Paris*, 'suggested by' Victor Hugo's *Hunchback of Notre Dame*. With the focus on Bara, Quasimodo's character became tall and handsome for the film, having had a little corrective surgery by Frollo, 'a scientist.' (Try to imagine a tall, handsome Quasimodo.) At the end of the film, Esmeralda and Quasimodo marry. Even the Disney version didn't go that far.

When her contract came up for renewal, William Fox raised her salary to $1,500 a week. The contract also required that she remain in strict isolation to preserve the mystery around 'the most mysterious woman alive.' Under its terms, she was prohibited from getting married. She could go out in public only if heavily veiled. She was forbidden to use public transportation, and she could travel only in a curtained limousine. (These curtains for the limo were made of fabric provided by an Egyptian relative, of course.) Even going to a public Turkish bath was forbidden her, although she was permitted to have one in her own home.

Eve Golden believed these contractual obligations are just another fiction cooked up by the publicity department. Yet Fox may have exerted pressures on Bara involving her personal life. Keenly aware that their fortunes were tied to their star performers, movie moguls sought to control their stars' private lives as well as their careers. Their fears were somewhat justified. Adoring female fans of Francis X. Bushman deserted their matinee idol when they learned he had divorced his wife to secretly marry his frequent co-star, Beverly Bayne. His career never fully recovered from the revelation.

Fox had invested heavily in the fabulous promotion around Bara, and likely he wanted to protect his investment. It is not unreasonable that Fox would require her not to go out in public in circumstances which would reveal the notorious vamp to be an ordinary woman. Bara obeyed the restrictions imposed on her, according to contemporary witnesses. However, Bara's isolation came mostly from her hard work schedule of making eight feature films a year. She rarely attended the type of parties Hollywood became famous for nor was she known to have had affairs with any of her leading men or directors.

"I have been a vampire of fiction, not fact," was Bara's way of putting it, but the public believed something else.

When the Catholic Federation in Cincinnati protested against the showing of *The Serpent*, it gave additional publicity to the film. This was quickly exploited as Theda Bara (or Fox publicity, using her name) wrote an open letter to the mayor of her former hometown:

"I cannot conceive how my appearances in pictures in Cincinnati theaters could give grounds for the protests now being published.... I cannot analyze or understand the purpose of those who would seek to attach stigma to my name because of the work I have done in *The Serpent* and other of Mr. Fox's pictures.... Quite the contrary. Every mother, every minister, every person with the well-being of the younger element of Cincinnati owes me gratitude for what I have accomplished through these pictures. Every picture in which I have appeared had a clear and understandable moral ....

Theda Bara dressed to kill. (Author's collection)

"To pillory me for trying earnestly, thru my pictures, to make sin and wrong-doing a thing to be shunned and avoided, presents an inconsistency which I am unable to fathom . . . .

"I have just as definite a place, just as high a mission as the best of your evangelists and the most beloved of your local ministers. Through the silent but expressive medium of the Motion Picture, I am saving hundreds of girls from social degradation and wrong-doing. I believe I am showing time and time again the unhappiness and misery that fall to the lot of transgressors, and the contempt and hatred which such people inspire in good society, and among the well-behaved people of the world. Furthermore, I am reaching one million people each day, an audience larger than was ever had by any man or woman in the world's history."

"Why should anyone declaim against the so-called sex drama?" she said in a press release defending *Gold and the Woman*. "Sex is the most vital influence in life. From the time a person is born into the world he is constantly under the influence of sex. When I use the word sex, I use it in its true sense, which is the best sense. Most people give the word sex a false meaning."

What was the meaning of the new style that swept the country? Women burned incense and practiced the 'Bara-look;' haughty, half-lidded gazes and sinister smiles of sexual promise. They engaged in slithery walking and languorous poses. White pallor paired with black outfits was the fashion. Bare shoulders and plunging necklines caused consternation among decent people. Parents watched in horror as their teenage daughters, who had been emulating Mary Pickford, now turned into 'baby-vamps.'

"After Theda Bara appeared in *A Fool There Was*," Mary Pickford herself observed, "a vampire wave surged over the country. Women appeared in vampire gowns, pendant earrings, and even young girls were attempting to change from frank, open-eyed ingénues to the almond-eyed, carmine-lipped woman of subtlety and mystery."

Bara was not the only movie star in the public consciousness. Fans traded cigarette cards, a precursor of bubblegum cards, featuring photos of their favorite stars. The faces of movie stars appeared on sheet music. Children played with Charlie Chaplin toys and Mary Pickford dolls. What the stars wore, on and off the screen, became important information in fashion news, and still photos of screen idols helped hawk merchandise in magazine ads. Bara even allowed a former business associate in Ohio to license her nickname 'La Bara' in a line of cosmetics.

For better or for worse (and the debate continues to this day), motion pictures were having an impact on society beyond being a mere novelty entertainment. Movies were influencing people in how they saw the world and themselves.

The trouble was that some of the public actually thought the stories about Theda Bara were true. Marriages were allegedly broken up over her. She received hate mail from credulous people who believed her to be the evil woman of film. One woman wrote her, "It is your type of woman that brings terror to the heart of a good woman, that disrupts homes and lures would-be faithful husbands through dark and hidden paths toward the goal of shame."

Theda Bara gently wrote back, "My Good Woman; We live by contrasts. One cannot exist without the other. You are one extreme; I am the other, as an actress only. If I acted as my heart dictates, and as perhaps you feel, my pictures would be an artistic failure. Furthermore, if I were the kind of woman you think me, I would not be doing what I am now, which, I assure you, is very, very hard work."

On an elevator in Washington, a woman with her husband recognized Bara. She ordered the elevator to be stopped at the next floor and dragged her startled husband away to save him from the toils of the Vampire.

Another woman was fined ten dollars for kicking in the face of a Theda Bara movie poster, writing to her to say 'it was worth it.' "How I hate you!"

"Why do people hate me so?" Bara mused in an interview. "I try to show the world how attractive sin may be, how very beautiful, so one must be always on the lookout and know evil even in disguise. I am a moral teacher then. But what is my reward? I am detested."

This guise took a psychological toll, however, if the stories of the time are to be believed. On one occasion in the streets of New York, a woman saw her child chatting with Bara. The woman called the police, crying "Save him! Save him! The vampire has my child!"

Another story has Theda Bara starting to enter a New York department store, only to be intercepted by the store manager who said, "Please don't come in, Miss Bara. We'll send the gowns to your hotel, but we can't stand any more of these riots." The day before, she had visited the store and examined a hat on display. After she had left, some women who had recognized her fought for possession of the hat, perhaps hoping to gain some of her mysterious powers over men.

Bara recalled another disturbing incident.

"I was walking near my home in Manhattan. I had a great big apple in my hand, and ahead of me I spied a little girl with thin legs and, oh, such a hungry look."

After giving the girl the apple, "Her eyes fell on my face and a look of terror came into hers ... Other little girls came up. 'It's the Vampire!' whispered the biggest, in a croaking way. Then they all ran, and I went home and sobbed like the littlest of them."

Going about veiled seemed preferable to being recognized as 'the wickedest woman in the world.'

One can doubt the veracity of such stories, likely concocted by Goldfrap and Selig or news folk unconcerned about journalistic integrity. On the other hand, even today there are soap opera fans who believe the characters on their favorite soaps are real people, and that the characters and actors are one and the same. Others hated Bara because they thought the roles she played and the movies she appeared in were lowering public morals. Some absolutely loathed Bara because she was an artificially created media sensation based on lies and hucksterism.

Mindful of how the 'vamp' image distressed their main star, Fox publicity had changed its tack for a while, releasing articles dispelling their own myths about their biggest star, with headings like 'Theda, the Misunderstood Vampire' and 'The Real Theda Bara— She likes Kiddies and Horses, not Vampiring.' This did not go over well with the public either, so the publicity department returned to calling her 'the Devil's Maidservant' and 'The Reddest Rose in Hell.'

Some normalcy for Bara could be found with the support of her family. Her mother, brother, and sister all moved in with her in a West End Avenue apartment to share in her success. Theda arranged for brother Marque to become an assistant director at Fox and helped sister Lori, with whom she was especially close, start on her screenwriting career. For years, Lori remained her closest friend and confidante. Meanwhile, Goldfrap and Selig wanted the public to believe that Theda Bara lived alone in Oriental splendor, attended by two aged Moorish servants.

It was hard to dismiss the success the vampire myth brought her. In just two years, Bara had gone from a complete unknown to being the third top box office star in the country; Mary Pickford and Charlie Chaplin took the #1 and #2 slots, but Bara jostled for third place with Clara Kimball Young, Anita Stewart, and Margarita Fischer, who aren't remembered today. *The New York Times* called her 'the flaming comet in the cinema firmament,' and estimated that half a million people a day were watching her films which were in continual release.

In November of 1916, as part of the publicity campaign for *Romeo and Juliet*, Fox issued a rather anachronistic press release.

"The coming of Theda Bara," it exclaimed, and newspapers across the country duly printed, "was prophesied by the ancient Egyptians! Rhames, priest of Set, writing on the stone walls of a tomb near Thebes, foretold the great emotional actress, who would lead men to destruction by her wiles. The inner walls of a recently opened tomb have disclosed to scientists new writings which give the startling prophecy to the world. While the hieroglyphics are in large part obliterated by the action of the 2500 years which have passed since they were engraved, there is still enough of them legible to form the amazing forecast.

"I, Rhames, priest of Set, tell you this." the inscription reads. "She shall seem a snake to most men, she shall lead them to sin and to their destruction. Yet she shall not be so. She shall be good and virtuous, and kind of heart; but she shall not be so to most men. For she shall not be that which she appears. She shall be called—'

"Here the inscription breaks off, and the rest of the stone is so worn and fragmentary that most careful investigation has been unable to decipher it. However, scientists say that the sudden insertion of the Greek letter, 'Theta,' was not without purpose, and that it was evidently the writers purpose to give the name of the woman he was prophesying."

This presumably indicates the Egyptian god of evil, although a little shaky on spelling, foretold the coming of Theda Bara.

Whether this convinced anyone to go see *Romeo and Juliet* is unknown, but it was prophetic in linking Bara with ancient Egypt. She was at the height of her career when, in the Spring of 1917, Theda Bara left New York to journey to sunny Southern California. There, she would film the movie which would become her most famous.

CHAPTER FOUR: 'SHAKESPEARE—MODIFIED SLIGHTLY'

In February 1917, after mismanaging the war, Tsar Nicholas II of Russia was forced to abdicate. In April 1917, the United States declared war on Germany, but needed time to organize a fighting force. Not waiting for the Yanks, the British army began its offensive at the Third Battle of Ypres, also called Passchendaele, a name synonymous with mud and misery. Meanwhile, in the Nivelle Offensive, the French used its army as a battering ram on the German defenses. Fed up with the senseless slaughter, some French troops refused to fight anymore. The mutiny was suppressed and hushed up. In the United States, women won the right to vote in the state of New York, but in Virginia, suffragists arrested for protesting at the White House were beaten and tortured at the Occoquan Workhouse by guards acting under orders from the superintendent.

In 1917, Vitagraph bought the Kalem film company, and Lubin studios went out of business. America's Sweetheart and the Little Tramp remained the top box office draws. First National Exhibitors' Circuit, Inc. formed First National Pictures to compete with Paramount, and late in the year, it signed Charles Chaplin to a million-dollar-a-year deal.

In January 1917, Fox announced his 'picture promises for 1917.'

"For the next year Mr. Fox will present to exhibitors and public 70 productions varying in length from 4,500 to 6,000 [feet]. These cinema features de luxe will be on a magnificent scale and will maintain the Fox standard."

One of the projects being secretly considered as a 'de luxe' picture was a movie about Cleopatra.

***

There were other Cleopatras during the Macedonian dynasty of Egypt, but the last of the line of Ptolemys is the best known, and she is the most famous woman of antiquity. Like Boudicca, Zenobia and Amanirenas, other warrior queens who fought Rome, what little is known about her was written by her enemies. Romanized Greek historian Plutarch, in writing about the life of Marc Antony, felt obliged to write about his ally, Cleopatra. Plutarch wrote that, contrary to popular legend, "Her beauty was not in itself incomparable, we are told, nor such as to strike all beholders; but to converse with her had an irresistible charm."

It was her intelligence and personality, rather than her beauty, which beguiled men into supporting her ambitions. The Romans despised her not just as a foreign monarch who challenged Roman power, but that she had lured their greatest leaders to assisting her. She convinced Julius Caesar to back her against her brother for the throne of Egypt and then later won Marc Antony's support.

When Antony abandoned his proper matron wife Octavia to be with Cleopatra, her brother Octavius rallied the Senate and the people of Rome against his political rival Antony, claiming that he had been seduced by that foreign queen. The legends about Cleopatra's excesses came from Octavian supporters trying to erode Antony's support by depicting him as under the sway of a sinister Oriental monarch. Capitalizing on Roman suspicion of alien customs, Octavius' propaganda machine harped on Cleopatra's threat to the empire, that she would undermine the Roman family and patriarchal social order by introducing strange religions and foreign ideas of Egypt and Greece.

Declaring war on Cleopatra (not on his real enemy, his political rival Antony; that would make it a civil war), Octavius defeated the pair at the naval battle of Actium. Their deaths in Alexandria ended the possibility of an Eastern-based Roman Empire until the rise of Byzantium centuries later.

Modern historians have been re-evaluating Cleopatra past the Roman disinformation. Instead of an overly ambitious sexpot whose excesses led to her downfall, a picture is emerging of a skillful monarch who challenged the might of Rome. The next wave of revisionism may picture her as something else yet. Although many regard Cleopatra as a failure, a Roman historian Dio Cassius, perhaps gave her the best summation: "She captivated the two greatest Romans of her day, and because of the third, she destroyed herself."

Two out of three ain't bad.

Cleopatra might have ended up a mere curiosity for historians if Plutarch hadn't written down her romances and tragic end, which were snapped up centuries later by an obscure playwright called William Shakespeare.

Frontspiece of a Victorian printed edition of William Shakespeare's Antony and Cleopatra. *(Author's collection)*

His *Antony and Cleopatra* guaranteed Cleo an immortality superior to all the arts of the mummy embalmers. She became the subject of art, plays and novels, a scheming queen imbued with great physical beauty superior to what she likely had in real life.

In the absence of facts, legends grew up about Cleopatra, making her an exotic sex symbol of ancient history, both sensual and dangerous. She could be seductive, smuggled before Julius Caesar rolled up in a carpet and offering herself to him gift-wrapped; she could be magnificent, appearing

A matronly-looking Cleopatra dazzles Marc Antony at Tarsus. Print based on Sir Lawrence Alma-Tadema's painting, The Meeting of Antony and Cleopatra, *1884 (Author's collection)*

dressed as Isis on a splendid barge before Marc Antony at Tarsus; she could be 'one of the guys' by joining Antony in ribald humor and playing practical jokes on him; she could be wanton and cruel, commanding a slave to be her lover for ten days, after which he must kill himself; she could be frivolous, melting a valuable pearl in vinegar and drinking it; she could be treacherous, abandoning Marc Antony at the battle of Actium; she could be callously murderous, testing poisons on slaves as the pursuing armies of Octavius neared.

Nowhere is Cleopatra more sensuous than when she is dying. Historians think she drank poison rather than suffer the painful death of the bite of an asp, but the romanticists wouldn't have it. In ways ranging from the titillating to the pornographic, artists from the Renaissance on nearly always depicted her baring an arm or more frequently a breast to the bite of the serpent, accepting penetration by death as her lover rather than submit to the degrading bondage of Octavius Caesar, the most powerful man in the world. In rejecting him, she remains undiminished, albeit dead, and no longer a threat to the social order.

Two thousand years after her death, when it came time for Cleopatra to be reincarnated and unleashed on movie screens, the handiest interpretation came from Shakespeare. Among the first screen Cleopatras was the first American movie star. Florence Lawrence played the Serpent of the Nile in a one-reel adaptation of *Antony and Cleopatra* for Biograph in 1908, though one must assume the storyline was abbreviated for the ten-minute running time.

While American filmmakers were still cranking out one and two-reel 'nickel shows,' Italians invented the movie epic with mammoth historical dramas with lavish scenes on gigantic sets. With an uncanny feel for the scope and spectacle movies were capable of, the Italians produced epics on a vast scale, such as the three-hour long version of *Quo Vadis?* (1913), *The Last Days of Pompeii* (1913) and *Cabiria* (1914). Enrico Guazzoni, whose *Quo Vadis?* proved an international hit, also directed *Marc Antonio E Cleopatra* (1913) and *Caius Julius Caesar* (1914), both of which saw wide release in the United States. These inspired American moviemakers to attempt the same kind of epic.

After *The Birth Of A Nation*, American movie producers went 'epic' crazy, wanting to repeat its box office success. D.W. Griffith made *Intolerance* (1916), an epic showing four stories in four different time periods. The biggest and most famous sequence, the Fall of Babylon to the invading Persians, was undoubtedly inspired by Italian epics. Universal had already put out its lavish ancient world epic as its first feature film, *Damon and Pythias* (1914). Thomas Ince had made a large-scale Civil War epic, *The Battle of Gettysburg* (1913), followed with another big scale antiwar film, *Civilization* (1916). Cecil B. DeMille made his own historical costume dramas, including *Joan the Woman* (1917), with DeMille's *Carmen* star Geraldine Farrar portraying Joan of Arc. DeMille's *Woman God Forgot* (1917), also starred Farrar, wearing suitably outrageous outfits in the midst of the struggles between Conquistadors and Aztecs, filmed in the splendor of Yosemite National Park. These were precursors to the epics that would become his most famous.

At Fox, Herbert Brenon had spent an alleged $300,000 on the costume drama *Two Orphans*, which may have been more of an indicator of why it did not make money even with Bara as a draw. Brenon's other Fox big-budget spectacular, *A Daughter of the Gods* (1916), starred the Australian swimming sensation Annette Kellermann. Brenon, who had directed

Scene from A Daughter of the Gods *(Author's collection)*

Theda Bara in four Fox films, had done such a good job on a previous profitable aquatic collaboration with Kellermann, *Neptune's Daughter* (Universal 1914), that Fox gave him free rein.

The result was Brenon going hog wild in one of those out-of-control, over-budget epic productions that give movie moguls ulcers. A bewildering fantasy involving mermaids, gnomes, witches and sultans, the picture had been filmed in Jamaica at a reputed cost of a million dollars, making it one of the most expensive movies of its time. Fired by Fox, Brenon walked off, leaving a hopeless pile of film to be edited.

To deal with the miles of footage, Fox hired an editor, H. G. Baker, whose work on another movie he had admired. To his surprise, a woman showed up, Hettie Gray Baker. After she successfully edited *A Daughter of the Gods* into a somewhat coherent movie, she was awarded the post of editor-in-chief at Fox Films.

Still furious with Brenon, William Fox removed his name from the credits. Prohibited from attending the premiere, Brenon was caught trying to sneak in wearing a false beard. Annette Kellermann, taking her seat, was heard to mutter, "A plague on both your houses."

Reviewers ignored the squabble and credited Brenon as the director anyway. He gained even greater critical acclaim in his next film, directing famed stage actress Alla Nazimova's first movie, *War Brides* (1916). Still angry with Brenon, William Fox managed to have the movie, an antiwar drama made shortly before America's entered WW1, banned as damaging to the war effort. Fox ripped-off the title to make *The War Bride's Secret* (1917), which kept the anti-German themes, but dropped the pacifist sentiments of Brenon's film.

Fox publicity may have boasted about the 'million-dollar mega-production' of *A Daughter of the Gods*, but it is unlikely there was much boasting about this figure in the Fox headquarters. In fact, epics were huge financial gambles, sometimes losing bets.

"*Civilization*, like *Intolerance*, was produced at enormous cost," commented Lee Royal in 1920 "Too expensive, in fact, to enjoy the same percentage of profits that is accorded the average picture."

Even success had a price. DeMille could point out his *The Ten Commandments* (1922), reaped more profit than a smaller budget film like his usual sex titillation comedies, such as *Old Wives for New* (1917) and *Why Change Your Wife?* (1920). His boss, Jesse Lasky, pointed out that three of DeMille's lower budget films earned more profit together than *The Ten Commandments* brought in on its own. Even so, epics were in DeMille's blood. *Male and Female* (1919), one of his sex comedies, has a fantasy scene with an Oriental monarch throwing Gloria Swanson to the lions, a prelude of such scenes in his *Manslaughter* (1922), *The Sign Of The Cross* (1932) and of course, his *Cleopatra* (1934).

Since modest budget pictures were inherently less risky than big-budget epics, it is no wonder studio heads shied away from epics in favor of more reliable potboilers. However, the allure of making screen spectaculars sometimes proved too much to resist. When an expensive movie about a wagon train crossing the continent during the old west was proposed, studio heads at Paramount, including Lasky, shook their heads, saying that Westerns, temporarily slumping at the box office, were 'out of style.' James Cruze argued it was not a Western, but an epic, and so won them over. *The Covered Wagon* (1923) proved a critical and box office sensation.

Not everyone was enamored of epics. In 1918, Randolph Bartlett in *Photoplay* commented on the epics that were changing the face of cinema, but not for the better.

"*Cabiria* was a huge success, in spite of the absence of personal interest in the story, because in its day it was a novelty. *The Birth Of A Nation* was a success, not because it was spectacular, but because its theme came right out of the heart of America's greatest crisis. *Intolerance* falls short of great success because it was too darned educational. *A Daughter of the Gods* despite its marvels of beauty, fell short, because the tale was purely artificial. *Joan the Woman* related an epic fable, but fell just a little short of the intimate, human touch."

Generally, Fox avoided making expensive prestige films. Most Fox movies were potboilers; 'purple' vampire pics, weepy melodramas, slapstick comedies, and Westerns. However, Fox did make some prestigious pictures, especially starring his favorite, William Farnum. Fox also made a few reform-oriented social justice pictures, such as *The Honor System* (1917), directed by Raoul Walsh, widely acclaimed for its theme of advocating humane treatment for prison convicts, and *The Price Of Silence* (1917), an exposé of child labor.

"What *Uncle Tom's Cabin* did for the negro slaves, William Fox's *The Price Of Silence*, will do for the underfed, ill-nourished, hard-working little factory slaves," declared *Motography*.

Motion Picture News told how 'The World's Greatest Showman' picked stories.

"William Fox has a private barber shop in his office. Every afternoon his staff barber arrives, and Mr. Fox retires to his barber chair. While the tonsor thus plies his job, a young woman enters . . . . Seated in a far corner of the room, she begins to read the scenarios. She has been selected because she has a metallic, unemotional voice that rarely fluctuates and never quivers."

"The ones I can remember when I get to bed, hours later, in the dark, are the ones I want," Fox explained "I don't weigh them by standards, arbitrary values or any other one thing. But I know that those that registered on my half-sleeping brain hours before, and still stand in relief, are the ones that will register on the brain of the audience in the theatre when portrayed."

Most sources list the Shakespeare plays *Antony and Cleopatra* and *Julius Caesar* as the primary inspiration for the Fox *Cleopatra*. The original idea came from H. Rider Haggard's novel, *Cleopatra*, first published in 1887. Haggard, like Kipling, is considered politically incorrect nowadays, with his exotic visions of the dark continent of Africa. He is best known today as the author of the novels *She* and *King Solomon's Mines*. Fox made the first screen version of *She* in 1916, starring vamp Virginia Pearson as 'She-who-must-be-obeyed.' A year later, Fox re-made the film with another vampire, Valeska Suratt, although one senses a lost opportunity to have Bara in the role.

Haggard's *Cleopatra* told of Harmachis, a fictional last descendant of the original Pharaohs. He tries to usurp the throne from Cleopatra, only to fall in love with her. This relationship results in the destruction of them both.

Whoever brought Haggard's book to William Fox's attention is unknown. It could have been Eva Fox, who continued to look for story ideas for her husband. Having read Victor Hugo's *Les Miserables*, she had recommended it for filming. As Glendon Allvine told it, "Here was a big book they could get for nothing, the copyright having expired, and it looked like a bargain, except for the title, which they considered changing to *In the Sewers of Paris*."

Hettie Gray Baker convinced them not to change the title.

It's possible, even likely, Bara herself, who had long dreamed of playing the role, suggested making *Cleopatra*. It could have been J. Gordon Edwards. In the course of his career, he had been steadily working on larger and more grandiose projects. Edwards had already made several historical costume pictures with Bara, including *Romeo and Juliet* and *The Darling of Paris*. They drew in critical praise, giving Fox films greater prestige needed to compete with other companies. *Cleopatra* offered Fox and Edwards a chance to work on a full-scale epic. Aside from disappointing returns on *Two Orphans*, the Bara costume pictures were successful, and with Brenon's *A Daughter of the Gods* being enough of a moneymaker, it gave Fox greater confidence in proceeding with *Cleopatra*.

Staff writer Ann Maxwell wrote a synopsis of the novel, apparently after being instructed to do so, since she regarded the project unfavorably. She remarked in her synopsis that a movie based on Haggard's *Cleopatra*, "would be valuable as a very costly spectacle, and it is doubtful if the interest created would compensate for the cost."

Noting that the story focused on Harmachis rather than Cleopatra, "the loves and treachery of CLEOPATRA comes third-hand to the audience … " Furthermore, "the love of ANTONY AND CLEOPATRA is only lightly touched upon while stress is laid on that of Harmachis and

Cleopatra and people are so imbued with the idea of the former was the grand passion of the Egyptian's life, that they'd hardly accept the readjustment."

Maxwell added, however, that one of the actresses Fox had under contract, Yiddish stage star Bertha Kalich, "would make a corking CLEOPATRA."

Yet it was only natural that the 'daughter of an Arab princess born in the shadow of the Sphinx' should play the Serpent of the Nile, which is how it was probably pitched to Fox.

Like Maxwell, Fox's staff worried that such a film would work only as an expensive epic, which they doubted would generate enough audience interest to pay back the extreme cost. They may have pointed out that although a sensation at the box office, *Intolerance* lost money because it cost so much to make; it took years for Griffith to recover. But Griffith didn't have Theda Bara, and first and foremost, William Fox intended *Cleopatra* to be a showcase vehicle for his superstar. Here was an opportunity for Bara to vamp and destroy great historical figures, wear gorgeous outfits and chew gorgeous scenery.

To play the role of Cleopatra had been a lifelong ambition of Theda Bara.

"It meant the realization of one of my supreme dreams. With emotions I could not describe I was told of a momentous decision." True, she wanted to play the 'mystic enchantress' on stage, but a spectacular movie epic would do.

Promotion began in early May 1917, proclaiming that Theda Bara was starring in a new "super de luxe picture under the direction of J. Gordon Edwards."

"Screen's Supreme Artiste Portrays Role of History's Greatest Sorceress..." Fox announced in *Motion Picture News*. "Never has an actress been given a vehicle in which to better display her versatility.

"Egypt's great queen was in many ways a refined and cultured woman; of wonderful charm and personality, but with limitless ambition. History has definitely fixed her position as a sorceress among the men of her time. She was a woman whom men might easily love, for she was active, plucky, high-spirited and dashing. She viewed life with a light heart, except toward the end, having a greater familiarity with laughter than with tears."

The blurb went on to say, "J. Gordon Edwards, who made *Cleopatra*, has presented some of the greatest scenic effects ever shown."

This before filming had even started.

As for Cleopatra's ethnic origin, Fox publicity merely stated:

"Cleopatra, Miss Bara found, was completely of Greek descent. It is to be supposed, therefore, that she resembled the Greeks in appearance more than the Egyptians. Most women of Macedon, the region from which the Siren of the Nile was sprung, are fair-haired and blue-eyed. It is logical to presume, therefore, that Cleopatra followed the race.

"Popular opinion, however, is deeply rooted in the belief that the Sovereign was a brunette, with dark eyes and hair. Miss Bara acted on this assumption when she devised her make-up for the character."

The announced budget of the film was $250,000 and the finished movie was expected to run seven reels, slightly over an hour in length.

Writers, then and now, have trouble getting respect in Hollywood, but during this period, they exerted a major influence in the maturing of cinema. In a 1920 pamphlet titled *The Romance of Motion Picture Production*, Lee Royal described the typical process for creating a scenario (today called a screenplay) at a major studio.

"The opinions of the producer, director, star and scenario editor are all taken into consideration when deciding upon a story to produce. After having arrived at a decision the story is given to one of the staff writers with the instructions to proceed with the continuity. Both men and women are employed in these positions. If the story deals with a subject most intimately known to women, a member of that sex is generally selected for this assignment. But if the plot is essentially masculine in the character, the job will unquestionably fall to a man."

Women wrote several of Bara's early scripts. Screenwriter Mary Murillo wrote six scenarios for her.

"Hats off to Mary Murillo," said *Motography* in a short article that praised her while at the same time belittling her. "A fair-haired little person in William Fox's scenario department, still in her twenties, has produced the scripts for twenty-five of his big feature photoplays during the past year.

"The phenomenal success of little Mary Murillo is probably without parallel among staff writers of any film company. She is a little woman with big ideas.

"She has herself written twenty-two scenarios to suit the needs of thirteen different screen and stage stars, in a year, for Fox Film Corporation."

This period was something of a golden age for women writers in film, as a little over one-quarter of screenwriters in the silent era were women. Anita Loos, Frances Marion, and Jeanie MacPherson were leading screenwriters of their era. 'Kalem Girl' Gene Gauntier was not only that company's star actress but its top screenwriter, penning Kalem's most prestigious film (and only feature), *From The Manger to the Cross* (1912), a story of Jesus Christ in which she also appeared as the Virgin Mary.

There were female directors as well, including pioneers Lois Weber and Alice Guy-Blaché. Mabel Normand directed a number of her Keystone comedies without credit, and she co-directed with Charlie Chaplin some of their films together when he was first starting out (for which he gave her no credit). Other actresses who occasionally directed include Margery Wilson, although some stars, like Mary Pickford and later Gloria Swanson, preferred to produce their pictures and leave the directing chores to others. The husband-wife team of Francis Ford and Universal's 'serial queen' Grace Cunard collaborated on writing and directing their thrilling chapter-plays in which they also co-starred. Another serial queen, Helen Holmes, directed some segments of her films. Carl Laemmle's Universal was especially liberal in hiring female directors, including letting Cunard, Ruth Stonehouse and Cleo Madison direct some of their own films, as well as at least six other women during the silent period.

It was still a world dominated by men, and women still had a tough time not only getting work but also getting respect. Frances Marion recalled when she applied to write for the Fox company. After being kept waiting an hour outside his office, she was admitted and she told Fox she was "dead serious about writing for your studio."

He waited as she rattled off story ideas she had, "until I finally ran out of breath," and she asked him, "Are you or are you not interested?"

"'Interested, yes. But answer me this question: For why does a pretty girl like you want to be a writer?'"

"'Because I like to write.'"

"He shook his head with mock pity. 'Now answer me *this*: Why ain't you in a dress from a stylish store? Why don't I see no jewelry?'

When Marion replied she had none, Fox tsked and said, "a girl like you should have rings on her fingers—'"

"'Bells on their toes?'"

"Ha, sassy! From a homely face I wouldn't take it. From prettiness it's cute. Do you know how you should look? In the most expensive outfits they got at Saks Fifth Avenue, earrings, bracelets, —no phonies, all the real stuff.' The look in his eye said more than his words. 'Well, what do you think?'"

"'I'm paid to think, Mr. Fox,' replied Marion, demanding $200 a week, with the proviso she would work two weeks for nothing to prove her worth.

Marion says Fox 'smiled indulgently,' and said, "Listen cuteness, don't try to be a foolish somebody. Nobody cares about female writers. Actresses—yes, they got glamour, but writers— the poor schlemiels!'"

When she persisted, he offered her $80 a week. Marion knew the top screenwriter, C. Gardner Sullivan, who wrote William S. Hart scenarios for Thomas Ince, made only $75 a week. She told Fox she would think it over, and she went next to World Pictures, where she was hired for $200.

There is also the case of Reatha Dale Watson, who was a scenario writer at Fox under the pen name of 'Folly Lyell.' No less a person than Mary Pickford advised her to become an actress as she was 'too beautiful' to be behind the camera. She did, and as 'Barbara La Marr,' she was promoted as the 'Girl Who is Too Beautiful.'

While never easy, it was easier for women to enter the motion picture industry during this period than a decade later. As Myrtle Gebhart wrote in the December 1923 issue of *The Business Woman*:

"Excluding acting, considering solely the business possibilities, the positions are held by women in the Hollywood studios as typists, stenographers, secretaries to stars and executives, telephone operators, hairdressers, seamstresses, costume designers, milliners, readers, script girls, scenarists, cutters, film retouchers, film splicers and other laboratory work, set designers and set dressers, librarians, artists, title writers, publicity writers, plaster moulders, casting directors, musicians, film editors, executives and department managers, directors and producers."

If women on the screen provided escapist fantasy for female audiences, those working behind the camera showed a surer path to self-determination and independence. Later, when the studio system was fully developed, and conservative moguls such as Louis B. Mayer ruled that a woman's place was in the home, women had a harder time finding work behind the camera.

The assignment of scenarist for *Cleopatra* was given not to a woman but to Adrian Johnson. Born in Knoxville, Tennessee, in 1883 of a prominent politically influential Kentucky family, Adrian R. Johnson (sometimes the middle initial is given as 'O',) had a Liberal Arts Degree from St. Mary's College in Belmont, North Carolina. His start in screenwriting was apparently at Metro. He also created two scenarios for the short-lived Mirror studio. Although he wrote for other Fox stars and directors, he seems to have been assigned to write Edwards-Bara Superproductions shortly after being hired at Fox in 1916. These included *Romeo and Juliet*, *The Tiger Woman*, *Camille* and *Madame Du Barry*, and was likewise chosen to write the scenario for *Cleopatra*. In all, he wrote fifteen scenarios for Theda Bara, more than any other single writer, along with other scenarios at Fox.

"There is one man in the motion-picture business that I should like very much to meet," Peter Milne wrote in *Picture-Play Magazine*. "He is Adrian Johnson, of William Fox's scenario staff. Mr. Johnson is a combination historian, research man, dramatist, and scenario writer. Sometimes I think he must be a syndicate, a mythical character, who gets the credit for the work of an entire staff. However, other scenario writers with whom I am personally acquainted assure me that he is flesh and blood—that there is a single man that will smile or frown when addressed as Adrian Johnson.

"Be that as it may, Mr. Johnson never seems to be at the club, at the Fox offices, or in any of the Gotham byways frequented by screen folk. As I know so little about the gentleman, I hope he will excuse me if I presume to know a lot. I will conjure before you Mr. Fox's office in New York, a modest, yet entirely comfortable, place."

Milne envisioned Fox sitting at his 'glass-top mahogany desk' and "Suddenly his face lights up." He summons Johnson to his office. Milne imagines the following dialogue:

"Adrian, let's make a picture around Cleopatra. We'll put Miss Bara in it and make it big. You write the scenario.'

"'Yes, Mr. Fox.'

"Mr. Johnson exits, and hurries to the public library, where he finds historical data on Cleopatra . . . . He returns with the completed scenario.

"'Very good, Adrian. Now how about this Caillaux case? Bolo Pasha, the ex-French premier and all that, you know. Let's put them in pictures. You write the scenario.

"'Yes, Mr. Fox.'

"Mr. Johnson exits, buys all the newspapers of the past month, and starts writing. He buys more newspapers each day. Before Joseph Caillaux's trial is over he presents Mr. Fox with an almost completed script.

"'Very good, Adrian. We'll add to it as the trial proceeds. Now how about putting the life of General Pershing in pictures? We'll call it *Why America Will Win*. You write the scenario.'

"'Yes, Mr. Fox.'

"Mr. Johnson proceeds to unearth data on General Pershing's early career, and also ventures to predict the manner in which he will walk through the streets of Berlin. He returns with the completed scenario.

"'Very good, Adrian. Now, Salome, that's a good name. Every one knows it. Every one knows Theda Bara. Combine the two of them in a picture, and we'll have a combination that even the war tax can't beat. You write the scenario.

"'Yes, Mr. Fox.'

"And so on — ad infinitum! What a diverse array of characters and subjects! Personages from ancient history — a traitor of the present day — one of the world's greatest heroes of the day. Does Mr. Johnson ever cry quits, throw up his hands, and exclaim at Mr. Fox: 'But how in the world am I to find out what General Pershing did when he was a boy? How do I know how many beads Cleopatra didn't wear?' Apparently not. Mr. Johnson's business seems to be to produce this material, and produce it he does."

Ann Maxwell's synopsis of Haggard's *Cleopatra* starts with an 'English professor' finding a scroll in the sarcophagus of a mummy in an Egyptian tomb. Returning to London, the professor reads the scroll, which turns out to be the autobiographical account of Harmachis.

In his notes for the scenario, Johnson pointed out, as Maxwell did, the focus of Haggard's novel was Harmachis, not Cleopatra, who would be the central figure in the movie. Haggard left out major parts of Cleopatra's life. To fill in some of the gaps, Johnson drew upon Shakespeare and also another interpretation.

Popular French playwright Victorien Sardou was known for his light comedies and his heavy, or at least pretentious, historical dramas. For Sarah Bernhardt's triumphant return to the Paris stage, he wrote *Fédora* (1882). He also penned *La Tosca* (1887) for Bernhardt, which would later be the source for Puccini's opera. Bernhardt also played the Serpent of the Nile in Sardou's 1890 play *Cléopatre*.

The writer of the English translation of *Cléopatre*, whose name is sadly lost to history (although his views on women's rights are faithfully preserved), sums up the theme of the play in the argument:

"The character of the voluptuous but crafty Queen of Egypt is a true type of those women who, straining beyond their sphere, seek to emulate the power and attributes of manhood, but, for lack of strength, are forced to resort to cunning. They mould men to their will 'tis true, but in the moulding they destroy the substance, and so the very vigor which they seek to use, in default of that which they do not nor cannot possess themselves, fails them at their direst need, and the house of cards they have built up tumbles about their ears for lack of foundation.

"Victorien Sardou has depicted this phase of female character with wondrous skill, and, though it may seem too daring that any modern writer should take up the theme so poetically handled by the poet of all time—Shakespeare— yet, exquisite as his work is, it somehow fails in the dramatic intensity so sought after on our modern stage, which is nothing if not sensational, and does not give the scope and verve enough to the talent of a great artist such as Sarah Bernhardt. Therefore Sardou may be pardoned for trenching on the ground already so worthily occupied by the great master of his art, inasmuch as he has given us a drama fit to display the genius of the greatest actress of modern times, clothed in appropriate language and fitted with the situation of climax of the modern school."

One contemporary critic described Sardou's *Cléopatre* as "fine history ruined by a music-hall writer."

Nevertheless, the play was enormously popular, especially when Bernhardt commanded the title role.

The chief matron of the Victorian era was Queen Victoria herself, wife and mother of the royal families of Europe, and wife and mother to the British Empire itself, whose people had known no queen besides Victoria for decades. When the glamorous exotic star played the glamorous exotic queen on the London stage, Bernhardt as Cleopatra was a startling apparition. During one performance, a matronly theatergoer reportedly exclaimed, "How unlike—how so unlike—the home life of our own dear queen!"

Sarah Bernhardt as Cleopatra in a stage production. (Author's collection)

As Margaret M. Miles observed in her book, *Cleopatra: A Sphinx Revisited*, "The purported remark, while expressing the sense of moral superiority of Victorian England, indicates that Cleopatra fascinated in that she embodied everything the Western bourgeoisie affected to abhor."

Sardou's play was adapted for a 1912 film version of *Cleopatra*. Helen Gardner, a teacher of pantomime, gained recognition appearing in movies, notably in the role of Becky Sharp in *Vanity Fair* (Vitagraph, 1911). Gardner became one of the first, possibly the first, movie star to form her own production company. Her Helen Gardner Picture Corporation built a movie studio at Tappan-on-the-Hudson in New York. She immediately started making one of the first American feature-length movies, featuring the Helen Gardner Picture Players. Vitagraph director Charles L. Gaskill

Helen Gardner in her production of Cleopatra
(Author's collection)

was hired to adapt Sardou's play as well as direct *Cleopatra*, with producer Gardner in the title role.

On its initial release, *Cleopatra* was very successful. Critics called it "probably the most stupendous and beautiful picture ever produced," and "a wonderful production." On the other hand, Robert Hamilton Ball, viewing it decades later, described it as "a complicated story of various loves and honours without real depth and with somewhat incomprehensible characters, indeed a sorry mish-mash."

Gardner produced several other pictures, including *A Sister to Carmen* (1913) but her films could not keep up with the changing tastes in cinema. She ceased work at her studio in 1914.

The September 1916 issue of *Picture Play Magazine* carried an article titled, 'Where are the Stars of Yesterday?' It queried in wonderment at how many of the great stars of only a couple years earlier had vanished from the screen, replaced by newer stars.

"Go back a few years and recall the vogue for Romaine Fielding, William Clifford, Paul Panzer, Fred Church, Harry Myers, Tom Stanschi, and

Walter Miller. How many get even passing notice to-day? . . . How many of you remember Linda Arvidson, Mary Malatesta, Isabel Rae, Adele Ray, and Joseph Graybill? Pictures patrons of five years ago had no greater favorites . . ."

Other names mentioned that are more familiar to silent film buffs include 'Bronco' Billy Anderson, Maurice Costello, King Baggot, 'Our' Florence Lawrence, Billy Quirk, Gene Gauntier and Helen Gardner.

"Helen Gardner is another favorite of yesterday whose popularity died a natural death because of lack of good plays and— Theda Bara. When this dazzling vampire of the Fox forces flashed upon the screens of a thousand photo-play houses in *A Fool There Was*, the death knell of Miss Gardner was sounded."

With the success of 'purple' pictures, Gardner turned into a rival screen vampire, but she soon faded to supporting roles. While some stars mentioned in the article experienced a resurgence in the movies, how swiftly most of them faded from view should have warned Bara and her contemporary stars 'all glory is fleeting.'

Gardner did not disappear altogether. Continuing to act in films, she made one of her last movies, *Sandra*, in 1924. Gardner died in 1968, but her *Cleopatra*, unlike the Fox film, still survives.

The makers of the Fox *Cleopatra* likely saw the original release and drew from it; as in the Gardner film, the Fox version uses the historical and Shakespearean character Ventidius to combine several characters in both Shakespeare and Sardou into one person. Several minor characters, such as hairdresser Iras and lady-in-waiting Charmian, also historical figures, were included in the interpretations of Shakespeare, Sardou and Haggard.

One character exclusively in the Gardner production is Pharon, who appears in neither Shakespeare nor Sardou. In the Gardner production, Pharon is a fisherman-slave who is 'entertained' by Cleopatra for ten days on the condition that he must destroy himself on the last day—apparently drawn from *Une nuit de Cléopâtre* (1838), a short story by the French writer Théophile Gautier. Both Haggard's Harmachis and Gardner's Pharon might be considered a replacement for Ptolemy, Cleopatra's brother and husband. History gave Fox considerable license to get sex, adultery and scandal sneaked past the censorship boards, but there was no way that bit of incest would glide past the censors of 1917.

In Adrian Johnson's copious notes for his scenario, he listed the books he consulted for research and inspiration. In addition to Haggard's *Cleopatra*, there was *Plutarch's Lives*, Shakespeare's *Julius Caesar* and *Antony and Cleopatra*, Sardou's *Cleopatra*, and George Bernard Shaw's play, *Caesar and Cleopatra*. Johnson noted that while Shaw treated his subject humorously, he thought others should read it. "Anything we read on this subject will do us all good, I figure."

Johnson read Lew Wallace's *Ben-Hur: A Tale of the Christ* (1880), chiefly for the chariot race and possibly the naval battle. He also read Jacob Abbott's biography, *History of Cleopatra, Queen of Egypt* (1879), which repeated Roman propaganda depicting Cleopatra as an evil sexpot. Johnson called Arthur Weigall's *The Life and Times of Cleopatra, Queen of Egypt* (1914), the "most accurate and concise historical record I have read on this subject..." Lauding Weigall's expertise in research in Egypt and the 'reliable classical authors,' Johnson added, "Weigall has neglected no point, however small, which might have a tendency to elucidate the subject. It is interesting historically, romantically, and dramatically..." and Johnson notes that he threw a light on Cleopatra's character different from that of derogatory critics. He recommended everyone should read Weigall's book because "it has sincerity, painstaking research and authenticity stamped upon it unmistakably."

While acknowledging Weigall as being "considered one of the greatest authorities of the period," Theda Bara had a completely different reaction to his book.

"In this I read that Cleopatra was nothing more or less than a royally born house-frau, with six or seven offspring, mainly interested in protecting her throne for her family."

Bara found no inspiration in this, because it ran counter to "the conception built up through the ages in the imagination of the world... I did not and do not believe Cleopatra was at all as the German (Weigall was actually English), without imagination or romance in his dry as dust nature, pictured her."

Bara couldn't believe such an ordinary woman would have made such an impact on history. Dismissing Weigall as a "dry-as-dust bookworm who in following the letter looses [sic] the truth of the spirit," Bara asserted, "It is not in dusty parchment rolls we discover the glory that was Greece, but in the poets and the dramatists...."

Adolphe Goupil's engraving of Jean-Léon Gérôme's painting, Cléopâtre et César *(1866), which perpetuated the legend of Cleopatra being smuggled in a carpet into Caesar's presence. (Author's collection)*

She believed 'that great soul' Shakespeare, "gifted with clairvoyant vision, with mind antenna reaching into the past, attuned to feel the still palpitating vibrations of old Egypt, of the thoughts and emotions of the queen who is now dust, was more reliable than a German deciphering hieroglyphics in a library."

Bara pushed for the romanticized version of the Cleopatra story, which she knew is what her audience wanted.

J. Gordon Edwards was also very influential in the writing of the scenario, as Johnson mentioned him repeatedly in his notes concerning the director's opinions and suggestions, and Bara also had some input into Johnson's scenario, as Johnson refers to some of her suggestions.

Johnson's scenario is filled with notes and queries for advice on how scenes should be handled, sometimes listing a variety of options, ending with 'PLEASE ADVISE!!!' Since he was already consulting with Bara and Edwards, he probably asked this of Fox staff writers or William Fox himself, probably being read aloud to him during his daily shave. An interesting quality of the scenario is how much it suggests several alternatives to the producer and director.

In the earliest days of cinema, there was no script at all. Films unreeled without any dialogue or description titles; audiences had to figure out what was going on without the assistance of any titles besides the name of the film. Actors and directors improvised. Stories were more in the form of outlines. Steadily, as films became more complex, so did the scenarios. When the sound era finally arrived, actors had to know exactly what lines to memorize, and 'screenplays' became more rigid in format.

For the opening, Johnson draws slightly from George Bernard Shaw's play. He dispenses with the Egyptian civil war altogether in favor of inventing a Roman invasion of Egypt, with Julius Caesar driving Cleopatra from the capital Alexandria. Johnson then uses the legend of Cleopatra being concealed in a carpet to get past Caesar's guards. Caesar is so dazzled by her beauty, he quickly falls under her spell. Cleopatra convinces Caesar to return to Rome and demand the crown of emperor. Believing "Caesar had strong Republican ideals . . . . " her seducing of him to claim the throne "was infinitely greater historically than that of Marc Antony." Johnson considered this to be "the greatest moment in the life of the Queen."

Most references list the primary source for the film as Shakespeare, since this was a very popular dramatic interpretation of the era. One invariably thinks of Shakespeare's dialogue for the assassination of Caesar and the funeral orations from *Julius Caesar*. However, Johnson used only events immediately surrounding the assassination. Although Cleopatra was actually in Rome when Caesar got shanked, Johnson leaves her in Egypt, yet

Art imitating art. Theda Bara's Cleopatra *emerges from a carpet, imitating the Gérôme painting. Egyptomania plus 19th Century historical and Orientalist art were major influences on* Cleopatra's *production design. (Author's collection)*

he wanted to establish "that it is her fascinating, alluring, ambitious influence" caused Caesar to demand the crown, resulting in his assassination.

Not regarding Calpurnia, Caesar's wife, 'of sufficient importance' Johnson introduces her only for a title card of her asking Caesar to remain at home because of her ill-omened dream, which Johnson noted as 'Shakespeare— modified slightly.'

Neither her warnings nor that of Antony sway from his ambition "which was activated by his love for Cleopatra."

About the conspiracy to assassinate Caesar, Johnson simply shows Cassius, Brutus and other conspiring senators meet in a secluded spot and raise their right hands in an oath.

Regarding Antony's funeral oration, "the 'friends, Romans, countrymen' stuff," Johnson selected a few lines, but he wanted to eliminate most of it. By having fewer title cards, "no matter how classic and Shakespearean, we have more time and footage to photograph ACTION. ADVISE!!!"

Harmachis / Pharon (Albert Roscoe) is crowned by his high priest father (actor unknown) in a secret ceremony not described in Johnson's scenario. (Courtesy of Academy of Motion Picture Arts and Sciences)

Although Johnson didn't have it in his original scenario, parts of Brutus' speech were possibly used as well, as production stills seem to indicate. Johnson skips over the Roman civil war between Caesar's assassins and Antony, reducing it to one title card explaining the defeat of Brutus and Cassius and the forming of the Triumvirate of Antony, Lepidus and Octavius.

From Haggard's book, Johnson tells of Harmachis, sent by his priest father to assassinate Cleopatra. Angry at a Nubian slave, Cleopatra orders his hand to be chopped off, Johnson wrote it "might seem cruel but it is a good character touch as Cleopatra demonstrates her imperial power here, her inflexibility towards anyone who may cast a slight upon her authority."

Johnson thought Harmachis might plead for the Nubian, but any leniency would make "her too soft and takes away from that awe in which we must regard her regard at times. Being a many phased woman, it is well to try and show a flash of all sides of her character— Advise!!"

Harmachis becomes Cleopatra's new astrologer (she having executed his predecessor for failing to predict Caesar's assassination). Edwards argued

Pharon interprets Cleopatra's troubling dream to her satisfaction, and she appoints him her new astrologer. (Author's collection)

Paulus, a Roman guard in Cleopatra's service, needed to be introduced at this point, as his dead body appears later in the film. Johnson didn't like this, but admitted if Paulus' death was important, then he had to be introduced earlier. Both Edwards and Johnson were in accord regarding the scene in which Cleopatra hires Harmachis.

"Mr. Edwards did not like— nor do I— the business of Harmachis producing the snakes with his wand as evidence of his magic power. This is 'trick stuff' and something misses 'getting over' as it should."

Edwards and Johnson instead adapted a scene in which Cleopatra tells Harmachis that she dreamed of the dead Caesar, and his favorable interpretation of the dream gets him hired, "without the magic effects specified by Rider Haggard. Please Advise!!"

Subplots include Cleopatra's handmaiden Charmian in love with Harmachis, and Iras in love with the captain of the guards, Kephren, but both men love the irresistible Cleopatra. Johnson changed another scene by Haggard, in which Cleopatra, informed by a jealous Charmian of Harmachis' true purpose, drugs him.

"To me, it seemed that Haggard missed the whole dramatic force of the scene," Johnson complained, wanting "the alluring qualities of this Queen, that she should stand up 'like a man' and seduce Harmachis with that One Great Kiss she gives him" that causes him to betray his cause "in that moment of supreme intoxication ... Let her fascinate him and cause him to forget his vows by the force of her own allurement rather than use the extremely antiquated drugged cup."

Believing this to be 'the supreme moment of his fall,' Johnson has Harmachis beg to be killed, but she spares him to be her plaything.

When Antony summons Cleopatra to appear before him at Tarsus, Johnson pondered how Cleopatra would deal with this, as she must yield without losing her queenly dignity. He thought the scene could create some audience suspense as she promises to go to war rather than yield. Promising to fight Antony, Cleopatra seduces Harmachis into helping her steal the 'sacred treasure' from the tomb of the high priest, Menkau-Ra. During this raid on the tomb, Harmachis is forced to kill his priest father, after which, Cleopatra betrays him by agreeing to meet Antony in Tarsus. Although Haggard had this betrayal in private, Johnson wrote, "if she came out flat and told him" in the throne room before everyone, "... it would show her imperious nature and also show that she is finished with him ..."

Johnson found disfavor with Haggard having Charmian constantly advising Cleopatra. "It appears, from his work, that Cleopatra never had or made a decision for herself ...."

Cleopatra betrays Pharon and orders his arrest, but spares his life, which allows him to seek revenge. (Author's Collection.)

Sardou's play begins with the arrival of Cleopatra in Tarsus, and he focuses on her relationship with Antony. Johnson adapts several scenes from Sardou. Johnson noted there was a difference of opinion as to whether Antony would board Cleopatra's barge, or she would leave the barge and meet him in the market place. Johnson believed that if Cleopatra came ashore and wowed Antony with her beauty, it would be better dramatically than impressing Antony with her glorious entrance on her barge.

"Cleopatra captivating the conqueror on his throne is wonderful," Johnson argued, "Her reliance upon her own charms— in this terrible situation— is fraught with drama."

Cleopatra immediately whisks Antony off to Alexandria. Although he admitted 'good water shots' could be obtained with a fancy scene on Cleopatra's barge, Johnson thought there was only time and budget for 'one entertainment' (that is, a feast or big banquet scene) and he placed it at Cleopatra's palace. Citing Sardou's description of the feast scene, Johnson thought the Fox version should also be "Bacchanalian

Cleopatra entertains Marc Antony (Thurston Hall) at a banquet at her palace in Alexandria. (Author's collection)

and risqué, as much as the Board of Censors will stand for. These Orientals were not particular as to where they let their passions run riot and Sardou becomes quite impassioned in describing the scenes between Antony and Cleopatra in view of the diners." He also thought the other diners should be 'doing a little loving' as well. He urged, "I wouldn't have any table with food on— food is always disillusioning—" although probably not as disillusioning as attending a feast only to find no food.

When Johnson has Cleopatra and Antony drinking from the same cup, he calls it, "an intimate love scene with a strong dash of Orientalism," and added, "These love scenes should be as strong and 'Oriental' as will be allowed—Cleopatra, when she did love, must have been a 'bear'—slang is sometimes not pardonable but always expressive."

At this feast, Johnson had Cleopatra dissolve the 'sacred pearl of Menkau-Ra' in a goblet of vinegar to impress Antony with her wealth, and the outraged Harmachis invokes the curse of Menkau-Ra on her. She has him imprisoned, although Charmian helps him escape and advises him to seek vengeance. Concerned there was too much focus on Harmachis, Johnson queried whether it was necessary to have a scene where Charmian confesses that she betrayed Harmachis's plot to kill Cleopatra as she helps him escape. He thought it would 'break up the tensity' of the recall of Antony to Rome and his parting from Cleopatra, but Edwards insisted that Harmachis' escape be told.

Only bits and pieces of Shakespeare's *Antony and Cleopatra* are used in Johnson's scenario: Antony's recall to Rome, the marriage to Octavia, Cleopatra beating the messenger who brings word about Antony's marriage, the rocky relationship after Actium, and their suicides following the victory of Octavius Caesar. Shakespeare's famous description of Cleopatra's barge at Tarsus is spoken through the mouth one of Antony's followers (and is word for word Plutarch, anyway). In the Fox film, this is depicted rather than described, right down to the cupids.

In Johnson's scenario, Ventidius arrives in Alexandria to inform Antony that Octavius is seizing power in Rome. Antony wants to remain with his love Cleopatra, but her ambition is greater. She advises Antony to go back to deal with Octavius in Rome. While she pines for Antony's return, a political marriage is arranged between Antony and Octavius's sister, Octavia. When Cleopatra learns of it, she savagely beats the messenger. Antony deserts Octavia and prepares for war against Octavius.

In Sardou, Cleopatra in the same scene both learns of Antony's marriage and receives a message from him, summoning her to arm her fleet and sail to Actium on the Grecian coast. Johnson split this into two scenes, and borrowed from Sardou of Cleopatra receiving a message from Antony carried by an ibis, 'the sacred bird of Egypt.' Johnson thought an ibis would be better than a messenger pigeon, as he did not think the Romans knew of them (they were known since the time of the ancient Persians). Sardou had Kephren, Cleopatra's loyal servant, shoot down Antony's ibis airmail with an arrow (although it was plainly delivering its message). Johnson thought it would be 'novel and effective' but thought shooting it with an arrow would be neither 'practisable [sic] nor humane,' yet he recommended special homage being paid to the bird by Cleopatra and her entourage. Surviving stills show the ibis being shot as Sardou described.

In Sardou, Octavia moves to intercede between Antony and Octavius just before the battle of Actium, but Cleopatra intervenes. Sardou set the scene of Octavia and Cleopatra vying for Antony in beautiful gardens, but Johnson reset it in Antony's tent, thinking it would be better than using an exterior setting, "because these big dramatic scenes are sometimes difficult to do in exteriors, as Mr. Edwards once told me . . ." but worried that audiences would think a land battle was about to occur instead of a naval battle. Edwards told Johnson that he wanted Octavia to convince Antony to make peace, and then after she leaves to report to her brother, Cleopatra arrives and wins Antony back. Octavia returns and the two women appeal to Antony, but his love for Cleopatra wins out.

When Antony accuses Cleopatra of having an affair with her captain of the guard, Cleopatra orders Kephren to drink poison to prove her loyalty to Antony (Antony stops Kephren before he drinks). The peace is broken. Johnson adapted the pre-Actium confrontation between Antony, Cleopatra and Octavia, but dispensed with the near-poisoning of Kephren. Bara and Edwards reinserted the poison cup scene.

Sardou has Cleo use sorcery in an attempt to destroy Octavius' fleet, but it fails, and Cleo flees. In Alexandria, Antony accuses her of treachery, but Cleo manages to win him back. Still, the lovers are doomed. Antony is mortally wounded, surprised in his sleep by Octavius' troops, whereas Shakespeare had him commit suicide.

During the battle of Actium, Johnson follows Haggard and has Harmachis' vengeful prayers to Isis cause Cleopatra's superstitious dread, so that when she hears an erroneous report of Antony's death on another war galley, she breaks off combat and flees. In Alexandria, she learns Antony is alive, and he blames her for his defeat. When he sneaks into the palace gardens to kill her, she successfully explains her desertion, winning back his love. The forces of Octavius march on Alexandria, and Harmachis sends a message to Antony claiming Cleopatra is dead. In grief, he stabs himself, and he is taken to the tomb in which Cleopatra is hiding, just as Octavius arrives.

Cleopatra had plenty of violence, but Johnson avoided too much bloodshed in his scenario. Although he wrote of the slaughter of the anti-Cleopatra conspirators as "savage and terrible scene of oriental political violence—" and luridly described the carnage of the battle of Actium, he felt the need to reduce the body count later in the script, asking whether Antony's lieutenant, Ventidius, needed to kill himself as well.

Throughout his scenario, Johnson questioned whether it was necessary to have both Charmian and Iras, urging that Iras be dropped entirely, as only Charmian was needed in the Haggard-based storyline. It is obvious from the stills and credits that Iras was kept. Surviving stills always show Charmian and Iras together, and the two actresses playing them had equal billing. (Except in the British release, where the actress playing Charmian got high billing while the actress playing Iras was not listed.) Outlines of the completed movie also hint that the importance of Charmian to the plot was reduced. Rather than Charmian betray Harmachis' supporters, it is Harmachis himself who does so out of his love for Cleopatra.

The historical debate over the exact method Cleopatra used to commit suicide entered the picture. Although he originally wrote the scene with Harmachis smuggling the asp to Cleopatra in a fruit basket, Johnson urged the asp to be dumped in favor of Haggard's having Harmachis bringing her 'slow subtle' poison instead. However, Johnson was apparently under the impression that an asp was a type of 'venomous insect' native to Egypt. Johnson objected to using 'the bug,' as he called it, as it would take "away from the dramatic nature of her Death scene and gives the audience the shivers generally..."

Perhaps Johnson was informed that asps were in fact snakes, or Edwards merely chose the more popular notion of death by asp bite. Hollywood has reinforced the 'asp notion' ever since. When in Hollywood, 'print the legend.'

One critic complained that Bara's Cleopatra doesn't age from being twenty-one at the start of the film to thirty-nine by the end of it, as the historical Cleopatra undoubtedly did. Just as Shakespeare and Sardou condensed events for dramatic reasons, historical events are condensed in Johnson's scenario as if in a trash compactor. Aside from two intertitle references to 'many moons' passing, one might easily assume that everything in the film happened within a span of a few months. This was yet another reason, along with the necessity of keeping the script length down, that Cleopatra's children by Caesar and Antony don't show up in the scenario— there wasn't time for them to be born. The main reason, one suspects, was because it was simply inconceivable to 1917 audiences that Theda 'Queen of the Vampires' Bara could be a mother.

Another aspect of the script is how it jumps from one scene to another and then back again, supposedly showing different events which were happening simultaneously. Called crosscutting, it was utilized by D.W. Griffith to heighten tension; although some find it jarring, disorienting and distracting. (It is certainly disorienting when, in *Cleopatra*, during the assassination of Caesar, it is simultaneously both morning in Rome and night in Egypt.)

In writing the scenario's dialogue, Johnson wrote, "it strikes me to have all the characters use the 'Thee' and 'Thou' style of discourse. Not only is it characteristic of them but lends an added dignity to the story."

Some dialogue was straight from Sardou, and occur both in the Gardner film and the Fox film. Other subtitles were drawn from Shakespeare, but these were pared down into silent 'sound bites' of the more famous lines and those more comprehensible to the average viewer, merely to keep the plot in motion. Transferring Shakespeare to the silent screen was always an awkward transition at best. Some reviewers commented about it being faithful to Shakespeare, but as Robert Hamilton Ball observed in his book *Shakespeare on Silent Film*, "Some of the subtitles were from Shakespeare. Yet the result must have been not Shakespearean but an eye-filling recreation of glamorous pseudo-history. The film enhanced Theda Bara's reputation and made an enormous amount of money for William Fox, and there's an end on't."

It is difficult to tell how much was changed from the original scenario into the final film. Dialogue was inevitably tailored before and even after shooting, in a way 'talkers' or 'talkies' could not be easily altered after filming was complete. Audiences preferred short, easy to read sentences in their title cards. The detailed synopsis published in *Motion Picture Classic* in 1917 suggests some of the lines that may have been changed. In Johnson's original, the lines "Who are you that enter Caesar's presence? You are more beautiful than the accumulated treasures of Alexandria," and "I am that Queen, O Caesar, whom your legions have driven from the palace of her fathers," may have been cut to "Who art thou?" and "I am Cleopatra, whose throne you have usurped."

On the other hand, the line "When I think that I, your queen, am a fugitive, and that yon palace on the Nile echoes to the footfalls of the conquering Roman, I could weep— I could kill ..." was apparently unchanged from the original scenario. Assorted lines were picked up from Shakespeare, Sardou and possibly from the Gardner film. The greatest detectable change to the story from the original scenario came at the end of the film. Johnson follows Haggard's lead in having Harmachis in disguise, delivering the asp to her as his final act of vengeance. Outlines of the finished film, as reported in *Motion Picture Classic*, describe the bringing of the asp as an act of kindness by the still love-struck Egyptian, unable to bear the thought of Cleopatra being humiliated in a Roman triumph.

In the *Motion Picture Classic* synopsis, the final line is, "Death, where is thy sting? Victory, where is thy grave?" This line wasn't cribbed from Shakespeare, Sardou or Haggard— it was from the Bible! New Testament, yet. (Corinthians 15:55.)

Lastly, the name of Harmachis was changed to 'Pharon,' the name of the fisherman-slave from the Gardner film. This change could have been made at any time, even late in post-production, when the title-cards were shot.

The change was necessitated by the decision not to pay Haggard for the filming rights to his book *Cleopatra*. Despite the fact that Haggard was repeatedly cited by Johnson while preparing the scenario, and the character Harmachis / Pharon was obviously drawn from the novel, Fox attempted to sneak by with the excuse Cleopatra was a historical figure not subject to copyright infringement. Although early press releases cited Haggard's novel as a primary source of the film, later press releases and reviews cited Shakespeare mostly, Sardou occasionally, and Haggard not at all. Some reviewers thought the scenario was closer to Plutarch than Shakespeare. The program given out at the New York screenings claimed the scenario was based on 'Shakespeare and other authoritative sources.'

Plutarch, Shakespeare and even Sardou were all dead and unlikely to take legal action. Haggard, however, was alive and kicking— and after the movie came out, alive and suing. Three years later Fox admitted the plagiarism and was obliged to pay Haggard £5,000 ($25,000). The experience did not sour Fox from buying Haggard's books, nor Haggard from selling screen rights to Fox; two more of Bara's films were based on Haggard novels while the suit was ongoing. However, the lawsuit gave Johnson pause, as his notes for his scenario for follow up Bara epic *Salome* (Fox, 1918) distances itself from Oscar Wilde's version of the tale, which was used in a popular opera still under copyright.

Johnson's ambition-driven Cleopatra may have been closer to the historical original than Haggard's perception of a treacherous and frivolous monarch, Sardou's wacko sorceress or Shakespeare's temperamental bimbo. Of course, the Fox film company knew audiences preferred to think of Cleopatra as ancient history's *femme fatale* and wanted her depicted as a power-mad sex-siren. In the words of Errol Flynn and Johnny Carson, 'Always give the audience what it wants.'

Reviews were mixed on Johnson's scenario.

"Historically the picture is incorrect almost without a single exception," asserted Randolph Bartlett in *Photoplay*.

"Historically *Cleopatra* is correct in practically every detail," claimed Peter Milne in *Motion Picture News*. "Adrian Johnson, who made the scenario, drew from Shakespeare's *Antony and Cleopatra* and *Julius Caesar*, and ancient history for his material and from them evolved a story that presents both the spectacular and the personal, and that is, as a consequence, unusually entertaining."

"The scope of the story embraces many of the historical facts covered by Shakespeare," concurred Edward Weitzel in *The Moving Picture World*, "and it is evident that Adrian Johnson, the author of the scenario, has gone to the English poet for most of his incidents, rather than to Plutarch.

"The author has furnished some original material, however, and has also borrowed a character and a striking scene from Sardou's drama on the same subject. Several of the subtitles are from Shakespeare.

"The result of this literary patchwork is a lucid and fairly authentic account of the love affair between Cleopatra and Julius Caesar, and the Egyptian queen's overmastering passion for Mark Antony."

However, the reviewer for *The Dramatic Mirror* thought, "The picture is a brave attempt to limn the outstanding features of Cleopatra's reign into some sort of a coherent pattern, but merely succeeds in being a tedious series of unrelated episodes plucked at random from the plays of Shakespeare. And, if the production cost $500,000, as is stated it did, it is a pity that part of this stupendous sum was not expended for a better scenario . . ."

Theda Bara wasn't just waiting for the scenario to show up on her doorstep. Even with her busy shooting schedule, Bara plunged into research.

"To essay such a role required practical preparations and study," wrote Bara, "So far as it is was possible, I wanted the background to avoid any possible anachronism." She wanted to research the costumes, jewelry, the manners and customs of the Egyptian court. Everything had to be correct and authentic, she asserted, "No flagrant error . . . or cheapness must mar the resurrection of that immortal tragedy."

Theda Bara meets the Mummy. Reputedly shot while Bara was doing research for Cleopatra *at the Metropolitan Museum of Art in New York. (Author's collection)*

She spent weeks doing research in the New York Public Library and the Metropolitan Museum of Art, which had an impressive collection of Egyptian antiquities. Albert M. Lythgoe, the first curator of Egyptian Art at the museum, whom Bara called "the Egyptologist who literally eats, drinks and sleeps with the Egypt of antiquity," provided Bara "every possible assistance" in her research. She even said he bore a certain resemblance "to the Egyptian type of physiognomy, as revealed by the mummies—but in this, Mr. Lithgow may be called quite a handsome man. With his help I dig up a plethora of material, including pictures and deigns [sic] for architecture, costumes, galley boats, war paraphernalia, the ensemble of the Egyptian court, jewels. These later guided the making of the film and were faithfully followed."

Bara had to do her research without Pharaoh Tutankhamun's treasures for inspiration, as his tomb would slumber undisturbed and undiscovered for another five years. She brought all of her materials to Edwards, as well as to Al Smith, who served as Edwards' assistant. Smith is practically invisible. There is no information on Smith, his background or fate, or even a job title, but Bara credits him as an energetic and resourceful subordinate, "Mr. Smith, as always, proved he never fails in anything he is asked to do."

Adrian Johnson seems to credit Smith with set design on *Cleopatra*.

Bara added, "In the picture there were a few minor anachronisms, an inevitable defeat in making any hisotircal [sic] spectacle, but on the whole the picture was accurate and gave an authentic picture as Egypt must have been at the time of the celebrated queen.

"That the star actress in such a film herself dug up all of this historical and archaeological material may surprise many people who thought perhaps all I had to do was to dress and follow the instructions of the director."

Bara came up with an unusual interpretation of her character in preparation for filming.

"I believe that Cleopatra was little different from the usual girl of today," she said to reporters before shooting started, "I believe that the story of her tragic life, if placed in modern setting, with its heroine a girl of the working class would be found almost commonplace. There would be little to distinguish it from the cases of a thousand girls of our own day."

It is hardly the typical interpretation of the great Serpent of the Nile.

Apparently, Weigall had some influence on Bara regarding the real-life Cleopatra, as Bara stated, "The deeper I delve into the personal history of Cleopatra the more I am convinced that history has made too black a case against her. Authentic historians, each and every one male, would have us believe that almost every woman ruler of distinction in history was at heart wanton and openly dissolute in deportment.

"From Cleopatra down to Catherine II of Russia, Mary Queen of Scots and Queen Elizabeth of England, they are painted as devils in disposition and demi-mondes by preference. Quite the contrary is true. Most of them were dispatched into life with a kick as it were, and had to fight for their birthrights and hold them against all manner of treachery and tremendous odds. Morally, they had not a chance from the day of their birth, and it was only natural intelligence of a superior order that preserved in them any honest or decent feeling whatever."

Talking about the murderous and treacherous dynasty of the Ptolemys, how Ptolemy XI murdered his daughter Berenice to regain the throne, and how Cleopatra gained the throne as a teenager and then was forced into exile before getting Caesar's backing, Bara added, "Altogether, I believe Cleopatra was more sinned against than sinning. Considering that she lived in an age when ethics were negligible, came from a non-moral race, was surrounded on all sides by intrigue and temptation, and had 300 years of bad blood in her own veins, I think she turned out remarkably well."

Motion Picture News reported, "Although Cleopatra's part in history is already well established, Miss Bara has come to the defense of Egypt's Queen and insists that she is a much maligned person, and should not be stigmatized by historians."

"Ambition was Cleopatra's life," declared Miss Bara. "She was willing to sacrifice all for her dream of world empire. Though her faults were many, she was not the woman of popular belief.

"To further her dream of empire, she deliberately captivated by her beauty, wit and grace, two of the greatest men in history—Caesar and Antony . . .

"Cleopatra was a brilliant, beautiful, charming woman, perhaps a bit unscrupulous at times, but she was not the daughter of His Satanic Majesty, who from her lair in the East attempted to entrap and ensnare the heroes of Rome for the pure love of conquest. She strove to unite Rome and Egypt into one vast empire, not alone for herself but for her people."

CHAPTER FIVE: 'INTO A NEW WORLD'

For *Cleopatra*, desert locations were needed, helping prompt the move of the production to California. This was part of an exodus of the film industry that had been going on for some time.

When exploring the Americas, the Spanish tended to name the places they found and the towns they founded after saints or other iconography of the Catholic religion. However, they had other inspiration they came to what they thought was an enormous island off the Pacific coast of North America. With its mountainous terrain and forbidding shores, they named it after a mythical island called Califerne, which is mentioned in the medieval epic, *The Song of Roland*. On this island there is said to have reigned a beautiful black queen, Calafia (possibly the feminine version of Arabic title *khalifa* or caliph), ruing over a tribe of fierce amazons. Calafia had gained further notoriety in Garci Rodríguez de Montalvo's popular fantasy novel, *Las sergas de Esplandián* ('The Adventures of Esplandián'), written around 1500 and eagerly read by Spanish explorers (and which Cervantes listed as first among the 'harmful books' burned in his novel *Don Quixote*). Before the first European set foot on its shores and centuries before the first click of a movie camera's shutter, California became a place linked to exotic fantasy—not least of which is the idea that California is an island.

While there was no tribe of Amazons, there were plenty of American Indians, more or less peacefully living out their California lifestyle. That is, until the arrival of the missionaries, who converted them to Christianity in time to give them Last Rites as they died of diseases the monks had inadvertently brought with them.

After the tribes were devastated by European diseases and their culture destroyed by missionary zeal, the other pattern was set; that of residents resenting the intrusion of newcomers arriving in California to find their fortune. Spanish settlers embraced the California lifestyle as their own, becoming Californios for whom life was one continuous hacienda party.

During the Mexican War of Independence, the Californios favored the royalists, preferring Madrid to Mexico City as capital since it was further away and less likely to trouble them. They were generally unaffected by Mexican independence, until California became an object of desire to a foreign power. The United States seized California during the Mexican-American War. It is unlikely Mexico would have been able to retain California anyway, once gold had been discovered in 'them thar hills.' 'California or Bust!' was the slogan of the hordes of 'forty-niners' who joined the gold rush; most experienced both. As always, California was a beckoning fantasy promising wealth and success, giving great prosperity to a few and unrewarding drudgery to the vast majority.

There were a few unpleasantries, including the state-sponsored genocidal campaign against the remaining Indian population and the cheating of the Californios out of the land they had stolen from the Indians. The new Californians made their money in agriculture, mining, logging and oil, troubled only by the usual shenanigans of unscrupulous businessmen and corrupt politicians.

Sacramento was the state capital, but the glamour capital was San Francisco, the largest city in California. When the well-heeled Angelinos couldn't go shopping in New York or Paris, they hopped on the train to San Francisco. With its economy based on oil and agriculture, the semi-arid region of Los Angeles in the early 1900s had all the exotic allure of Tulsa, Oklahoma.

However, it attracted the attention of the growing American film industry, which saw it as an ideal place for movie production. Southern California had ocean, beaches, deserts, mountains, cliffs, forests, ranches, farms, small towns and cities—a vast variety of locations. Los Angeles had not yet been overwhelmed with urban sprawl. There was plenty of space to build new motion picture studios, eclipsing acres of citrus orchards and farmland in the process. Best of all, California had sunlight—lots of it, more good weather than bad; a vital consideration when the sun was the main source of light for the slow film stock of the period. There would be no more disruptive snowstorms like the one that fell on 'Spain' at Fort Lee.

However, the original reason filmmakers came to Southern California was the Patents War. They tried to evade the Motion Picture Trust's spies, lawyers and thug hirelings by keeping within a hop, skip and hightail of the Mexican border. Edison's main competitor, 'Colonel' William N.

Selig, moved main production from Chicago to California in 1907, and two years later, he established the first movie studio in Los Angeles. After the 'War' was over, California offered filmmakers plenty of reasons to stay on.

In 1913, the recently formed Jesse L. Lasky Feature Play Company dispatched Cecil B. DeMille and Oscar C. Apfel to Flagstaff, Arizona, to start work on *The Squaw Man*. Not finding Flagstaff to their liking, they followed the rail line to its terminus in Los Angeles. Arriving in the village of Hollywood, they looked around and declared, like Brigham Young, 'This is the place.' Other production companies followed.

Eager to gain this new source of revenue, the Los Angeles Chamber of Commerce knew what line to pitch to lure the film industry to the Golden State.

"Environment certainly affects creative workers. You realize surely the importance in such essentially sensitive production as the making of Motion Pictures the vital importance of having every member of an organization awake in the morning and start to work in a flood of happy sunshine.

"Cold rain and slushy snow do not tend to the proper mental condition for the best creative work. Environment affects every member of a film producing organization from the stars, directors, and cameramen to extras and general helpers. Every film man should carefully consider the above bit of psychology. It is important to success.

"No other city in the world offers seashore, mountains, desert and city civilization within an hour of the studios. There is no cessation of the growing season. Gardens and orchards can be filmed twelve months of the year. Snow scenes may be had within a few miles.

"Cheap electric power is available in any quantity. We can assure you that Southern California is the most ideal city for producing films."

Southern California residents were less welcoming of the film industry into their quiet communities. For them, it was like the circus had come to town and then refused to leave.

Angelinos dubbed the motion picture personnel 'movies,' the term confusing the personnel with the product. Newspaper ads for apartment rentals of the period included provisos, 'No dogs or actors allowed' and 'No movies.' Yet the flood was irreversible, accelerated by wartime coal shortages on the East Coast reducing electrical power availability. Moreover, in 1915, New York City banned film production in its streets as a 'public menace', which helped prompt a search for a city more welcoming to movie producers. The exodus became a stampede as actors and production personnel deserted New York and Chicago. In 1915, there were 12,000 film industry people living and working in Southern California; in 1917, there were 20,000. They were joined by increasing numbers of movie hopefuls beginning to spurn 'the Great White Way' to make it instead in 'flickers.' Meanwhile, World War I devastated European film production. In 1912, only about one-fourth of American movies were being filmed in California. By 1919, eighty percent of the movies being produced in the world—that's in the world—were being made in southern California. Hollywood, a sleepy agricultural village, began a strange transmogrification.

Los Angeles was still fairly rustic. Without the new Mulholland aqueduct providing a steady flow of water, the city would have remained a desert community with an ocean view. Even palm trees, the icon of Southern California, were not very commonplace in 1917. Originally brought by Spanish missionaries (to provide fronds for Palm Sunday), palms remained relatively rare in the dry, dusty Los Angeles basin of the time, but many more were planted as the city rapidly grew.

"In 1919, Hollywood was still a village. Hollywood Boulevard could have been any main street in America," California-born screenwriter Lenore Coffee remembered. "The heat was a clear desert heat. The sky, a strong, deep blue and the mountains like a cardboard cutout—you could hardly believe they had any backs to them. Behind those mountains was the San Fernando Valley, as yet unexploited, save for Universal Pictures having built Universal City ... On the corner of Hollywood Boulevard and Vine Street was a large and beautiful orange grove, and one street down was the Lasky studio with its front lined by a row of lovely pepper trees."

Dirt roads were all that connected the scattered communities, and director Fred J. Balshofer remembered how bad the roads could be. He had driven out to the prospective site of Universal City and had argued against the company building a studio there.

"Cahuenga Boulevard, leading out from the little town of Hollywood to Lankershim Boulevard, was about three miles of tough going over a narrow dirt road with ruts so deep that once the wheels of a car got into them they stayed right there until the car reached the top of the grade."

The glitz and glamour of 'Hollywood' simply didn't exist yet.

The Roman Forum in sunny California, built on the Fox backlot for Cleopatra. *Note the telegraph pole in the distance. (Courtesy of Kevin Brownlow Collection)*

"After nine o'clock at night," recalled actress Viola Dana, "you could shoot a cannon off on Hollywood Boulevard and never hit anybody."

"When you talk about wild parties, they took place in the 30s— the 20s and 30s—" noted actress Enid Markey, "but not too much in the 1910s."

The movie work schedule of sometimes twelve hours a day and six days a week, left little time for play in any case. On Thursday nights, some stars did get together at the Hollywood Hotel for dancing and conversation.

William Fox knew the future of production was on the West Coast, sending companies to film there in 1915. He originally leased the old Selig studio, but soon production out-grew it. So he acquired the studio Thomas Dixon had built on the corner of Sunset Boulevard and Western Avenue for his preparedness epic, *The Fall of a Nation* (1916). Fox also bought up the adjoining land, eclipsing groves of lemon trees. He paid $215,000 in 1916, and nine years later he boasted he turned down an offer of $1.5 million for the same land. He also bought up other property in Southern California amid the land rush gobbling up real estate.

Production began at the Western Street facility in 1916, interrupted by a fire that swept the lot late in the year. Repairs and replacements began

Caesar is assassinated in the Roman Senate at Fox Western studio. Note the awnings above the set to diffuse sunlight. (Author's collection)

immediately. The following year, the lot had two wooden stages and six open-air stages, along with various workshops and bungalows used as offices. Also being built were glass stages, including a gigantic steel and glass studio 60 feet wide and 120 feet long, being constructed for the production of *Cleopatra*.

During the early days of the silent era, there was no need for sound stages— all sets, including interiors, were built out in the open. Takes were not ruined because of flubbed lines but because a reflector or the set was jiggled by wind or birds flying through the set. Many stages had glass roofs—resembling glass barns or greenhouses—to protect the sets against the whims of weather and birds.

As the Western Fox studio grew, Fox contract personnel began arriving from the East Coast to join those already there. These were William Farnum and his brother Dustin Farnum, Jewel Carmen, June Caprice, Gladys Brockwell, George Walsh, and Jack Mulhall. Theda Bara resisted going West. She didn't want to leave the stylish and refined New York she loved, to live in far-off Los Angeles, which she and many others considered a cultural backwater.

A dedicated 'head-to-foot' New Yorker himself, Fox remained East to run his growing empire. Nevertheless, in February 1917, he made the journey to California; the first time he went further west than Buffalo, New York. Hollywood legend has it that when Fox arrived to inspect his new studio, cowboy star Tom Mix was waiting for him at the front gate. Former rodeo champion Mix had risen to fame in adventuresome Westerns at Selig Polyscope Company. Realizing Selig was going under and he would soon be out of a job, Mix had staked out the studio gate and convinced Fox to hire him.

Fox himself perpetuated this myth in *Upton Sinclair Presents William Fox*, but film historians point out that Mix's contract with Fox was announced a month before Fox arrived in California. This is only one example of the massive amount of misinformation about Tom Mix's career generated by Mix and others, giving Theda Bara's press agents a run for their money in the telling of tall tales.

Waiting around in front of movie studios sometimes worked in early Hollywood. Wearing their cowpuncher duds, wannabe movie cowboys hung out on Gower Street at the corner of Sunset Boulevard. They hoped that casting agents from the nearby studios would come by and pick them as background players or bit parts in Westerns being shot that day. Many of them had been real cowboys. Finding working in movie Westerns more lucrative than punching cattle or riding the rodeo circuit, former cowpokes haunted the greasy spoons that lined Gower Street, cheekily dubbed 'Gower Gulch.' That name is now attached to a strip mall at the corner of Sunset and Gower, built in 'Old West kitsch' style.

Dramas were filmed on the west side of the Fox Western Street lot, comedies were filmed on the eastern side of the lot. William Fox also inspected the comedy unit being set up under the direction of newly hired Henry 'Pathé' Lehrman. The Viennese-born Lehrman got his nickname 'Pathé' when in 1909, he tried to bluff his way into a job with the Biograph studio by claiming he had formerly worked for the Pathé Frères. He fooled no one, but got the job anyway, eventually leaving in 1912 to join Mack Sennett's newly formed Keystone Company. He famously tried to direct Charles Chaplin in the latter's first films (but no one directs Chaplin but Chaplin himself). Also bickering with Sennett, Lehrman left Keystone to join Universal, later forming his own unit there, L-KO. It stood for Lehrman Knock-Out, although it could easily stand for Lehrman's Knock-

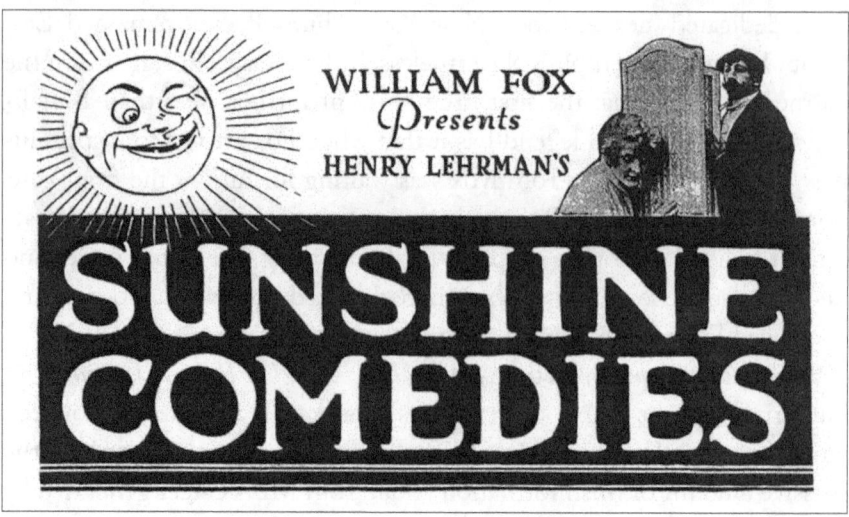

Sunshine Comedies (Author's collection)

Offs, as he made imitation Keystone comedies. Lehrman gained another nickname, 'Mr. Suicide' for forcing his performers to do dangerous stunts, but all slapstick comedy in this era was knockabout. After disputes with Universal, Lehrman left L-KO and Fox hired him to take charge of his new Sunshine Comedies. Fox advertised, 'Laugh with Lehrman, the Wizard of Wit.'

One of the problems of movie moguls who tried to manufacture films as if on an assembly line is that wit and creativity were essential in making comedies—or the product would not be funny. If William Fox, the former clothing manufacturer did not understand this, William Fox, the former vaudeville comic, did.

"Comedies have become a necessary part of every motion picture exhibitors' program and are eagerly booked by vaudeville houses as well," Fox stated in a press release. "The exhibitor must offer a comedy to round out the program properly.... We will make the best comedies on the market, or we will stop trying altogether."

Reviews of comedies from this era repeatedly claimed that they were stale, repetitious or even dreary. So how were the Fox Sunshine Comedies? A Chicago theater owner wrote to *Motography* about one of them, *A Milk Fed Vamp* (1917), "The monkey incident in this two-reel comedy received the biggest laugh I have ever heard in our theater. The first three Sunshine comedies are certainly laugh producers."

Not all Fox-Lehrman comedies were successes, but enough of them were for Fox to keep ordering them. Lehrman seemed to favor lions frightening characters in unusual places, such as *Roaring Lions and Wedding Bells* (1917), *Roaring Lions on the Midnight Express* and *Hungry Lions In A Hospital* (both 1918), all starring former Kalem funnyman Lloyd Hamilton. Among the other performers at Fox-Sunshine were Henie Conklin and assorted Keystone alumni, including Hank Mann, Slim Summerville and Ford Sterling. Also appearing in the Sunshine Comedies was a pretty ingénue, Virginia Rappe, who became romantically involved with Lehrman. Her untimely death in 1921 created the scandal that destroyed the career of Roscoe Arbuckle.

Abraham Carlos headed the West Coast studio, but his reign was troubled; one reason Fox visited California. In October 1917, on Hettie Gray Baker's suggestion, William Fox sent his 27-year old private secretary, Sol Wurtzel to replace Carlos as head of the West Coast studio. It may have been to Wurtzel who asked how he, an unknown quantity, could get the employees to respect him as the studio boss.

"Easy," replied Fox. "The minute you get out there, fire everybody. Call them in one by one and fire every single one. After a day or two you hire them back, one by one. Then they'll know who's boss."

Of course, Fox was the real boss, who let Wurtzel know that in a series of blistering letters castigating him for bad decisions and wasting money. In fact, Wurtzel efficiently ran the studio. Soon after his arrival, he uncovered a scheme siphoning off raw film stock from the company. Nevertheless, Fox heaped abusive tirades on him, which Wurtzel passed onto the studio personnel who crossed him.

While Fox was in California, President Woodrow Wilson asked Congress to declare war on Germany. Overnight, America went from a peacetime nation to one at war. Many inside and outside the film industry were shocked or ambivalent, but William Fox knew what to do.

"Mr. Fox employs in his various departments several thousand men," reported *Motography*. "His studios and offices throughout the country are now seething with martial activities.

"William Fox, now at his Los Angeles studios, is major of four home guard companies formed there. He has telegraphed to the adjutant general of the California militia for authority to enroll the platoon.

"Mr. Fox will supply the complete equipment for his men and has already placed an order for two machine guns. Three squads will be excused from work each day for rifle practice at the Eagle Rock near Los Angeles. The entire force will drill one hour nightly. A transportation corps has already been formed.

"In the east the same enthusiasm prevails. An infantry company has been organized at the Fort Lee studio by Director William Nigh. Drilling will be under supervision of Director J. Gordon Edwards, who spent several years in the Canadian Mounted Police."

About 200 men were enlisted under 'Colonel' William Fox, with 'Spanish War veteran' Tom Mix commanding a troop of scouts. The Fox group was later absorbed into the Lasky Home Guard, commanded by the resplendently uniformed 'Major' Cecil B. DeMille*, and the unit was officially designated the 51st California Home Guards. In August 1918, the governor of California reviewed the troops, which were ready, one supposes, in case the German army suddenly appeared marching up Hollywood Boulevard. Although mostly for show, the Lasky guard did serve as a reserve unit of the Coastal Artillery. The Lasky Home Guard was just one of many militias raised in factories and small towns throughout the country to drum up martial spirit and parade the flag.[1]

After spending a couple of months in California, Fox started for the East. Edwards and Bara rushed to complete their latest film at Fort Lee before heading West to film *Cleopatra*. However, another type of drama at Fox headquarters indicated a different kind of collision course.

As a struggling actress getting her first real break, Bara may have consulted her spirit guides, but she hadn't consulted a lawyer when she signed her first contract at Fox. She just kept signing the updated contracts being handed her, after some modest negotiation, because William Fox kept promising to take care of her. In this her third year, she was very aware that while she was the chief moneymaker at Fox studios, stars at other studios were making more money.

Bara had gone to a lawyer on another matter, and as an afterthought, had him look over her contract with Fox. He discovered that while Bara had been contracted to one of Fox's companies, the movies she made were

---

1   Some sources state DeMille was a 'Captain,' but C.B. was not above a little self-promotion.

at another of his companies. Technically, the contract was invalid. Armed with this knowledge, Bara forced a renegotiation of her contract.

"There was a tremendous flurry of excitement," Bara remembered. "I was offered almost anything I wanted."

Fox was in a bind; his top box office star could walk out the door and go to any studio, which would gladly pay anything for the 'Queen of the Vamps.' Other big stars were leaping from one studio to another, always looking for more lucrative contracts or more artistic freedom. The trade magazines frequently complained about how star salaries were rising out of control (just as the Trust predicted). Some editorials demanded an end to the 'star system.' This end was frequently predicted, but never came to pass, because people didn't just go to the movies to be entertained, they went to be entertained by their favorite stars.

Fox did have something Bara wanted: *Cleopatra*. She could go to another studio, but only Fox was ready to shoot *Cleopatra* on the epic scale it deserved. Even if another studio had been willing to make the epic, Bara would have to compete with the established stars on their roster for the role. If she stayed at Fox, she would play Cleopatra. That role, which she felt predestined to play, was by no means certain if she left Fox.

The truth was, he needed her as much as she needed him. Everything was geared to creating the movie around Theda Bara as Cleopatra. No other star in his roster was suitable for the role, not even his back-up vampire stars, who lacked sufficient box office pull to guarantee *Cleopatra* would be a success. Epics were risky ventures; why add additional risk?

With her new contract, Bara would receive $3,000 a week, which would be raised to $4,000 a week in 1918, as well as a percentage of the income from her movies. She felt well pleased, unaware of how infuriated Fox had become over the matter. Fox was the head of his family, and he considered the above the line talent at his studio part of that family. Like a lot of movie moguls, he considered any resistance to his will on the part of these 'extended family members' as a personal betrayal. Instead of accepting what she had agreed to, Bara had used a legal loophole to squeeze concessions out of him. It permanently damaged relations between them, but the final reckoning was still to come.

With her new contract signed, Bara embarked for California on that 'momentous day,' as Bara recalled in her memoirs, "Clothed in grey, with a

Valeska Surrat (Author's collection)

grey veil floating yards behind me, I boarded the train feeling I was going forth into a new world."

As Bara headed West, Fox mulled over his desire to find more stars to turn into superstars to overtake or even replace Bara. He was not having much success. Having signed Broadway star Valeska Suratt at $2,500 a week, Fox had high hopes for her as a vamp star, but as *Wid's* reported, "The attempts of Miss Surratt to act . . . were very painful, and several times she had all the appearance of a man dressed in woman's clothes . . . ."

Although an accomplished stage actress, Suratt had a mannishly strong chin that she tried to hide in publicity stills, and in movies, attempted to overawe viewers with her bizarre costumes. *Wid's* declared that she depended "upon her weird clothes to attract the women. Nobody ever

Pearl White (Author's collection)

has any hunch that she will be a good as an actress . . . . Surratt could act for half an hour straight ahead and it would be impossible to tell any one emotion that she had registered."

Nor did his other vamp stars, Virginia Pearson and Madlaine Traverse, generate much box office appeal.

Perhaps a big star could be made bigger. Fox contracted Pearl White, famed for her serial adventures. He put her in features, but White's star was already fading and her Fox films were flops.

Perhaps another exotically contrived background would work. Fox signed American actress Gretchen Hartman. Since German-sounding names were out, Fox publicity gave her a new name, Sonia Marakova. A phony biography was created about how she fled the Russian Revolution and "escaped the turmoil on an ammunition ship," and that letters of introduction from the Russia embassy introduced her to William Fox. *Motography* swallowed this whole and unchewed, but *Photoplay* spat it out.

"William Fox captures the 1917 prize for effrontery without a close competitor. Sonia Markova, whom he is advertising as a Russian star, is none other than Gretchen Hartman.... This bit of bunk would be less impudent if it were not for the fact that Miss Hartman has already been seen upon the American screen, and will be recognized immediately by thousands of picture fans.

'The big guffaw,' *Photoplay* added, was that Markova was suffering 'nervous prostration' due to the anxiety she felt for her relatives in danger in Petrograd, and 'to sooth her temperamental nerves,' some scenes of her first Fox film were shot aboard the ship during the voyage to New York.

"This is a harmless indoor sport, of course, as the public cares very little about the nativity of players, but it illustrates a deplorable and too prevalent viewpoint maintained by a few producers."

Bara, on the other hand, found the trip westward validating not only her increased salary but also her status as a superstar.

Since the cross-country trip took days, there were several rest stops, but there was no rest to the 'wickedest woman in the world.' Al Selig had scheduled her to be interviewed by reporters. As Bara observed, "for the business end could not be ignored and commercially the Fox company wished to take advantage of the trip. For publicity purposes, the vampire was to be exhibited as she was in real life."

This didn't appeal much to Bara, but she knew it was essential to have publicity, and, "after all, I was being paid" for it. "My interviews with reporters were staged with all the props and settings expected of a movie vampire."

Bara stopped two days in Chicago, where a memorable press conference was arranged at the Blackstone Hotel. Bara is reported to have emerged from a white limousine, attended by 'Nubian' footmen. A suite had been arranged for her: A dim room hung with red and black velvet over the windows. Bara remembered, "The room in which I was received was draped with Oriental tapestries, redolent with incense fuming from a great brazier, and banked with roses."

Among the reporters was 35-year-old Louella Parsons, a gossip columnist and entertainment reporter for the *Chicago Record Herald*. In her 1946 autobiography *The Gay Illiterate*, she wrote "head and shoulders above all vamps of prewar No. 1 was Theda Bara. Later on Theda was revealed to be a home-loving, tender-hearted Jewess with an appetite for corned beef and cabbage, and a homespun soul. But in those days she was the original mystery woman . . . . Greta Garbo is an out-and-out flagpole sitter compared to Theda—or rather to the act put on by Theda—and the old Fox company.

"The charmer from the land of the Sphinx did not grant many interviews," said Parsons, recalling that she waited to be 'admitted to royal chambers' with William Hollander of the *Daily News* and Mae Tinee of the *Chicago Tribune*.

'Mae Tinee,' (from 'matinee;' get it?), the *Tribune's* film critic from 1915 to 1966, was actually the pen name for a number of different reviewers, which indicates how indifferently the *Tribune* regarded entertainment reporting. Her real name in 1917 was either Mrs. Zack Elton or Frances Peck. Mae Tinee was criticized for her witty reviews sneering at pictures, giving them 'frivolous treatment', or so complained *Motography*. It said she "apparently has never outgrown the 'Oh, girls' style of writing, or else she fails to appreciate that the motion picture industry is a big and serious one, as it ranks fifth of the industries of the nation."

Motography added that exhibitors did not object to her bad reviews of films, only her 'inelegant levity.'

'Mae Tinee' wrote scathing reviews of Bara's movies, eventually having to respond in her column to complaints that she was 'just jealous' of Bara.

"Daring the ire of those who always abuse me when I have aught but praise to tender Miss Theda Bara, I must say that in *Her Greatest Love* I believe her worst picture . . . .

"Taking it as burlesque, I may say that as an unintentional comedienne I think Miss Bara has Charlie Chaplin backed off the boards. If you ever in your life saw anything funnier than Theda Bara thus garbed rolling around her beblackened eyes in horror at the sight of her harridanlike mother lighting a cigarette, or Theda Bara's supposed misery at the sight of a one piece bathing suit, or Theda Bara staggering naively about in her first high heeled slippers, I miss my guess."

"The day was hotter than the proverbial hinges of the proverbial hot spot," Parsons continued in her account, as the three waited and sweated in the stifling anteroom of Bara's hotel suite. Hollander had just voiced the

Theda Bara dressed warmly. Actually, a still from the film When Men Desire, *but you get the idea. (Author's collection)*

opinion that it was so hot the Vamp had probably melted into her own eyelash goo when the press agent appeared in our midst and said: 'Miss Bara will be a moment longer. She is not yet acclimated to the Northern weather!'

"No more were the words out of his mouth than the door of an adjoining room began to open noiselessly and seemingly without the aid of human hands— and there, exposed in unbelievable splendor, sat the Queen of the sirens draped to the teeth in magnificent furs.

"'Miss Bara,' declaimed the press agent in the manner of a circus barker, 'was born in the shadow of the Sphinx, you know. It is very, very hot, and she is cold!'"

"I reclined on a Madam de Maintenon couch as I talked to the reporters," Theda recalled. "To have stepped out of the role of the vampire at that time would have been disastrous. It would have shattered a sedulously if artificially created motion picture illusion."

Bara dressed and acted the role of a Vamp much as she did before studio cameras. She wore an especially made gown of lustrous black velvet "which swathed me in long sweeping lines from a collar of chinchilla which high up under my ears to my toes" embroidered "with scarlet roses with stems and leaves of gold."

According to Bara, the reporters had been accompanied by curious friends "who scrutinized me as though I were some monstrous rarity that would have added to the discoveries of Barnum. All seemed bent upon fixing my image in their minds and to carry away a full impression of that extraordinary freak, the vampire."

"It was an interview to go down in the annals," remembered Parsons, "and Mae and Bill and I did the best we could to make it immortal on our typewriters. Bara didn't talk—she merely grunted. She looked as ineffably bored as we felt."

Bara: "I was perforce compelled to preserve a very worldly-wise, supercilious, languidly bored attitude, employing those various movements of the shoulders and upliftings of the eyebrows identified with the vampire of the films. Beneath it all I was secretly amused, but having the role to play I hope I played it perfectly."

Parsons: "Finally, and probably because she couldn't stand the furs any longer, she gave a wave of her hand, dismissing us, and we left the shuttered, smoldering room gasping for fresh air and chance to howl our lungs out."

After the last of the reporters left, Theda threw off her wraps, tore off her dress and flung open the windows, gasping, "Give me air!" Then she sat down and laughed at the absurdity of it all.

Parsons reported about this interview back at her office, to much amusement.

"Dick Little, our dramatic critic, picked up the Bara catch phrase, 'It is very, very, very warm in Africa,' and used it profusely—particularly when a bit of the flush from the bottle that cheers that had colored his own face. 'Well,' he would philosophize, 'you know how it is in Africa.'"

Parsons repeated this story in her *Los Angeles Herald-Examiner* column in July 1948, prompting Theda to refute it in a letter to *Los Angeles Times* gossip columnist and old friend Hedda Hopper, who was in a long-standing feud with Parsons.

"You've always been very decent to me, too," Bara wrote, "never made up yarns that humiliated me to make copy—as did recently the Lady on the other paper; and so utterly ridiculous! We came to California to make pictures, years ago, only, as everyone knows, in the winter, in order to take scenes that could not be filmed in the Eastern cold—and I certainly was entitled to wrap myself up in furs to avoid those biting blizzard winds in Chicago when we passed thro' en route to LA—even an Esquimo couldn't have taken it! If it were ever made an issue that Lady would perspire profusely in Chicago's zero-est weather trying to pull that fable out of the morgue—our first meeting was on the set in Fort Lee when I was making *Carmen*."

Some attribute this interview to the publicity attending to the release of *A Fool There Was*. There is no record of Theda Bara, once she became Theda Bara, being in Chicago prior to May of 1917 (not the dead of winter.) She confessed to journalist Agnes Smith about such an interview in the 'Confessions of Theda Bara' article in *Photoplay*.

Hollander had a completely different take on the interview (if it was the same interview). Writing in the *Chicago Daily News*, Hollander said that Theda "made her hearers forget the vampire of the screen during her dissertation."

Asked if she preferred vampire roles, Theda responded, "it isn't a matter of preference. The theatergoers want it and their wishes must be gratified. I have departed from these parts in one or more pictures and instantly I received hundreds of letters asking me to return to them."

While Bara told Hollander she was happy in her career, he observed that Bara became irritated when asked stupid or impertinent questions. She indignantly denied receiving hate mail.

"I have my inspirational moments, and sense when I am doing my best. No matter how extravagantly I am praised after a scene is taken at the studio, if the bell within me fails to ring, I am not satisfied that I have achieved good results."

As for Mae Tinee, who never lost an opportunity to ridicule Bara, there is no mention of any kind of such an interview in the *Chicago Tribune*. Probably she wasn't there, possibly on Bara's insistence.

Maintaining the mystique. (Author's collection)

While in Chicago, Theda Bara 'stopped vamping long enough' to drop by the headquarters of the Motion Picture Exhibitors' League, promising to attend their exposition.

"I'm glad to hear it," said Chairman Schindler, "because that will mean an enormous attendance of women and girls every night you are there, to guard their husbands and sweethearts."

"Cease chaffing," snapped Bara, dubbed 'the world's champion vampire' by *Motography*, "If people only knew how un-vampirish I am—but then, what's the use? The more I say I am not, the more everyone will think I am. Why, I positively begged managers to let me just once more play a different role and they figuratively hit the ceiling. Once I almost 'vamped' a press agent in an effort to persuade him to say something nice about me, and he said, 'Aw, be reasonable. I've been telling all the newspapers that you're the only real vampire in captivity and I dassent back up.' So bring on your husbands and sweethearts and I'll be conservative as possible."

Bara couldn't resist vamping for reporters. While headed for the next destination, Selig informed Bara that the train would be stopping in Kansas City for an hour or two, and arrangements had been made by telegram inviting reporters from various papers to interview her at 8 o'clock in the morning in the private drawing room of the train.

"I replied that no honest-to-goodness vampire would be up and about at eight in the morning, especially after months of hard work at 'vamping' and a long and tiresome trip."

"That is true," Selig replied. "What will you do?"

"'Well,' I said, game up to my special role, 'I'll receive in bed, a la Du Barry.'

Selig thought this "a brilliant idea, an innovation in the art of giving an interview. It would be great publicity. So the next morning, as the train drew near Kansas City, I draped myself in a clinging robe of black crepe silk. Alas and alack, the reporters arrived too early and found the vampire eating a hearty breakfast of buckwheat cakes and deerfoot sausages. I should, of course, have been delicately tasting *pate de foi gras* or breakfasting with relish on French snails."

As these reporters left, another, 'a very young man,' arrived late and alone, looking very timid and nervous.

"Naturally, I held out my hand, but he refused to shake hands with me—dropped my hand as though it had been a snake," Bara recalled with amusement. The reporter requested an autographed photograph of Bara but assured her he was engaged 'to a very nice young girl.' With great anxiety, he finished up the interview, and hastily left her compartment.

"After he was gone, I made a little bet with the press agent, 'That reporter thought I was going to kiss him.'"

Theda signs photos at a public appearance. (Courtesy of Robert S. Birchard)

He feared more than that. Later, Bara found the article he wrote in a batch of newspaper clippings sent to her. The reporter had once interviewed Ziegfeld stage star Anna Held. She had jumped up and kissed him on both cheeks. If Anna Held did that to him, what would the notorious vamp Theda Bara do?

Mostly, Bara was met not with cynical sneering nor flustered fear, but the kind of love that fans showered on movie stars. In Albuquerque, a huge adoring crowd awaited her arrival. She was "pelted with roses, virtually a rain of flowers," followed by a more formal presentation of bouquets. Bara was so overwhelmed by the cheering thousands that she was moved to tears and could not speak. An attempt to pass out autographed photos nearly led to a riot as people surged forward, so Selig called out that anyone who wrote to Fox studio would get an autographed photo of Bara, resulting in a deluge of requests.

She had been forced into isolation not only by the terms of her contract, but her hard work schedule, disturbing incidents of surprise recognition on the street and hate mail, so she had practically no social life. She had no idea how truly popular she was. Fans turned out by the thousands to greet her whenever her train stopped, showering her with flowers and love.

After her years of unrewarding struggle and the grueling studio schedule, Bara "found a reward surpassing my wildest dreams." The adoration

Theda Bara is welcomed off the train in Los Angeles. (Courtesy of Robert S. Birchard)

moved her "as few things have ever moved me in my life," and she said she would remember this for the remainder of her life, "this perfect memory of a people's love, life giving as the sunshine, sweet still with the fragrance of the wreaths and roses which then they freely gave."

Bara arrived in Los Angeles June 2, 1917, at the Atchison, Topeka & Santa Fe Railway's La Grande Station at 2nd Street and Santa Fe Ave. This station, which opened in 1893, featured unusual Moorish-inspired architecture and appeared in a number of movies. The grandeur of the station was overwhelmed by the huge crowd that showed up to welcome Theda Bara. In a panic, Bara's maid hastily finished packing and turned the luggage over to the porters as Bara's party left the train.

"Bringing with her seventeen trunks of clothes, five servants, and a parent or two, Miss Theda Bara, most popular of the Fox stars and world-famed for putting the 'ire' in vampire', arrived yesterday via the Sante Fe," reported Grace Kingsley, columnist for the *Los Angeles Times*. "She was met by a delegation of Fox co-workers, who enthusiastically welcomed her with cheers, flowers and fruit."

Among those greeting Bara at the station was J. Gordon Edwards, as well as Abraham Carlos, whose little daughter Gertrude presented Bara with a bouquet of American Beauties.

"Facing a battery of cameras and a crowd of admirers," noted *Moving Picture World*, "Miss Bara descended from her overland journey looking like some demure Quaker maiden in her soft gray cloak and long gray veil."

"This is Miss Bara's first trip West, the effete east having always claimed her," noted Grace Kingsley. "It is even said that she was born on the edge of the Sahara Desert. Be this as it may. Miss Bara declared the part of the trip which principally interested her was the desert, and that she knew it for what it was the moment she spied it, on account of the number of desert pictures in which she appeared."

As Bara's party was pressing through the crowd to leave the station, Bara was dismayed when she saw a porter running after her with a hot water bottle that her maid had forgotten to pack. Believing this was taken care of, she boarded a car, and like Cleopatra arriving on her splendid barge in Tarsus, Bara and her entourage "motored slowly through the crowded streets" in what Bara called 'a truly royal reception.' Movie stars arriving in Los Angeles was then still a big occasion.

Bara checked into, appropriately enough for her role, the Hotel Alexandria, then the most luxurious hotel in the city. Bara's queenly dignity suffered a jolt when a bellboy followed her solicitously holding up that same hot water bottle.

"Pretending not to notice this I hastened my steps, seeking such a distance from that hot water bottle as if it had been the plague."

Kingsley reported that Bara "is spending her few days of leisure prior to beginning work on her most ambitious picture . . . in long and joyous motor trips through Southern California."

Bara claimed it was her first visit to the state, but being nervous behind the wheel, she left all the driving to her chauffeur.

"I am going to have a house," Bara told Kingsley shortly after arriving in Los Angeles. "I shall select a house not too close to my neighbors as I must have solitude and quiet after my hard day's work. I think if more workers along artistic lines would realize the value of being alone in their leisure hours, working out their ideals, many more of them would succeed in their chosen fields."

Theda Bara rests at her new home. (Author's Collection)

The house she picked was at 649 West Adams Boulevard in the fashionable West Adams neighborhood. It belonged to wealthy businessman Randolph Huntington Miner, who as a retired naval officer reenlisted in the Navy when America declared war. His wife, famed socialite Tulita Zoila Wilcox, a descendant of one of the original Californios, opted to devote the war years volunteering for the Red Cross in France. She leased out the house to the world famous vamp. Neighbors, who included oil-barons and the crème of Los Angeles society, were appalled that an actress, the notorious Theda Bara at that, had moved into their ritzy neighborhood.

Worse, in keeping with Bara's vamp image, a room of the house was decorated with astrological charts, tiger-skin rugs, crystal balls, skulls, mummy cases and 'anything else that looked mysterious and sensual' for use in doing interviews with bewildered reporters. Eve Golden and other Bara biographers have long thought that Fox property personnel decorated her home. Perhaps they did, but decades later Joan Craig found the same types of items—maybe exact same items—in Bara's Beverly Hills home, suggesting they may have actually belonged to Bara all along. Fox publicity claimed that in her new abode, she practiced her two favorite hobbies of astrology and distilling her own perfume—which actually might have been true. Otherwise, the quiet and charming Bara never gave her neighbors justification for their concerns.

"The Fox star lives on West Adams street, in a colonial house which is surrounded by lovely gardens," noted Grace Kingsley, "and it is because of the gardens, she declares, that she took the house. A dainty Japanese garden, with its pool of goldfish under spreading trees, is her favorite lounging place; and it is here she thinks, studies, reads and plans."

"This garden has brought me luck," Bara told Kingsley.

"Aren't you afraid of being kidnapped by some energetic admirer?" Kingsley asked. Bara acknowledged being a bit afraid at first, "but now has a big dog which keeps her company on her strolls. For recreation she improvises dances to the music on her phonograph when she tires of reading or writing or planning."

Kingsley reported that, "Moonlight nights too finds her in her garden, as there is something in the mystic light which aids peculiarly in her visualizing of a role."

"Theda Bara, the world-famous William Fox screen artiste" told a reporter from the *Los Angeles Herald* very much the same thing, describing "her love for the pale, cold light of the heavenly orb has been intensified by the beauty of the moon in a picturesque and romantic corner of the beautiful gardens that surround her..."

"The moon has a tremendous fascination for me," said Miss Bara, "and its cold rays seem to harmonize with my very soul. It seems to look upon this terrestrial globe with a cold unblinking stolidness, mixed with a certain stern cruelty that fits in with my mood while I am portraying the role of Cleopatra."

CHAPTER SIX:
'IN SUPPORT OF THE DIVINE THEDA'

The May 5, 1917, issue of *Motion Picture News* reported that, "Theda Bara, premiere vampire of the screen, has completed in secret a production of *Cleopatra* which will be released by the Fox Film Corporation on June 4."

The article stated that Bara and director Edwards had been filming for several months.

"The picture is complete, with the exception of the final cutting. Because of the elaborateness of many of the sets, which were exceedingly costly, the length of *Cleopatra* has not yet been determined . . . Miss Bara has done the best work of her career as *Cleopatra*, so those who have seen parts of the production say."

The most interesting thing about this article, of course, is that it wasn't true. The movie would not be released on June 4th. No one had seen footage from the production, because not one frame of film had been shot yet.

Why the fabrication? What possible reason for the ruse? It may well be that William Fox, who had no qualms about racing into production competing versions of *Carmen* and *Romeo and Juliet* to get them into theaters before his rivals completed their films, didn't want any rivals rushing to make their own version of *Cleopatra* before the Fox version could get to theaters. Fox obviously didn't think turnabout was fair play. This might explain why certain films based on stories in the public domain, like *Madame Du Barry*, were kept under wraps until completion, while other movies adapting licensed copyrighted works were proclaimed far and wide by Fox publicity during production.

Fox was only partially successful in staving off rival productions. There were no new Cleopatra movies, but in 1918, Helen Gardner released an upgraded version of her *Cleopatra*, with new scenes added. George Kleine also dusted off the Italian production, Guazzoni's *Antony and Cleopatra*, which he had distributed in America in 1914, and re-issued it as *Cleopatra*.

Clare West (Author's collection)

Both capitalized on the Fox publicity campaign, but neither seriously competed with the Fox epic, except in the case of confused moviegoers who went to see the wrong film.

From the time William Fox greenlighted *Cleopatra* to when Theda Bara arrived in California, there had been feverish activity in pre-production. Al Smith, the chief assistant to J. Gordon Edwards, arrived in Hollywood loaded with research materials handed him by Bara, Edwards and Adrian Johnson. He set to work conjuring sets and props into existence. Plasterers made sphinxes, and Egyptian style furniture was constructed. Practically everything had to be made from scratch.

Usually, studios relied on the actors to supply their own costumes for films in a contemporary setting, but for *Cleopatra*, the studio was forced to supply all of the costumes— not an easy task in Los Angeles at the time. Most studios did yet not have well-established costume departments, but there were a few costume suppliers that sprang up to fill the gap. There was (and still is) Western Costume Company, which, as the name suggests, supplied costumes for Westerns, although they later also carried other period clothing as well.

For her costumes, Bara had asked Fox to hire the person who designed the Babylonian costumes for *Intolerance*. To her surprise, Fox acquiesced. A telegram was sent to Smith to find the designer and hire him or her for *Cleopatra*.

"We hardly expected success, as the discovery of this woman, after so long a time, would be like finding a needle in a haystack," remembered Bara. "Yet upon my arrival, the woman was on hand."

For the movie industry back then, and researchers today, Clare (sometimes spelled 'Clair' or 'Claire') West was something of a mystery. She is sometimes erroneously identified as being born Clare Frances Whitney on May 10, 1889, in Kansas, and dying in 1980. According to Jay Jorgensen and Donald L. Scoggins in their book, *Creating the Illusion: A Fashionable History of Hollywood Costume Designers*, she was actually born Clara Belle Smith on January 30, 1879, in Missouri, the sixth of eight children. A farm girl, she married salesman Otis Oscar Hunley in 1898, and moved to Billings, Montana. When they divorced in 1902, Clare was awarded custody of their one-year-old Maxwell. A year later she married musician Marshall Elmer Carriere in Tulare County, California. Their son, Leonard, was born in 1908 in Bakersfield. The family moved to Missoula, Montana, where Carriere opened the Carriere School of Music. He co-owned and operated the Star Theater, likely showcasing traveling vaudeville acts. In 1912, Carriere sold his interest in theater, and with their new son, Lester, the family moved to Los Angeles, where Carriere found work playing piano at movie theaters. He and Clara divorced, and after this rootless, nomadic existence, a single mother in the big city with her three young children, Clara did what many people do when arriving in Los Angeles with nothing. She reinvented herself. She became Clare West, the fashion designer.

There is no record of how she became a fashion designer. She claimed she sold sketches to fashion magazines 'when she was still wearing her hair in a braid.' She also apparently claimed she had graduated from college and went to Paris to study fashion. None of this can be verified. It is conjectured that she learned sewing as a Missouri farm girl and costuming at her husband's Montana theatre. She probably found work as a seamstress and began sketching designs. It is not known how West actually acquired her design skills, but what she lacked in formal training, she made up for in talent and imagination. Whether she actually sold her designs for gowns to clothing manufacturers is anyone's guess. Regardless, she had landed in the right place at the right time, as motion picture studios sprang up around her, with a pressing need for a wide range of costumes.

About 1914, West started emerging from the mists—but only partly.

"West, who had developed a penchant for sketching gowns, began selling her designs to makers of fine clothes and peddling her artistic talents to the film industry," Jean Mowat wrote in 1927. "Miss West had been an ardent picture fan, and the idea came to her that a unit in costuming would greatly improve a picture. She presented her dress plan to David Griffith and 'sold' him the idea so well that she was given the opportunity to costume *The Birth of a Nation*."

Although Robert Goldstein's costume rental house in Los Angeles supplied Griffith with authentic surplus Civil War uniforms and other costumes, West designed costumes for the female leads. West created Mae Marsh's tattered post-war dress, dressed with pieces of cotton referred to as 'Southern Ermine' in an attempt of recapturing antebellum splendor.

"Though a meticulous researcher, even in this early film (*The Birth of a Nation*), West's attractive costumes seemed lived in and not just 'in period,'" says one of the authors of *Costume, Makeup, and Hair*. "West is arguably one of the first costume designers to merge historical precision and tailoring that appealed to a modern audience."

West also designed the iconic Klan uniforms (one writer suggesting she got the idea after witnessing 'confraternal processions in the streets of Europe'). While the actual Klansmen of the postbellum South wore a variety of outfits to disguise themselves and terrorize others, the costume for Griffith's hooded nightriders immediately caught the public's imagination. Klansmen adopted much of her design as the Ku Klux Klan resurged in the wake of *The Birth of a Nation*, although West can hardly be blamed for that.

West was rewarded with a permanent position with Griffith's studio and, something new in motion pictures, credit as 'costume designer.' Whether it was West's imaginative reinventing of her life or Hollywood hyperbole, *Motography* announced in its March 11, 1916, issue, "Madame Clare West, a trained Parisian designer, formerly head of 'The Maison Clare' in New York, is now head of the Fine Arts costume department."

Noted the authors of *Creating the Illusion*, "Other than the fact that West had indeed been hired by D.W. Griffith studio, nothing else in the announcement is true. West never lived in New York, nor had she ever left the country."

Motography added, "She designed the gowns Dorothy Gish wears in *The Pennsylvanian Dutch Girl*," which was later released as *Little Meena's Romance* (1916). A more daunting project commanded her attention, Griffith's ambitious *Intolerance*. Stung by charges of racism and glorifying Klan violence in *The Birth of a Nation*, Griffith responded by accusing his critics of intolerance. His *Intolerance* depicted four stories set in different eras; the Fall of Babylon, the last days of Jesus, the St. Bartholomew's Day Massacre of 1572 and a tale set in modern America. The logistics were enormous. Griffith handed West his research to create thousands of costumes from scratch. West came through, and she was assigned the title 'studio designer' after she completed *Intolerance*. Her Babylonian costumes were especially appreciated.

"West's *Intolerance* designed concepts were advertised as influencing off-screen fashion trends," Adrienne L. McLean commented, "an April 1917 *Photoplay* article was entitled 'Back to Babylon for New Fashions.'"

Although *Intolerance* was a box office sensation, the tremendous costs in making it could not be recouped in ticket sales, and Griffith was forced to shut down his studio. West reports she was 'resting'—Hollywood-speak for unemployed—when she got the phone call from Al Smith, asking if she was interested in working on *Cleopatra*. Even before she met Bara at the station, West had been hard at work designing and making costumes. Some of Bara's designs must have preceded her to California, and West had ten or fifteen women as seamstresses making Bara's costumes alone, with many others in charge of making costumes for the multitude of actors and extras. One of these seamstresses was teenager Laura Augusta Meyer, later with the married name of Pettus, who told her children and grandchildren she made all of Bara's Cleopatra costumes.

Theda Bara wearing the peacock gown (Author's collection)

West had been working a month already on the Cleopatra costumes before Bara arrived in California. One of these costumes was the 'peacock dress.' Bara claimed the tail feathers of 230 peacocks were used for the detachable train, "representing an immense and magnificent peacock tail outspread, undulated twenty-five feet back of me as I walked." Calling West 'a keenly intelligent woman,' Bara said the two of them devoted many hours to discussing the patterns for the costumes as well as in fittings and alterations.

In an interview in the 1920s, West described her work methods.

"I make a sketch first—an idea of what I have in mind—something that expresses to me the character I have read in the script, as she would be interpreted by the girl who is to play the part. Then I buy the materials, take out the manikin that belongs to the girl concerned, drape fabric on it—and cut!"

In addition to the costumes, Bara's Cleopatra needed footwear. One morning, five men "in impeccable Prince Albert dress" visited Bara in her hotel room to measure her feet for sandals.

"*En grande* function, surely!" Bara recalled. "One measured, one who looked on passed the exact measurement to another who nodded and painfully impressively made his record as if the fate of a world depended upon it."

Later, the estimate arrived: Six pairs of sandals for $950. According to Bara, the best sandals in New York would have cost only $25 or $30 a pair. "The retinue of five did not receive the order."

Adrian Johnson commented on Cleopatra's jewelry, saying Haggard "specifies priceless rings upon her fingers and UPON HER TOES— This is a little outre, is it not?"

Bara personally attended to the matter of Cleopatra's jewelry, which she considered as important as the costumes. Where to find a modern jeweler capable of making jewelry that looked of the period?

"I have said certain fairies come to my aid when I am in any quandary," Bara stated. "Surely these fairies led me, as I was in Los Angeles one day, into the shop of a little old man . . . an extraordinary artist, as adept in the classic art handcraft, and when he learned what I desired he was inspired to a poetic fervor."

This was Austrian-born jeweler Adolph Feil, who reminded Bara of Benvenuto Cellini, Italian goldsmith and artist during the Renaissance.

Bara recalled receiving numerous compliments on jewelry she wore in *Cleopatra*.

"While they were not made of gold, but of copper, white metal and silver, and while the stones were simply very excellent imitations, those jewels were things of beauty, exquisite, and unique examples of the ancient jeweler's craft."

To play the part of Cleopatra, Bara had to feel the part, and she credited the jeweler as contributing to her performance.

Had she "been compelled to wear some tawdry modern sham jewelry, some meretricious counterfeit, the 'antique art' of Broadway," Bara wrote, she could never overcome the feeling "that something was out of harmony, fraudulent, false and through the whole play would have run my sense of a conscious flaw."

Finding this jeweler filled Bara with 'mystical meaning,' firmly believing that her spirit guides led her to Feil's shop. Her spirit guides didn't have to work too hard, as Feil's shop was just a block away from Hotel Alexandria in the heart of the what is still the downtown Jewelry District, what was

The iconic image of Theda Bara as Cleopatra features Adolph Feil's cobra crown with pendant pyramids and coiled snake breastplates plus fancy belt and armband. (Author's collection)

then the 'Rodeo Drive' of the era. It was nevertheless quite fortuitous she found Feil. According to Mark Shoemaker of the Art Deco Society of Los Angeles, Feil gained his skills during the 'pre-Weimar Werkstaette' art movement, influenced by the Art Nouveau 'Sezessionstil' or Secessionist jewelers of Vienna.

Immigrating to America, he set up shop in San Francisco in 1903 to some success, only to have his store and entire stock wiped out in the 1906 earthquake. Starting over in Los Angeles, he custom-designed jewelry for well-to-do clients, and then a famous movie vamp walked into his shop. Discovering their shared interest in Egyptian designs, she commissioned him to make jewelry worthy of an Egyptian queen. Bara possibly collaborated on the designs, sharing her research on ancient Egyptian decorations with him. Feil made finger and toe rings, necklaces, bracelets, headdresses, crowns, anklets and more for Cleopatra and possibly other characters in the film. The most famous piece Feil created for Bara was a metallic bra whose cups looked something like pretzels, but on close inspection, they are revealed to be the figures of coiled snakes. The fittings for the infamous snake-bra became something of a Feil family legend.

"The whole costume echoes the sinuous, avant-garde Art Nouveau gold jewelry made by such European artist-dealers as Lalique and Fouquet," noted the authors of *Hollywood Jewels: Movies, Jewelry, Stars*. According to them, the costume 'oozed sensuality.'

Feil was paid $300 for his creations, which Fox publicity claimed to be worth $150,000. A grateful Bara inscribed photos to Feil 'in recognition and sincere appreciation of the exquisite artistic and authentic jewelry' he had made for her, and Feil presented her with a ring at the Los Angeles premiere of *Cleopatra*.

While in the jewelry district, Bara naturally did some shopping for herself.

"The sparkle of diamonds fascinates me. But only through the [shop] window," Bara wrote for a newspaper column in 1916. "I do not care for diamonds as a personal decoration."

In their book *Hollywood and History: Costume Design in Film*, the writers commented on Bara's vamp screen image and how it influenced fashion in her time.

"In the 1910s one of the most important fashion influences was the style of the femme fatale, or vamp, and no one personified it better than she. She wore paste bangles and slave bracelets long before the modern concept of costume jewelry and, indeed, her sequined overskirts, jeweled stomachers, and beaded shawls helped to set the stereotype for a host of exotic screen ladies yet to come."

They also commented on the costumes of the three main Hollywood Cleopatras, namely Bara, Claudette Colbert in the 1934 version and Elizabeth Taylor in the 1963 version. "Bara's makeup, typical of the silent era, was heavily applied in contrast to the more subtle styles used for Colbert and Taylor."

During the production of *Cleopatra*, photos were taken of Bara in her various costumes, her arms twisted in 'Egyptian-like' postures, for publicity shots. The 'fifty distinctively different costumes' hyped by Fox demanded a new costume in every scene Bara appeared in. The actual number of Bara's costumes, barring the discovery of stills from hitherto unknown scenes, was twenty-eight, one complete costume per scene she appears

Clare West's costumes for Marc Antony, Cleopatra, Charmian and Kephren (Author's collection)

in. The poor woman could not go from one room to another without a complete change of clothes.

Looking at the surviving stills, the authors noted, "one can see that the costumes, hairstyles, and makeup were more in line with Theda Bara's contemporary screen image than with the dress for a queen of ancient Egypt.

"Bara wore metallic fringes, pearl-embroidered brocades, and rhinestone-encrusted chiffons. Her ideas about such decorative devices undoubtedly came from a variety of sources, including Leon Bakst's designs for the Ballets Russes, Paul Poiret's orientalism, and George Barbier's drawings for the periodical *La Gazette du Bon Ton*, all initially introduced in Paris.

"While these clothes were exciting to see on the screen and certainly did not resemble everyday wear, they did not represent serious attempts to re-create period dress." They criticized the use of lace in Bara's costumes, because lace did not exist in ancient times. Likewise, Bara's costumes were embroidered with a large number of pearls, but in ancient Egypt, pearls were rare. "They were however, the vogue in 1917, and during the next few decades continued to be used in costumes for films depicting ancient times."

So much for Bara's scholarship regarding Egyptian fashion, but the writers go on to point out faults in the subsequent movie *Cleopatras*, for all their claim of rigorous research and authenticity, more attuned to the hairstyles of their own period than ancient times.

"As was common in the 1910s and 1920s, Bara's hair completely covers her forehead. In one scene she wears sausage curls. Both Colbert and Taylor wore smooth, black pageboy wigs with straight bangs." The writers argued that the real Cleopatra would have had her head shaved to wear a tightly coiled wig. "So much for history!"

The Hellenistic Ptolemys didn't follow all the hairdressing customs of the Egyptian pharaohs of a millennium earlier. Portraits in coins and busts show Cleopatra kept her natural hair. Furthermore, mummies of many Bronze-Age royals still have their original hair.

Although Bara's costumes seemed more Martian than Egyptian, many of the costume elements featured Egyptian designs, more so than in Helen Gardner's film. (Gardner also designed her outfits for her role, remaining faithful to the Greek mode of dress.) Moreover, Bara's multitude of dazzling gowns made up for their lack of authenticity by sheer exuberance, such as the fabulous peacock dress. This spectacular costume reportedly created a short-lived fad of peacock-feathered hats. Bara repeatedly claimed that she helped designed the outfits herself, something she restated in a 1934 radio interview.

While Bara supervised the making of her costumes and jewelry, she was also consulted in the building of sets, many based on sketches made at the Metropolitan Museum. She said there was as much labor involved in building the set as in the building of a modern skyscraper, employing "thousands of people, the making of plans and sketches for buildings, courtyards, exterior views, landscapes, costumes, jewels. Hundreds of sketches are made only to be discarded." Bara recalled that often, "after a set was finished, Mr. Edwards and I found some detail that was incorrect," and the set had to be torn down and rebuilt.

Some of the sets for *Cleopatra* were built on the Fox lot, including the Forum of Rome, the Roman Senate, and interiors of Cleopatra's palace. Construction crews were sent ahead on location to build pyramids, a sphinx, the waterfront at Tarsus and Alexandria, and Cleopatra's pal-

The court of Cleopatra, where an emissary delivers Anthony's message summoning her to meet him in Tarsus to answer for her crimes. (Courtesy of Academy of Motion Picture Arts and Sciences)

ace exterior. In contrast with the desire to make the sets look big for the epic film was the Fox usual film practice of scaling down sets for Bara's films to make her appear taller and more formidable (thus achieving that childhood ambition to be 'tall.') Overall, the result was not as awesome

The banquet hall where Cleopatra entertains Antony and dances in the peacock gown for him. (Author's collection)

Ruth St. Denis in 1913 (Author's collection)

as the Babylonian sets of *Intolerance* (which are awesome even today) but impressive to the eyes of 1917 moviegoers nonetheless.

Fox property men toiled on making ancient furniture, armor, weapons, and as Bara recalled, "Tropical gardens grew up out of the barren sands within a few days, with constructed fountains, imported palm trees and vegetation." Background actors were trained 'in the arts of ancient warfare,' and "Vast choruses were instructed in Egyptian dances."

The dancers were led by famed choreographer Ruth St. Denis, considered one of the founders of modern dance, somewhat ironically, for she cast back to the ancient past for inspiration. She had been initially inspired by a picture of Isis enthroned on a poster advertising Egyptian

Deities cigarettes. Since nothing is known about the actual movements of Egyptian dance, St. Denis improvised, adapting and incorporating elements of European folk, Asian and Middle Eastern dance. Photos of her show her arms twisted to resemble figures in Egyptian wall paintings.

After seeing her perform in 1911, another dancer, Ted Shawn became her student, and in 1914, her artistic partner and husband. In 1915, they founded Denishawn School, 'the cradle of American modern dance,' in a house in Los Angeles. There they trained students and formed a troupe of dancers which toured the remainder of the decade and throughout the 1920s.

Their strategic location meant that Hollywood soon came calling to hire St. Denis and Shawn as choreographers and dancers in movies. New York's *Dramatic Mirror* (May 13, 1916) claimed D.W. Griffith sent seven female actors, including Lillian and Dorothy Gish, Blanch Sweet, Mabel Normand and Mae Marsh, to Denishawn to learn dance.

"I also joined the Denishawn Dancing School, studying under Ruth St. Denis and Ted Shawn," Lillian Gish recalled. "Their large living room had been converted into a studio with mirrors and practice bars ..."

Other actors who studied dance for film roles at Denishawn included Louise Glaum, Carmel Myers, Ruth Chatterton, Constance and Joan Bennett, Myrna Loy, Colleen Moore, Lenore Ulric, Ina Claire, and Florence Vidor.

St. Denis and her troupe of dancers also performed in films. St. Denis danced in *The Lily and the Rose* (1915), produced and written by Griffith and directed by Paul Powell. Ted Shawn performed as the faun in Cecil B. DeMille's *Don't Change Your Husband* (1919). Denishawn dancers performed in *The Lily and The Rose, The Victoria Cross* (1916), *A Little Princess, Conscience, The Legion of Death, Joan the Woman* (all 1917), *Hidden Pearls, Wild Youth, Bound in Morocco* (all 1918), *Pettigrew's Girl, Backstage* (both 1919), *Sex* (1920), *Look Your Best* (1923), and probably many more films. For St. Denis and Shawn, Hollywood provided much-needed cash to finance some of their more esoteric (and unprofitable) dance projects, but no more than that. Neither mentioned their film work in their autobiographies. Shawn even denied appearing in these films.

Their biggest film project was *Intolerance*, and their most famous scene was the Babylonian sequence that featured hundreds of extras wearing costumes by Clare West and performing dances choreographed by St. Denis and Shawn.

Theda Bara as Cleopatra performing a dance for Caesar. (Author's Collection)

St. Denis choreographed Bara in at least two dance scenes, maybe more, in *Cleopatra*. One was when Cleopatra rolled out of the carpet before Julius Caesar and performs a dance. Judging from Bara's costume and poses in stills, the dance looks very much like a Middle-Eastern style 'belly dance'. The second dance was at a banquet, in which Cleopatra in her fabulous peacock dress dances before Marc Antony. Since St. Denis was famous for performing a peacock dance with a similar trailing gown, she presumably taught Bara her peacock dance, which Bara performed in *Cleopatra*. Louise Glaum is reported to have borrowed St. Denis's peacock dress and performed the peacock dance later in one of her films. Bara called upon St. Denis and Shawn again to choreograph her 'dance of the seven veils' in *Salome*. St. Denis denied she doubled for Bara.

The Denishawn troupe also performed in *Cleopatra* in the banquet scene (and probably other scenes, such as the mysterious 'Feast of Isis'), but since none of their faces can be seen in the surviving stills, identifications are difficult. St. Denis and Shawn likely performed, but the only other dancer credited as being in the film is Edith Emmons, who later established a dance school in Carmel, California. Other Denishawns who may have been in *Cleopatra* include Vanda Hoff (later third wife

Fritz Leiber and Virginia 'Bronnie' Bronson Leiber as Julius Caesar and his wife Calpurnia (Courtesy of Academy of Motion Picture Arts and Sciences)

of Paul 'King of Jazz' Whiteman), Florence Andrews (who changed her name to Florence O'Denishawn and starred in the Ziegfeld Follies in 1921), Margaret Loomis (who acted alongside Sessue Hayakawa in several of his movies), Carol Dempster (who became D.W. Griffith's leading lady in a number of movies of the 1920s), Chula Monzon, Claire Niles, Yvonne Sinnard (later a model), and Ada Forman, who trained Bara in Javanese dance for her role in *The Soul of Buddha* (1918). Dancer and later actress Louise Brooks barely missed being in *Cleopatra*, not joining the Denishawn school until 1918.

The other actors cast in *Cleopatra* began showing up at the studio for costume fittings and rehearsal.

Famed Shakespearean actor Fritz Leiber was cast as Julius Caesar. Leiber was born on January 31, 1884, in Chicago. Among his stage credits was touring in 1903 with Sybil Thorndike and future *Maltese Falcon* villain Sidney Greenstreet. He also starred in David Belasco's *Van Der Decken*, based on the legend of the Flying Dutchman. Like other stage actors, he was lured into the movies between theatrical engagements. Leiber had made at least two other appearances in films before *Cleopatra*, in the role of Mercutio in the Metro version of *Romeo and Juliet*, and as the Indian Brain Elkhorn in the Fox film *The Primitive Call* (1917).

"Fritz Leiber as Caesar possesses the features and stature that are generally accepted as correct," Peter Milne wrote in his review for *Motion Picture News*. "His acting is exceedingly good . . . ."

Leiber declined to sign a long-term contract with Fox. For him, "silent films were simply a summer job, an easy way to make money."

Also picking up some extra dough was his wife, actress Virginia 'Bronnie' Bronson Leiber, who frequently acted on stage alongside her husband. She was conveniently cast in the uncredited role of Caesar's wife Calpurnia. She remembered that "Fritz was very impressed with Bara's vampish quality," but apparently he was even more impressed by her costuming or lack of. He reportedly commented, "There was nothing on under those beads."

Bara seemed to have an even more profound impression on Leiber's young son, also named Fritz.

"I had often been backstage with my parents, watching the actors in costume standing in the wings among the stagehands in their work clothes. Even at my young age I understood the difference between the real world and the theater. Although sometimes the theater was more real for me than the regular world.

"One very hot day when I was about seven, my mother took me on a streetcar to see my father in a long high building with skylights," Fritz Jr. remembered. "My father was there, wearing a toga. I had already seen him in this costume because he had worn it in our hotel room while posing for a sketch done by an artist."

Each time he performed in a new role on stage, Fritz senior commissioned a portrait made of himself in costume. It seems he carried this over to his film roles.

He introduced his son "to a woman who seemed very tall, but now I guess that's because I was a young boy then and she was wearing a dressing gown and some type of headdress. She really wasn't tall. She had thick black hair and dark eyes with makeup, and I was a little bit intimidated . . .

"But she was absolutely nice to me and not in any way scary once I'd gotten used to her. She was Theda Bara, though I remember one of the men calling her Theo. When she took off the dressing gown she was dressed as Cleopatra, and even at my young age I knew a little bit about

The marriage of Antony and Octavia. In foreground from left to right: Henri De Vries as Octavius, Genevieve Blinn as Octavia, Thurston Hall as Marc Antony, and Herschel Mayall as Ventidius. Filmed at Henry T. Hazard's Greco-Roman gardens in Los Angeles. (Courtesy of Academy of Motion Picture Arts and Sciences)

who Cleopatra was, but she didn't act regal or snobbish at all except when the camera was running . . .

"When she finished her scene with my father, Theda Bara kissed me. She was absolutely nice to me and not like Cleopatra at all. Later on, I read all that nonsense about how she was raised by cobras and so on, but she certainly didn't act like any of that. Some actresses start believing their own press notices. She wasn't that type."

When the day's shooting was complete, he saw her dressed in street clothes with her makeup off, and he was, "impressed by her dark brown eyes which seemed to me very deep and hungering. I wrote a story years later called *The Girl with the Hungry Eyes* and maybe that's where I started to get the idea. From Theda Bara."

There are several problems with this. Fritz Jr. was six years old when *Cleopatra* was filmed, and he related the story more than fifty years later. He had been grown up to be a noted science fiction writer, essentially making a career of fabricating stories. Worse, the man who recorded the story was F. Gwynplaine MacIntyre, another science fiction writer who was notorious for writing film reviews of lost films, claiming he had viewed them in 'private archives' but refusing to name where. It caused confusion regarding the survival status of these films. After his bizarre death, his brother stated much of Gwynplaine's autobiographical information was false. Then again, nothing in the Fritz Leiber story has been proven to be untrue.

The part of Marc Antony went to another stage actor, Thurston Hall, born Ernest Thurston Hall on May 10, 1882, in Boston. Instead of going to Yale, Hall took to a stage actor's life, making his debut in 1901 in *When We Were Twenty-One*, under producer William Morris. Hall worked in stock theater in New England until migrating to the New York stage. A handsome man with a big rich baritone voice, Hall had the title role in *Ben Hur*, played opposite Lillian Russell in *Wildfire*, and also acted with future movie stars Marguerite Clark and Charlotte Walker in other productions.

In an interview in *Pictures and The Picturegoer* in 1923, Hall stated, "When I played Marc Antony, I was quite new to movies. It was my first picture, and I thought everyone had forgotten it."

He had apparently forgotten the movies he previously appeared in, at least seven short dramas for Lubin, starting in 1915, including *Sweeter Than Revenge* (1915), which survives. When Lubin folded in 1916, Hall went to Fox.

"I had been in a play with Irene Bordoni, and I hurried out to Fox studios, and made that one film between the end of that play and the first night of a new one," Hall recalled. "I quite took to screen work, and made up my mind to have another shot of it later."

Cleopatra was his first feature.

"Didn't see the beauteous Theda, excepting on the set," Hall confided,. "Those days she was very much the woman of mystery to the public, and her publicity people made her keep up the mystery business always."

Even so, Hollywood, then and now, thrust virtual strangers into very intimate scenes at short notice. Reporter Kenneth Beaton visited the set during the shooting of a love scene between Cleopatra and Marc Antony. With Edwards looking on, Bara and Hall went through their paces.

Sent to assassinate Cleopatra, Pharon (Albert Roscoe) instead falls in love with her. (Author's collection)

"He had her in his arms crying for air, and they came up and breathed deeply, and went down again. And the director said, 'That's all right.' And they broke and Antony went over and sat on the running board of a Ford and lighted his pipe."

The part of Pharon went to Albert Roscoe, who has several different dates for his birth. Some sources list his date of birth as August 23, 1887, or 1888, or 1889, all in Nashville, Tennessee. Studio publicity claimed that in 1898 he ran away from home to serve in the army during the Spanish-American war, but as that would have made him around nine or eleven at the time, this seems dubious. If he was, as stated, eighteen when he joined the army, then he must have been born around 1880, or he served in the army after the war was over. At any rate, Roscoe said his army service was beneficial to his movie career.

"It was a great experience and what little success I have won I owe to my years in the army, for it taught me self-discipline, self-control and patience, which are required in motion pictures."

There were claims that he started his stage career at the age of twelve when J. Gordon Edwards spotted him at his father's drugstore. Edwards, then with the Boyle Stock Company, persuaded Roscoe's father to let his boy appear on stage as Little Lord Fauntleroy. Then, depending on what source one uses, Roscoe attended Vanderbilt University, served as a scout in the Philippines, or continued acting on stage.

After some more stage work, which included directing, he broke into film acting in Chicago in 1915, then trying to rival New York as the leading center of movie production. His first movie, a one-reeler at Essanay called *A Pound For a Pound*, which allegedly took a single day to complete. Roscoe recalled, "We took the exteriors in the morning, the interiors in the afternoon, developed and cut it that night and by morning it was completed. Can't you imagine what a terrible picture it must have been?"

Wallace Beery had the lead role, and Beery and Roscoe became lifelong friends. Roscoe continued at Essanay, where he made six more movies, appearing with stars Beery, Francis X. Bushman, Beverly Bayne, Lester Cuneo and Nell Craig, among others. One of the films was the six-reeler *Gaustark*, with Bushman, Bayne and Cuneo.

Roscoe got tired of the factory technique of making motion pictures, and dropped out of movies for about two years, going back to the stage. He returned to movies in 1917, making at least one movie for Lasky. One source says he had also worked as a film director, but this may have actually been stage directing. Roscoe's first known film appearance for Fox was as Armand in *Camille*, opposite Bara and under the direction of the man who allegedly first got him on stage, J. Gordon Edwards. Then it was on the train west to Los Angeles to make *Cleopatra*. In all, Roscoe made seven pictures with Bara, frequently as her love interest.

To prove she loves no one but Antony (Thurston Hall, center), Cleopatra orders her love-struck bodyguard, Kephren (Art Acord, left), to drink deadly poison. (Author's collection)

"With no exception that I can remember, the men who acted opposite me were worthy of the attention I lavished on them," wrote Bara in an article in *Cinema Chat* magazine in 1920, commenting on her leading men. "Consummate actors and consummate gentlemen all. What better combination can a screen siren ask? . . .

"I look upon *Cleopatra*, for instance, as a milestone in my screen adventures; it is so elaborate and so overwhelming in its play upon the senses and emotions. Also because there I had three district screen loves—Julius Caesar, Antony, and Pharon, played respectively by Fritz Leiber, Thurston Hall, and Albert Roscoe, under the watchful eye of the camera, it is lucky to have such splendid fellows in the retinue.

"Albert Roscoe also played with me in *Salome*, and though, as John the Baptist, he did disdain me so cruelly, I think too well of him to have cut his head off were I not absolutely obliged to by historic precedent."

When Grace Kingsley reported Bara had arrived in California to film *Cleopatra*, she also announced, "Monroe Salisbury has been engaged in a leading role in support of the divine Theda."

While almost completely forgotten today, even by silent film buffs, Monroe Salisbury was not only a movie star but a matinee idol who appeared in DeMille's original *The Squaw Man*, *Ramona* (Clune, 1916), and numerous other westerns. He was under contract to Universal Studios around this time. No other sources link him with *Cleopatra*, and it is highly unlikely he would perform in an uncredited role at this point in his career. What role was he supposed to play? It is possible that Salisbury was to be cast in the role of Kephren, Cleopatra's stern but love-struck captain of the guard. Whatever the case, this role was assigned to Art Acord.

Appearing mostly in Westerns, Acord (sometimes spelled Accord) was a rollicking rough and ready type with a reputation as a brawling drunkard, very different from the grim Kephren seen in movie stills.

Although he could be a 'gentle, friendly' man, he was a belligerent drunk, picking fights with friends and foes alike. Acord became notorious for once attacking friend and rival cowboy star Tom Mix in a drunken fistfight at Mix's house. Other cowboy stars he duked it out with while in his cups include best buddy Hoot Gibson and bitter rival Buck Jones. He allegedly broke Victor Fleming's nose when the director questioned whether Acord had ever been a real cowboy.

He had been a real cowboy. Born Artemus Ward Acord in 1890 in Utah to Mormon parents, Acord went from being a cowpoke and ranch hand to rodeo performer. His first film appearance may have been doing stunts for the Bison Film Company about 1909 in California. However, it was on the rodeo circuit he made his name, as a bulldogger, bronco rider and roper. He toured with Dick Stanley's Wild West Show around 1910. He didn't appear regularly in movies until after 1912, acting primarily in Westerns, including *The Squaw Man*. He is even reported to have contributed to the writing of scenarios.

In 1915, Acord began making westerns for the Mustang company, a division of the American Film Company, known as the Flying 'A', based in Santa Barbara. *Moving Picture World* of June 17, 1916, reported Acord was severely injured performing a stunt in a scene for *Sandy, Reformer* (1916) in the Santa Ynez Mountains. He was riding down a steep and rugged grade when his horse slipped and rolled over him. Undaunted, he nevertheless entered 'The Stampede' at the Sheepshead Bay Speedway in New York in August 1916, and broke his nose when he was thrown from a horse.

In late 1916, Fox signed Acord to a contract, but didn't put him in many films, none of them Westerns. With Dustin Farnum starring in most of the studio's Westerns, plus the hiring of cowboy star Tom Mix, it left Acord in semi-limbo. Acord had a role in *The Battle of Life* (1916), a crime drama. Early in 1917, he appeared in *Heart and Soul*, with Theda Bara. Adapted from H. Rider Haggard's novel *Jess*, the setting was moved from South Africa to Puerto Rico (although some reviews named Hawaii or Cuba). For the tropical locations, wherever they were supposed to represent, J. Gordon Edwards took Bara and his company south to Florida to film. Acord's role is undetermined; likely he had a supporting role that involved riding stunts in the adventure-romance movie.

According to fellow rodeo performer Tex McLeod, Acord "got in a big picture with Theda Bara and went down to Florida with her one winter, and he was spinning a rope—he couldn't spin a rope much—but he was doing his best. And the chauffeur said, 'Oh, a Montgomery Ward cowboy, eh?' And Art half heard him and he said, 'What did you say?' 'I just said a Montgomery Ward cowboy.' 'Oh, did you.' Art went over and grabbed him by both lapels and jerked him out of the car and threw him on the lawn and beat three hells out of him. And Theda was so pleased— she hated the chauffeur— that she started being very friendly with Art. And I believe they were sweethearts for a while. I wouldn't guarantee it, but I think they were."

No other source has suggested a romance between Acord and Bara. It is difficult to imagine an odder couple than the intellectual, timid, and spiritually inclined Bara with the hard-drinking, hard-fighting and rough-hewn Acord, but stranger pairings have been made in Hollywood and elsewhere. (Marlene Dietrich and John Wayne? Really? Bela Lugosi and Clara Bow?) It sounds more like cowboy talk around coffee shops of Gower Gulch.

Acord's casting in *Cleopatra* was apparently primarily due to the stunt work he was to perform in the chariot race scene, along with other chariot scenes. Most of the film, however, demanded that he stand around on guard and look stern—when he wasn't gazing love-struck at Cleopatra, even when she orders him to kill himself. This probably suited Acord fine, as he was still recovering from his injuries, but in one scene he had to carry 135 lbs. of limp Theda Bara after her character of Cleopatra had fainted.

Hector Sarno as the Messenger tells Cleopatra that Julius Caesar has seized her palace. Behind are Dorothy Drake as Charmian and Delle Duncan as Iras. (Courtesy of Academy of Motion Picture Arts and Sciences)

When *Cleopatra* came out, a columnist for *The Billboard* wrote in dismay, "The funniest thing about that *Cleopatra* carnival of licentiousness was good old Art Acord, the greatest cowboy that ever risked a bronco or took a prize at a Stampede, all dolled up as Cleopatra's slave! Art never had on less in public in his life, even down at Coney, and we venture to bet it took some salary to make that boy promise to drink poison, even for the Serpent of the Nile."

The role of Antony's loyal lieutenant Ventidius went to Herschel Mayall. In his description of Ventidius, Adrian Johnson wrote, "The story demands that he be played that war-grizzled veteran— dog-like in his devotion to Antony."

Mayall acted in some of Thomas Ince's best films, including *The Battle of Gettysburg*, *The Typhoon*, and *The Wrath Of The Gods* (all 1914, the latter two directed by Reginald Barker), as well as a starring role as the warmongering king in Ince's acclaimed antiwar film, *Civilization*. The burly Mayall had also previously appeared in a number of Westerns starring William S.

Hart, usually playing the 'heavy.' These included *In the Sage Brush Country*, *On the Night Stage* (both 1914), *Keno Bates, Liar* (1915), and one of Hart's best, *The Aryan* (1915). Because they had similar facial features, Mayall was cast several times as the father of George Walsh's characters in Fox films.

Dutch actor Henri De Vries played Octavius. A foreign accent was no problem in silent movies, but the casting of a middle-aged man as the youthful Octavius is curious. Naples-born Italian army veteran Hector V. Sarno played a messenger.

There is little information available on the female supporting players. Canadian actress Genevieve Blinn, who had the role of Octavia, came from a venerable theater family from New Brunswick. Actresses Dorothy Drake and Dell Duncan were cast to play the roles of Cleopatra's handmaidens, Charmian and Iras, apparently because both were very short, so Bara would appear 'tall' alongside them. Other actors with notable roles in the film cannot be identified. Although the supporting actors got little attention from other critics, Edward Weitzel simply named the entire known cast in his review.

"A gratifying feature appertaining to the male members of the cast is their ability to wear the costume demanded by the time. This is notably so in the case of Fritz Leiber, who plays Julius Caesar, and of Thurston Hall, the Antony; of Herschel Mayall, as Ventidius and Henry de Vries, the Dutch actor, as Octavius. All four are to be credited with impersonations of the first rank. Albert Roscoe, Dorothy Drake, Dell Duncan, Genevieve Blinn, Hector V. Sarno and Art Accord are useful members of the cast...."

In his denunciation of *Cleopatra* in *The Billboard*, Theodore A. Liebler praised 'legitimate' stage actors appearing in the film at the expense of movie actors.

"Another point of interest to the people of the legitimate is the demonstration of the fact that picture trained and stage trained people mix as badly as oil and water. The legitimate players in this picture had all the best of it, and in some cases threw secondary parts into such prominence that the balance of the cast seemed disturbed."

CHAPTER SEVEN: A DAY IN THE LIFE OF CLEOPATRA

Theda Bara in costume for Cleopatra. *(Author's Collection)*

When writing notes for her autobiography, Bara commented that she had received hundreds of letters from female fans who opined what a 'wonderful' experience it must have been, "an exalted and intoxicating dramatic carousal, a revelry in pomp and glory, palatial surroundings, gorgeous costumes . . . a sort of emotional bacchanalian revel . . . to create the stellar role in such a picture as *Cleopatra*."

Bara admitted that there was "the truest joy any artist can know" in performing a great role, and that there "is intellectual satisfaction that far exceeds any purely material reward or enjoyment . . . which is unique and apart from the ordinary feelings of every day life."

Theda Bara studying the scenario. (Courtesy of Robert S. Birchard)

However, in the actual making of *Cleopatra*, "there is certainly little if any physical pleasure, no more joy in appearing amid the dazzling surroundings."

Bara wrote that there was a tremendous amount of labor, "physical suffering and mental strain, wearisome rehearsals, hours and hours of work overtime and into the night. . . ." Bara thought no labor union would tolerate such hardship for a common laborer.

Bara thought many young women aspiring for movie stardom imagined a life "of ease, of joy rides, of rolling in millions of dollars, would have their ardour dampened if confronted by such actual labor as is required."

Thurston Hall and J. Gordon Edwards (both right) wait as wardrobe assistants help Theda Bara adjust the Peacock Gown on the banquet set. (Courtesy of Robert S. Birchard)

Bara asserted the hardest part of playing Cleopatra was wearing the costumes, designed to dazzle, not for comfort.

"For two hours and more at a time, as my dressmaker will testify, I had to stand on my feet while a costume was being draped, altered and sewn upon me." While being costumed "in itself painfully tedious and tiring," there was also the process of applying make-up and having her hair done, "of arranging my headdress and getting on the elaborate jewels. Every detail had to be perfect."

After she was made up and dressed in costume in her dressing room in a 'charming bungalow across a street from the studio,' she needed help to get on set. Bara wrote that many of her costumes were so heavy with metal trimmings, three wardrobe assistants had to escort her across the street to the studio, with probably one more to deal with motorists, although the sight of Bara dressed as Cleopatra would have stopped traffic in itself.

"Theda Bara, who, we are sure, needs no introduction to our readers, while playing a scene for Cleopatra the other day, almost came to grief when—but the story must be told from the beginning," *Motion Picture*

Wardrobe assistants struggle to prevent Theda Bara's costume from completely falling off while J. Gordon Edwards directs Hershel Mayall on how to exhort Antony to return to Rome. (Courtesy of Robert S. Birchard)

News reported. "Be it known that the costumes she wears in this picture are very, very frail. They are made of thin materials trimmed with a few beads and jewels. Now if one bead on any one of the chains was to become fatigued and if it subsequently cracked under the strain, the entire garment would commence to disappear rapidly....

"Miss Bara is followed about by three dressmakers equipped with beads, needles and thread and a maid armed with a large gray cloak ready to be thrown over the shoulders of the actress should any of the beads become unruly. Well, the other day, er, the other day, that is while a scene was being made, one of the beads did begin to weary and let go its hold on its neighbor. That started things going—and—well—well, here's the place where the dressmakers and the maid play their parts. They fixed things up of course. What did you expect?"

"There was a costume which was deservedly called 'my agony dress,'" wrote Bara, "and a diadem called 'my agony crown.' The costume was kept in place by small invisible wires which stuck into my flesh like a thousand needles. The diadem was of heavy metal and represented an asp, its body coiled about my head and the head extending over my forehead."

When it came time to shoot the scene, Bara found the diadem was a size too small. There was no time to alter it, so she forced it down on her head.

"For three hours I went through a scene in which, for sheer pain, I could hardly see, feeling as though a band of red hot iron were being forced into my brain. When I removed the crown, blood trickled from a deep cut, as of a knife, across my forehead."

A friend of hers visiting the set remarked, "Well, screen acting certainly isn't what it is cracked up to be."

Bara experienced California sunshine in its fury as "the heat beat into the studio with a torrid intensity." Bara felt as if she was going "through some such Babylonian furnace as tested the strength of Daniel ... my skin felt as if it were being scaled and blistered off my body."

By late afternoon, temperatures dropped as heavy fog and cold wind came in from the Pacific, and, "after roasting by day, for several hours I'd go through the sensations of freezing to death."

Before any scene could be shot, the actors had to rehearse it repeatedly, and Bara wrote, "One can easily imagine that resources of energy and enthusiasm were required to carry one through the final filming...."

Describing J. Gordon Edwards as "successor to Herbert Brenon," *Photoplay* added. "Director-in-chief to Miss Theda Bara, vamp-in-chief to the William Fox film forces. Maker of the Fox undressed version of *Cleopatra*. Miss Theda Bara's boss 'round the lot in *Du Barry*, and other Foxy chronicles of crime. Perfectly cool and dispassionate while directing *Cleopatra*—which was why he directed *Cleopatra*. ... Miss Bara is calm because she knows what's coming, she's done it so often; J. Gordon, because he's told her how to do it so often."

Bara enjoyed working with Edwards, who allowed her considerable artistic freedom.

"J. Gordon Edwards was the nicest director I ever had," Bara remembered. "He was kind and considerate."

"In all of my experience, I have never met so remarkable a woman as Theda Bara," Edwards told a reporter. "I have watched her work with a feeling akin to awe ... Miss Bara has developed into one of the foremost artistes of the dramatic and silent stage, and ... she will go down to posterity as the greatest actress of her time."

Vanda Krefft wondered if Edwards was simply toeing the Fox publicity line about Bara's acting abilities, but he may have been sincere, or at least, a gentleman.

"I rate Mr. Edwards one of the finest gentlemen I have ever known," actress Betty Blythe related to Kevin Brownlow in his book, *The Parade's Gone By*. "Mr. Edwards wasn't English, but he was the same sort of person. He was such a scholarly man, just as fine as silk.

"And he had a lot of power. If he wanted something done, it was done— right, boom. But he had this love of the theater, love of the entertainment world. It was just part of his vibrations that he put into these wonderful pictures."

Blythe worked with Edwards on *The Queen of Sheba*.

"We worked side by side for six months on *Sheba* and until the last day, it was still 'Mr. Edwards' and 'Miss Blythe.' We never sat around and talked or laughed. He was always thinking, thinking of the next scene: Was this right? So one was very quiet on the set ... There was something quite powerful about him. He was always watching and thinking, so I never wanted to intrude ... Under his direction, depth and sincerity came to the fore—and all on of your knowledge of screen etiquette ...

"The wonderful thing about Mr. Edwards was this: no matter how dramatic it was, it was never hammed."

Edwards did not call directions to his actors while the scene was being shot, as some other directors did. His philosophy of directing was simple.

"I believe that the less directing a director does, the better the picture will be— other things being equal. Let the actress do a scene in her own way, let her have a chance with her temperament— that has always been my idea. Then you obtain grace, naturalness, the living thing, the thing that makes pictures as well as drama."

"Before starting a scene Director J. Gordon Edwards," noted the *Los Angeles Herald*, "generally gives three terse commands. They are: 'Quiet.' 'Music.' 'Camera.'"

Film historian Paul O'Dell noted in his book *Griffith and the Rise of Hollywood* the way different directors regarded scenarios. "While [Thomas] Ince was always to insist upon the detailed use of scenario, if Griffith was given a script, the first thing he would do was tear it up."

Griffith would often direct a movie with only a two or three-page outline and improvise his way through the production. Raoul Walsh also

During filming at Fox studios, Theda Bara and Thurston Hall consult the scenario as J. Gordon Edwards tries to grab it and throw it away. (Courtesy of Robert S. Birchard)

apparently directed off the cuff, also dispensed with scenarios and scripts, "The man with the scenario brain," according to *Motography*. "Some go as far to say that he wouldn't recognize one if he saw it."

Johnson's massively detailed scenario even specified close-up and long shots. Edwards followed the Griffith approach to directing, and what happened to Johnson's scenario may be perceived by Edwards's statement, "I read the scenario once: then I throw it aside and never look at it again. A slavish following of its dictation would hamper me at every turn, making that which should be fluent and living into something static and dead."

So it was a journey of two thousand years from the original Cleopatra, ground through Octavius' rumor mills, through Plutarch writing down the rumors many years later, translation from a French translation by Sir Thomas North, processed by Shakespeare, re-processed by 'music hall writer' Sardou, through Haggard, Gardner, Johnson, Fox, Edwards (who, presumably, read it once then threw it away), then to Bara and cast. The actors had the freedom to interpret their characters and scenes as they saw fit.

"I have always prepared myself for a new character on the screen by going deeply into its emotional needs, by creating the part for myself in a broad way, regardless of the scenario," Bara said. "Scenarios are traps in which the movie-actress, who is striving to express herself artistically, is constantly entangled. They seem to be devised solely to show how badly an artistic theme can be put together. Magnificent tragedies, such as *La Gioconda*, when transposed to the movies become painfully inartistic attempts. Under another name, no one would recognize their source. The scenario is usually my natural enemy, something I strive to overcome with artistic enthusiasm. Directors, even, have conspired with me to do this, against their better judgment, perhaps, but very much to my advantage as an actress."

During the filming of *Camille* at Fort Lee, extra Ethel Rosemon watched Bara and Edwards consulting with each other.

"One realized at a glance her success was due to no trick of the camera, no guidance of a clever director, but to the intelligence and thought that shines from those deep gray eyes. They plainly said that Theda Bara does not take her art lightly, that she is ever reaching out for perfection. In short, the real woman behind the screen vampire has a mind that makes itself felt, that causes one to know intuitively that she would succeed in any line she undertook. Her voice as she talked to the director had that soft, low quality that made even the most loquacious extra stop and listen.

"The fact that Mr. Edwards greeted all of her suggestions with a hearty 'fine!' put a stamp of approval upon my first reading of Miss Bara. Evidently he knew from the past that his star had come on the set with a wealth of ideas gained from a careful study of the script, that would prove profitable to even his wide experience.

"Perhaps the Fox press-agent will not thank me for presenting his star vampire in such a unvampirish light. Probably I should have her ranting up and down the studio and making things generally interesting. I will leave that to him and, tho not questioning his veracity or that of any man following the same calling, will simply state that I am pledged to tell the truth on the honor of an extra girl and that here you have a realistic picture of Miss Bara taken from the sidelines."

However, Bara could be a prima donna at times.

"You can't put anything over on Miss Bara," Rosemon overheard another extra remark. "Just heard the property-man throwing a fit because he had to go 'way down to the heart of New Jersey to get camellias. She wouldn't wear fakes."

"She's right. Why should she?" answered another.

How Edwards directed some of the larger crowd scenes, such as the feast at which Cleopatra entices Antony with her peacock dance, may be indicated by how he handled a similar scene in the subsequent *Salome*. As observed by one reporter on the set, assistant directors passing from group to group, giving instructions to "handsome youths wearing Roman tunics. They were stationed down in front near the cameras, where there were several girls without partners. 'Make friends with these girls,' said the director, 'and when the feast gets going, make love to them.'

"One bashful Roman took a place on the divan near a buxom looking extra of the opposite sex.

"'How do you do?' she said, putting out her hand. 'My name's Robinson,' he said. 'Glad to meet you. I guess I'll have to make love to you— if you don't mind.'

"'I should worry,' the girl replied.

When Bara arrived on the set, there was a flurry of interest.

"A hush fell over the scene. 'Look!' said a hundred voices. 'There she is!' All eyes turned to the throne.... 'Oh, isn't she lovely?' cried several girlish voices. Miss Bara inspected the scene.... King Herod got down from his throne, and even the great Edwards came down and consulted with her.

"Rehearsal started. The crowd drank their grape juice. They got to their feet and shouted the health to the king. But it is too tame. Assistants passed here and there, talking, exhorting and urging them to greater efforts.

"They tried it again with no greater success.

"And then Edwards, heretofore silent except when he gave orders to his assistants, got into the game. He stood on the edge of his high platform.

"'Get life into this!' he shouted. 'Remember where you are. You are back in Jerusalem, over 2000 years ago. You are at the palace of the king. You are having a feast. You are glad— you are merry— you are carefree. Now! Drink, drink! Laugh! Talk! Drink to the health of the king! Drain your glasses. Drink again!'

"The scene livened up. Edwards was making them believe it. Music from an orchestra hidden somewhere on the sidelines was heard. Edwards talked and exhorted again, and miraculously— the whole thing became real! . . . The bashful Roman youth whose name was Robinson threw his arms around the buxom extra girl and kissed her.

"The scene was alive. The crowd was hypnotized by the thing."

Silent movie acting was much different than stage or 'talkie' acting. Title cards showing dialogue or describing situations slowed down the pace of a film and thus were used sparingly. Actors, rendered mute by the lack of sound, had to rely on facial expression and gestures to convey the emotions and intentions of the characters. Movie acting proved very disorienting to those used to the stage.

"The staging and methods of the moving-picture people were a revelation to me," said Frederick Warde in an interview in *The Brooklyn Eagle*. Warde was a famed stage actor who made his movie debut in *Richard III* (Film d'Art, 1912), one of the first American feature films.

"I thought I knew all the tricks of acting, but their work was simply amazing to me. The director of the company simply told the other actors what to do, telling them when to look glad and sorry, when to shout and when to fight, without telling them why they did any of these things."

Warde said he "had to suppress all sense of the ridiculous to go on with the thing in such surroundings." He continued appearing in films, however, including the lead in a version of *King Lear* (Thanhauser, 1916).

Originally, films were shot entirely in long shots (showing the entire actor from head to foot) so to convey an emotion the actor would use their entire body in broad pantomime, as if on a stage. Most early films look like they are shot on stages, the camera facing the actors straight on as if viewed by a member of a theater audience.

The lack of recorded sound sometimes led the actors to improvise their dialogue when speaking their lines for the camera. One famous actor was notorious for uttering obscenities to his leading lady during love scenes, and the actress had to endure it while wearing the expression of one listening to sweet nothings. Stage producer Oliver Morosco, while a guest on the set during the shooting of an early movie version of *Macbeth*, was appalled when he heard the actors spouting such ad-libs before the camera as "Wal, I'll be hornswoggled if it ain't my old pal MacDuff!" and "To arms, men! We'll slaughter the lousy buzzards!"

The growing number of lip-readers in the audience made this more and more hazardous, who complained about profanities and ad-libs at odds with the dialogue on the title cards, especially as more close-ups were used. *Moving Picture World* commented in 1917 that the 'days of actors saying just anything are over.' Johnson's scenario for *Cleopatra* specifies dialogue even when there were to be no titles, indicating that the actors at least mouth the words.

"I had never seen a movie being made before, and at the start I thought this was a rehearsal because my father was acting without an audience," Fritz Leiber Jr. remembered. "We didn't have to be quiet, and I recall my mother saying something out loud from the side of the set while my father and Theda Bara were speaking their lines. Of course I'd seen movies before this, but I didn't realize yet that here was one of them being made. I don't recall the dialogue but I remember they stayed in character. A few years later I saw another movie being made, another silent movie, and the actors were just talking about the ball game while they were pretending to speak their characters' lines. But my father and Theda Bara were actually being Caesar and Cleopatra even though nobody could hear their dialogue. My father projected his lines as if he was speaking from the stage, but Miss Bara just spoke her lines normally."

Fritz Jr. noted there was nothing special about her voice, that while Bara could have had a career in talking movies, "My mother and father both had trained voices, and I could tell she hadn't taken elocution lessons."

In Chicago, Bara had been trained in the Delsarte System of acting. Disdaining the flamboyant mode of acting he had seen in Paris, François Delsarte developed a system in which emotion was registered through a series of distinct gestures. Delsarte sought to convey the real emotion of the scene. However, the system, which became very popular in America, devolved into a code of gestures. It wasn't necessarily bad acting, but it moved away from the emotional content Delsarte was seeking to project. The Delsarte method was popular in early cinema, because lacking the conveyance of emotion through voice, actors could pantomime the fixed series of gestures that audiences understood.

"Lacking words, the picture people adopted a sort of shorthand code of gesture to represent different emotions, and the faithful fans have learnt this code by heart," commented Dorothy Donnell in *Motion Picture Classic*. "When the persecuted heroine clutches her chest and rolls her eyes, they know she is not having an attack of acute indigestion but a pang of unrequited affection. When the hero beats his brow and clenches his fist, they know it is not the bill for his wife's new hat that troubles him, but the fact that he has just dropped a couple of millions in Wall Street. Jealousy has its bitten lip; revenge, its flashing eye and set jaw.

"When Theda Bara lets down her back hair and runs her hands thru it, in a sort of vampirish shampoo, it is a sign that she is being very naughty. I don't quite know why back hair is as naughty as it is, but when a movie actress lets hers down, it's one of the surest things you know that trouble is brewing."

With the introduction of medium shots and close-ups, a more subtle style of acting was permitted. Later, use of different camera angles, advanced lighting techniques, and the improved art of editing did more to convey the mood and tell the story, with less reliance on actors' miming and title cards. This presented a problem for those trained in the Delsarte method, which increasingly was seen as old-fashioned and unnatural.

Bara's acting came out of the period moving away from the broad pantomime into a more subtle style. Since hardly any of her films survive, none from the height of her success, the style of her performances must be judged from commentaries of those who witnessed them.

Reviewing *Sin*, the *New York Morning Telegraph* said of Bara, "That she is an uncommonly good actress will be admitted by anyone who has seen her ... "

In its review of *Destruction*, the *Telegraph* commented, "Miss Bara has a way of making the most of her parts. At no time that she is on the screen does she fail to hold the attention of her audience."

"Miss Bara does most of her real acting through a marvelous control of her features," said the *New York Evening Journal*. "Her mouth can express a hundred expressions, her lips are provocative even when they are parted cruelly, her eyes are wistful when they are wicked. There is an intelligent foreign element about this actress that savors of the real thing ...."

"The 'Vampire' required an actress of the scope and ability necessary to play the part of a woman who lures a man to dissipation and finally a degrading death in her arms," *Motion Picture Classic* stated. "The character must suggest snake-like subtlety and beautiful weakness, mingled with an exotic quality of attractiveness that will prove fatally irresistible to her luckless prey. Theda Bara depicts all these qualities in a manner that causes her audiences to be suddenly attacked with chills— splendid tribute to her genius."

The Brooklyn Daily Eagle, in its review of *The Devil's Daughter*, said, "Mlle. Bara's facial expression is wonderfully brutal and fiendish, but every physical movement shows grace and charm."

The Brooklyn Daily Eagle later denounced Bara and her films, calling her a 'second rate actress' who relied on emotional scenes to throw fits instead of genuine acting.

"She gives the spectators their money's worth in exactly the same fashion that a prizefighter delights the devotees of the ring when he pounds an opponent into a pulp. Theda Bara pounds emotion until there isn't anything left of it. In most of her work she is a maudlin emotionalist who daubs the colors on her palette with a shoe-brush. There is nothing easier for an experienced actress than the vampire type of character. It is hysterical acting raised to the nth power; it is sheer emotionalism gone mad; it is, in fact everything except great art. Simplicity, intelligence, and restraint are the three qualities that go into making of any lasting success on the legitimate stage. She has none of the three."

Lynde Denig in her review of *Destruction* thought, "Miss Bara is not to be blamed for the picture's failure as emotional melodrama, for she acts precisely [as] in the past and that, no doubt, is what the Fox Company wants."

Bara herself said that she preferred the more subtle stage acting style of Eleanora Duse's 'bloodless cheek of chaste renunciation' to the more flamboyant displays of passion as performed by Sarah Bernhardt. Bara's few surviving films show her giving restrained performances rather than the histrionics of which her critics accused her. Her performance in *Cleopatra*, however, seems to have been very broad.

Directors had no trouble getting energized performances out of Bara, as she threw all of her energy into her role.

"It is impossible to act without feeling," Bara told Archie Bell. "When I play a part, I live it. I am nobody else, and my companions often remind me that I say strange things and do strange things afterward, for I am still in the character. Sometimes I do not regain full self-possession until after I slept."

"She throws herself into a part so forcefully, and puts so much of her whole nature into the role that it is like reality to her," said Stuart Holmes, who acted in at least four movies with Bara. "When she throws herself

The impressions of a cartoonist visiting the set during the filming of the scene when Cleopatra is informed of Antony's marriage. (From the Los Angeles Times, July 29, 1917)

into [my] arms, in a scene, it is real. I have to brace myself, she comes with so much force."

This type of acting proved physically draining for her.

"After I played a few big scenes, I was like an invalid," Theda related. "I got into the automobile, went home as quickly as possible. My maid gave me a little warm milk or a light lunch, and I went to sleep and rested until far into the night. Then I felt like myself again and studied and read."

Sometimes the intensity of her performance got the better of her, especially in fight scenes, which in silent movies were much more rough and tumble before the advent of sound effects. In *Carmen*, with director Raoul Walsh jumping up and down and screaming encouragement, a fight between Bara's Carmen and another gypsy woman became so heated that the other actress fainted.

"What a terrible woman," she was heard to mutter when she slunk off the set, never to return to films. While filming *Cleopatra*, Bara lay so violently into Hector Sarno, the actor playing Antony's messenger, he fled the set in alarm, bleeding from the scratches inflicted on him.

Bara later told Grace Kingsley, "when I was supposed to beat the messenger, I didn't realize, for some reason, so engrossed was I in my work, that I had given him more than a couple of gentle taps. I complained to the director that he had run away without getting a beating. Then I looked over at the poor fellow. There were welts on his arms and shoulders. 'God!' was all he said—and he groaned that, as much as to say, 'What does she think a beating would be like?' I had in my zeal whipped him much harder than I realized."

"It was the emotional expression of Cleopatra's rage," Bara explained.

There was also another hazard. Bara, along with other stars, was known for her 'soulful eyes.' It was ex-vamp Nita Naldi who revealed their secret.

"We were all blind as bats. Theda Bara couldn't see a foot ahead of her, and poor Rudy [Valentino] groped his way through many a love scene, and I really mean groped."

Further aggravated by the bright lights and sunlight reflectors shining straight into her eyes, the myopic Bara occasionally blundered into parts of the set or (as bitter rival Miriam Cooper claimed) even into the camera. To avoid this, she rehearsed every scene until she knew exactly where every piece of furniture was on the set before shooting. Hitting her marks by memory, she rarely strayed beyond the chalk lines marking the limits of the camera's vision, even though she could not see them.

Edwards apparently allowed Bara to select her costumes for the various scenes. The most famous outfit worn by her she picked for the scene in which Cleopatra seduced Pharon, causing him to betray himself and the other conspirators in the assassination plot against her.

"It was a scene which called for a consummate portrayal of all of the queen's vampire wiles," remembered Bara. "And I knew I had to be properly dressed for the part."

"Tomorrow I must wear less than I have ever wore before," she told Clare West, who replied wittily, "It can't be done."

"Well, we'll see."

'Skirmishing about the closets,' Bara picked out pieces made by Adolph Feil, including a metal snake crown with pyramid dangling on the sides like earrings, and the two jeweled coiled snake breastplates. To these, she added "a piece of beautiful gossamer material, iridescently spangled, in which was achieved one of the most striking costume effects in the picture," which West fashioned into a see-through panel skirt held by a jeweled belt. Bara hesitated to wear the breastplates with shoulder straps as it "seemed to me to suggest nothing but a harem dance in a Broadway musical show."

"I've got it," I said to Mrs. West. "I'll glue them on."

"'Good!' she exclaimed, 'that has never been done before.'

"So the next day, clothed in 'less than I had ever worn before,' we attached the breast plates with Royal glue. Needless to say, the removal was not so facile or painless as the putting on."

Later to become renowned as an Academy Award-winning set designer, George James Hopkins is sometimes erroneously credited with designing costumes for *Cleopatra*. Some modern sources credit him with designing and decorating the sets, but there is no hard evidence supporting this. A native of Pasadena, California, Hopkins got his start designing scenery on stage after studying design in college. He had been a costume and set designer in New York for showman Florenz Ziegfeld's Follies and stage producer Charles Frohman. His mother, Una Hopkins, was an interior designer 'in the tradition of Elsie de Wolfe'. She convinced Oliver Morosco, theater magnate, for whom she designed sets, to hire her son to design

When Cleopatra snatches the dagger of Menkau-Ra from her would-be assassin Pharon, her breastplates stay on, thanks to Royal glue. (Courtesy of Robert S. Birchard)

costumes, so her son could be with her in California. In 1916, mother and son were also hired to work at Realart Studios in Hollywood.

Hopkins recalled, "At the time of my first studio experience, most sets were being constructed out of painted canvas. No one had ever heard of a set decorator. Prop men scraped together what furniture they could lay their hands on, and stuck it in front of the painted walls."

Describing himself as a 'New York sophisticate,' he wondered. "What kind of place was *this* for someone like me?"

In 1917, he started working for Fox at the old Selig studio. By his own admission in his unpublished autobiography, Hopkins' first encounter with Theda Bara was as a visitor on the set, being introduced by Ryszard 'Richard' Ordynski, a Polish stage producer, director and writer who arrived in the United States in 1915.

Hopkins recalled, "the set inside the tent was supposed to be Cleopatra's throne room. To reach it one had to wade through dust half a foot deep. There were hundreds of extras blocking our way. What I could see from a distance surprised me. Cleopatra didn't seem to have a particularly good figure ... Her Cleopatra consisted of a beaded skirt and two brass serpents entwined around not very impressive breasts."

Even so, he found her, "Remarkably self possessed and not at all glamorous. I don't remember what we said but I immediately liked her. The liking was to become mutual for many years."

Even if he designed nothing for *Cleopatra*, as a Fox employee, it seems likely he was drawn into the production that demanded all the resources of the Fox California studios, especially in the days when an employee could have many duties.

"Aside from the painters and carpenters none of us were subject to union restrictions." Hopkins remembered. "I designed sets, dressed them, supervised costuming, and even wrote original screenplays and titles. I forgot to mention acting—in which we all indulged upon occasion."

So Hopkins may have helped dress sets and assisted West in costuming supporting characters and extras—and possibly appeared in some of the 'mob scenes' in Rome and Alexandria.

Whoever dressed the sets in Cleopatra's palace got complaints from some reviewers.

"J. Gordon Edwards, the producer of this big film," complained Randolph Bartlett in *Photoplay*, "has crowded his settings with bewildering heaps of fabrics and properties, and thereby has lost his great opportunity and wasted a large amount of money. True magnificence is simple, dignified, not a clutter of expensive decorations. The eye is impressed most strongly not by a multitudinous detail, but by vast spaces— a long vista with a collonade of pillars would express Egypt much better than all Mr. Edward's rugs, divans, tapestries, hangings and what not."

Hopkins and Bara hit it off so well that he would go on to design her costumes in other films. Bara called him 'Neje,' a nickname that stuck.

"Miss Bara is very easy to design for," Hopkins commented in 1919. "Her peculiar type adapts itself ... Costumes have a motif, as much as music or drama. For [Bara's] sirens, I use flame colors, for sirens are burning fountains of passion."

"Cameramen felt for some strange reason that color was distracting, that it would detract from the actors," Hopkins recalled, retorting, "This is a black-and-white film."

The objection cameramen had to Hopkins' choice of color had more to do with how it would register on film. In 1917, black and white

Theda Bara checking her make-up. (Author's collection)

orthochromatic film was the standard, but when prints were struck, red appeared black, while blue appeared as white. Directors and cameramen would look at a scene through a viewfinder with a blue glass filter to determine how a shot would look in black and white. This remained the situation until the introduction of panchromatic film, which could record blue better.

Orthochromatic film did not record Caucasian flesh tones well, so when the film was projected faces looked darker than in real life. To overcome this, White actors coated their faces with white or yellow makeup so it would register as 'normal' on orthochromatic film. Noël Coward, making his film debut in D.W. Griffith's *Hearts Of The World* (1917), noted the experience "left little mark on me beyond a most unpleasant memory of getting up at five every morning and making my face bright yellow."

For Bara, baring more skin than most actors, it was more of a chore.

"For some roles I have had to literally be painted white," Bara related to the *Boston Post* in 1920. "My maid always did this; and I told her once that if she ever left me she could certainly get a job whitewashing, for she'd had plenty of experience. Getting rid of this white afterward was not easy, but

Close-up of Theda Bara in make-up for Cleopatra. *(Author's Collection)*

it was nothing compared with the ordeal of removing the brown I used when I played a dark part. Two or three baths were sometimes needed to take off this color."

To her white makeup, Bara added kohl, framing 'those perilous eyes.' In poorly reproduced heavy contrast photos, it gave her a dark mask like that of a raccoon. For her lips to 'look' red, she applied brown makeup with a thick grease pencil. She must have presented an odd spectacle to any visitor on the set, yet she still managed to beguile movie audiences of the day, although she might have benefitted from a make-up artist who wasn't myopic.

Critics are divided on her use of make-up. One reviewer said in 1916 that Bara "can apply make-up so skillfully as to obtain excellent results, something quite rare in filmdom." Others complained she used too much make-up.

Still, with her dark eyes, she was better off than blue-eyed actors, whose irises looked white on film, giving them a bizarre alien look in close up. While having pictures of costume tests taken, starlet Mary Miles Minter asked photographer James Wong Howe if there was any way in which she could be photographed so her baby blue eyes would look less freakish. Howe hung a black curtain in front of his camera with a hole just large enough for his lens, and set up his lights to illuminate Minter from the sides. Staring at the black cloth in front of her, Minter's pupils dilated, making a more pleasing appearance when photographed. The actress praised Howe to everyone she met, and soon all of Hollywood was talking about the Chinese photographer working his mysterious Oriental magic behind black curtains. Thus was launched the career of one of Hollywood's greatest cinematographers.

Cleopatra was shot on black and white film, but *The Gulf Between*, the first feature film using a color system later known as two-color Technicolor, was released in 1917. Gaumont, a major French film company, came out with a three-strip additive color system called Chronochrome in 1918. *The Toll Of The Sea* (1922), starring Anna May Wong, and Douglas Fairbanks's swashbuckler *The Black Pirate* (1926), were entirely in two-color Technicolor, but the process was expensive and far from perfect. More often this Technicolor was used in one or two scenes to make a splash in otherwise black and white films, such as *The Ten Commandments* in 1923, *Ben Hur* and *The Phantom Of The Opera* (both 1925). . In 1933, improved three-strip Technicolor was introduced, and full-color feature films slowly became more commonplace.

Rial Schellinger, John W. Boyle and George Schneiderman are credited as Cleopatra's cinematographers, but 'cinematography' in 1917 was basically making sure there was enough light to expose the film as they cranked the cameras. Presumably, one man operated the main camera while another operated the 'safety' camera to produce the negative for the foreign prints or a back-up for scenes where there might have been a problem with the main camera's footage. There were additional cameras operating for the major crowd scenes.

At the Western Fox studio, taking advantage of the California sun, muslin awnings diffused direct sunlight, or huge aluminum reflectors could direct sunlight onto either the open or glass-roofed stages. When there wasn't enough natural light, artificial lights were used, mainly klieg lights, invented by the Kliegl brothers (spawning the in-joke 'Who knocked the 'l' out of Kliegl.') Actress Olga Petrova recalled the problems with klieg lights "which often melted one's make-up, blistered one's skin, made one's hair so brittle that it cracked and fell out. . . . worst of all were the major or minor attacks of klieg eyes."

Klieg lights caused eye-irritation in the form of ultra-violet burns of the retinas. Enid Markey, an actress at Ince Studios (she played the first 'Jane' to the first movie Tarzan) recalled the harsh effect of the lights, "The next day you would have no 'eyes' at all. That was the only time we had off, when we had Klieg eyes."

She went on to say, "The remedy was a grated potato and a bandage of cheesecloth bound around your eyes. And you would stay in bed with this and it would draw the fire out of your head. It was a dreadful thing."

Petrova also had a bad experience with 'Klieg eyes.'

"I had been in bed that night for some hours when I was awakened with the most excruciating pain in my head. My eyes felt as if all the sand of the seven seas were behind my eyelids. Tears were streaming down my cheeks . . . I pressed the button of the lamp beside my bed. No light. I felt my way to the nearest wall button and pressed that. Still no light. I felt my way down the corridor. I knocked on Dr. Stewart's door. 'I've got some sand or something in my eyes,' I said, 'The lights are off in my room and I can't see to get it.'

"In great agitation Dr. Stewart followed me. 'Why, the lights aren't out,' he said. 'They're all on, full on.'

"Although the actual blindness didn't last long, the pain and weeping continued."

Klieg lights also created the fashion of movie stars wearing sunglasses; at first to combat the ultra-violet rays, and then to disguise their identities, then as a trend.

One of the advantages of shooting with artificial lights was the use of lighting to create the mood of a scene. Most cameramen were only

Edwards employed atmospheric lighting for the scene of Cleopatra consulting her astrologer, who assures her Julius Caesar has been crowned king in Rome. (Author's collection)

worried about was getting enough light on the set for the slow film to record the image. While working on *The Warrens Of Virginia* (1915), Cecil B. DeMille and his cameraman Alvin Wickoff embraced Chiaroscuro lighting to escape the flat lighting most commonly used.

"What I was after was naturalism," remembered DeMille, "if an actor was sitting beside as lamp, it was crudely unrealistic to show both sides of his face in equal light, so, with portable spotlights borrowed from the Mason Opera House in downtown Los Angeles, we began to make shadows where shadows would appear in nature."

This type of illumination was dubbed 'Rembrandt lighting,' and then promoted as 'Lasky lighting.'

Most scenes in *Cleopatra* were filmed with flat lighting, but in a few scenes, Edwards employed 'Rembrandt lighting' to set the mood, such as Cleopatra consulting her astrologer, in the temple of Isis and the plundering of a mummy's tomb.

Pharon and Cleopatra enter the tomb of Menkau-Ra. A spotlight provides the illumination for Pharon's torch. (Author's collection)

Music was sometimes supplied for the benefit of actors playing their scenes. Some argued for music to 'set the mood' for the actors; others said it was to keep the action in pace with music; still others thought it was all a humbug. Mostly, the music drowned out the chattering noise of the camera, and the various other distracting sounds emanating around the open air set, from traffic noise to the racket of nearby sets being constructed or torn down. Before the advent of 'talkies' and recorded dialogue, there was no need to say, 'Quiet on the set.'

Some big stars demanded orchestras; others were satisfied if they merely rehearsed with the sound of the camera cranking with no film in it, so as not to be distracted by the camera's grinding during the actual filming. Music became an issue over which stars could flex their muscles at the studio. At Goldwyn Pictures, the rivalry between actresses Pauline Frederick and Geraldine Farrar caused Fredrick, upon learning Farrar had three violinists to provide the mood for her scenes, to also demand three violins. Not to be outdone, Mabel Normand demanded a jazz band (five-piece, instead of fifteen-piece as sometimes claimed) playing red-hot numbers during her scenes. Previously, neither actress had required music during filming.

Most stars settled for a piano and/or violin accompaniment, which is what many audiences heard during performances. Alfred A. Cohn, writing in *Photoplay*, noted, "Even Bill Hart likes to have a violin about when he is doing some emotional stuff. Perhaps it's some memory of his youth that makes him particularly susceptible to 'Sweet Bunch of Daisies' and he can squeeze out a tear any old time the violinist starts that almost new song hit of *Oh Boy*, entitled 'Til the Clouds Roll By.'"

According to Cohn, D.W. Griffith "does not hesitate to invoke the aid of Orpheus when any of his players is particularly responsive to music. He has found the mob especially responsive in big scenes and during the filming of *Intolerance* he had a big brass band on the lot for three days playing for the battle scenes. It will be news to many archaeologists that Cyrus was repulsed at the walls of Babylon to the stirring strains of the 'Marseillaise,' 'Tipperary' and 'The Star Spangled Banner.' In the wonderful dancing scenes in Belshazzar's court the dancers got all their cues from the music of the band. In rehearsals Griffith has used a phonograph many times to get unity of action by music cues."

J. Gordon Edwards allowed Betty Blythe her choice of music while shooting *The Queen Of Sheba*.

"He never talked during a shot; he left us to it." Blythe recalled. "But he always had a five-piece orchestra on the set. . . . Mr. Edwards would never suggest what music to play; he would say to an assistant, 'Ask Miss Blythe if she wants a change.'"

"I first discovered the inspiration given by music—the right kind—when playing in pictures directed by Mr. Herbert Brenon," recalled Bara. "Music was almost a mania with Mr. Brenon, and I remember one occasion when, directing a scene, he became so absorbed he turned about and directed the music." At this, the cast and crew broke up laughing.

"There were times when music made continuance in work almost impossible—that was when, in some tragic scene, we were assailed by the cacophony of a jazz band taking part in a jazz picture on an adjacent stage to mine."

Edwards also allowed Bara to pick her music for filming.

"Music became the vogue at Fox's western studio when Theda Bara came west to do *Cleopatra* and *Du Barry*," Cohn reported. "Theda Bara also likes 'Elegie' for emotional scenes. A three-piece orchestra— violin, harp, and cello— played it during the death-bed scene in *Du Barry*."

"Miss Bara was never in doubt as to the sort of music she wanted and quite often interrupted a selection to get a change of air, so to say. In *Du Barry*, the court scenes were usually filmed to the sound of Paderewski's 'Minuet' and the 'Elegie' was played for the death of Charles XV, Du Barry's meal ticket, as it were."

Although some scenes in *Cleopatra* had "a string orchestra to play airs from *Aida*," Cohn went on to say. "A lone harpist furnished nearly all the music for the emotional scenes in Theda Bara's *Cleopatra*."

"While the redoubtable Theda vamped Marc Antony, Octavius, Caesar, et al, a young lady in modern garb and solemn mien picked the strings of a harp with grim determination. The theme was usually the same for the intimate scenes and to the openly curious it was declared that it was an old Egyptian chant that had been dug up with some mummified Rameses, or carried down through the ages by Cleopatra's posterity, if she had any."

While Fox publicity announced the music performed was based on an ancient Egyptian chant, Cohn claimed it was actually modern dance music by Gabriel-Marie called *La Cinquantaine*, or 'The Golden Wedding Anniversary.'

"Imagine Marc and Octavius being vamped to a golden wedding anniversary song," quipped Cohn, but Bara insisted the music originated in ancient Egypt.

"In keeping with my conception of Cleopatra, with the sensuousness, the plaintiveness, the beauty and tragedy of that atmosphere, I asked as accompaniment only the music [of] ancient Egypt—the music Cleopatra heard. Its silver notes rippled as moonlight rippled on the Nile when Cleopatra lay in Antony's strong arms; it voiced, as a silver fountain leaping to the stars, the heights and rapture of Cleopatra's love; its plaintive sobbing, whispered grief made moan through all the palace hall the night when Cleopatra died. Unobtrusive, poignant as are subtle things, it is the magic music to conjure a mystic mood."

A *Los Angeles Times* correspondent, visiting the set during the scene of the messenger reporting Antony's marriage, wrote, "Miss Bara vamps to the soft music of a harp—when the harpist began plucking 'The End of a Perfect Day,' she called, 'Oh! Tell her not to play that—play something spirited!'"

In costume, dog-lover Theda Bara delights in the gift of a husky puppy, 'Admiral Peary,' named after the polar explorer. (Courtesy of Robert S. Birchard)

Bara had another method for creating the proper mood on set, according to *Motion Picture News*.

"The perfume Theda Bara uses in aiding her portrayal of Cleopatra, in William Fox's coming release, was made for her by Anne Haviland, 'famous psychic perfumist,' from a 2,000-year-old formula. The fragrance is so strong that it would not be strange if it were detected on the screen."

Bara backed up this claim, or part of it anyway. In 1917, she called Ann Haviland the 'poetess of perfume.' Legend had it Haviland learned the art of perfumery as a girl living in Smyrna, Turkey. Born in Millington, Maryland and educated in Philadelphia, Haviland also claimed she trained in Paris with famed French perfumer Eugene Charabot. Honing her naturally sensitive olfactory abilities, she gained the tagline of "the woman with the most wonderful nose in the world." In 1909 (or 1912, sources differ), she had established Haviland Laboratories at West 57th Street, New York. One 1920 newspaper article claimed that Haviland "makes individual perfumes to order and can distinguish more than 400 varieties when she is blindfolded," adding that she was "recognized today as the one woman owns her own perfume laboratory in New York." Her company was bought out in 1970, and the Ann Haviland line of perfumes ceased production in 1974.

Apparently, the perfume concocted by Haviland for Bara was never commercially available. The description of the formula may have been more easily deciphered from an ancient Egyptian text than from Bara's manuscript and her poor typing skills, "My Cleopatra perfume may be likened to the music of a harp—a melody wherein all elusive notes are beln[?] [blended]."

Bara wrote that the perfume blended "the essences of herns [herbs?] and flowers that grow in the Mediterranean shores of Egypt, occluding sweet bassil [basil?] the poetic flower of Greece, saffron, the flower of courtesans, Cleopatra's known favorite a rare balsam from Palestine, aloes, cumin and male incense from Arabia, fragrant as insidious flowers at evening, with a subtle suggestion of musty spices, grown musty in the sepulchres [sic] of sueens [queens, or maybe eons], this very rare and wondrous invention, as a magic . . . conjuring, called up the phantomed personality, the rustling robes, the light passing [word illegible; feet or foot?], the sighs that ghosts are said to breathe within there [sic] tombs, of Cleopatra.

"It was indescribable. It breathed of Cleipatra's [sic] chambers. It was as ghostly palapable [sic] as the touch of Cleopatra's spirit hand. It enfolded me, wrought enchantment, carried me centuries into the past, brought Cleopatra into my fibre and my cells, changed my blood pressure and my heart beat. For the moment I was—Cleopatra. Whenever people came into the studio, the odor was so peculiar, they would go looking about, and then ask—'What is this wonderful smell?'"

Bara claimed she did not seek to reincarnate the queen, but rather "A woman, a most womanly woman, supreme in her love and self immolation, embodying both evil and good, strength and weakness, realizing what all women desire, as Shakespeare puts it 'the amorous pinches' of Phoebus, the light giving power of the universe, the love that is life—such was Cleopatra as I sought to recall her from her 'enchanted halls' of dead Egypt and bare the secrets of her heart through the vehicle of a modern art."

Even after hours of dressing and getting made up, hours of rehearsing and more hours spent in shooting scenes, Bara's labors did not cease when filming ended. Bara and the rest of the cast had to stay on to shoot 'still' pictures while they were already in costume and on set.

Actors and extras freeze in position mid-fight for the photographer to capture the image of the final battle as Octavius' forces storm Cleopatra's palace. (Author's collection)

For most productions, one of the Fox photographers would take 'stills' of the actors in costume on the sets, or Bara would be sent to the studio of a portrait photographer to pose for additional shots. However, for this special production, Fox hired Los Angeles glamor portrait photographer Albert Witzel and his assistant, Walter Frederick Seely, to take stunning stills of Bara and the cast on the actual sets in Hollywood.

According to Mary Mallory, Albert Walter Witzel "possessed a dead-on knack for capturing the public's eye with his vibrant, elegant portrait photographs." Beginning as a photographer's apprentice in Seattle in 1894, Witzel and his brother Charles moved to Los Angeles in 1909, setting up their own studio at 811 S. Hill Street. Hollywood came calling, and Witzel was commissioned to take portraits of stars at his studio, sometimes in costume. He would take Keystone bathing beauty cheesecake photos on location, but drew the line at doing photos at the movie studios themselves.

"Motion picture companies periodically approached him to shoot stills," wrote David S. Shields in his book, *Still: American Silent Motion Picture Photography*. "Knowing his forte was portraiture and that production publicity consumed inordinate amounts of time, he discouraged invitations. Yet when the project promised a high quotient of visual novelty, he said yes. Apparently the prospect of capturing on film the gaudy exoticism and bare-navel vamp sexuality of Theda Bara proved irresistible."

Trained as a landscape painter, Seely became a photographer's assistant in Eureka, ending up working for photographer Fred Hartsook in Los Angeles about 1911. In 1916, Witzel hired Seely away from his competitor Hartsook, and the next year, notes Shields, Witzel and Seely "crawled over the faux Egyptian sets, shooting close-ups of Cleopatra lolling on divans, rugs, and pillows wearing nothing but diaphanous harem pants and pretzeled metal asps on her breasts. Rarely in early cinema had a major actress been made to seem so exotically vulgar."

The stills were taken for promotional purposes, to advertise *Cleopatra* in newspapers and magazines, as well as to create posters and lobby cards for theaters. Bara states that a complete set of stills were taken for every scene in the picture, sometimes the actors posing frozen in the dramatic situations they had just filmed.

Scenes with the extras or background were shot first. The the extras were then dismissed, and Bara and the other principal actors would pose in in twenty or more tableaux of the scene. Then the other actors were dismissed for the day, but Bara was kept at work, posing in costume, "expressing various attitudes, and emotions in the scene, was needed to complete the set. As anyone knows who has posed for their photographs through an afternoon at a photographers, this is not a pleasure. Each day I posed for thirty to forty photographs, and it required my utmost ingenuity each day to think out different poses and effects."

"Asked if I was tired, I would always say— 'Go ahead, take as many as you want.'"

It's a good thing, too, since practically all that survives of *Cleopatra* are the still photographs. Witzel and Seely apparently did not follow the company out on location, as none of the location photos bear the Witzel stamp and there are no Witzel portraits of Bara in her costumes on location, so likely the task was handled by a studio photographer, and the record is sadly much slimmer. Cameraman Boyle probably took some still

In a Cleopatra costume, Theda Bara poses for a photograph intended for use in promotional art and newspapers. (Author's Collection)

photographs himself, but his cranking job likely kept him busy. In all, more than five hundred still photographs related to *Cleopatra* survive, and the number taken during the production probably numbered more than a thousand.

After they completed their day's work, Witzel and Seely went home, but Bara, still in costume, and Edwards viewed the 'dailies'; the processed footage from the previous day's work, watching "12,000 to 18,000 feet …

in the dark unventilated" projection room for three-quarters of an hour or more. Viewing the footage, they decided what to keep and what had to be re-shot.

"This daily inspection of the previous days work was necessary to keep fully in mind the continuity of the story, to seek out and so remedy defects. Sometimes part of the previous day's work was pronounced unsatisfactory, and all the labor of the day before had to be gone through again on the morrow."

After the screening of dailies, Bara could finally go home.

"After all this, too tired to undress or even rid myself of my jewels in my bungalow, I'd wrap myself in a heavy cloak and be driven to my home, and it was a rare and lucky day when I got there—without dinner, without any rest during the entire day—by nine o'clock."

After a hot bath and a light dinner, she would try to sleep.

"Invariably I was unable to sleep from sheer exhaustion. Or if I did sleep, I had nightmares in which I felt my body crushed under heavy garments as resistless as the shields which crushed the Sabian women, or I'd feel myself bitten by a thousand asps, or my body pierced by countless needles, or my head compressed in a red-hot iron crown."

CHAPTER EIGHT: 'WE CAN GET AWAY WITH MURDER HERE'

Theda Bara in costume for Cleopatra. *(Courtesy of Academy of Motion Picture Arts and Sciences)*

Cinema had an advantage over the stage, in the field of background scenery. Whereas the stage had to build a set or paint a backdrop or just let the audience imagine something, movies could be filmed anywhere a camera could go—provided the cast and crew came along with it. That itself was a great logistical problem; add to that the whims of weather, and shooting on location was fraught with peril. William Fox had authorized the shooting of *A Fool There Was*, *Under Two Flags* and *Heart and Sou*l in

Florida, somewhat necessitated by the exteriors involved and the winter conditions at Fort Lee. However, after his experience with *A Daughter of the Gods*, he began suspecting other motives of directors who wanted to shoot on location: a desire to get away from studio control.

Fox blasted the new West Coast studio head, Sol Wurtzel, when the latter reported that a company had arrived in Truckee, California, to film snow scenes only to find no snow. "You know from past experience, that nothing suits a director any better than to hop on a train with his company and go somewhere, no matter where it is, as long as he can get away from the studio."

In Los Angeles, a lot of shoots on location involved just loading up the film truck and relocating the cast and crew a few blocks down the street from the studio to shoot scenes on public streets, sidewalks and in public parks. Some stage actors had trouble with the transition to acting in motion pictures, such as shooting on location in the days before the movie industry developed effective crowd control. Movies like *A Fool There Was* plainly show curious bystanders become unpaid extras in the background as they watched the filming. Stage star Tyrone Power found 'acting on the sidewalk' taxing on his concentration.

"I am, invariably more rattled than a stage struck girl in a first appearance in her hometown." Power told *Photoplay*. "I can't get used to having my fervor dodge a streetcar or sidestep a baby carriage. I feel like an actor doing Hamlet with the scenery indecently falling down around him, or a leading lady losing her skirt in the midst of a grand rage ... I am embarrassed because my audience is continually walking in and out on me, or just past me, which is worse. It's so hard for one to be a sincere murderer when a boy carrying a ham and whistling 'Tipperary' sidesteps into a gutter so as to not interfere with the foul deed, and goes on his vulgar way— just beyond the line of vision— unheeding, unmoved and utterly disconcerting."

Nevertheless, he saw a bright future for movies.

"The field of the camera transcends the area of the stage in every way except the personal appeal of the human voice....

"I was, as one might say, reared behind the footlights, so my loyalty to the stage is very sincere; yet there is that about the motion picture industry which makes me believe we are only groping at its dawn; perhaps none of us will live to see the splendor of its noon."

Power lived long enough to make one Talkie with his big booming voice; his son, also named Tyrone Power, became a movie star during Hollywood's so-called 'Golden Age' of the Thirties and Forties.

Of course, scenes for *Cleopatra* were not shot on the sidewalks of Los Angeles, but as the Chamber of Commerce had boasted, there were plenty of scenic locations nearby.

While Bara was searching for a house and arranging for costumes and jewels, Edwards began filming the scenes set in Rome that didn't involve her. A huge replica of the Roman forum was built on the backlot for Caesar's arrival at the Senate and the post-assassination speeches of Brutus and Antony. A huge set was built for the interior of the Senate on the massive new 'Cleopatra' stage. For additional Roman scenes, Edwards went on location.

California pioneer Henry T. Hazard went from being a farm laborer and mule drover to being a highly successful land developer, patent attorney and leading citizen of Los Angeles. During the anti-Chinese riots of 1873, he leaped from a barber's chair "with his face covered with lather" and confronted the mob. He mounted "a barrel in the middle of the street and remonstrated with the crowd," trying to stop the violence. "He was rewarded by being shot at."

Surviving the incident and prospering, Hazard served in city and state government, including as mayor of Los Angeles from 1889 to 1892. When he retired, he built "one of the most beautiful of the new residential show places of Los Angeles," south of Third Street, between Vermont Avenue and New Hampshire Avenue. It was "an Italian villa and five acres of sunken gardens" of stately classical design, with Greco-Roman features, including pergolas, fountains and a Greek temple. Widowed and in his seventies, 'Governor' Hazard, as he was styled, allowed filming in his gardens just to see them in such a prestigious movie, but the studio also made a donation to the Red Cross in his honor. It spared Fox the expense of building additional sets and gave Edwards more naturalistic scenery as background. The scenes included Julius Caesar with his wife Calpurnia at their villa, the meeting of the Triumvirate of Antony, Octavius and Lepidus, and Antony's wedding to Octavia. These were filmed just in time, for the patriotic Hazard was pulling up his flowers to grow vegetables for the war effort.

Giant Sphinx built in the sand dunes with a person (probably Theda Bara herself) for scale. This Sphinx had no paws, because in 1917 the forepaws of the original Sphinx in Egypt had not yet been excavated. (Courtesy of Robert S. Birchard)

A location to double for the deserts of Egypt had to be found. Spurning actual desert sands, Edwards picked seaside sand dunes in Ventura County, near the town of Oxnard, seventy miles from Los Angeles. In the dunes next to vast bean fields, set builders erected scaled-down replicas of the pyramids and the Sphinx. With these in the background, Edwards filmed the scene of Cleopatra's encampment after her army was chased out of Alexandria by Caesar. Also filmed was the exterior of an Egyptian temple for a tomb-robbing scene.

Newspapers had announced that Fox Hollywood studio manager Abraham Carlos was looking for camels for *Cleopatra*, not something that was in ready supply in the United States. Although Fox publicity claimed the production had '300 camels,' Carlos likely gathered only a few. Surviving stills reveal at most five camels, but since hardly any crowd scene stills survive, one can't be sure. Some camels may have been rented from the famed Selig Studio Zoo (which had more animals than the Los Angeles Zoo), but additional camels were obtained from other

Theda Bara looks uncomfortable on location, dressed in the mantle for the tomb-robbing scene. (Courtesy of Robert S. Birchard))

Pharon guides Cleopatra through the secret entrance of the tomb of Menkau-Ra (Author's collection)

sources. This included the famed 'Topsy,' who had a more interesting life than any camel has a right to have.

A Bactrian (two-humped camel), possibly born on the Silk Road, Topsy was allegedly one of the camels brought from the Middle East in the 1850s for the United States Army Camel Corps for use in the American deserts, ranging from Texas to Los Angeles. This experiment, fostered by then Secretary of War Jefferson Davis, had mixed results; the camels performed well, but their strange appearance and smell spooked horses and mules that were the mainstay of the army. With the outbreak of the American Civil War, some camels were turned loose in the desert (where they inspired the legend of the Red Ghost of Western lore). Others were put to use by the Confederate Texans, including 'Old Douglas,' a dromedary-mascot who was killed by a sniper at Vicksburg.

The US Army auctioned off the remainder of its camels in the mid-1860s. A number of these were taken to Nevada and put to work carrying salt, firewood and other cargo to the Comstock Lode silver mines. Because they continued to spook horses, Nevada banned camels from the highways, forcing the herd to relocate to Arizona.

Hadji Ali, nicknamed 'Hi Jolly,' born of Greek and Syrian Christian parents, but who self-identified as Turkish, had been one of the original camel herders brought to America with the camels. He started a camel cargo caravan service from Los Angeles to desert towns in Arizona. One time in Los Angeles, upset he hadn't been invited to a German-American birthday party in Griffith Park, he disrupted the picnic by driving his camels through the festivities. When 'Hi Jolly' went bust, he turned some of his camels loose in the desert, but others, including Topsy, were sold to Ringling Brothers Circus. Topsy entered show biz, bearing noisy children with the same stoicism she showed bearing firewood. Her circus career ended in a train crash that crushed one of her humps and killed her companion camel. Ringling Brothers sold the slightly damaged but fully functional camel to Fox Studios to perform background work in *Cleopatra*.

To take an entire company on location in Oxnard was an enormous logistical effort, akin to a military operation. Not only did the cast and crew have to get there, but so did cameras, lights, reflectors, costumes, tents, chariots, props, animals, plus feed and equipment for taking care of the animals, plus a way had to be found to feed the cast and crew as well

In the sand dunes near Oxnard, California, J. Gordon Edwards (on horseback) directs the costumed background actors at Cleopatra's desert encampment. The Bactrian camel in the foreground might be the famed Topsy. (Courtesy of Academy of Motion Picture Arts and Sciences)

as deal with their waste. There were also materials for building the Sphinx and a couple of pyramids.

Motion Picture News reported the desert scenes were shot in early July. "Two special trains and a dozen automobiles" were used to transport the cast, crew, extras, and equipment, along with "several hundred animals, including camels, burros and Arabian horses."

Fox reported that 2,000 extras were used filming the desert scenes, although one has trouble finding them in the surviving stills.

J. Gordon Edwards was an avid equestrian, and when out on location, he took advantage of a studio-rented horse and spent his spare time between takes riding about the still undeveloped countryside. In fact, production stills show Edwards directing crowd scenes on horseback, as if he was a Napoleonic general commanding troops into battle. It meant Edwards really wore jodhpurs, the flared riding britches often ascribed to movie directors of the period. Modern active wear being non-existent, wearing jodhpurs and riding boots suited location shoots in rough terrain. Besides, no gentleman would be caught dead wearing dungarees or 'blue jeans,' which were strictly common laborer apparel. At the studio, Edwards wore a business suit, and he would sometimes take off his jacket when it got hot, but never his tie.

"On the sands of Oxnard, a beachside city of Southern California, William Fox erected the most marvelous replica of the sphinx and pyramids that has ever been attempted," observed *Motography*, "Word that Miss Theda Bara, the William Fox screen artiste, was to make certain scenes on this location for the superpicture *Cleopatra*, had been noised about, and tourists and natives flocked to this out-of-the-way place to witness one of the most gorgeous spectacles ever attempted. As one approached the sands of the desert he saw looming up in the distance, the inscrutable head of the sphinx and the triangular pointed pyramids in the background. One can safely believe that he had made a trip to the Egyptian deserts and was gazing upon the handiwork of the ancient Egyptians.

"Long before the arrival of Miss Bara on the scene, an army of men were marshaled together and decked in the multi-colored costumes prevalent in the days of the 'Siren of the Nile.' More than two thousand men, mounted and unmounted, were scattered over half a mile of desert sands, which were dotted here and there with gaudy colored tents.

"In the foreground was the tent of the queen, wonderfully comparisoned [sic] and decorated with a body-guard of giant Nubians whose black glistened in the sunshine. War chariots lined the streets, while the silver-pointed spears of Cleopatra's picked soldiers threw off scintillating rays.

"To the casual observer all seemed confusion. Hoarse orders were being shouted while squads of soldiers were being drilled as to the proper manual of arms of the day of Cleopatra. Seated on a nervously prancing steed, sat Director J. Gordon Edwards, darting hither and thither, issuing instructions, and getting order out of chaos; all the while upon this scene the face of the sphinx looked on unblinkingly, and gave one the feeling that behind its mask was the vision of by-gone glories and pageantry.

"Everything was in readiness, and when Miss Bara, arrayed in the ancient garb of the great Egyptian Queen, appeared, the word was given for a 'take.' Her gaudily decked chariot drawn by four black horses, dashed to the front of Cleopatra's tent, and Miss Bara started her journey to meet Caesar. At a given signal, thousands of soldiers lined the tented street, and with spears waving and vociferous shouting, Miss Bara, drawn by four horses, dashed through the sands toward the sphinx and pyramids. At another given signal, the tents were folded as if by magic, and her body-

Bound for Alexandria to confront Caesar, Cleopatra addresses her troops, "Rise, my soldiers! This night will your queen sit upon the throne of Ramses or her body shall float amongst the rushes of the Nile!" (Courtesy of Robert S. Birchard)

guard of horsemen and foot soldiers fell in line and followed their queen until the entire body disappeared over the sandhills."

While it is irresistible to think of Theda Bara dressed as Cleopatra driving her chariot down the Pacific Coast Highway, the real ride home proved harrowing. On the way back to Los Angeles from Oxnard, it is reported, the car in which Bara was riding was nearly forced off the road by a reckless driver coming from the opposite direction, "crowding the Bara car to the edge of the mountain highway, which overlooks a deep canyon with a sheer drop of a thousand feet. A heavy fence built along the edge served to prevent the car from going over the cliff."

The Fox publicity department certainly wasn't above inventing stories of its star in life-threatening situations to gain additional attention of a gullible public. Fox publicity released a dubious story about Bara and *Cleopatra* every week during production. However, there are enough hazardous mountain roads and reckless drivers around Los Angeles for the story to be true, and reason enough for Bara to spurn taking the wheel herself, letting her chauffeur drive.

Waterfront of Alexandria with Cleopatra's palace. (Courtesy Kevin Brownlow Collection)

In fact, 'jovial' Mike Miggins, a twenty-six-year-old assistant director (or 'Chief Gimme' as *Cinema News* dubbed him), was severely injured late July when he crashed his car on Lookout Mountain in Los Angeles. Whether he recovered in time to continue working on *Cleopatra* is unknown, but he survived to assist Edwards on other films, including *The Queen of Sheba*. Miggins was adept at organizing crowd scenes.

Betty Blythe recalled, "He was a character of the world, and as clever as anything. He had been with Mr. Edwards through the Theda Bara films, so that if a mass formation was needed, he could do it very well."

The next location was for the scenes set at the waterfront of Alexandria and the exterior of Cleopatra's palace. The massive set was built on the edge of the corporate limits of Los Angeles at wetlands called 'Nigger Slough.' Calling it 'the Nile of California', "The banks of the almost stagnant body of water are ideal for this setting, inasmuch as they are overflowed at every rain in this section," *The New York Times* reported, "Upon the marshy soil of a beachward plain in Southern California there rises an imposing Egyptian palace behind which towers an obelisk, while in the dim distance fringing the horizon are the peaks of pyramids and the kiosks of temples. Before this background Theda Bara has been posing as

J. Gordon Edwards on horseback directing a scene at the Alexandria set. (Courtesy of Robert S. Birchard)

Cleopatra, and recently 3,000 supers knelt in homage before this modern Queen of the Nile, while the camera clicked away the footage."

The sets were based on various sources, including a picture postcard Edwards had provided Al Smith, who found an illustration he liked, 'the gate of the temple at Karnak.'

"The buildings erected are from ancient drawings, copies of which were secured from museums. . . ." *Motion Picture News* added, "Members of the Fox organization state this is the most elaborate setting ever built for a Fox production, and one of the most costly ever erected on the West Coast . . ."

"Cleopatra Bara's palace," continued *The New York Times,* "was built with a stone platform leading down to the water's edge, so that when she landed from her barge she might not get her feet wet. The palace, it is said, is an authentic reproduction of the one frequented by Caesar, Antony, and the other boys."

In a scene on the streets of Alexandria, Cleopatra orders a child torn from her mother for execution (according to the *Los Angeles Times*— the scene is described differently in Johnson's scenario). Filming was interrupted when two half-starved gray kittens wandered into the scene. A production assistant moved to kick them out, but devout animal lover

Costumed background actors cheer a military parade in Alexandria. (Author's Collection)

Bara stopped the filming, scooped up the kittens and gave them to her maid, with the instructions, "Here, Marie, take them to my tent and give them milk!"

The shoot resumed with a crowd scene, noted the *Times*, "the sun was at its hottest, with mobs and soldiers rehearsing until it would appear they must be ready to drop, when the command came from Director Edwards to 'shoot!'"

A frail old woman on the fringe of the crowd was overcome by heat and exhaustion. She dropped on a big stairway. A young woman, 'picturesquely clad', stopped to help her.

"Never mind me," said the old lady, "I'm old. You're young. Get in the picture, dear, get in the picture!"

The street fight between Pharon and Cleopatra's Nubian slave was filmed, in which Pharon's robe was torn off. Adrian Johnson was anxious that Pharon not be too bloody after the fight, so Cleopatra can cast an admiring glance over his manly figure. However, reviewers and moviegoers both noticed something odd about his bare chest.

"It was quite noticeable that Albert Roscoe, who played the part of Pharon, had been wearing a modern-cut bathing suit this summer," commented one critic, "because when he appeared before Cleopatra for the first time, stripped to the waist, two well-defined streaks of tan were in evidence. Surely something could have been done to offset this, because his tan shoulders will make everybody think of the beach, losing entirely the atmosphere of Cleopatra's riding thru the streets...."

A *Los Angeles Times* article noted, "The remarkable feature of the extra business, the makers of the film say, was the excellence of the types to be obtained in California. This is the best department store in the world for talent. Go over to the counter and take your pick— Romans, Egyptians, Nubians, Greeks, Persians,— they are all at hand just as you want them.

"Mexicans are being used in the picture for Egyptians in many instances, fair-haired Americans for Romans, and real negroes for the Egyptian slaves. The Nubian types are really of a startling stature. Other nationalities and races were adapted with astonishing ease to the needs of the feature."

Fleeing the Jim Crow laws and customs of the American South, an increasing number of African-Americans moved to California, and some appeared in movies, including *Cleopatra*. Race relations weren't that much better in California, and the roles offered to Blacks were usually limited to slaves and servants. Fritz Leiber Jr. recalled, "There was a Negro man in the scene with (Bara), dressed as a slave I guess, and she was perfectly nice to him even though people often weren't so nice to colored people in those days."

The names of the Black background actors in *Cleopatra* are lost, along with those of the Whites. Noble Johnson, who is thought to have appeared in *Intolerance* as a Babylonian soldier, may have appeared as one of Cleopatra's Nubian or Ethiopian warriors. Rex Ingram (the actor, not the writer-director) might have as well, but he may not have arrived in Hollywood until 1918. He is credited in some sources as having the role of Naaman, the executioner, in the Fox *Salome*.

There were serious concerns in the African-American community about how Blacks were depicted on screen. Apparently, *Cleopatra* offered no objectionable scenes, but William Fox was criticized for *The Nigger* (1915). It starred William Farnum as a newly elected reform governor, out to protect the Black community from cheap liquor, which drove Black men 'wild.' Liquor interests blackmail him with the knowledge that he is mixed race, forcing him to resign. The main objection to the film was the title, and Fox would have had done better to distribute the film under its alternate title, *The New Governor*.

Greater controversy surrounded D.W. Griffith's *The Birth of a Nation*. His vision of Reconstruction had Black men engaging in vote fraud, electing corrupt officials and attempting to rape White women. The White males organized into the Ku Klux Klan, who lynched uppity Blacks and rode to the rescue of White women in threat of being violated. White American audiences cheered and praised the film, making it the first feature blockbuster. Appalled, African-Americans protested. They did not have much political clout, but they convinced censors in several cities and states to ban *The Birth of a Nation*.

The White-owned Ebony Pictures Production began making all-Black slapstick comedies in 1918. It went out of business in 1922, in part from hostility from the Black press for its depictions of African-Americans. If African-Americans wanted movies showing more positive images of Blacks, they would have to do it themselves with their own productions, but these were limited by small budgets and poor distribution. The Lincoln Motion Picture Company was the first African-American owned and operated film production company, starting in 1916 and folding in 1923. The even more short-lived Frederick Douglass Film Company was located in New Jersey. Prominent African-Americans founded the Democracy Film Company in California to produce a feature depicting the patriotic role Blacks had played during WW1. They hired screenwriter-director, Captain Leslie T. Peacocke, a white officer who had led Blacks in battle, to write and supervise the production, of which there is no further information. The most famous and successful was the Micheaux Film Corporation. Founded in 1918 by Oscar Micheaux, pioneering Black producer, it continued production through 1940.

Other minorities were also concerned with presenting positive images of their race. There was the Japanese-American Film Company, and the Mandarin Film Company, among others. These companies struggled against the overwhelming odds of competition from other film companies and the prejudices of distributors, exhibitors and audiences. Founded in 1917, the Japanese Photoplayers' Club of Los Angeles encouraged producers not to make racist depictions of Japanese and discouraged its members from accepting demeaning parts. The most famous Japanese-

American star was Sessue Hayakawa, who, fed up with stereotyped roles, started his own production company. There he cast himself in a variety of roles, including as an Arab and as a Mexican, but he too continued to make movies with Asian stereotypes, in roles that the American public was most comfortable seeing him.

The famous scene of Cleopatra's barge arriving at Tarsus drew special consideration by Adrian Johnson, citing a 'wonderful' illustration Smith had. However, there was a problem Johnson was concerned about. He thought the barge scene should be filmed in New York, because he knew of no lake or river of any size big enough in Los Angeles for the barge scene to be shot. A 'Mr. Bach' of the Fox organization apparently suggested a lake in Los Angeles, but Johnson was dismissive. Johnson said this lake was not large nor deep enough, and besides, he doubted a permit could be obtained to film there for a major scene, and furthermore, it had been 'shot to pieces' by Keystone comedies. Echo Park Lake certainly would have been too small and too near a residential neighborhood to substitute for the Cydnus River, but Johnson's concerns about the lack of an adequate body of water to film the scene at Tarsus and other water scenes were addressed by the proximity of the Pacific Ocean. *Motion Picture News* noted, "Preparations are now being made for the staging of naval battles in the vicinity of Balboa Beach, approximately fifty miles down the coast from Los Angeles."

In June, laborers offloaded tons of lumber from flat cars and trucked it all to Balboa Bay (now Newport Bay) in Orange County to build sets and ships. Fox Film Company leased the East Newport Pavilion for a shipyard to make 'reproductions of the oared galleys antiquity.'

"Two hundred fifty thousand feet of lumber was used to make the boats and transform them into the type used in 31 B.C.," according to *Motion Picture News*, "The battle of Actium was one of the first naval battles of any great consequence in the world's history and Director Edwards sought to reproduce this according to the best reports in history.

"The making of these scenes was a gigantic undertaking because it required transporting the men, costumes, properties and implements of warfare for the scenes. The nearest railroad station to the location is a distance of ten miles and from here auto trucks accommodated the needs of Director J. Gordon Edwards and his staff."

Modern surf bathers greet the arrival of Cleopatra's barge at Balboa Bay. (Author's collection)

The number of galleys actually built varies in different sources. Johnson notes that Edwards 'specifies fifteen,' but another source says twenty-nine. Fox publicity boasted fifty galleys, then bumped the number up to eighty 'full sized' galleys as the actual number. Apparently, no miniatures were used, but the boats built were scaled down from the massive Roman and Egyptian ships to more humble size. Roman triremes had triple banks of oars, the galleys seen in stills only have single banks. Of course, the real battle of Actium was waged with more than nine hundred ships, so absolute authenticity suffered from budgetary restrictions at Fox. Also, had they had eighty full-sized galleys in the rather small Balboa Bay, it would have been less the Battle of Actium than the Parking Lot of Actium.

Meanwhile, Edwards filmed the famous arrival of Cleopatra's splendid barge at Tarsus to wow Antony. Johnson's concerns about the lack of a river for the scene at Tarsus were resolved when a huge set was built for the Tarsus waterfront on a spit of land called Balboa Island inside Balboa Bay. In fact, the river Johnson was so adamant about was adequately substituted by the bay, since the River Cydnus in Asia Minor isn't much of a river either.

Locals were dressed in ancient garb for the scene at the waterfront in Tarsus to greet the arrival by barge of Cleopatra, just as they had earlier greeted the arrival by train of movie queen Theda Bara, whom the *Orange*

Cleopatra enraptures Antony on her barge at Tarsus. (Author's collection)

County Register hailed as having "more sybaritical splendor and fury than any other beauty of the flickering films."

Not everyone was so hospitable. The night after the Tarsus scene was filmed, it was reported that someone stole some of Bara's 'jewels and costumes worth $1,000.'

"I enjoyed Balboa immensely," Bara later told Grace Kingsley, "and used to delight is hiring a rowboat by night, and skimming the bay."

On one outing, her boat nearly collided with another manned by two boys, one calling out to his companion, "Don't you dare spill Mrs. Cleopatra!"

"I had another mishap down there; for I ventured out on a rocky point to read, and before I knew it the strip of beach on which I had come over was covered with water. I had to climb a nearly perpendicular rock to reach the mainland, and even then I was very nearly marooned. In another hour I should have been entirely cut off from land."

Along with the naval battle and the Tarsus waterfront, there were battle scenes with horses and chariots, plus a dramatic chariot race, in which Cleopatra personally drives a chariot to victory. Part of the chariot race was evidently filmed near the Ventura county desert site instead, since

Edwards wanted the Sphinx and pyramids in the background during the scene. Tom Mix is alleged to have staged the race. He had previous experience staging chariot races for rodeos and movies. Another possibility is Art Acord, who had similar expertise. In fact, the casting of Acord probably had a lot to do with his driving chariots for *Cleopatra*. The big chariot race was drawn from Lew Wallace's novel, *Ben Hur*, which Johnson enthusiastically endorsed as reading material for those involved with the production. Although Edwards loved this chariot race scene, as he later had one in *The Queen of Sheba*, Johnson had misgivings about including it in *Cleopatra*. Not denying it would be 'spectacular' and mean excellent 'double stuff' for Bara, Johnson cautioned how colossal and spectacular the movie was already. Was a chariot race needed?

"PLEASE ADVISE! AS TO MOTIVE AND NECESSITY!"

He goes on to advise that 'NO BRONCHOES' be used. News sources indicate the chariot race was filmed, although no stills survive to confirm this. At the time of release of *Cleopatra*, Fox issued the following story which was printed in numerous newspapers.

"A thrilling chariot race, with four horses abreast, followed by more than five hundred mounted men, speeding around dangerous mountain roads above the rolling Pacific, forms one of the most spectacular scenes in the Theda Bara super production, *Cleopatra*....

"For many days Director General J. Gordon Edwards had been rehearsing his tactics employed by warriors of past centuries. The mountain sides and the ocean front of Balboa bay, in California, where the scene was to be filmed, were lined with thousands of sightseers. Not the least interested of these was Miss Theda Bara herself.

"At intervals of a quarter of a mile, perched on the edge of crags more than 200 feet high, were a dozen cameramen, like so many gazelles, ready to 'shoot' the approaching charioteers and horsemen when they appeared around the bend in the road a thousand yards away.

"Director Edwards, his legs swinging over the side of the cliff, the rest of his body silhouetted against the sky, shouted to the bugler far below to give the signal for the race.

"The shrill notes of the bugle sounded and a dozen chariots began their race.

"Ten feet from where Miss Bara was seated in her automobile, the first chariot, drawn by four coal-black horses, swerved and started down the embankment to the water beneath. Miss Bara's shriek could be heard above the clattering hoofs of the passing riders.

"It seemed that horses, chariot and rider would be hurled to death. The young cowboy who held the reins reckoned differently, however. With the genius that comes from being in the saddle for years, he guided the sliding horses back to the roadway."

Whether the myopic Bara actually drove a chariot is unknown, but in the days before rear screen projection and other special effects, the alternative was using a double.

The re-enactment of the battle of Actium was hindered by another major conflict. The war on Germany resulted in shortages for the movie industry of both material and manpower. Despite the difficulties, the sets for *Cleopatra* were built. However, war fever had swept away many of the able-bodied men who rushed to join the real army, and it became harder to fill the ranks of the armies of Antony and Octavian. Just as the generals of ancient times had to struggle to gather up enough troops to man their ships before the battle, Fox production assistants were hard pressed to fill up their fleet. They rounded up every available extra in Los Angeles and sent them to Balboa, augmented by bums scrounged from Los Angeles's skid row, and further supplemented by obliging Orange County locals, especially fisherman adept at boat handling. The extras were paid three dollars a day, plus lunch. An alleged 2,000 costumed extras appeared in the battle of Actium, a number Fox publicity inflated to 30,000.

The quality of many of these recruits filling up the Roman legions was substandard, according to the *Newport News*, which noted, "Some were short and some were tall, some knock-kneed and some bow-legged. Others were pigeon-toed and some suffering from flat-feet. Several of them looked so hard and tough that their faces must have ached. One old fellow tottered up the hill, and it seemed that the gentle breeze which was blowing would topple him over into the bay. Another Roman gladiator with lead pencil legs, looked like he might have been borrowed from a museum...."

"The scenes made at this point show the camp of soldiers of Cleopatra and Antony," stated *Motion Picture News*, "which consisted of Romans, Egyptians and Nubians, and also the encampment of Octavius Caesar. Thousands of horses with chariots and other vehicles were required, together with thousands of tents."

Cartoon spoofing production of Cleopatra *at Balboa Bay. (From the* Los Angeles Times, *August 9, 1917)*

Cleopatra and Antony confer on her barge prior to the battle of Actium. (Author's collection)

Local schoolgirl Adelaide Perrin recalled, "The filming took weeks on end. Cleopatra's fleet was towed in stately procession to the 'lakes'. Thousands of extras were hired as galley-slaves and soldiers. A great camp was made on the bluffs above the lakes, with camels and horses, chariots and tents. Hanging around constantly as we did had its reward, for one memorable day my friend Lucille and I were invited to mount a real, live camel on which we rode around the bluffs for a few dazzling moments." Topsy may have been pulling double duty.

Meanwhile, other scenes were filmed around Balboa Bay. One scene featured Octavius' army on the march toward Alexandria, another featured seven hundred Roman soldiers rushing down a slope to the galleys. (Considering the steepness of the slope, one hopes they did this in just a few takes.) Antony and Cleopatra's troops camped in tents along the shore, until the additional extras for Octavius's force arrived from Los Angeles on thirteen rail cars. An additional three busloads of African-Americans were brought in from Los Angeles to augment Cleopatra's force of 'Nubians.'

After several delays while the 'troops' were massed, shooting the battle scene began on August 8 and required eight days to complete. *Motion Picture News* reported that four 'auto trucks' were required to bring lunches daily from the railroad station to the location to feed the cast and crew.

The battle was filmed in upper bay, also called the 'lakes.' According to the recollections of one resident, the upper part of Balboa Bay at that point in time was "really pretty much of a mudhole. It was filled with water only at high tide. At low tide it was just a mudflat . . ." Cleopatra's barge "could only be moved at high tide since it actually sat on mud at low tide."

Why not film in the open ocean? First of all, the rolling sea would have rendered nearly all of cast and crew seasick. Secondly, most could not swim, certainly not in armor, and there was less chance of drowning in the upper bay that was only a few feet deep. Lastly, the galleys were not seaworthy—they were scarcely bay worthy. Built to last only a week or so and then be burned, some were only kept afloat by air-filled barrels lashed to the hulls.

"At the sound of a trumpet, the triremes of Cleopatra swept into the upper bay, each propelled by a row of sixty brawny oarsmen," Orange County historian Ellen K. Lee wrote, "Those aboard were a number of Newport fishermen suitably costumed with shields, helmets, swords and sandals. As few actors could swim, the fishermen were to enact the dangerous roles requiring falling or being thrown into the bay."

One extra dove head first into two feet of water, became stuck in the mud and had to be rescued before he drowned.

With wooden swords flailing in the close-up shots and the ships maneuvering in the long distance shots, the filming of the battle proceeded. Vanda Krefft says Edwards, "refused to posture with a megaphone as Brenon had, instead gesturing with his arms to communicate instructions at a distance." Unable to direct the battle from horseback, he stood on the beach or more often in a small boat maneuvering around the battling fleet. In the days before the invention of the walkie-talkie, buglers were also used for signaling and directing the crews on the galleys. Upon viewing the film, some critics complained it was odd to have put all that money in the building and the burning of the fleet, then shoot the battle from so far off as to make the ships look like 'toys.'

"Thousands of people daily drove to Newport Bay from Los Angeles to witness the scenes," said *Motion Picture News*, "The autos parked along the

'Eighty full-sized oared galleys of antiquity' re-enact the battle of Actium in Balboa Bay. There may have been other vessels, but this is the only photograph of the battle that is known to survive. (Courtesy of Academy of Motion Picture Arts and Sciences)

roadside on the border of the bay extended for several miles, and the Palisades, which surround the bay on all sides, were covered with machines at every point where an advantageous view could be had."

Sightseers crowded the east side of the upper bay to watch the spectacle. At least once, naval aviators on a training flight from the San Diego base flew overhead to view the ongoing battle. Many cameras were employed on the nearby cliffs or in flat-bottomed boats circling the clashing fleets. To conserve manpower, some galleys were fitted with oars only on the side facing the camera, and were assisted in navigation by hidden outboard motors or launches.

Local resident Warren F. Morgan, whose brother served as one of the warrior extras, later recalled, "To make the battle as realistic as possible, the colored men were told that the whites were actually going to fight, not pretend, and that they had better be on their guard against roughness. The white men were told the same thing. The result was a very real fight picture."

Generally, Blacks portrayed the Nubian soldiers of Cleopatra, while whites played the Romans of both Antony and Octavius, so the staging of the battle does not appear to have been along strictly racial lines, with

Whites pitted solely against Blacks. Still, worse things have happened in Hollywood to get 'proper realism.' However, the 'proper realism' would have lasted less than an hour. Even with wooden swords, many of the extras would end up in the hospital, which would have delayed both a resumption of hostilities and filming. Even without being egged on by the assistant directors, there were numerous casualties as the two sides clashed as the untrained extras hacked at each other, but fortunately, there were no deaths.

For the grand finale of the battle, Adrian Johnson noted in his script:

"I have thought it best to stage this fight at night to give the full value to the smoke pots, the Grecian fire, and the mask of night to hide— if desired, the paucity of vessels which we have, unless we intend to build fifty. I believe Mr. Edwards specified fifteen. The title at the lead takes the affair into night easily. It seems to me what with the night tint and fire effects and distant shots, we can get away with murder here."

Motion Picture News reported, "The boats were equipped with catapults and the scenes made at night showed these machines throwing fire-balls from one boat to another until eventually practically every vessel of the two fleets caught fire. Some spectacular water night scenes were filmed."

Adelaide Perrin watched the filming of the finale.

"The climax to weeks of filming came one fine night when the fleet was burned. Great torches were lighted to illuminate the scene. We sat for hours on the bank above the lakes until the rehearsal was over and the ships were burning and the galley slaves screaming and jumping into the water."

Most of the fleet burned after being covered with hay and 5,000 gallons of smudge pot oil, "the most magnificent and spectacular scene ever taken on water," said one witness.

"The payroll on the last day required $35,000," noted *Motion Picture News*, "This amount was all in silver dollars and was given to the men as they boarded the train for Los Angeles after completing their work. From ten to eighteen cameramen were used on the scenes every day, the amount of film exposed exceeding 100,000 feet."

"J. Gordon Edwards has furnished the picture with a production that belies detailed description," said Peter Milne in his review of *Cleopatra*, "On settings, including entire cities, costumes and the handling of the tremendous mobs, not still mobs, but fighting, raging mobs, he has demonstrated his ability as a manager of the spectacular as never before. His work also includes some effective desert scenes with pyramids rising in the background. The photography by Rial Schellinger and John W. Boyle needs no criticism . . . ."

Vanda Krefft credits William Fox's organizational skills for making the filming of the epic a success.

"His preparation and oversight paid off. Production of *Cleopatra* proceeded with remarkable efficiency, economy and goodwill. Although Edwards had the incalculable advantage of a nearby company town, with experts available to solve any problem, he still had to manage a movie that was significantly larger in scale than A *Daughter of the Gods* and that had the logistical challenges of equal complexity. Edwards' cast numbered twenty-five to thirty thousand, compared to Brenon's cast numbered twenty-one thousand; and every day, he had to supervise ten to eighteen cameramen instead of six."

The promotional campaign boasted Fox had spent $500,000 on *Cleopatra*, which is just as much a fantasy figure as all the others. The announced budget, for what that's worth, was $250,000. In his book on the Fox Film Corporation, Merrill T. McCord quotes the figure $197,237 for the final cost of the film. Film historian Robert S. Birchard said the final cost of *Cleopatra* was $293,471, adding, "there was a lot of production value for the money spent on the screen." The latter figure might include promotional and distribution costs. If the epic ran over budget, William Fox was still satisfied with the result. In 1919, when Fox was berating Sol Wurtzel for the high costs of various productions, he added he saw no problem with J. Gordon Edwards productions, for he knew, "Mr. Edwards does not spend a single penny more than he has to, for he, as you know, has my explicit faith and confidence."

After filming was completed, a few of the galleys survived for years as curious relics in East Newport, while Cleopatra's glorious barge got caught in the surf near the mouth of the lower bay and was wrecked on the shore. Abandoned by the production company that soon packed up and left, the hulk could be seen from the highway for years as it slowly rotted away.

CHAPTER NINE: 'DRESS YOUR USHERS IN ROMAN TOGAS'

Upon her return to Los Angeles after the completion of filming, Theda Bara attended a birthday party for Eileen Percy, just making her start in movies. Mr. and Mrs. Douglas Fairbanks hosted the party, and other guests included Charles Chaplin and William S. Hart.

Theda Bara catches up on her paperwork at her West Adams home. (Courtesy of Robert S. Birchard)

"I am quite pleased with the picture," Bara told Grace Kingsley in her first interview after completing *Cleopatra*, "In fact, though one sees flaws in her own work, I believe it compares favorably with anything I have ever done. The character is such a wonderful one—so many-sided—and the company has been so generous with its money, that one could hardly fail to be effective in it.

"No, I shan't tell you about the asp we used in my death scene—you must wait to see that. I have taken a liberty with natural history, however, and so die peacefully, and in accordance with the poetic, rather than with the realistic ideal. Of course one dying of the asp's sting expires in convulsions."

Kingsley added, "Regarding *Cleopatra*, Miss Bara is attending the cutting of the picture, her director, Mr. Edwards, having gone away on a short vacation trip."

Such was the working relationship between Edwards and Bara; how many times in Hollywood have any directors left the editing in the hands of their leading lady? Likely Bara was simply choosing the best shots with the Los Angeles editor, but she may have played a more active role. The Internet Movie Database credits Edward McDermott as the editor on *Cleopatra*; Kevin Brownlow cites an unknown source that Arthur Ripley was the editor. It is likely there were several editors; at least one on the West Coast and one on the East Coast.

Final approval, of course, went with William Fox, who claimed to have scrutinized every reel that bore his name before it went forth to the movie-going public. As the miles of footage were edited into a coherent storyline, Fox watched the incoming reels for problems with Hettie Gray Baker. It is not known if Fox demanded retakes or other changes, but often he relied on his 'right hand man' Baker. In 1922, Baker described her process.

"I take all the parts of the film which the film editors have considered unnecessary or unsatisfactory and have those run off for me on the screen. I pick a piece here and insert it there, clip a part from here and substitute it for another. Finally, I have the whole film run off as I have revised it. Then, if it looks almost censor-proof and yet retains enough interest and spice to hold the public, I let it go."

Last to be filmed would have been the title cards, which were literally hand painted cards and shot with a regular movie camera, processed and edited in. None of the original title cards are known to survive. Along with the opening titles, identifying the film and production company (Such as 'William Fox Presents Theda Bara as Cleopatra, the Siren of the Nile'), and the end title (which might just say, 'The End.') There were also intertitles used to relay information, called 'subtitles' in the silent era. Those used to provide related descriptive/narrative material are referred to as 'expository intertitles'. In the absence of the spoken word (being, of course, a silent movie) dialogue was made into subtitles called 'dialogue titles.'

Titles for *Cleopatra* may have featured designs with an ancient Egyptian motif; pyramids, palm trees and a sphinx, and perhaps hieroglyphics— something for fast readers to look at while the slow readers finished reading the text. Title cards for the scenes in Rome may have had Roman designs. These elaborately decorated title cards did not become commonplace until 1919, but a big production such as *Cleopatra* might have used them in 1917.

Writers were often brought in after production wrapped to create additional intertitles or ones different than originally intended by the scenarists, especially if directors like Edwards simply threw out the scenario and worked out the action with the actors. Changes in the script required modifications in the titling. Sometimes additional titles were needed to explain the situation on the screen which the original writer or director thought self-explanatory but upon screening proved vague or confusing. At other times, the job of titlers was to inject humor into the titles of a dull movie, to spice them up to further entertain audiences or tone them down to satisfy the censors. Sometimes, titlers could get creative, show-

In Adrian Johnson's scenario, when Cleopatra learns of the assassination of Caesar, she turns on her astrologer (actor unknown) and says, "Your life shall answer for the false counsel you have given me!!" This still suggests she said this or expressed similar sentiments in the finished film. (Author's collection)

ing different fonts for different moods, or big letters or all capitals for exclamation, and even tried animated titles on occasion, but producers found these expensive and audiences found them distracting. Titling was considered such an important job that title writers often had equal credits with the original scenario writer. If there was a title writer in addition to Adrian Johnson, that name is lost.

Title cards often had the movie studio's name or logo shown prominently as part of the industry's attempt to reduce the bootlegging of their films. Crooks sometimes made unlicensed copies of popular films and distributed them without paying the royalties, much the same way bootleg videos today are copied and sold. Company logos on title cards were supposed to discourage this, although it was not always effective.

Although filmed in black and white, *Cleopatra*, like other films of the era, was given color through one of a variety of processes. One method was to apply colors to the finished film. In France, Pathé hired hundreds of women to carefully hand-tint each frame of a film using a stenciling process called Pathecolor. Others imitated the process with less success, when sloppily done, the result when projected were fluttering blobs of color distracting the audience from the action of the film. It was also hugely expensive to individually color thousands of frames of film. L. Frank Baum squandered a fortune having his own movie versions of his *Oz* novels hand colorized. *The First Auto* (Warner Brothers, 1927) utilized red hand coloring to create fire effects for a car engine to burst into flames during a road race.

More often, Hollywood opted for another method of providing color called tinting and toning. Entire scenes would be toned in a color appropriate for the mood or setting; blue for night, amber for interiors, red for fire scenes, etc. Ordinarily, the choice of tinting was left up to the editor, in consultation with the director, but Adrian Johnson specifies certain tints in his *Cleopatra* scenario; 'tint night,' 'tint moonlight,' 'tint sunset,' and 'tint evening' for particular scenes.

One method replaced the silver on film by dipping footage in vats containing a witch's brew of toxic colored metallic compounds such as ferrocyanide. Technicians could get quite clever with coloring. In a scene tinted blue, a man could enter a dark room and switch on a light, and the tint would shift from blue to amber. Combining toning with tinting could produce a two-color effect, although this could be used only for select

Reconciled, the lovers Antony and Cleopatra await the wrath of Octavius. This atmospheric shot suggests the excellent production values of Cleopatra. *(Courtesy of Academy of Motion Picture Arts and Sciences)*

scenes (such as a night scene in blue with actors reflecting red firelight) the effect could be quite striking.

Tinting was abandoned with the coming of sound, because the coloring interfered with the optical soundtrack. It became a lost art, and a missed one, especially as old movies reprinted without the tinting lost some of their original power. A night scene, which would have been tinted blue, in ordinary black and white shows a man skulking about as if in the dark while in obvious broad daylight. More confusingly, close-ups shot at night were intercut with long shots filmed during the day. Modern-day preservationists often try to reproduce the tinting in the films they restore, now using more environmentally friendly food coloring for the process.

Big productions like this were filmed with multiple cameras, including two cameras side by side for most shots. This was done in part as a safety, in case of problems with the film in one camera, but it was also done because Hollywood studios were actually making two movies simultaneously.

In this period, American studios made two or more versions of their movies, using their best takes for the domestic release version, and a least one foreign version would also be made from the secondary takes and out-takes. Assigned to different editors, the result could be a slightly different picture distributed abroad. Reasons for doing this varied. For one thing, repeatedly striking a new prints eventually wore out the negative. Having two original negatives would slow this process down. Also, European censors were far more lenient on depictions of nudity and sexuality on the screen, allowing for spicier versions being sent overseas, while the tamer domestic versions battled prudish censors with the worst offending scenes already excised. So when a foreign release print of a lost film is found and screened, it isn't exactly what American audiences saw during the original domestic release. Considering the censorship problems of *Cleopatra* in America, one can only wonder what might have been in the foreign release print.

Ever since the announcement of the project and throughout the production (or rather, 'the stupendous photodramatic William Fox photoplay') the Fox publicity department released press statements to keep *Cleopatra* in the public mind. As usual, these statements tended toward the bizarre.

"Theda Bara, the incomparable William Fox artiste, soon to be seen as Cleopatra in a film classic made by J. Gordon Edwards, wore throughout the picture a scarab ring which archaeologists declare to be an antique of extraordinary value."

There were other dubious claims as well. The script called for Cleopatra to dissolve a pearl into a glass of vinegar in an attempt to impress Antony with her wealth and extravagance. Fox publicity claimed that Bara, "just to satisfy her natural curiosity," tested the veracity of the scene, dropped a $5,000 pearl earring into a glass of white vinegar.

"With silent amazement Miss Bara watched the peerless pearl slowly melt in the white fluid. All that was left of her valuable bauble was the gold setting."

That wasn't all. It was revealed to the press that Theda Bara had received an illuminated card bearing strange cabalistic symbols, supposedly deciphered by Bara herself (who was, of course, well versed in 'Egyptology') and translated as: "Homage to the beautiful lady Theda Bara, sacred woman chosen for the service of the Gods. O protect Thou her body against all things evil."

A letter accompanying the 'ancient blessing' was from the unknown admirer, who claimed to have made a lifetime study of ancient Egypt. He also claimed that he was the reincarnation of one of Cleopatra's courtiers. His studies in Egyptian tombs and reading ancient papyrus rolls had convinced him that Theda Bara was the reincarnation of Cleopatra.

Bara topped this herself shortly after filming was completed.

"I felt the blood of the Ptolemys coursing through my veins," she declared, "I know that I actually am a reincarnation of Cleopatra. It is not mere theory in my mind. I have positive knowledge that such is the case. I live Cleopatra, I breathe Cleopatra, I am Cleopatra!"

William Fox must have thought this didn't go far enough, so to promote *Cleopatra*, he called in a heavy hitter.

Working as a creative press agent for various stage performers and Broadway impresarios, Edward L. Bernays was known for a variety of outrageous publicity stunts. He linked Henry Miller's revival of the stage play, *Daddy Long Legs* to charities for orphans. He fabricated press stories about how opera idol Enrico Caruso protected his superb voice. To promote Diaghilev's Ballets Russes, he had star Flore Revalles photographed wearing a tight fitting outfit while posing with a giant snake at the Bronx Zoo. Just the man Fox needed.

Unable to join the army because the medical examiners diagnosed him with flat feet and defective eyesight, Bernays contributed to the war effort by getting his Broadway connections to organize war bond rallies and recruitment drives. When William Fox invited him to his office, Bernays was intrigued. Like others, he was smitten by the fantasy ideal of the motion picture.

"I was thirteen when I first went to the movies to watch elves and fairies flickering on the moon, to the accompaniment of a tinkling piano," remembered Bernays in his 1965 autobiography. Disillusionment awaited him.

Arriving at the Fox offices in "a seedy-looking building," Bernay found Fox in "a partitioned private office, which was part of a chopped-off loft. . ." He described Fox as "a dark-complexioned, pudgy, moon-faced man with thinned-out black hair . . ." Bernays thought he looked like 'a saloon keeper.'

"Young man," said Fox, "I want you to handle the publicity for a great pitcha, *Cleopatra*, with Theda Bara—super colossal," he said with enthusiasm and conviction. "The greatest pitcha of all time. It's got more elephants, tigers, camels, soldiers and dancing girls in it than any other pitcha made yet. A hot box-office attraction. You make it hotter."

Bernays remembered, "I had thought of Fox as an impresario, like Diaghileff, or a producer like Henry Miller. It was a disappointing beginning."

However, Bernays was beguiled by the prospect of doing promotion for *Cleopatra*, because of Theda Bara.

"To be considered for such an assignment was as exciting as it would be for a young man to be asked to handle Brigitte Bardot. A vamp then had more allure than a love goddess today can equal."

So with his interest piqued, Bernays said he visited Fox in his Mount Vernon, New York, home, where more disillusionment awaited him. He said Fox greeted him wearing an undershirt and red suspenders, reminding Bernays of something his father has said, that no gentleman wore visible suspenders. Sitting at a large table full of dirty breakfast dishes, Fox "repeated with gusto how colossal *Cleopatra* was."

Vanda Krefft has doubts about Bernays account of these meetings.

"Fox didn't live in Mount Vernon in 1917; and it's inconceivable that, otherwise so prideful about decorum, he would have greeted a professional colleague in such a slovenly manner. Bernays also wrote that at the time of his hiring, Fox had been 'rapidly increasing the number of his storefront movie houses' when Fox by then owned some of the city's plushest theaters. And Bernays claimed to have visited Fox in his office in a 'seedy-looking building' on West Forty-Ninth Street. In 1917, Fox Film headquarters were located in the smart, relatively new Leavitt Building, at 130 West Forty-Sixth Street."

Part of the problem was that Bernays was writing nearly half a century after the events, but Krefft suggests something else which may have affected his memory.

"Having always known privilege, Bernays was a fearsome snob who regarded his low-born, uneducated employer with contemptuous sang-froid."

It didn't prevent Bernays from accepting Fox's money. Agreeing to Bernays' fee of $150, Fox told him to 'start on Monday.'

A print of *Cleopatra* was screened for Bernays, who was asked to make recommendations. Possibly he started earlier, as the publicity drum had been beating all the summer of 1917.

"Looking back, I am surprised at the glowing report I wrote. Apparently my Broadway years had aligned my viewpoint with Broadway's box office," remembered Bernays, "My memorandum pointed out that *Cleopatra* offered 'all those features that delight movie habitués—for instance, students of Egyptian and Roman history.'"

Fox had urged Bernays to focus on the spectacle of *Cleopatra*. After all, he had spent huge sums of money producing the epic. He wanted the promotional campaign to reflect that. Bernays thought that it was Bara's sex appeal that would sell the film.

"I raised questions the public might discuss: 'Is Theda Bara just in her portrayal of the Egyptian queen as a woman of lust, voluptuousness and sensuousness?'"

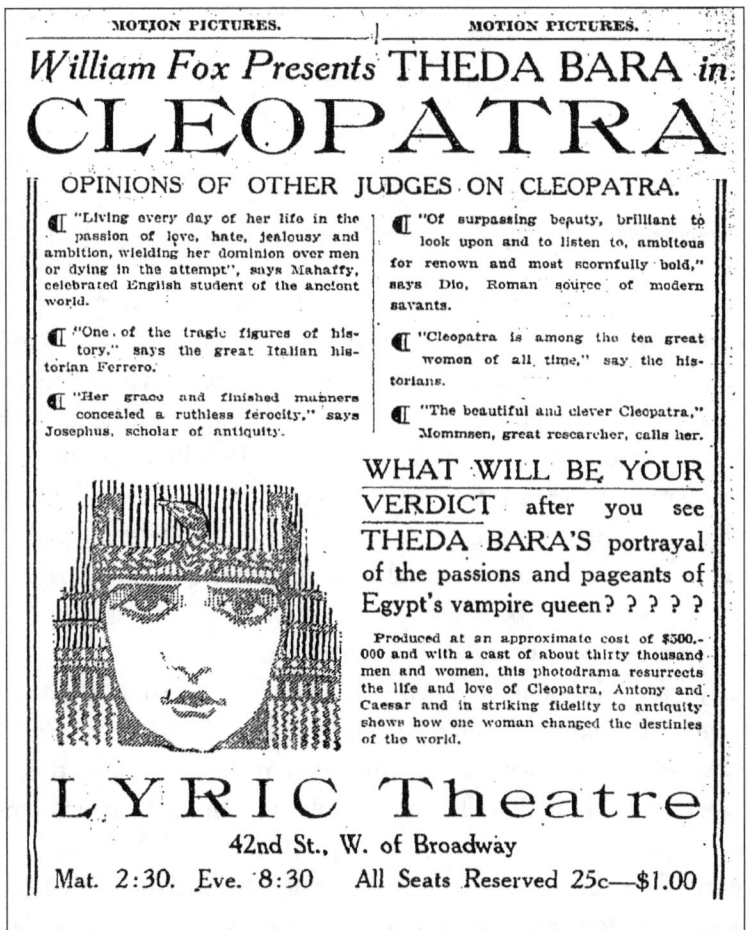

Advertisement for Cleopatra *in* The New York Times, *October 15, 1917.*

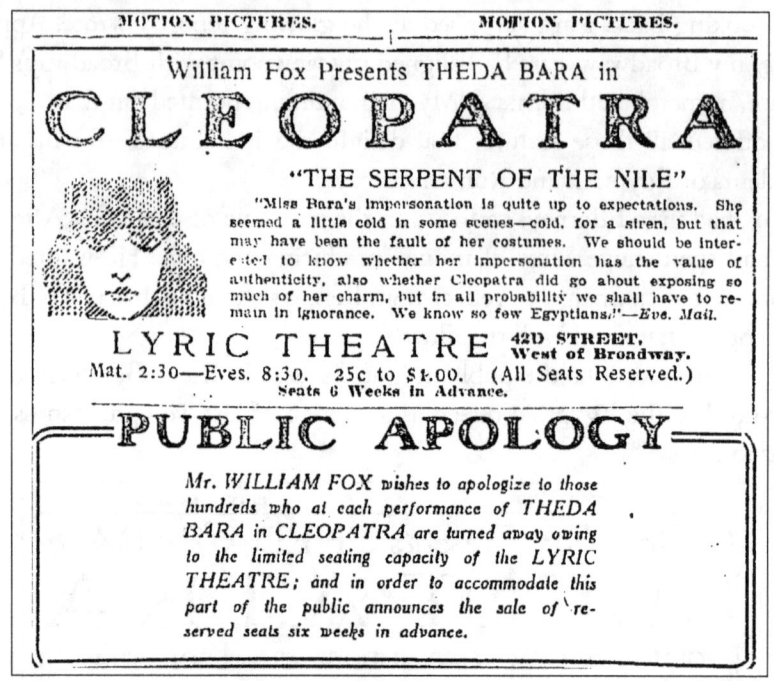

Advertisement for Cleopatra *in* The New York Times, *October 17, 1917.*

Bernays balanced his campaign both as a sexploitation piece and on presenting the film as serious history worthy of scholarly interest. "I looked for social values in *Cleopatra*." He stressed the educational aspects of the film as a way of teaching ancient history. He suggested the advertising program include references to classic and modern literature on Caesar and Cleopatra. He pitched that "Milliners and dressmakers will find it an inspiring source of new ideas for fashions." Fox publicity men would turn these ideas into free articles for publication. Among the newspaper stories he proposed, "one about Cleopatra's couch in art throughout history, another to reveal how armored men make love!"

Bernays' advertisements featured "—a silhouette in profile of Cleopatra reclining in her native costume, which later became the picture's trademark. We advertised Theda Bara as the 'siren queen of today' or the 'vampire queen of yesterday.' . . . These one-column, one-inch advertisements stimulated public interest."

Newspaper advertisements featured scantily clad drawings of Cleopatra fondling a snake or posed alluringly—some ads simply featured a representation of Bara's 'perilous' eyes, but others, showing drawings of Bara

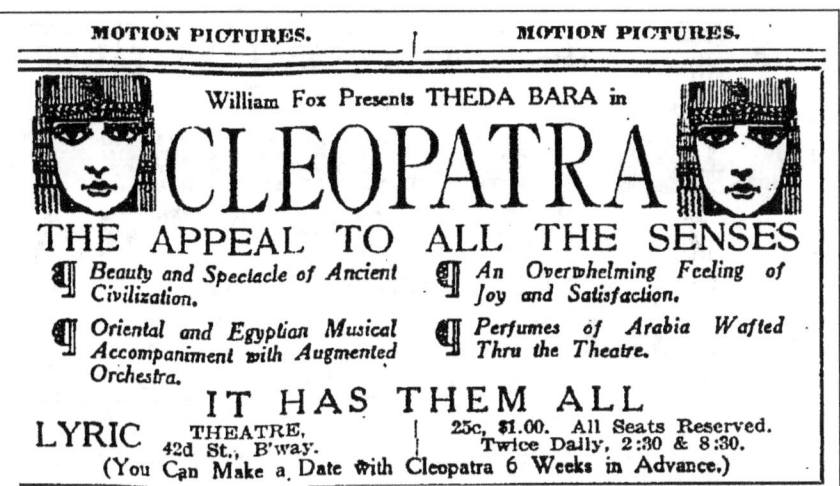

Advertisement for Cleopatra *in* The New York Times, *October 30, 1917.*

nearly naked or even topless, were censored by some papers. Bernays also apparently wrote the copy for the newspaper ads.

"*The New York Times* turned down my advertisement for the film in which I claimed it was the hottest summer resort in New York. It was in December."

Fox publicity department also released the following 'facts' about *Cleopatra*, which were sent out to newspapers in cities where the movie was about to screen.

"It was photographed in California.

"It portrays the world's first naval battle—the Battle of Actium—and the first naval conflict ever filmed," for which "80 vessels were especially constructed... and later burned to the water's edge.

"Miss Bara wears fifty distinctively different costumes.... To match each costume the Siren of the Nile wears a complete set of jewels—fifty dazzling and different sets of baubles.

"Before and during the production ten seamstresses were constantly working on the star's costumes.

"2,000 persons who do not appear on the screen were active in the work of production—carpenters, masons, painters, hostlers, ship builders, and the like.

"3,000 horses were used in the battle and desert scenes."

Because of all the Fox publicity lies, there is no reason to believe any of this. The publicity department couldn't keep its lies straight in additional

Advertisement for Cleopatra *in* The New York Times, *November 3, 1917.*

press releases. Another blurb claimed that *Cleopatra* employed 10,000 cast members, 500 horses (not 3,000; another blurb says there were 2,000 horses), 300 camels (where the heck did they get 300 camels?), 2,000 special costumes and 31 chariots.

While this may have been the first full-scale filming of an ancient sea fight, Actium was hardly the 'world's first naval battle.'

Bernays is credited with having invented the pressbook, specifically for use in promoting *Cleopatra*—but the wise film historian hesitates in unequivocally declaring anything the 'first' in the murky world of film history. Twice the size of a daily newspaper, it "contained stories and illustrations embellished with lurid headlines. 'The loves of Cleopatra bared on the screen' had a subhead 'Outlines of the story that stirs men's blood.' 'The high cost of kissing the modern Cleopatra is cheap compared with the price Caesar paid,' said another."

"I shrink from them today," Bernays admitted, "but my friend, Arthur Mayer, the movie historian, tells me that they expressed the accepted attitudes of the movie editors of the times."

Surviving examples of the pressbooks are loaded with advertising suggestions, and the exotic appeal of the movie was expounded to exhibitors:

"Egypt! Alexandria! Rome! The immensity of the Desert! Mystic Sphinxes and centuries-scented Pyramids! Bizarre Obelisks!

"The Mediterranean and the Nile are highways for quaint ancient vessels. Caravans wind their heavy-footed way like multi-colored ribbons on the deserts monotony. Armies of gallant ancients rush at each other with

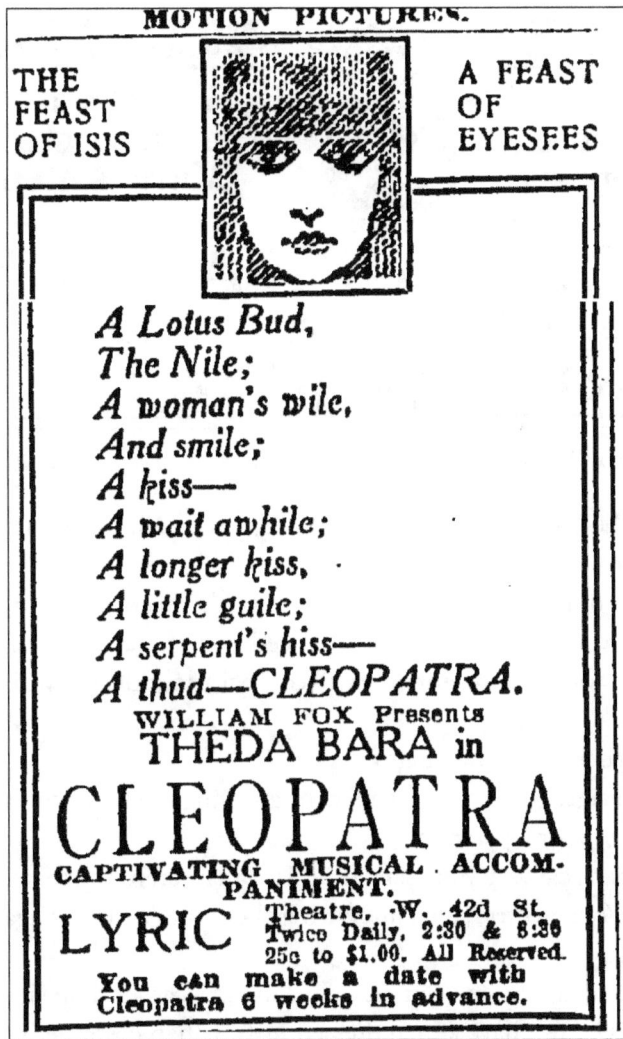

Advertisement *for* Cleopatra *in* The New York Times, *November 7, 1917.*

the impetuosity of a mountain torrent. There are hand-to-hand conflicts. The phalanx is wielded like a mighty spear.

"Were there ever more opportunities for a sensational lobby display than in this stupendous wonder film?

"*Cleopatra* leaves a free hand for extravagance. Nothing is extreme in effect. Your most strained efforts will give only a suggestion of the grandeur that scintillates on the screen.

"Festoon your lobby with many-colored drapings [featuring the] silhouettes of camels, sphinxes, and pyramids forming the border. Let the

Advertisement for Cleopatra *in The New York Times, November 16, 1917.*

gold-brown of the Sahara and the orange of Egypt's sky predominate in the color scheme.

"Two obelisks (of paper, wood or concrete, with the word 'Cleopatra' on them drawn to resemble hieroglyphics), placed one on each side of the main entrance to your theatre, not only will compel attention, but will give fine 'atmosphere.'

"Dress your ushers in Roman togas.

"If you have a stage, give it a desert effect by strewing the floor with sand and using an obelisk or a pyramid.

"At any rate, you can set your screen in a Roman arch, supported by Doric columns. Your electric sign announcing the show can be set against a Sphinx outline.

"If you have a menagerie and can secure the use of a camel, drape it with appropriate signs— and have a man dressed in Egyptian costume parade it through the streets.

"Remember that *Cleopatra* has immense educational value: It is historically correct, so far as humanly possible. The settings are absolutely faithful. The Shakespearean Julius Caesar and Anthony and Cleopatra are aptly illustrated by this picture. Make these facts a source of profit.

"Invite the principals and teachers of all your local schools— elementary and high—as well as the librarians, to a special performance of *Cleopatra*. Get their opinions and give these publicity.

"Start a composition contest in the various school grades on such subjects as: 'The Assassination of Caesar,' or 'The Battle for Actium,' or 'The Dress of the Ancients.'"

These latter suggestions are a curious idea, especially as censorship groups subsequently denounced *Cleopatra* as being unfit to be seen by children.

In the days before electronic mass media, elaborate publicity campaigns were by no means rare. Exhibitor trade journals were filled with suggestions of how to decorate their theaters with eye-catching displays. Triangle's *The Captive God* (1916) was set in Aztec Mexico and starred William S. Hart in a rare non-Western role.

"This play affords every Triangle exhibitor unlimited opportunity for effective lobby display, promotion, press work," the studio assured, "It will not be hard to obtain a figure of an Indian god—anything ugly, prehistoric type will do, and it will be a big hit in the lobby."

Trailers (so-called because they originally appeared after the feature film when first introduced in theaters) were not commonplace during this era. Instead, slides with colorful artwork advertised the exhibitor's upcoming film presentations. These, along with slides discouraging whistling, spitting, loud talking and wearing of large hats, or slides with local advertisements, were projected on the screen while audiences were taking their seats before the show, or in theaters with only one movie projector, while the projectionist changed reels.

Poster art was also flourishing during this period. Still photos, lobby card and posters of varying sizes beckoned passers-by into the theaters. Lobby cards, first introduced in 1913 by Universal, were originally printed in black and white and usually depicted scenes from the movie being advertised. In 1917, colored lobby cards were introduced, with scenes being tinted, even though the movie was in black and white. Although posters of the period did not have the inventiveness of later eras, they were colorful and lavish, and William Fox made sure that his posters were some of the best. He was prompted in part by the fact he had only a couple major stars, such as Bara and Farnum, competing with studios that boasted more stars. Eye-catching Fox posters today are highly collectible, so a large number of them survive. Many boldly proclaim the virtues of movies that no longer exist.

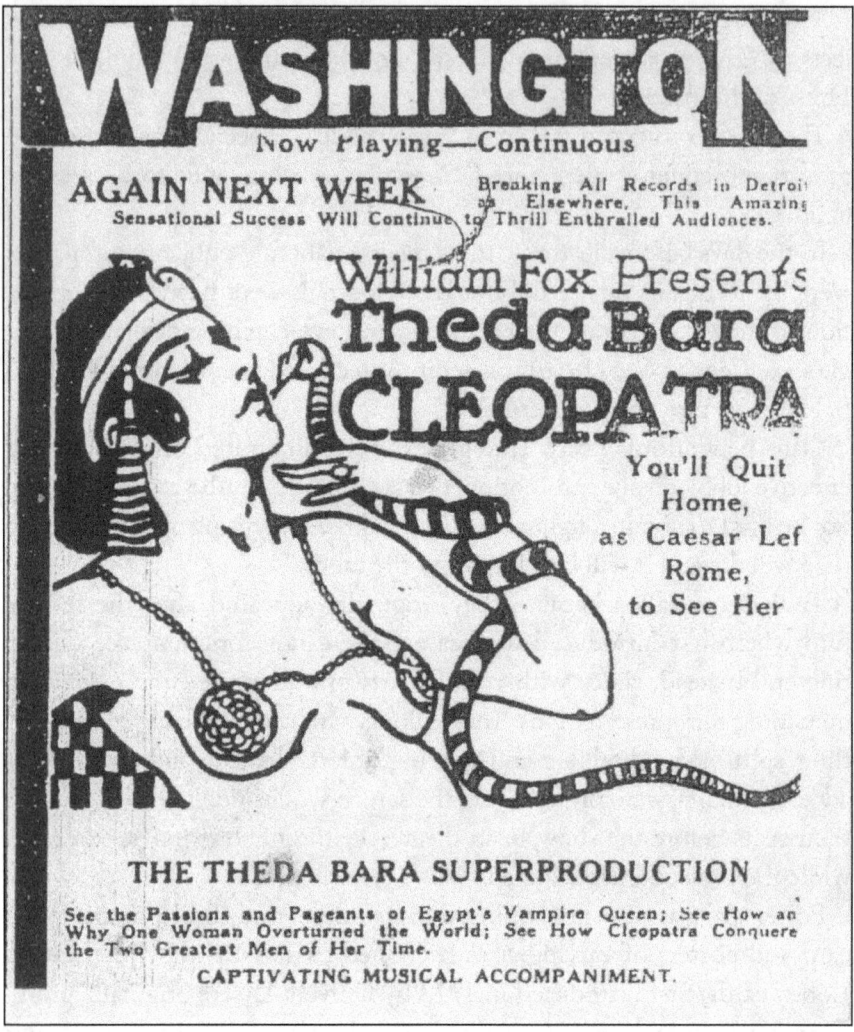

Advertisement for Cleopatra *in a Detroit newspaper, date unknown. (Author's Collection).*

Bernays did not remain long at Fox after he outlined the publicity campaign. He was asked to coordinate with Winfield Sheehan, who several times kept Bernays waiting outside his office. Saying he wasn't being paid to wait, Bernays quit in a huff.

"Fox carried out the program I suggested and for two years the picture ran as a great box-office success."

In an ebullient mood, William Fox told *Motion Picture News* that Theda Bara "had advanced to the very top of artistic achievement and of trade

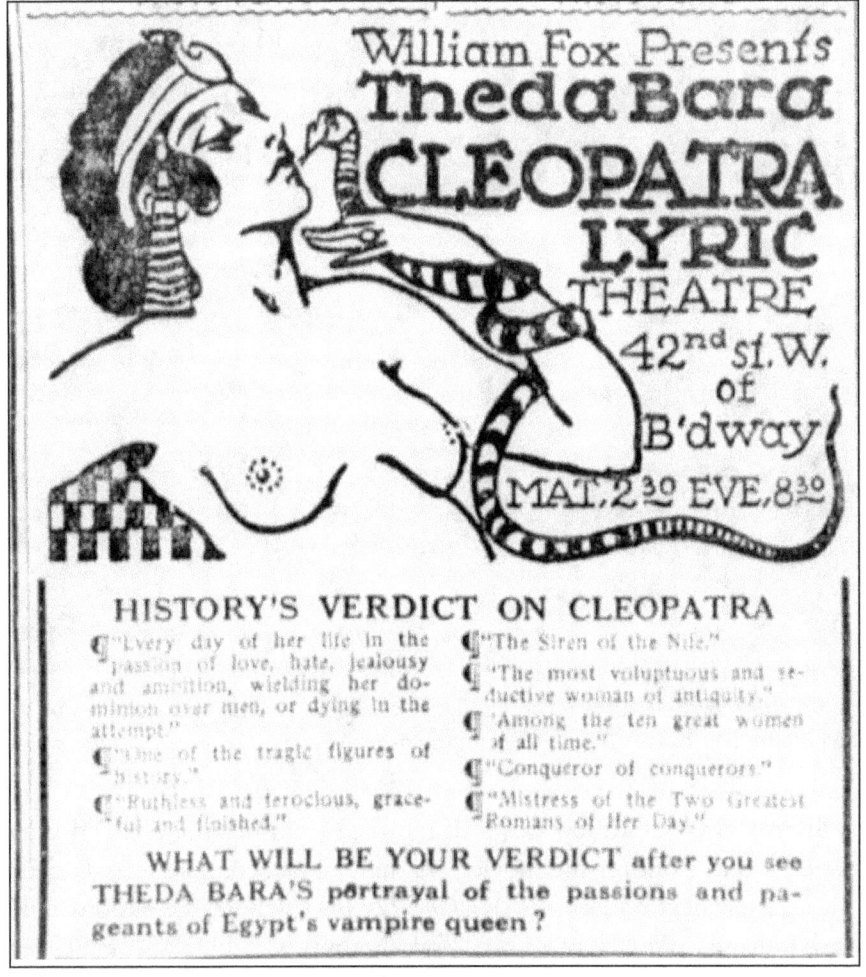

Advertisement for Cleopatra *rejected by a number of New York newspapers. (Author's collection)*

popularity, and I decided that we would give her the very best we had in us. She posed in a version of *Cleopatra* which looked so very good that we decided to lay this picture on our shelf also, to save temporarily for our own private enjoyment."

He said this in late July, when production was still ongoing.

Fox added, "Then I began to think hard. We had three more big subjects for Theda Bara, so we cast everything to the winds and turned her loose, with the result that we have piled up in our private storeroom a group of pictures better than I had ever seen anybody make before."

Theda Bara emerges from her Hollywood bungalow wearing a costume for Madame Du Barry. *The people standing next to her are unidentified, but on the steps behind them is George James Hopkins.*

Shortly after J. Gordon Edwards returned from vacation, he and Bara were hard at work on the movies Fox had announced had already been made. Their next project was *Madame Du Barry*, about the famous mistress to King Louis XV of France. Now chummy with Bara, George James Hopkins designed her costumes for *Du Barry*.

"I'm afraid I paid very little attention to historical detail," Hopkins admitted. For Du Barry, "I just got the silhouette correctly and filled in the rest myself. I hope to capture the spirit of that time, the luxurious abandon."

Certainly, no one would mistake his Art Nouveau costumes for Bara's *Salome* for historical accuracy, although the costumes for Nazimova's *Salome* (1923) were even more outlandish.

Bara vamped again for *The Rose Of Blood* (1918). She portrayed a Russian revolutionary sent to assassinate the aristocrat who previously spurned her love.. Hopkins' friend Ryszard Ordynski wrote the story and also had a role as a Russian revolutionary.

Finally, in the autumn of 1917, Bara boarded a train bound for New York to attend the premiere of *Cleopatra*. She headed East with misgivings.

"In the little book which I compiled before I entered pictures, in the days of my struggles, called 'When My Ship Comes In,'" Bara remembered, "I made this entry—'One day I shall possess jewels that belonged to Cleopatra.' Well, even this was accomplished, albeit the jewels were those of the picture *Cleopatra*."

After *Cleopatra* wrapped, Bara feared that the jewelry and costumes she had helped bring into being would be simply stored in the wardrobe department, and be re-used in lesser movies. "I could not bear the thought that these exquisite creations, works of love of the old artist and precious to me, should be handled so roughly, carelessly, and worn by extras."

It didn't matter that they weren't really Cleopatra's jewels, "Beauty is holy, whatever its guise. . . . Yes, I would be a thief . . . to save them from desecration."

She 'appropriated' the ones she wanted to keep and brought them with her East. It is unknown if there were the same costumes and jewels reported stolen at Balboa Bay, but since that theft was done near the end of filming, it is possible. She had promised the Metropolitan Museum of Art to bring the clothes and jewels she wore on *Cleopatra* so they could be put on display, but this would be tricky if they were 'stolen property.'

Bara fretted about it on the train, and then she decided to write a story that Fox could turn into a movie for her in exchange for the costumes and jewels.

Newspapers were filled with accounts of the trial of Mata Hari, convicted as a German spy. Her real name was Margaretha Zelle. Trapped in a loveless marriage with an abusive husband in the Dutch East Indies, she devoted herself to Balinese culture. Returning to Europe and getting a divorce, she re-invented herself as Mata Hari, a Javanese princess, who had been taught from childhood sacred Indian dancing. Throughout Europe, she performed Balinese-influenced versions of modern dance, in the same mold as Isadora Duncan and Ruth St. Denis. As a citizen of the neutral Netherlands, she could cross wartime borders easily, which would be very useful for espionage. She had apparently agreed to spy for the French, but they came to believe she was a double agent, and they sentenced her to death. Historians believe that she was a victim of the machinations of others, but others have labeled her an archetypical *femme*

Theda Bara wearing one of the costumes she rescued from 'desecration.' (Author's Collection)

fatale; an exotic woman who seduced and used men to her own ends: in other words, a vamp. Historian Julie Wheelwright described Zelle as "an independent woman, a divorcee, a citizen of a neutral country, a courtesan and a dancer, which made her a perfect scapegoat for the French, who were then losing the war. She was kind of held up as an example of what might happen if your morals were too loose."

Theda Bara as a Javanese temple dancer in The Soul of Buddha, *a role which she wrote for herself. (Author's collection)*

Nurse Edith Cavell, a proper English matron who was executed by the Germans for helping Allied POWs to escape, was revered as a martyr. In contrast, the idea of an exotic dancer working as a lethal double agent, using her powers of seduction to extract military secrets from her many lovers, made Mata Hari an enduring archetype of the *femme fatale*. Like Cleopatra, this is the myth that prevailed in the subsequent movies made about her.

That's not the story Bara chose to write, as one would expect, nor one of an innocent victim. Bara wasn't interested in being 'good' or 'bad,' she just wanted to be exotic, just as Zelle had re-imagined her life as Mata Hari—the interesting similarity in their names gives one pause to wonder if Theodosia had heard of or even seen Mata Hari while in Europe before the war. With Mata Hari's faux background as inspiration, Bara wrote on the train ride back, "the plot of *The Soul of Buddha*, a vampire story, the chief character being a Javanese temple dancer who becomes an outcast through her love of a man."

The dancer forsakes her vows to marry a Scottish officer, but is stalked by the vengeful high priest of the temple. She winds up leading a dissolute existence in Paris. When she performs a sacred dance in her stage debut, the high priest, disguised as a statue of Buddha, strangles her mid-performance to the applause of the audience, who think it is part of the act.

When Bara arrived in New York, she made an appointment to see William Fox. This may have been with some trepidation, for the last time Bara was in New York, she had strong-armed contractual concessions from Fox.

"I have a trade to make with you," she told him.

"What is it?"

"I have stolen the jewels of *Cleopatra*."

"Possession is nine points of the law, isn't it," Fox replied, "And they are only a lot of junk, after all."

"'Yes, but I do not want something for nothing, and I have written a story which I will give you in exchange.'"

She read him the outline she wrote, to which Fox said, "That is splendid!" and the bargain was struck.

Fox could afford to be gracious. He was in a good mood. He had seen *Cleopatra* and knew it was going to be a surefire hit. Besides, it would not do to have his top star hauled off to the hoosegow on the eve of the premiere of their biggest movie. The costumes and jewelry were of little value to him now the *Cleopatra* was finished, and their loss certainly offset by the publicity value of Bara writing her own story.

Some have wondered why Bara wrote herself another vampire story when she was continually beseeching Fox to let her play other kinds of roles. Obviously, she had to write something that pleased Fox to make the bargain, but the real question was why didn't she, already a playwright, write more of her own stories? Perhaps she did, but there's no record of them. More likely, the demands of being not just a movie actress but also a famous star, whose workload included photo shoots and personal appearances, didn't leave the time to focus on writing. As it was, she sighed with relief that Fox accepted her story. She met with Lythgoe at the Museum of Art to show him the costumes and jewelry to be displayed, and then she prepared herself for the premiere of *Cleopatra*.

After the film came out, a colleague wrote to Lythgoe, "Somebody mentioned seeing Theda Bara in *Cleopatra* and I began thinking about the stir at the Museum when she came and wanted you to design her costumes for this very movie. It's really a pity you didn't. It wouldn't have taken up any of your time for all she wore was a pair of sandals—one in one scene and one in another."

Cleopatra premiered at the Lyric Theater on 42nd Street, in New York on October 14, 1917. Bara's presence attracted considerable attention of fans and the press. At eleven reels; two hours and five minutes in length, *Cleopatra* was nearly twice as long as most other feature films, at the average length of six reels.

While waiting for the film to start, audiences could peruse the souvenir program, which was available at the special $1.00 reserved seat performances of *Cleopatra*. Included in the program was an article titled, "Is Theda Bara a Reincarnation of Cleopatra?" Among the compelling evidence cited to support this proposition was "the character of Theda Bara and the character of Cleopatra are similar in many respects," that "in appearance, so far as can definitely be ascertained, Miss Bara and the 'Siren of the Nile' were similar," that "Miss Bara's last name is similar to an Egyptian word meaning 'Soul of the Sun'" and lastly, perhaps irrefutably, "the prophesy of Rhadames [aka Rhames] fits Cleopatra as easily as Miss Bara."

The lights dimmed, the orchestra started up, and the movie began. The opening of the film, as described by Alice Brown in the *Columbus Journal*, starts with an opening shot of the vast expanse of a desert "stretching out illimitably, with the Sphinx in the distance. Then we come closer to the Sphinx until at last there is a close-up of the enigmatic lady, and lo! her face is that of Theda Bara, who opens her eyes, twists her mouth and raises one brow in the manner familiar to film fans..."

Just hours after the premiere, Margaretha Zelle was executed by firing squad in France. It is said she blew a kiss to the soldiers before they fired. An even wilder legend had her opening her coat to reveal herself nude to

Agreeing to meet Antony in Tarsus, Cleopatra proclaims peace, not war, between Egypt and Rome. (Author's collection)

the firing squad, declaring, "A harlot, yes; a spy, never!" which somehow escaped the notice of the reporters present to witness the execution. Like Cleopatra, *femmes fatales* not only had to be punished, but also had to be sexy in receiving death.

The Fox Film Corporation's press department asked the public: "What will be your verdict after you see Theda Bara's portrayal of the passions and pageants of Egypt's vampire queen?"

The verdict of reviewers was varied. Most praised the lavish scenery and costumes. The critic for *The New York Tribune*, was "completely overwhelmed," saying, "the spectacle simply beggars description. The photoplay is the greatest of all film spectacle plays. Flawless in its settings, magnificent beyond compare, and the performance of Miss Bara is at all times interesting. She has never before looked so regally beautiful, and if the original Cleopatra was just half so lovely, we do not blame Antony for renouncing Rome."

The *New York Telegraph* said, "The scenes are so gorgeous that they brought continued applause. Miss Bara gives a striking performance in a luxurious production. She is probably the first actress to play the role whose eyes looked the part. Needless to say, the photography and other technical points are above criticism."

When mentioned at all, the actors in the supporting roles were praised, but most of the attention focused on Bara's performance. *New York Review* declared "Proud, defiant, willful, emotional, sinuous by turns, Miss Bara makes a representation the most auspiciously successful of her career."

Reviewers were critical, however, what they thought was a weak story and poor editing, which served to detract from the huge spectacle.

"*Cleopatra* should have been a magnificent spectacle; the Fox picture is merely garish," Randolph Bartlett wrote in *Photoplay*, "Cleopatra herself was an irresistible siren; Theda Bara is merely brazen in a ponderous manner.... Yet there is one inspired moment which redeems the entire production. Cleopatra, returning from the defeat at Actium, believing Antony dead, is bowed with grief. Several scenes in this episode are classics. They might have been animated paintings by Alma Tadema. Miss Bara rises to heights of tragic expression hitherto unsuspected, not by ravings and hysteria, but by sheer grace of despair. Had the entire picture been done in this spirit, *Cleopatra* would have been a thing of joy."

Some reviews are so illuminating— or at least, entertaining— about the movie as to deserve to be printed virtually in their entirety.

"Cleopatra of Egypt was among the earliest of the vampires of history," said *The New York Times*, "if not the earliest, and it was therefore but a matter of time until the siren Theda Bara should duly attend to the transfer of that temptress to the movie screen. The result is 'Cleopatra,' an uncommonly fine picture which was unreeled for the first time at the Lyric Theatre last night before an audience which included the dazzling Miss Bara herself. The star, by dint of much rolling of eyes and many other manoeuvres, contributes a thoroughly successful portrait of 'the serpent of the Nile, the siren of the ages, and the eternal feminine,' in the words of the screen, and thus does the ill-starred Queen of Egypt become the well-starred queen of the movies....

"From a scenic standpoint, also, it is quite a triumph for the director. The Sphinx, the pyramids and a goodly section of Rome are duly duplicated, and the larger scenes are handled in a way that suggests D.W. Griffith. The naval battle at Actium is made most impressive, and the handling of the chariots also furnishes many a thrilling moment.

One of 'fifty' outfits worn by Theda Bara in the course of the film. (Courtesy of Academy of Motion Picture Arts and Sciences)

"Miss Bara, to quote the program, 'wears fifty distinctively different costumes,' many of which are so thoroughly in attune with the period that they are likely to cause not a little comment..."

"Those who like to see Theda Bara should not fail to take advantage of the opportunity afforded in *Cleopatra*," said *The Dramatic Mirror*, "for, certainly, they will never see *more* of her, nor—on the other hand, will they ever find their adored one running truer to form.... Miss Bara, as Cleopatra, moves throughout the long two acts with all the grace of a hula-hula dancer, investing the Egyptian lady with accomplishments in her amours that she probably never dreamed of possessing. And were Cleopatra to return to earth and witness the performance she undoubtably would thank her interpreter 'for the compliment.'

"Much attention has been devoted to the mob element and to the spectacle of an ancient naval engagement. But the total force of it all is lost through the absence of a good interesting story."

"It is a stupendous offering with many magnificent scenes and gorgeous costumes, imbuing a rich Oriental atmosphere," Helen Rockwell said in *Motography*, "Some few thousands of people are represented in the big scenes which are especially noteworthy, some scenes of the 'Feast of Isis' being particularly beautiful. Everything has been done on a very large scale. The scenes in the desert are very effective as is the vivid picturization of the naval battle of Actium. Theda Bara as Cleopatra gives to her representation a Winter Garden touch which is not traditional. At no time does she appear queenly and dignified, but she makes a striking picture and wears some daring gowns which will occasion many gasps from the spectators. She is the type that is nothing if not seductive and in this respect fills the role of the notorious queen to a nicety— if the term may be used without calling forth a smile.

"The whole production is one of great lavishness and moving picture fans will undoubtably receive it with a great deal of enthusiasm. J. Gordon Edwards has directed the big scenes with a degree of skill which shows a careful study of his subject, but in a few minor details he hasn't been quite as consistent. The photography generally is good, the water scenes being exceptionally well done. . . .

"The progress of the story is at times a little slow but interest is sustained by the sumptuousness of the spectacle and Cleopatra's frequent appearances...

"The production is not an artistic triumph, due to the overdressed interiors and historic shortcomings on the part of some of the cast, but this is of little commercial importance, as the picture is of the type to attract attention and it will be a good picture from the box-office viewpoint."

"*Cleopatra* is a magnificent picture as a spectacle, vastly entertaining as a drama and mighty interesting as to Theda Bara," wrote Peter Milne in *Motion Picture News*, "And this ought to signify that it will be a constant

Another spectacular costume. (Courtesy of Academy of Motion Picture Arts and Sciences)

source of revenue to both Mr. Fox and exhibitors for many weeks, months and even years to come. Anyone who attempts to stroll by the Lyric Theatre, where it opened a week ago Sunday, will stand witness to these statements without a second thought. The line extending from the box office is liable to get tangled up with the Rialto clientele a few hundred feet away and around the corner if the rush for tickets keeps up.

"Here, having disposed of its glorious fate in one paragraph, we must reach the question: Do the people flock to see *Cleopatra* because of

'Cleopatra' or because of Theda Bara? With due deference to Egypt's queen it must be confessed that Theda Bara wins.

"Mr. Fox realizes this. In his billing he presents Theda Bara as Cleopatra, and not even *Cleopatra* featuring Theda Bara. When one frees himself from the Lyric push and proceeds into the rarefied atmosphere of the subway where there is space to think it is the star that occupies the thinking quarters first. His mind will drift back to the first half of the picture when Miss Bara wore a different costume in every episode. Different pieces of costume rather; or better still different varieties of beads. His temperature will ascend with a jump when he recalls the easy way on which the siren captivated Caesar and Antony. If he knows the picture business he may wonder about Pennsylvania and Chicago and other places with censor boards that have no appreciation for the female form in a state that so nearly approaches nudeness that only a few strings of beads stand in the way. He might suddenly realize that his mother back in Hohokus would shut her eyes once or twice for fear the beads might break or slip, but then— mother never did understand Egyptian history after all . . . .

"The last half of it, wherein the proud queen comes to a realization of her love of Antony is really the best dramatically. Here in these scenes of repentance Miss Bara rises to heights we have never seen her attain before. As a seductive, snakelike adventuress, whether of the present or past she generally excels, but such characterizations are dangerous in that they go to extremes in their effect. Some they awe, others they amuse, a few they turn away. But when she is allowed the opportunity for acting that is more mental than physical she surpasses her usual self. So it is the final half which depicts the overthrow of Antony and Cleopatra before the forces of Octavius that presents the greater range of appeal."

"There have been many mimic Cleopatras since the birth of the drama but never before has a feigned 'Serpent of the Nile' been given such a massive and artistic setting as the one furnished by William Fox for the ten-part production in which Theda Bara acts the Egyptian vampire," noted Edward Weitzel in *The Moving Picture World*, "The scene shifts from Alexandria to imperial Rome, and several historical moments that have been immortalized by the brush of some famous artist, are reproduced with impressive fidelity . . . . all these historical situations are thrown on the screen with an accuracy that necessitated the employing of one of the largest forces of actors, extra people and other essential workers ever used

Cleopatra prepares for her journey. (Author's Collection)

in a photo-spectacle, and the building of a correspondingly large number of edifices of ancient Rome and Egypt, with streets, waterways and interiors that truthfully reflect the period.

"J. Gordon Edwards, who directed the production, has held his work well in hand and brought out a series of rapidly shifting pictures that tell the story with a force in keeping with the subject and ambitious attempt to make it live on the screen. Toward the end the action would be strengthened by condensing it, the movement up to this point having been firm and engrossing.

"The cast is exceptionally able. Theda Bara as Cleopatra is always satisfactory to the eye, save that a certain grade of spectators will criticize unfavorably the very frank display of her physical charms and some of the seductive wiles she uses to ensnare her lovers. Technically her acting commands respect without ever reaching any great tragic outburst, and is best in the lighter scenes of the part. Her dressing of the Egyptian is remarkable for the variety and beauty of garments employed."

Wid's Daily found a 'very bare Bara' who "Wore many marvelous creations which left her much undressed; had time of her life vamping; if

'The very frank display of her physical charms.' (Author's Collection)

authorities let it get by, will certainly register as her greatest bit of multiple love-making. Producer J. Gordon Edwards has certainly delivered in the matter of providing a superb background for Theda Bara's supreme attempt at vamping.

"As spectacle this is excellent, although not supreme, and Miss Bara's 'baring' of quite considerable of herself on most every occasion will prove most interesting generally if the authorities decide that it's all right because Cleopatra did it.

"As drama this doesn't make much of an impression. It fails to stir and never hits a tempo that brings you to the edge of your seat to watch the swinging action. The one opportunity for this, which was the battle of Actium and the scenes showing the rushing Roman troops hurrying to Alexandria, was killed utterly by a number of titles which anticipated what was to come, so decidedly that there was no interest whatever in the scenes, except to see that they used a lot of people."

The reviewer thought the overuse of titles explaining events giving away too much information and killing any suspense, "the titles told us that it was all over but the shouting...."

"Of course, I understand that this situation is history, but I'll tell you that not one in a thousand knows the details of it, and certainly it is legitimate to create an element of suspense by showing your action without telling what is going to happen in titles which kill any interest in the scenes except as considered from a spectacular viewpoint of seeing thousands of extras chasing around.

"I don't suppose that anybody really cares whether this is good drama or not. It shows Miss Bara quite bare, in a wonderful background, and, despite the fact that the action slumps very decidedly at times, the production is big enough to make anyone feel that they have seen an unusual and decidedly distinctive production.

"The death of Caesar was rather well handled, and some of the dramatic situations were well played, but there was that unfortunate and unescapable repetition of Cleo's love-making, which tended to weaken the effect of the various individual scenes.

"The supporting cast was more than satisfactory. It was decidedly well balanced and all of the parts were played in such a manner as to please anyone...."

Considering the 'The Box Office Angle' the reviewer opined, "This will undoubtably make a mint of money. It is big enough as to atmosphere and spectacular effects to register as a production, and it will only be necessary to announce Theda Bara as Cleopatra and show a few of the costumes which she wears to guarantee business. Many may say that it's awful, but the chances are that they will go back a second time so that they will be able to detail fully to their friends why the aforesaid friends should not go.

"Of course the historical story is a wonderful alibi and provides the necessary dignity to offset much criticism." Noting the movie ran over two hours in length,

"I believe that this will get by, as a special road show, because the presence of Miss Bara, a modern vamp, offsets the costume element, and the fact that it is a story of Cleopatra dignifies it sufficiently to pull many who would turn up their noses at an ordinary Bara production.

"There are many places where editing would help, because at times, at the end of a scene, the crowd was allowed to close in, so that we saw how many extras were working; whereas trimming would cut this before the bare places showed— I mean the bare places on the ground— which would have made a better impression generally. The same thing is true in this of Miss Bara's work; because there were a few scenes in which she didn't screen to advantage. These naturally discounted some of her better scenes, and if the poorer ones could be eliminated it would leave a better impression on the whole.

"Be sure that you don't play up too strongly the snake death of Cleo, because this is a decided anti-climax. Everyone is waiting to see the big scene, and they of course expect Theda to let the snake crawl all over her just to prove that she's a real vamp. As it is handled, the snake is hardly in evidence to the eye— at least, I couldn't see him; and I looked pretty hard— and that gives a touch of artificiality to what should have a very big dramatic climax."

Others hated the production. *The Cleveland Press* thought, "Caesar and Cleopatra are posturing and raving even when they are alone, and pose as stiffly as a citizen in a boiled shirt before the camera of a village photographer."

One critic decried the waste of resources to make such an expensive film during wartime shortages.

If some reviewers hated the production but liked Theda Bara, there were at least some reviewers who simply hated Theda Bara. *The Brooklyn Eagle* said, "She makes a burlesque of the Serpent of the Nile and is never for one moment convincing. She could never tempt a man to be late for dinner, much less give up the throne of Rome. When she is not repulsive, she is funny."

The Cleveland Leader claimed Bara substituted, "a low-cut gown for any attempt at clever acting ... doing odd sorts of squirms... instead of trying to portray seductiveness," and added unkindly that Theda Bara appeared to have gained weight and dubbed her 'Feeda Bara.'

The Billboard magazine was so offended by *Cleopatra* that in its October 27, 1917 issue, it not only gave it a bad review, but also included two additional articles denouncing the film.

"*Cleopatra*, a nine-reel Fox feature, exploiting the physique of Theda Bara and purporting to reproduce the famous old story of Antony and the Siren of the Nile, is a mechanically monstrous production. It boasts in the printed matter, which accompanies its presentation, 30,000 players and 2,000 people who are not on the screen, but who have helped in the carpentering and masonic work. It is a colossal succession of magnificently arranged mob scenes without a touch of divine genius, which impresses other than with enormity.

"Featured as Cleopatra is Miss Theda Bara, who goes thru her sensuous scenes almost completely stripped of clothing and places on the record of the screen the most vulgar and nauseously disgusting exhibition which has yet been allowed for showing outside the private dining rooms, where bibulous gentlemen congregate for stag parties and to see the much coveted films which are constantly being wrenched from public exhibition by the cruel hand of the law.

"The limit is reached with a calm assurance. Miss Bara walks and lies about, draped in a few strings of beads and once in a while a bunch of tulle, which if entirely left off would have produced a less shocking effect. Present-day audiences, being, however, incapable of the passé emotion of a shock, must rely on their repugnance to what is wholly licentious . . . .

"The Fox Film Company has evidently spent an inordinate amount of money in producing what is up to the present time the prize smut film."

Theodore Liebler, in his column, 'The Legitimate Stage,' takes director Edwards to task for making *Cleopatra*, then focuses on his real target.

"Talking of prima donna directors in pictures another has been added to the list in Gordon Edwardes (sic), of the Fox staff, who is heavily featured in the advertising of the Theda Bara *Cleopatra* picture now being shown at dollar prices at the Lyric. Edwardes is another recruit from the legitimate, as he was director of the stock company that used to disport at the old Academy of Music for many years. His big picture is interesting in that it challenges foreign picture producers in a field that has been hitherto considered their own. In our opinion Mr. Edwardes has not succeeded in giving to his spectacle the dignity and majesty of some foreign historical pictures of note, but he was obviously working under severe handicaps.

"In the first place one can hardly conceive of a large mouthed woman, who makes up her lips as a possible Cleopatra, especially when the conventional Egyptian style of head dress is utilized, unless one reverts to the medieval conception of the Serpent of the Nile as a lady of color. Miss Bara has proven herself an artist of caliber in pictures such as *The Clemenceau Case*, but her selection for the name part of this spectacle scarcely seems good judgment. And in a picture like this there is no second consideration."

The *Billboard* gossip columnist for 'Tea With The Ladies' also chimed in.

"The Serpent of the Nile is spending a resplendent fortnight over at the Lyric. Reincarnated by Theda of Fox fame and vampire tendencies, she shows twice daily to near capacity jams who want to see as much of her as possible.

"It takes two hours and a quarter to witness all of what the program says is a wardrobe of fifty 'costumes'—a misnomer, since costumes, according to Webster, are a covering for the body, and these aren't that by some . . . . matinee audiences have been so eager to sacrifice themselves to it that all complimentary tickets were suspended and ticket scalpers poked their heads out of doorways behind the back door of the Rialto and offered seats before the box office could be reached.

"That's what Theda Bara, in *Cleopatra*, is doing.

"We used to think that Valeska Suratt held the candle for crazy clothes. It isn't diplomatic to mention the two of them in the same breath—they never do it around the studios where diplomacy is observed—but it's a fact that for colossal daring in draperies and disgusting coarseness in their exploitation Theda's got it over her fondest rival this time.

"Just plain, frank nudity would have been easier to stomach."

Different reviewers had entirely different reactions to Bara's performance. One thought she "rolls her eyes and her hips in that manner which the circus side-show has taught us is thoroughly Egyptian" while another praised "the brilliant work of Theda Bara, who grasped the subtleties of the character in a most wonderful way . . ." *Motion Picture Magazine* thought, "Theda Bara is excellent and does some of the best work of her career."

Other reviewers preferred to focus on her nearly nude state, "If Cleopatra didn't look like Theda Bara her contemporaries were the losers, and if

The death of Antony. Bara's performance in this scene drew critical praise. (Author's Collection)

she didn't dress like her then she failed to take advantage of a warm and pleasant climate."

"How does she compare with other Cleopatras?" wag Edward P. O'Day asked in his review, answering, "She outstrips 'em all."

The *Manchester Guardian* in Britain, while condemning the crosscutting between Alexandria and the Senate of Rome ("the effect is often of an unpleasantly switchback kind . . .") also believed, "The acting of Miss Theda Bara as Cleopatra reaches a standard rarely seen on the screen. She has the intensity that acting in a silent medium demands, while her gesture is both significant in its allusiveness and musical."

Some reviewers were dismissive of Bara because of the Fox phony publicity campaign. Louella Parsons in the *Chicago Herald* pitied the original Cleopatra, "Poor lady, resting in her queenly tomb. All these ages and ages, she had little idea her system of vamping the men of her time would pass down through the centuries and be preserved in the moving pictures by filmland's chief vampire."

In November of 1917, Theodosia legally changed her name to Theda Bara. Her parents and siblings also abandoned the Goodman name and took the surname Bara, their seal of approval on her career as 'the Wickedest Woman in the World.'

Theda Bara as Cleopatra. (Author's Collection)

CHAPTER TEN: 'IT'LL NEVER SHOW IN PENNSYLVANIA!'

In 1918, the Americans in force joined the slugfest on the Western Front. On July 17, the imperial Romanov family was executed by a Bolshevik firing squad in the basement of a house in Siberia. Early in 1918, a new form of influenza was detected in the United States. Concerns of some health officials about spreading the disease were ignored as the Army shipped troops overseas. The so-called 'Spanish Flu' infected 500 million people around the world, killing between 50 to 100 million (three to five percent of the world's population), making it far deadlier than the world war that ended in November.

In 1918, the Edison Manufacturing Company, the producer of the first American films, released its last production and went out of business. The Balboa Amusement Producing Company, based in Long Beach, California, and boasting it had the largest studio in the industry, went bankrupt. Selig Polyscope, founded in 1896 and one of the original American film companies, also ceased production. It struggled on as an amusement park and zoo, the main attraction being the animals originally gathered for use in movies.

Also in 1918, the Warner brothers produced their first feature, *My Four Years in Germany*, a 'hate-the-Hun' propaganda film. They also opened their first studio on Sunset Boulevard in Hollywood. Charles Chaplin opened his Hollywood studio near the corner of La Brea and Sunset.

In 1918, Fox leased the rights to make a series of cartoons based on the Mutt and Jeff comic strip from creator Budd Fischer. Fischer was credited as a producer even though his association with the series ended with his cashing the check. Among the cartoons in the series was *Mutt And Jeff Meet The Vampire* (AKA *Meeting Theda Bara*), which combined live action and animation.

"Probably for the first time the history of films, a real life personage and cartoon characters meet and act together on the screen," commented

Motography, ignoring *Gertie The Dinosaur* and numerous other examples of combined live action and animation.

The plot of the cartoon had Mutt and Jeff trying to become movie producers. Jeff wants Theda Bara to do any 'vamping' in their picture. Mutt points out Bara was under exclusive contract to Fox. The cartoon may have used an outtake from one of Bara's films, but reviews indicate Bara interacted with the cartoon characters. The short is not listed on filmographies of Bara.

The start of 1918 found Bara and Edwards back at work at Fort Lee making Theda Bara Superproductions. *The Forbidden Path* found Bara as an artist's model, out for revenge against the man who seduced and abandoned her. *The Soul of Buddha* featured her in the role she wrote for herself as a Javanese temple dancer. Bara missed California sunshine, or at least preferred it to the klieg lights necessary for filming back at Fort Lee. She especially missed California when, while going to the studio at Fort Lee, her limousine became stuck in the snow. While she waited in the car, her chauffeur trudged through the snow to get help. Help did not arrive until late in the day, and after being rescued, she went home without reaching the studio.

In January 1918, *Motion Picture News* reported that *Cleopatra* "has met with such success at the Lyric Theatre, New York, and in other cities where it has been shown, that William Fox has determined to put out forty road companies.

"This drama, it is said, not only caused great comment and talk, but broke all business records in New York, Washington, Buffalo and Schenectady, and has been booked for return engagements.

"In the four cities in which *Cleopatra* has been shown there was a great diversity of audiences. In Washington, the most fashionable people of the city attended, it is said, and the business increased each day until toward the end of the week it was impossible to obtain seats. In Schenectady, it played to the industrial classes, and both days were sell-outs."

"Do not let cruel fortune cheat you of this final opportunity to view superb splendors, opulent wonders, congregated marvels that have staggered and stunned the imaginations of all beholders," William Fox declared in a press release.

"Facts refute press agent publicity, and the woeful lack of patronage at the Academy of Music, New York, where the spectacle, *Cleopatra*, is presented, demonstrates that salacious stories on the screen have met their

Waterloo!" declared *The Billboard*, "The public—the invincible arbiter and censor—has shown its repugnance at this brazen display. 'Tis said that women's hands have rewritten the pages of history—beginning eons and eons ago—and today emancipated women have set their seal of disapproval on screen plays whose only appeal is to the sensualist and decadent.

"The argument proffered by producers that such pictures as *Cleopatra* are replicas of the world's historical figures may be true, but such characters teach nothing—why exploit the EVILS of the world?"

Again denouncing *Cleopatra* as a smut film, "nothing worse has taken place of this undraped serpent of the Nile. Witnessing a performance on Thursday afternoon, a reviewer of *The Billboard* was more impressed by the rows of empty seats than by the sartorial beauty of the screen play. Why did not the public come to see the widely advertised picture? Surely for the small admission charged a feast of beauty, barbaric splendor and oriental extravagance was offered in return. Listening to the giggling remarks of those present the answer came out—the American public will not accept such expositions seriously.

"From the Bronx to the Bowery the public prefers to wash its dirty linen in the privacy of its own houses. Fourteenth street and the mixed population thereabouts respect their women and children, and courageously show their condemnation of the vulgar, licentious Egyptian by remaining away from the theater. The actress who attempts a portrayal of this famous courtezan lacks the sinuous suppleness of Egypt's queen, and falls an immeasurable distance from a visualization of the subtle, exotic siren. Her draperies consist of a veil and beaded breast plates, and in the earlier scenes even the solemn Sphinx opened one eye for a peek, then closed it quickly in disgust."

Bara returned to California to shoot *Under the Yoke*, which cast her as a Filipina loyal to American interests and a handsome American captain over those of a Filipino rebel leader, and then her next epic, *Salome*. She arrived in Los Angeles in time for the West Coast premiere of *Cleopatra*.

"Theda Bara appeared last night at Clune's Auditorium in the much-heralded William Fox production of *Cleopatra*," reported Anthony Anderson, writing for *The Los Angeles Times*, "The occasion was a distinct triumph for both the production and the famous photoplay actress. The huge auditorium was packed with 'fans' and the fashionables, and everywhere be could

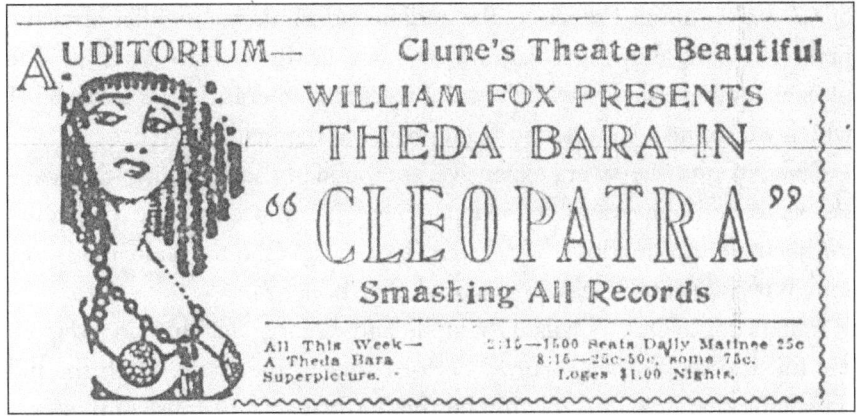

Cleopatra ad in the Los Angeles Herald, *date unknown. (Author's Collection)*

seen the faces made familiar to us by the screen. Everybody was on the qui vive, eager-eyed, expectant, full of curiosity and enthusiasm.

"And the enthusiasm grew as the play—or rather the pageant—moved swiftly forward in all its oriental splendor and gorgeous impressiveness. All agreed, with shining eyes and sometimes with whispered words, that the pageant-photoplay was an overwhelming success, and that Theda Bara has again scored one of the splendid triumphs of her conquering career....

"We see the sumptuous splendor of Alexandria, the stately beauty of Rome, the devastating carnage of Actium. We see vast armies dealing death and terror, and we watch the passing of empires. And at last we see how a queen, though heartbroken, crushed, vanquished, may still die like a queen.

"The pages of history have been blazoned for us in gold and purple and red, and, reading it thus, we shall never forget what we have seen."

This big-budget spectacular had anything but a standard release. As sometimes the case with a studio's major releases, it played in roadshows, screening only in the biggest theaters of major cities. A symphony orchestra traveled with each print, supplemented in each city by the 'best local musicians.' Such a presentation would have had musical numbers as entertainment to warm up the audience, instead of the usual short subject films, before the feature started. Admission for these prestigious roadshows varied from 25¢ to $1, compared with the usual 10¢ or 15¢ admission.

The expense of the roadshow often outstripped the profits of exhibition. After Sol Wurtzel advocated a three week run instead of a two week run of *Cleopatra* in San Francisco, the audience turnout was smaller after the first two weeks, allowing a disgruntled Fox to acidly write to Wurtzel, "The pleasure of playing *Cleopatra* the third week in San Francisco costs us $521 which we are now subtracting from profits of the first two weeks . . ."

Even though they were expensive, the publicity surrounding the roadshows made them overall a good value. Fox continued to have roadshows for his major productions. *The Queen Of Sheba* lost money on its roadshow tour, but its general release was a box office bonanza.

Italian conductor Nicola Donatelli and George Rubinstein adapted the musical score for *Cleopatra's* performance at the Lyric. With the full orchestra, there would probably be the performance of musical numbers instead of or in addition to some short films, to warm up the audience before the feature. The Los Angeles performances featured a 'sextet from Luci' and a xylophone solo. When the roadshow run for *Cleopatra* was complete, the prints were passed to large theaters that had organ accompaniment. Smaller theaters had a pianist and violinist; really cheap theaters had just a player piano.

Cleopatra went into mass release in August 1918, just as the second wave of 'Spanish flu' unleashed a deadlier strain of the disease, forcing theaters to close as a precaution in infected areas. Even so, people risked death and flocked to see *Cleopatra* where it was playing.

The journey from major city movie palaces to small-town theaters may have taken up to three years, at which point, *Cleopatra* was re-released in the major cities again, repeating the process.

The term 'silent movies' as used to describe cinema before the arrival of 'Talkies' is a bit of a misnomer. Although they did not have synchronized soundtracks, films were almost never shown in public without accompanying music.

"It was the aim of the exhibitor to eradicate silence from silent pictures," noted Kevin Brownlow in *The Parade's Gone By*, "A first-class orchestra could make the dullest picture bearable, and careful scoring, combined with good playing, could provide an extra dimension to the magic of the movies."

A first-class orchestra was not always available. Vachel Lindsay, a well-known poet and part-time film commentator, wrote in *The Art of the Motion Picture*, "Unfortunately, the local moving picture managers think it necessary to have orchestras. The musicians they can secure make tunes that are most squalid and horrible. With fathomless imbecility, hootchy kootchy strains are on the air while heroes are dying. 'The Miserere' is in our ears while the lovers are reconciled. Ragtime is imposed upon us while the old mother prays for her lost boy."

He noted an instance where the pianist repeatedly played 'In the Shade of the Old Apple Tree' during the screening of a Civil War drama. When asked why she did not play, say, 'The Battle Hymn of the Republic' during *The Battle Hymn Of The Republic* (Vitagraph, 1911), she replied that she didn't have a copy of the sheet music for that and played what may have been the only melody she knew over and over again throughout the film.

Lindsay thought, "the perfect photoplay gathering place would have no sound but the hum of the conversing audience. If this is too ruthless a theory, let the music be played at intervals between programs, while the advertisements are being flung upon the screen, the lights are on, and the people coming in."

Chicago movie accompanist Mildred Maginn Fitz Patrick wrote an article for *Motography* instructing musicians on how to play for movies:

"Next to good films, the most important feature of a picture theater is good music. Of course, it is very important to have good pictures, but very often an inferior picture will be shown. It is then more necessary to make your music more interesting than the picture, so the audience will be pleased by the music into overlooking the faults of the film . . .

"If it is possible to view a certain picture before you play for it, do so by all means. You have no idea how it helps you . . . Very often this is impossible. After you have had enough experience, you will find you can play a picture, following it properly, just as easily as you would read a sheet of music.

"The first time you play a new picture, pay strict attention to the story. If it is a dramatic picture with little or no comedy running through it, introduce some light number whenever you have the opportunity so that the monotony will be broken. . . . Now, by this I do not mean to play 'Yankee Doodle' for a funeral procession.

"While you are playing the picture for the first time, think of what music you will play for each particular scene for the next time. You are then able to arrange your music so that when a hurry scene appears you won't have to stop in the middle of some pretty number and stumble into your hurry music . . . .

"Whenever you can connect a sub-title with the name of some particular song or piece, play that song or piece. But do not carry this idea so far as to burlesque a dramatic picture."

Sometimes a score was specifically written for a movie. *L'assassinat Du Duc De Guise* (France, 1908) is the first film known to have its own score, but more often musicians worked from cue sheets that lifted phrases from classical works and crazy quilted them into something resembling a score. Some piece of music would be used for a fight scene, another for a love scene, another for suspense, and so on. Some solo musicians simply watched the movie and improvised a score— at every additional performance fine-tuning their version.

Composer Max Steiner, who called William Fox "one of the finest men in the world I have ever known," credited the innovative mogul with helping establish music scores for films. Steiner was the conductor at the Riverside Theater, which was showing the Fox film *The Bondman* (1916), starring William Farnum.

"Until about 1915 there was no special music written for motion pictures. We just used to take albums publishers put out and would play 'Hurry #1, Hurry #3, Love Scene #6.' I said to myself, 'This is a lot of baloney. I'd like to do something new.' I talked to Mr. Fox and told him I wanted to write music for the picture... And I went down and wrote the music for William Farnum's *The Bondman*."

For his preparedness epic, *The Fall of a Nation*, Thomas Dixon spared no expense (one of the reasons he lost money) and hired noted composer Victor Herbert to compose the score. Herbert demurred at first; a dedicated Irishman, he did not want to compose music for an anti-German (and therefore pro-British) film.

Often associated with the presentation of silent movies, organs were just beginning to supplant pianos, and mostly in large movie palaces, where they provided more volume than an orchestra could belt out. Moreover, a single organist was cheaper to hire than an entire orchestra. Organs had the added benefit of producing a variety of sound effects, such as thunder, car horns, waves crashing on the shores, the wail of a steam locomotive whistle, and many more. There were a number of manufacturers, but it was the Wurlitzer organ which was most fixed in the public mind. It was a show in itself; forget the movie.

"Few wonders of the movie palace brought more shivery pleasure to audiences (or caused more breast-beating among crusaders for culture) than the Mighty Wurlitzer," Ben M. Hall wrote in his book, *The Best Remaining Seats,* "Part one-man band, part symphony orchestra, part sound effects department, the Wurlitzer was one of the most versatile instruments ever devised by man . . . . to the average movie goer if it rose up out of the pit at intermission with a roar that made the marrow dance in one's bones, if rows of colored stop-tabs, lit by hidden lights, arched like a rainbow above the flawless dental work of the keyboards— if it could imitate anything from a brass band to a Ford horn to a choir of angels— gee, Dad, it was a Wurlitzer!"

Ben Hall describes one organ that above the row of stops containing the standard ranks of the organ had an additional row of tabs:

"Each of these was marked by a spot of color—violet, blue, green, red, pink, yellow, orange— and these were inscribed with a catalogue of emotions and situations that would make the most brazen scenario writer blush for shame: 'Love (Mother)'; 'Love (Passion)'; "Love (Romantic)'; 'Quietude'; 'Jealousy' (green spot); 'Suspense' (blue); 'Happiness'; 'Hate'; "Mysterious' (gray); 'Gruesome' (black); 'Pathetic'; 'Riot'(red) — to list only a few. Each of these tabs controlled preselected combinations of ranks which produced tones suitable to the indicated mood— it was up to the organist to supply the melody."

There was also the photoplayer, an automatic mechanical orchestra, usually a piano with percussion instruments, sometimes with a pipe organ, but all using a paper roll system akin to a player piano, except it had two rolls, so one could play while the operator loaded the next roll. The operator also had a selection of sound effects such as sirens, carhorns, bells, drums and even gunshots. Some theaters owners tried to combine the job of projectionist with photoplayer operator, which would have made for a very busy projectionist.

Some theaters even had sound effect technicians on hand for every performance, provided the sound of galloping hooves, gunshots with special blank firing revolvers with eight to twelve shots in each cylinder. These and other effects were later adapted for radio dramas. Slapstick comedies especially benefited from the adding of sound effects for the various pratfalls and conks on the head. Now more closely associated with the sound effects connected with the slapstick of the Three Stooges, they are in fact holdovers from silent slapstick sound effects.

***

The main obstacle in releasing *Cleopatra* was censorship. This was before the Hays Office, and then the Breen code, and their iron-fisted rules over what could not be shown; therefore what could not be made. Consequently, motion pictures were made and shown without restriction in the early days of cinema. Soon enough, in communities around the United States, censor boards sprang up to combat vice and indecency in movies. Chicago established the first censor board in 1907.

Trying to stave off federal regulation and defuse local censors, producers, distributors and the Motion Pictures Exhibitors of New York State formed the National Board of Censorship of Motion Pictures in 1909. Although the board could not ban or censor any movie, it could decline to approve a film, which might give an exhibitor cause— or at least pause— not to book it.

This board managed to stave off federal censorship, except in one federal law in response to the race riots sparked by the 1909 Jeffries-Johnson boxing match. Any films depicting a prize fight were prohibited. It took effect in 1912 and stayed on the books until 1940, but this was apparently ignored much of the time. In 1916, the National Board of Censors changed its name to the National Board of Review of Motion Pictures, Inc., whose seal of approval was required by some state and local governments. As an attempt to thwart official censorship it failed, as many communities retained their own censor boards, although a federal censor board never came into being.

Instead, censorship varied throughout the United States. Ohio, Pennsylvania, Maryland and Kansas each had a state censor board, and many cities had their own boards to pass or reject films for public presentation. Even if a movie passed the tough Pennsylvania state board, the tougher Pittsburgh censor board might block it. The censor board of Kansas, composed of three women appointees, reportedly inspected fifty movies a day, with the board watching three or four movies simultaneously.

Freedom of speech was not considered a legitimate argument against censorship. In 1915, in *Mutual v. Ohio*, the U.S. Supreme Court ruled that movies were not covered under the First Amendment because movies were a product of a business and not a form of speech. This remained in effect until 1952, when the court reversed itself.

Clara Williams and Margaret Thompson, bathing beauties of Ince Studio, rather than Keystone. (Author's collection)

As motion pictures became more sophisticated, so did the censorship codes, as did moviemakers' methods of getting around the codes. At Keystone Studios, Mack Sennett conjured up the idea of having sexy women caper about in swimsuits amid the antics of Sennett's comedians and Keystone Cops. He hired a bunch of beautiful young actresses. Tossing out the wardrobe department-supplied 'mother hubbard' swimsuits of black stockings, bulky tunics and 'ballooning sleeves,' he had the girls dressed in "some bathing suits that showed what a girl looked like," namely one-piece suits with bare arms and calves.

"The whole studio turned conservative on me," Sennett wrote years later, "Even the comedians complained I was risqué. But I went ahead and put the girls on film in the most abbreviated suits possible forty years ago. When the studio received hundreds of letters of protest from women's clubs, I knew I had done the right thing."

The Keystone bathing beauties were a terrific success and were imitated by other studios. However, they were not as daring as Sennett would have one think.

"Women didn't even have bosoms in those days, not on the Keystone lot anyway," remembered Phyllis Haver, a bathing beauty who went on to stardom, "According to the Keystone style all the girls had to bind their bosoms like mummies and wear waistlines halfway down to their knees."

Even so, the movies showing frolicking, semi-scantily-clad beauties risked running afoul of more stringent censors, so they appeared only in scenes which could easily be cut without affecting the plotlines— making make their appearances in Keystone comedies to modern eyes all the more incidental and thus baffling.

There was a surprising amount of nudity in silent film. While nudity was more commonplace in European films than in puritanical America, Hollywood studios managed to sneak in shots of naked and half-naked men and women in some of their historical epics, including D.W. Griffith's *Intolerance* and *Orphans of the Storm*. *Ben Hur* (MGM, 1925) featured a sequence with topless maidens strewing flowers in the path of Ben Hur's triumphant parade for the European release version, with an alternate version depicting the maidens more modestly attired for the American release.

Not only nameless extras appeared nude. Popular leading lady Margarita Fischer was even more popular after her nude scene in *The Pearl Of Paradise* (Mutual, 1916), Fox's June Caprice shed her good girl image and her clothes for a nude swim in *The Ragged Princess* (1916), and writer-director-actress Nell Shipman had a brief nude sequence showering in a waterfall in *Back To God's Country* (Canadian Photoplays, 1919). Such scenes were often made in such a way that the storyline would not be affected when more strict censors cut the offending footage. However, Lois Weber's allegorical drama *Hypocrites* (1915) featured a young woman

Artist's model Audrey Munson in her work clothes (Author's collection)

as 'The Naked Truth.' Unattired accordingly, she wandering about, holding up a mirror to hypocritical characters throughout the film.

"Mayor Curley of Boston handed down a decision regarding the playing of *The Hypocrites*," noted *Photoplay*, "The Mayor, after viewing the picture, said that it could be placed on public exhibition if the producers would drape the naked figure of Truth in the film."

Model Audrey Munson posed in various stages of undress for art's sake, including works of public art. She posed nude for much of the sculpture

Right: Annette Kellermann wearing a one-piece bathing suit. (Author's Collection)

Below: Annette Kellermann not wearing a one-piece bathing suit in A Daughter of the Gods. *(Author's Collection)*

created for Panama–Pacific International Exposition of 1915. Nicknamed the 'Panama–Pacific Girl,' Munson is now considered 'America's first supermodel.' With producers sensing a way to get by the censors, several films were made to capitalize on her fame and her ability to be nude. Thus she played an artist's model in *Inspiration* (Thanhouser, 1915) and *Purity* (American, 1916), appearing nude in these and other films. *Purity* also had fantasy sequences in which she appeared in re-creations of famous works of art, including statues she had posed for in real life.

Censors seemed to have been put in a dilemma; if the statues she posed for were not obscene, how could her posing for them be obscene? Most concluded that since she was playing a nude model, her on-screen nudity was permissible, although how much nakedness was allowed and how much was cut varied from censor to censor. Some reviewers also went out of their way to say how tasteful her nude scenes were, although *Wid's Daily* noted, "While all this is done in rather an artistic manner working logically into the story, the fact remains that the picture will have its chief appeal because of the display of the nude."

Display of the nude also figured in *A Daughter Of The Gods*, starring the frequently naked Annette Kellermann.

"There are long passages where Miss Kellermann wanders disconsolately through the film all undressed and nowhere to go," one reviewer quipped, "Audrey Munson, as exhibited in the short-lived *Purity*, has nothing on Miss Kellermann, and as observed elsewhere, neither has Miss Kellermann. This business is carried rather far in the life in the palace of the Sultan where the picture suffers so much from overexposure that you can scarcely say *A Daughter of the Gods* is merely released. It is positively abandoned."

As an indicator of how flexible censors could be, this nudity was often allowed, because as a fairy tale about magical beings, a witch and gnomes, it was considered a children's movie, therefore not of prurient interest.

Censors were usually less concerned with nudity itself than the context in which bare skin appeared; sexual situations were often ordered cut from films. Suggestive dialogue also was ordered clipped. So were other scenes affronting the social mores of the time. Shots of women smoking were often ordered deleted. Both 1915 versions of *Carmen*, in which Bara and Farrar smoked cigarettes, ran into censorship troubles on that account.

Sea nymphs frolic in the 'children's movie' A Daughter of the Gods. (Author's collection)

Crime was a major concern of censors, who believed that any depiction of criminal activity would encourage children and perhaps others to imitate what they saw on the screen. In a speech made in the late 1920s, William Fox remembered, "if a boy was arrested for stealing, his attorney found the most convenient defense to be that he learned to commit this crime because he witnessed motion pictures. If a man was arrested for wife beating, his lawyer said that he acquired the habit because he was a regular patron of a motion picture theatre."

Not everyone agreed that censorship was necessary. *Photoplay* quoted a New Jersey newspaper that opined, "Remedy does not lie in attack upon films nor in regulation by the censor, but with the public itself, and is a matter of education. Producers of films are not foisting upon the public emotional, cheap or sensational ideas. They know such efforts would be short-lived."

As a film producer, Fox originally tried to make only family friendly fare, cleaning up plots of early releases he thought would please audiences and avoid censorship trouble, with only modest returns of his investment.

Along came *A Fool There Was*, which became a box office smash, followed by Bara's other vampire movies, loaded with lust, crime, greed, and other sins aplenty, and Fox was raking in the dough.

Still, Fox remained the final judge of what his company put out. When director Sid Franklin convinced Sol Wurtzel to write Fox urging that he reverse his decision cutting a risqué scene with Jewel Carmen in his film, *The Bride of Fear* (1918), Wurtzel incurred the wrath of Fox.

"I am not interested in the comment Franklin makes," Fox wrote in a blistering letter to Wurtzel, "nor am I interested in the comment you make. The final judgment with reference to any picture . . . is left with me and not with you or Mr. Franklin. . . . You know that there never was a scene that I ever cut out of a picture that met with the director's approval. Each director thinks the scenes he photographs are the most wonderful in the world, and I never followed the policy of consulting a director when I thought a scene should be eliminated. If I had done that, the Fox Film Corporation would have been on the rocks long ago. . . . I am not interested in any further controversy in this matter. . . . This matter is now closed. You are to blame for it being necessary for me to write this note."

Yet Fox knew that sex, crime and violence sold tickets, so he permitted writers and directors to come up with increasingly risqué and daring subject matter. It wasn't just Bara's films; other Fox films were replete with depictions of sex, violence, crime, and sin as well, resulting in Fox being denounced as 'the whorehouse film company.'

Fox's battles with censor boards were practically nonstop. Kansas banned Bara's first four movies outright, at least until cuts were made. *Sin* got by Kansas censors after some objectionable scenes were eliminated, only to be banned in Topeka.

After Kansas censors rejected *Gold and the Woman*, Fox submitted the film to the Appeals Board, which passed the film on the condition that all objectionable scenes be cut or reduced to a 'flash,' meaning a shot lasting less than a second in which a viewer might be able to glimpse and recognize what was going on but would not be subjected to or titillated by the shot lingering on the screen. Among the Kansas dictated eliminations:

"Reel 1, eliminate two murder scenes; shorten one to a flash; reels 2, 3 and 4, shorten all persuasive scenes between guardian and vampire; reel 4, eliminate all love scenes between vampire and guardian except one, which

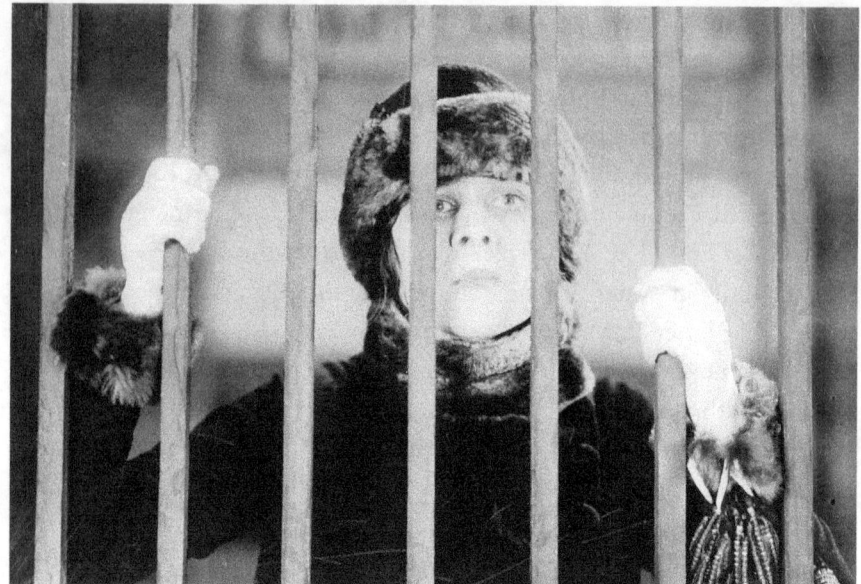

Theda Bara in trouble with the authorities again. From When Men Desire *(Author's collection)*

is reduced to a flash; eliminate all cigarette scenes; reel 5, eliminate all scenes of vampire and shorten drinking scene of guardian to a flash."

No amount of cutting could please some censors. *Gold and the Woman* was simply banned outright by New York, Cleveland and even by Bara's hometown of Cincinnati.

Sometimes dialogue proved offensive, as when the Kansas censors ordered the following dialogue intertitles cut from Bara's 1919 movie, *When Men Desire*, although what was so offensive about them is obscured by lack of context in the film:

"I admit it, Dearest Elsie, I intend to keep you here for myself."

"This couldn't be better. It isn't Strassburg, where, like a fool, I thought I'd have to marry you to possess you."

And "Marry you— marry you."

The Kansas board kept the censored footage to prevent it from being re-inserted in the film, with the result that when the print of the movie moved on to another state, the Kansas-ordered cuts remained in the film.

Pennsylvania also had a tough censor board. Director Raoul Walsh recalled that there was a saying at the studio whenever a risqué scene was shot, "It'll never show in Pennsylvania!"

"Everybody had battles with the censors. They went out of their way sometimes to make it pretty tough for us. A kiss could only last three seconds. You weren't allowed to take any love scenes if there was a bed visible, even if it was a mile down the road.

"We battled on and battled on. Sometimes we'd take maybe six or seven risqué scenes, a-bit-off scenes, hoping they'd leave two. That's how we worked."

Hettie Gray Baker observed, "If it [a film] is so fixed that it *will* pass the censors—Lord help the people. It is usually so slow and stale that a church deacon would have a hard time not imagining that he is listening to the minister's sermon, and you find him sound asleep—mouth open and all."

Despite the fact D.W. Griffith toned down Dixon's novel *The Klansman*, and he cut several scenes depicting black males assaulting white women from the finished film, *The Birth Of A Nation* was banned in Kansas and elsewhere for its racism and incitement to violence. A black legislator in the Illinois House of Representatives sponsored a bill prohibiting 'lynching and illegal hangings' in movies, which passed by a vote of 111 to 2.

In part due to his experience of battling those trying to stop the exhibition of *The Birth Of A Nation*, Griffith became a dedicated opponent of censorship, publishing a pamphlet *The Rise and Fall of Free Speech in America* in 1915. He also traveled to speak against censorship, lecturing to state and city governments considering establishing their own censor boards.

Infuriated by the perceived 'intolerance' of those denouncing his work, Griffith titled his next movie *Intolerance*. During production, Jews learned the Pharisees were depicted as the persecutors of Jesus during the 'Passion of Christ' segment. Also worried about intolerance, leading Jews threatened protests against the film. They were able to coerce Griffith to make changes, destroying footage he had already shot, so in the movie, there is the abrupt appearance of Romans taking Christ to Calvary. Griffith also apparently toned down the anti-Catholic aspects of the 'St. Bartholomew's Day Massacre' segment to avoid offending Catholics. Nevertheless, some French critics denounced that sequence and his *Orphans Of The Storm* for being anti-French.

Griffith's contempt for those urging censorship appears in *Intolerance*. In the story set in modern times, he compared the 'Uplifters' advocating reform to the Pharisees persecuting Jesus, and he made a cheap shot at women reformers with a title card stating, "When women cease to attract men, they often turn to reform as a second chance."

Whether Maude Murray Miller was attractive or not is unknown, but she certainly was a woman of ability. She served as president of the Ohio Newspaper Women's Association and business manager of the *Morning Times*, Springfield, Ohio, before being appointed to the Ohio Board of Censors. She led— some say dominated— the two men who also served on the board, although they voted to ban *The Birth of a Nation* when she, a Southerner, supported exhibiting the film.

"I have been put here," she told W. Stephen Bush of *Moving Picture World*, "by the Governor of Ohio to protect the women and children of Ohio. Ohio wants censorship, and the whole state is back of us. I have seen so many pictures of the vilest description that I was ashamed to think men and women would pose in such pictures."

She insisted that the film industry wanted state censorship to prevent more censorship on the local level.

"Oh, I'm not opposed to good pictures," Miller added, "*Quo Vadis* is all right, although if it were not a classic I should cut a good deal out of it, for you know there is murder, seduction, abduction and debauchery, not to mention suicide. Such things I would, of course, eliminate from a modern feature."

Miller banned Lois Weber's *The Hypocrites*, calling it 'indecent.' Her statements made her a lightning rod for anti-censorship tirades, such as when Miller commented to a reporter that an "exhibitor showing an unapproved picture in Ohio might easily accumulate a life sentence if he runs a continuous show from 10 a.m. to 11 p.m."

"The rest of the population of Ohio might think a picture is harmless, but if Mrs. Miller thinks otherwise, the picture goes back to the reel and stays there as far as Ohio is concerned," W. Stephen Bush wrote an editorial, "If Mrs. Miller objected only to things that she believed immoral or indecent, few would be inclined to criticize, but she goes so much further. It would seem that she is, or aims to be, a censor of the odious type, the medieval type of bigot which 'censored' Galileo in an effort to disapprove one of the most important discoveries in astronomy. Mrs. Miller rejects any subject which does not fit in with her own pet social theories. Here is the real monstrosity of censorship."

The denunciations of Miller were mild compared to those leveled against Chicago's appointed film censor, who was the Second Deputy Superintendent of Police. His name, appropriately enough, was Metellus Lucullus Cicero Funkhouser, and was addressed as 'Major' for his Spanish-American War service. Chicago's broad censorship law prohibited movies that depicted crimes, or that made the authorities look bad or foolish, or insulted ethnic groups or religions. These movies could be banned entirely or had so many scenes cut as to be rendered unintelligible.

Funkhouser took censorship to the most absurd extremes. He didn't just ban Audrey Munson's films, he ordered all footage of nude statues and paintings cut out of films. After a woman complained, he also had Albin Polasek's male nude statue *The Sower* covered up and removed from display at Chicago's Art Institute. It would remain covered and in storage until 2005. Other nude works of art were also prohibited from display.

Funkhouser's censorship could be wildly arbitrary. He cut footage of either men or women wearing one-piece bathing suits— even though such suits were permitted on Chicago beaches. No women could be shown in movies knitting baby garments, because that would be suggestive of pregnancy. Funkhouser banned an instructional film showing modern dances such as the hesitation waltz, the turkey trot and the tango, on the grounds young people might go to public dance halls to try these scandalous dances, or even be lured into drinking liquor. Furthermore, no couples in movies could dance together closer than six inches. After one moviegoer complained about a rattlesnake appearing in a William S. Hart Western, Funkhouser banned all snakes from movies.

Theda Bara movies did not fare well under the Major's reign; Funkhouser banned *The Tiger Woman*, *Camille* and *Madame Du Barry*, among other films.

Even literary classics when filmed were not safe. Charles H. Tarbox states in his book *Lost Films*, "*Othello* was turned down completely on the ground that its central theme was murder. *The Scarlet Letter* was condemned because of its theme of adultery. Mary Pickford's film, *Tess Of Storm Country*, was disapproved because the parentage of the baby was in dispute."

Among the Chicago-ordered cuts in a movie version of *Macbeth*: "incantation scene showing witches…"

"If the witches are cut the scene showing the cauldron may remain…"

"...cut out scene in the bedroom and title which follows, 'who would have thought the old man had so much blood in him...'

"...shorten the banquet scene and eliminate ghost of Banquo...

"...cut out scene of Lady Macbeth in nightgown..."

Hamlet fared no better with the censor, with the following cuts demanded:

"...scenes showing Hamlet, Horatio and Marcellus carrying deadly weapons must be cut to a flash...

"...scene between Hamlet and his mother must be cut as tending to discourage respect to parents and to encourage the murder of old men..."

"...scenes in graveyard must be shortened..."

"...scene of Laertes and Hamlet in grave must be cut out..."

"...last act must be shortened by elimination of fencing match and stabbing of the king..."

"...body of Hamlet on stretcher may be shown in flash only..."

Lastly, incredibly, "the name of Shakespeare must be eliminated from the film because it is suggestive to impressionable youth and savors of violence...."

"Major Funkhouser, we makers of moving pictures don't know just how to please you," Universal's Carl Laemmle started calmly in an open letter in the *Chicago Tribune*, "We have tried hard to do business in Chicago, but we don't seem to be able to measure up to your standard...."

Then Laemmle openly mocked him (calling him 'General' and 'Admiral') and his censoring decisions, adding, "You have made Chicago a laughing stock."

In another open letter, Laemmle blurted in all caps, "HOW LONG ARE YOU INTELLIGENT ALDERMEN GOING TO STAND FOR THIS STUPENDOUS NONSENSE?"

Although the city government was embarrassed by his actions, Funkhouser thwarted attempts to oust him, as women's groups demanding more film censorship and a crackdown on vice supported him.

The decisions of other censors could be just as arbitrary. The theater license of a movie house in Holland, Michigan, was revoked for showing the Keystone slapstick comedy, *Tillie's Punctured Romance* (1914). A Cleveland theater manager was arrested for showing slides opposing censorship. The Ohio board of censors ordered Fox to change the title of *The Devil's Daughter* on the grounds "the Devil had no daughter," to which

Theda Bara as Cleopatra. (Courtesy of Academy of Motion Picture Arts and Sciences)

Photoplay observed, "They would have had a much harder time in proving that Balaam's ass never had any direct descendants."

Even after the name change, Ohio demanded 1800 feet snipped from the film— which probably left very little of Bara doing anything offensive on the screen, and likely made the resulting movie incomprehensible.

A Chicago newspaper wondered why censor boards cracked down so heavily on movies, but not stage productions. The reason was simple— it was difficult to censor stage shows, and easy to force film companies to have their movies inspected before release, and charge them fees for the process.

And then along came *Cleopatra*.

"The spectacular drama, Mr. Fox states, has passed every censor board in the United States," announced *Motion Picture News*, "and has received the commendation of the National Board of Review, which issued a special report on *Cleopatra*, saying: 'This story, true to the main facts of history, shows the ambitious and beautiful Queen Cleopatra using her sex to juggle with the political history of Rome and Egypt. The cast is excel-

Cleopatra seducing Julius Caesar (Author's collection)

lent and intimate details are handled with reserve. The picture abounds in magnificent settings of desert, palace and sea.'"

Of course, *Cleopatra* hadn't passed every censor board in the country. There were probably no shots of Cleopatra smoking cigarettes; there were plenty of other scenes in *Cleopatra* that caught the censors' attention. Even though movies such as *A Daughter Of The Gods* and *Purity* revealed more female anatomy than Bara in her Cleopatra outfits, it was the context in

Knowing of his plot, Cleopatra seduces would-be assassin Pharon, and then snatches his dagger from him. (Author's collection)

which Bara wore the revealing outfits that infuriated censors. Her near nude state merely added to the censors' dismay at observing the overt sexual advances Cleopatra made on the leading men in the movie.

To pass the Kansas state censors, Fox had to: "Eliminate: suggestive advances of Cleopatra on Caesar; all close-ups of Cleopatra in the arms of Caesar; all close-ups of Cleopatra in the arms of Caesar; close-ups of exposed limbs, breasts, and abdomen; all close-ups of Cleopatra luring Sharon [Pharon] and lying on a couch and in arms of Sharon [Well, it's 'Pharon' or this is an entirely different movie]; close-up of Cleopatra and Anthony in embracing scene on couch, where Cleopatra's body is exposed."

Chicago's Major Funkhouser didn't bother to order cuts— he simply banned *Cleopatra*.

At the Chicago Press Club, criticizing those who criticized *Cleopatra*, William Fox assured the costumes were historically accurate, and also stated, "I have always opposed censorship of any kind that would deprive the screen, meaning the public, of the worthwhile, artistic photoplay."

Whereas Laemmle used argument to sway opinion, Fox used legal action. Fox sued Funkhouser and the mayor of Chicago.

For the added publicity value, he prompted Theda Bara to sue Funkhouser as well. There were two slander suits against Funkhouser, one by Bara for $100,000 and one by Fox for $25,000.

"That is a company matter," Bara replied to a reporter asking about the affair. "Really, I would rather not discuss it."

Then she lashed away at Funkhouser, saying he "doesn't know the least thing about art. If he did he would have appreciated the production. It was historical and the heroine was one of the foremost women of ancient history."

On December 7, 1917, Chicago Aldermen met to see *Cleopatra*.

"Cleopatra trotted out all her wares again for the aldermen yesterday," reported *the Chicago Tribune*, adding that they "took another chance on their eyesight by looking at the Fox Film company's *Cleopatra*, showing Theda Bara in various stages of undress.

"The committee is considering curbing the censorship of Maj. Funkhouser . . . who has declared that the photoplay cannot have a permit unless most of the nearly nude scenes are eliminated. It was learned that the major might deny the film a permit entirely on the grounds that it is immoral, as it glorifies the acts of a vicious woman—Cleopatra, not Theda Bara."

The aldermen "thought it looked pretty good and wanted to see more.

"'What you have seen now,' said the major, 'is without the cutouts ordered by the censors.'

"'Bring on the cutouts. Let's see them all,' said several aldermen."

The cutouts were shown, and "It was pretty well agreed that Miss Bara had no hidden charms, because she did not wear enough clothing to 'pad a crutch,' as one alderman said."

The ban remained in effect, and more legal maneuvering ensued.

On her way to California, Bara stopped a few days in Chicago and invited the censor and the aldermen to her hotel room to reason with them.

"Theda Bara is in town on her way to the coast, where she will immediately start work on another humdinger," reported 'Mae Tinee' in the *Tribune*, adding that the censors and aldermen had been invited "may have a chance to meet the lady personally."

Cleopatra beguiling the ever-gullible Pharon (again). (Author's collection)

"Her managers want the censors to see that Miss Bara in real life is not the vampire she is in reel life, and to correct any impression possibly obtained by them through her pictures, such as *Cleopatra*, etc."

Bara refused to leave her hotel room to meet with them; they had to come to her.

"Her representative asserts passionately and vehemently that she will not leave her room," Mae Tinee reported cheerfully, "He wishes to goodness she would leave her room, as he knows he would get a thundering good story could he persuade her to call on the critics and sech—regarding whom he says she thinks of most kindly, and against whom she bears no grudge of anything."

"The idea of all concerned is that censors, aldermen, critics, have audience with Miss Bara where she rests in rapt seclusion .... She will greet them with tea and open arms."

Whether any of the city officials responded to the siren's call, and then to her charms, is unknown, but a month later, in its March 16, 1918 edition, *Exhibitors Herald* listed the 'Official Cut-Outs by the Chicago Board of Censors':

"Reel 1, three scenes of the Queen posing before Caesar with her navel exposed, ascending stairs to throne and suggestively leaning against him, two scenes of Queen laying on couch with Caesar standing near.

"Reel 2, Queen in objectionable costume turning as she embraces Caesar, first and last scenes of Queen at astrologer's table looking into crystal.

"Reel 3, first scene of Queen at harp and on couch before she goes to dais, two closeups of Queen on dais bending over, two full length views of Queen in chariot exposing her legs, two views of Queen on couch awakening from sleep.

"Reel 4, entire incident of Queen's meeting with Pharon except scene at beginning of conversation at point where she raises cloth as she starts towards balcony to where she leaves Pharon, all front views of Queen showing her breasts outlined by snake breast plates, closeup of Queen in spangle costume at doorway as she descends stairs and approaches Pharon, closeup kissing scene between Queen and Pharon and Queen's actions following, scene of Queen and Pharon before couch where she turns and exposes legs, three scenes of Queen in objectionable costume before and after Pharon raises knife, two closeups of stabbing guard, all scenes of Queen coming down stairs, two scenes of Queen on low couch, two scenes before and two scenes after taking parchment from Pharon, Queen on couch taking Pharon's hand and scene following embrace, Queen standing while Pharon reads parchment, Queen advancing towards Pharon, closeup of Queen seizing knife and all views of it descending,

"Reel 6: five closest views of Antony and Queen showing her breasts,

"Reel 7: Queen standing before Antony, Queen on couch after Antony leaves, three scenes of Queen in leopard skin costume with one breast exposed, full view of Queen in leopard skin costume on couch.

Cleopatra and Antony's lovemaking interrupted by affairs of state. (Author's collection)

"Reel 8: the intertitle "Antony, one last word. Will nothing save you from this wanton?" etc., four scenes of Queen and Antony on couch before curtains are drawn aside.

"Reel 10: Queen walking to throne in costume exposing body."

Finally, after legal wrangling, on April 10, 1918, Funkhouser issued a 'white' permit (for general audiences) to see the censored *Cleopatra*, and Fox and Bara dropped the two slander suits against him.

Other boards were more lenient.

"After a careful review of the film *Cleopatra*," Maude Murray Miller stated, "I decided to release it for exhibition in Ohio without any eliminations. The producers have followed history in a remarkable way, and Miss Theda Bara's interpretation of the character is so skillfully and convincingly done, that I feel justified in passing the picture as it was brought to the censor office."

When official censors hesitated, independent groups would sometimes pressure the authorities to act. Private organizations such as 'better films committees' and women's clubs exercised considerable muscle in having films banned or withdrawn from exhibition. The careers of actresses Mabel Normand and Mary Miles Minter were damaged by such groups demanding the actresses' films be banned because of their alleged involvement with director William Desmond Taylor, even after police exonerated them of Taylor's murder. These groups, chiefly composed of matrons, were not puritanical, at least in the religious sense. They were less concerned about vamps leading astray their 'cantaloupe-headed' husbands than the effect of vice depicted in films on their children and the institution of the family.

One such group, the Better Films Committee of the Women's Club of Omaha, Nebraska, routinely met to approve or disapprove of movies showing in their fair city. When *Cleopatra* arrived for its roadshow special engagement, it resulted in the committee having their most 'exciting' and contentious meeting ever. Some argued it had value in teaching history, but others denounced Bara's 'wicked, suggestive' performance.

"I never let the thought out of mind that she was a pagan, not a Christian woman," Mrs. Benjamin Baker said at the meeting about *Cleopatra*, "but I must confess to being shocked at the movements and few clothes worn by the actress. She was certainly Hooverizing on clothes!"

"Go to the producers and censor films before they are released," demanded Mrs. J. H. Dumont.

Some defended the movie, and when it was argued that movies drawing away people from church on Sundays, and so showing movies on Sunday should be banned again, Mrs. E. G. Bailey retorted, "If the movies interfere with church attendance, bring movies into the church."

In the end, the Better Films Committee voted to declare *Cleopatra* unfit for either children or adults.

"Women of Omaha, Neb., have manifested their contemptuous disapproval of *Cleopatra*," rejoiced *The Billboard*, "and their positive condemnation of Theda Bara's interpretation of the Egyptian queen. This echoes the public sentiment and offers the best argument for clean pictures."

Winfield Sheehan happened to be in Omaha on business a few days after the meeting. Asked by a reporter to comment on the Committee's decision, he smiled patronizingly and said, "If the women condemn a picture, they are right."

He added that had Cleopatra lived in Omaha in winter instead of balmy Egypt, she probably would have worn more clothes than Bara in the movie, but even so, "The women are always right. It makes no difference to me what they do or say, they are right. They are beautiful — and they are right."

"It is with a great deal of reluctance that I make this statement," Bara responded to the controversy in a telegram to the *Omaha Daily Bee*.

"It is not the mission of the artist to explain her interpretation, for if the interpretation is perfect it explains itself, but once this attack has been launched at my head I feel that in justice to myself and my manager, Mr. William Fox, that some idea be given as to the underlying and educational motive of my portrayal."

Bara explained how much research she had done into authentic costumes.

"Mr. Fox, myself and my director, J. Gordon Edwards, were unanimous in agreeing that this production must be historically accurate both as to my portrayal and the scenes involved. I played Cleopatra according to history as a woman who used the prerogative of her sex to gain political supremacy. In direct contrast did I show her with the same human feelings that dominate any other woman—her wonderful and true love for Anthony, for whom she eventually sacrificed her life. This was the spiritualization of the character, so that I progressed from the low, sensual love attributed to Cleopatra, to the spiritual love, which was the regeneration of the woman."

Bara added that according to "eminent archaeologists, Cleopatra appeared on many occasions without any clothing whatsoever." She cited as further evidence the many works of art depicting Cleopatra wearing far less than Bara did in the movie.

"In giving the portrayal of Cleopatra I have been faithful first to myself as an artist, then to myself as a woman and heart and soul so with the public."

All the cacophony from critics, censors and film committees was music to William Fox's ears. He knew that all of the censorship battles were nothing but good publicity. When the Better Films Committee condemned *Cleopatra* as obscene, it helped sell out every performance for its entire Omaha engagement.

The censor reports mostly survive, the newspaper and magazine reviews survive, but what was the response of the average moviegoer to seeing *Cleopatra*? For all the naysayers, dismissive critics and censor boards, audiences voted approvingly of the Fox epic by buying tickets, making *Cleopatra* the undisputed box office smash of 1918. Mary Pickford overall was

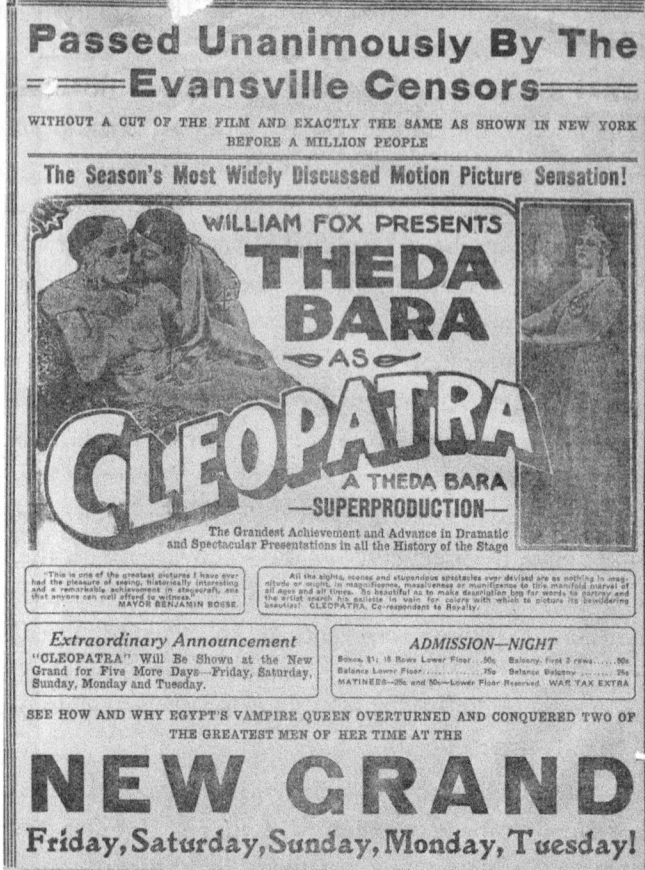

Newspaper ad for the censor-approved Cleopatra *in Evansville, Indiana, date unknown. (Author's collection)*

still the top drawing star with her movies, but *Cleopatra* was the most talked about and seen movie of the year.

Some individual impressions survive.

"I wanted to go see Theda Bara in *Cleopatra* at the Washington Theatre," John F. D. Carrico of Detroit noted in his diary on Sunday, February 3, 1918, "I got to the theatre at about seven-thirty and there was a crowd lined up across Washington Blvd. waiting to go in. I stood in line for over a half hour and then managed to get in the lobby but could not get a seat until the second show. The picture was fine and had some grand scenes."

Mrs. E. Schiefelin of Los Angeles recalled that one the *Cleopatra* costumes created quite a stir, as the fabric from which it was made cost $1,000 a yard and Theda seemed to be wearing only ten cents' worth.

Cleopatra had an even more lasting impact on a twelve-year-old boy in Nashville, Tennessee. The son of immigrants, Hermes Panagiotopoulos became enthralled with Theda Bara after seeing her in *Cleopatra*. Believing all the publicity stories about her exotic background and mysterious ways, he wrote to Fox studios, asking for a photograph of Bara.

"A few weeks later, the glossy still arrived in the mail with an actual signature scrawled across the bottom. I was enchanted."

Advertisement for Cleopatra *in a Detroit newspaper, date unknown. (Author's collection)*

Later, Hermes shortened his surname to Pan, became a dancer and then a choreographer, famously working with Fred Astaire. Hermes Pan choreographed many other films as well, as such the 1963 version of *Cleopatra*, including the spectacular scene depicting Cleopatra's entrance into Rome.

***

'Political correctness' was alive in the 'teens, although it was not called that. Japanese were so offended by *The Cheat* (Lasky, 1915) that when the film was reissued, the villain was changed in the titles from a Japanese to a 'Burmese' — apparently because Burmese had less pull in Hollywood.

Produced by William Randolph Hearst, chief promoter of the 'Yellow Peril,' the serial *Patria* (1918) told of a conspiracy between Mexico and Japan to infiltrate and take over the United States. In the throes of its revolution, Mexico was in no position to protest this depiction, let alone invade the U.S. Japan, as one of America's allies against Germany, could protest, and it protested loudly. The Wilson administration successfully pressured Hearst into editing out Japanese flags and title cards referring to the Japanese in the remaining episodes. Hollywood would be less sensitive about portraying Japanese during the Second World War.

When America entered the war, it was not popularly supported in the western states and sizable German-American communities. Woodrow Wilson established the Committee on Public Information (CPI), to promote the war effort. It was headed by journalist-reformer George Creel, who said he opposed censorship, preaching that the press and others should exercise 'self-censorship.' Congress passed draconian laws that held a giant club over anyone opposing the war. The Espionage Act of 1917 gave stiff penalties for espionage, sabotage or making 'false statements with intent to interfere' with American military forces, 'promote the success of its enemies,' or 'cause insubordination, disloyalty, mutiny, refusal of duty' among enlisted personnel, or to discourage recruiting or enlistment. The Sedition Act of 1918 could punish anyone who criticized the government's war effort, or who organized labor strikes against war-related industries. Although Creel insisted there was no federal censorship, between 1,000 and 1,500 people were prosecuted for violating the vague restrictions of these laws.

Many of the heads of the American film industry were immigrants or sons of immigrants from Central Europe, especially from Germany or Austria-Hungary. Aware their foreign origins might cause a backlash, they immediately and enthusiastically declared their support for the government war effort to belie any doubts about their loyalties. They only had to regard the case of Robert Goldstein.

Inspired by *The Birth of a Nation*, Goldstein, son of Jewish-German immigrants, made *The Spirit of '76* (1917), set during the American War of Independence. Its patriotic themes seemed perfectly attuned to the times. However, his villains were British soldiers committing atrocities against American colonists, including raping and murdering women, and a soldier bayoneting a baby. These scenes were deemed damaging to the British-American alliance. He was convicted of violating the Espionage Act (for inciting disloyalty and insubordination among US soldiers), heavily fined and sentenced to ten years in the pen. He could have saved himself a lot of grief if he simply re-titled his film to identify British soldiers as 'Hessians.'

Little wonder producers were initially cautious about making movies that would be costly failures if banned or even land them in prison. Already, movies with pacifist themes, like *War Brides* and *Intolerance*, were banned in more hawkish cities. The movie industry was quick to offer support in other ways. The most significant contribution to the war effort was its participation in the Liberty Loan drives. Mary Pickford, Douglas Fair-

In a very rare public appearance together, Theda Bara and William Fox lend their support at a Liberty Bond rally. (Author's collection)

banks, Charles Chaplin, Sessue Hayakawa and many other stars appealed directly to crowds at Bond rallies, even at the risk of being mobbed by their fans.

In October 1917, Theda Bara promoted the sale of Liberty Bonds at a rally in front of the New York Public Library. She sold $70,000 worth that day, for which President Wilson personally congratulated her. Bara was so popular that the Stage Women's War Relief asked her to attend another bond rally in November, where she sold another $300,000 worth of Bonds. In April 1918, when she attended the West Coast premiere of *Cleopatra* in Los Angeles, she sold an additional $56,950 worth of Liberty Bonds at another huge Bond Rally.. She also accepted an invitation to be the godmother of the 158th Infantry, who presented her with a golden horseshoe. Bara also visited military hospitals. The façade that she was a wicked woman in real life became impossible to maintain.

Although this generated publicity for Bara and Fox Films, both Vanda Krefft and Merrill T. McCord believe that Fox and Bara were sincerely patriotic and were keen to do their bit for their country, as were others.

"I left instructions here in California that we must do all things that would help our cause, regardless of profit and gain; that sequences should be written into our pictures that would arouse patriotism," William Fox asserted to Upton Sinclair, "We sold Liberty bonds from the stage of every theatre we had, many times much to the annoyance of our patrons, who came there to be entertained, and not to be reminded that there was a war. They came to forget there was a war, which we never allowed them to do."

Once Hollywood understood its role, it reaped the benefits of working hand in hand with the government as part of the propaganda campaign. The film industry also contributed to making propaganda shorts, promoting 'hooverizing' (slang for economizing) measures. Stars posed for photographs turning their flower gardens into vegetable gardens, knitting socks for soldiers, or even more grand gestures, such as donating ambulances to the Red Cross. Whether they continued doing any of this when there were no cameras around is anyone's guess.

Everything German was frowned upon. German language classes were banned, sour kraut became 'Liberty cabbage', and frankfurters became 'hot dogs'; even though the slang term 'hot dog' originally refers to the questionable origin of the sausage meat.

Geraldine Farrao achieved her first great success in Berlin and had been friends with the Prussian imperial family. When she did not cut her German ties, she was denounced for being 'pro-German.' German-Americans actors had to alter their names or risk the enmity of the American public. Margarita Fischer, voted Most Favorite Actress of 1914 by readers of *Photoplay* magazine, was obliged to drop the 'c' from her name in favor of the more 'American' name of Fisher. Romantic leading man Norman Kaiser changed to the less offensive Norman Kerry. Annette Kellermann became Annette Kellerman. Fritz Leiber felt the pressure to change his name (he refused; but in Britain, his screen credit was changed to Frank Love). Actor Gustav von Seyffertitz switched to the less-Teutonic sounding screen name of G. Butler Clonbaugh, not resuming his real name until 1920.

After some hesitation, Hollywood ventured into making patriotic war movies. These were recruitment films, made to inspire men to enlist, and spy movies, crime dramas with spies instead of crooks. Mary Pickford starred in *Joanna Enlists* (Paramount, 1918), about a country girl aiding troops bivouacked nearby, or *Joan Of Plattsburg* (Goldwyn, 1918), with Mabel Normand in a very similar role.

The most notorious of Hollywood's output were the 'Hate-the-Hun' movies, designed to stir up hatred of Germans. One finds frequent denunciations of 'Prussianism'—whatever that was. It was deemed *de rigueur* for German officers to sexually assault women that they encountered, whether attempting to seduce them, coerce them into exchanging their favors (to save the male hero from the firing squad, for example) or simply raping them. Kaiser Wilhelm II was singled out for special abuse. There was *To Hell With The Kaiser* (with the Devil directing Kaiser Wilhelm's every move), and *The Kaiser: The Beast Of Berlin*. Movie patrons were encouraged to hiss the Kaiser as if he were the villain tying damsels to railroad tracks in nickelodeon melodramas of a decade earlier. America's entrance in the war caused a wave of anti-German feelings, cheerfully stoked by Hollywood in a number of hyper-patriotic films that depicted Germans as evil incarnate. No atrocity was beyond 'the beastly Hun.' The movie moguls jumped fully on the bandwagon with their pro-American anti-German films.

"There has been no more effective ammunition aimed at the Prussian empire than these pictures depicting German atrocities," claimed Louella Parsons, "The followers of the cinema have seen with their own eyes how German militarism is waged against civilization. They have seen the rape of Belgium, the devastation of France and the evil designs against America."

President Wilson and George Creel pleaded with Hollywood, the press and other hate-mongers to curb the vicious 'Hate-the-Hun' rhetoric. Fearing hate propaganda would cause Americans to demand harsh punishment of Germany, hindering Wilson's vision of a postwar world, he instructed the Creel Committee "to try to stop the atrocity pictures because they made the job of securing a just peace yet more hazardous."

The CPI avoided vicious anti-German propaganda, as Creel wanted to influence the vast German-American population to contribute to the war effort, not alienate them. Others deplored the ham-fisted hate propaganda being shoved at them. Yet the temptation to demonize the foe was irresistible for others, playing into the racist and xenophobic elements of society in America already honed from putting down blacks, Hispanics and Asians, with European immigrants already in their sights. Raoul Walsh directed *The Prussian Cur* (Fox, 1918), which featured German-Americans conspiring against America and getting their just desserts by a hooded mob of loyal American vigilantes. The Wilson administration pressured Fox to pull the film from release.

One of the reasons Hollywood loved anti-Hun films was it seemed to give free rein for them to show salacious material under the guise of making patriotic films—one explanation for the preoccupation with rape. The American film industry had successfully fended off attempts at national censorship, but state and local censor boards had frequently banned or demanded cuts from movies. Now Hollywood could let loose the most sensationalistic movies, wrapped in patriotic wartime sentiments, showing an unprecedented amount of rape, cruelty and carnage, and so long as Germans were depicted doing the foul deeds, it defied censors to act upon them—those who did were denounced as 'pro-German.' When local censors continued to ban or cut films, the movie industry felt secure enough to counterattack.

"KEEP YOUR HANDS OFF OF WAR PICTURES," the *Exhibitor's Trade Review* warned censors, "THESE PICTURES ARE A PART OF THE FIGHTING FORCES OF THE UNITED STATES .... SUPPRESS ANY PART OF ANY ONE OF THESE PICTURE MESSAGES AND— WHETHER YOU ADMIT IT OR NO— YOU ARE PLAYING THE GAME OF GERMANY AS LOYALLY AS IF YOU WERE THE PAID HIRELING OF THE WILHELMSTRASSE .... If you adapt and persist in a policy of interference, you will be dealt with accordingly— and you will speedily cease to interfere. Your patriotism, your Americanism, is on trial. See to it that it is and remains above suspicion."

One censor who did not get the message was Major Funkhouser. He had banned *War Brides* and other 'pacifist' dramas with the declaration of war, and he demanded cuts from *The Spirit of '76*, but as 'hate-the-Hun' films started appearing with German atrocities, he censored them as well. He banned Cecil B. DeMille's *The Little American*, which had America's Sweetheart Mary Pickford imperiled by raping, pillaging Germans because, "it would offend the Germans here, who did not start this war."

'Mae Tinee' of the *Chicago Tribune*, blasted his decision.

"Let us hope that the Major will rub the sleepy seeds from his eyes in the near, near future, discover that the United States is at war with Germany, and that the picture in question is not only anti-German but is pro-American."

She campaigned to have Washington pressure Funkhouser to ease censorship.

Fox's *The Spy* (1917), which starred Dustin Farnum as an American secret agent captured by the Germans, had a prolonged and graphic torture scene. Reviewers dismissed it as crude propaganda. When Funkhouser banned *The Spy*, William Fox sued him and the mayor of Chicago, 'virtually charging them with treason.' Funkhouser demanded certain scenes be cut, and, according to *Motography*, "Mr. Fox . . . would not consent to the elimination of the scenes desired because they were vitally necessary to the patriotic mission of the piece.

"President Wilson has specifically requested that film producers and distributors organize and mobilize to co-operate with the government in waging war and in bringing it to a successful conclusion.

"In producing *The Spy*, Mr. Fox . . . is warning America to the perils within her own gates. He is trying to assist the Government by having people ferret out the thousands of spies in this country who are obtaining information about the movements and plans in the army and navy, for use by the Imperial German Government."

Later in that same issue, *Motography* reported that Fox won the right to show *The Spy* in Chicago.

"Mr. Fox established the point that Funkhouser's power to condemn a photoplay was limited to pictures which were in some way obscene or immoral, and that *The Spy* was obviously not within that classification."

Funkhouser fought back, not only banning the Fox-Bara film, *The Rose of Blood*, with its tale of revolutionaries in Russia, but he also tried to get the Department of Justice in Washington to ban the film nationally on the grounds it was damaging to the war effort. After a special screening for the CPI and the War Department, it was determined *The Rose of Blood* threatened neither public morality nor national security, and the movie was released uncut— by the federal government, anyway.

Funkhouser ordered the following cuts: "Reel 2 two scenes of a young man holding a bomb and the throwing of it and the intertitle, "They still live, but next time", in Reel 5, the intertitle "Nothing less than death", in Reel 6, scenes of the shooting of the general and the servant doping the wine, and in Reel 7, five riot scenes including a soldier killing a young man and a soldier clubbing an old woman, the intertitle 'When are you going to pay me?'; two scenes of women taking bombs from a chest, and the lighting of the fuse."

Funkhouser aroused more outrage by cutting graphic scenes of violence from Edison's *The Unbeliever*, and Warner Brother's *My Four Years in Germany*. When Funkhouser had scenes cut showing German soldiers committing atrocities in D.W. Griffith's *Hearts Of The World*, letters and telegrams were sent to President Wilson denouncing Funkhouser as a German sympathizer. Funkhouser denied the charge, saying he was born in St. Louis and was not of German origin. It did no good. It quickly turned into an ugly campaign to have 'Herr Funkhouser' fired. Still smarting from Funkhouser's censorship, Hollywood led the mob demanding his dismissal. Although abhorring the hate films, Wilson and Creel did not intervene.

Funkhouser was suspended as a film censor, brought up on what Chicago newspapers concluded were trumped-up, politically motivated charges, and he was finally dismissed from the police force. One of the first acts of his successor was to restore footage he had cut from the anti-German film, *My Four Years In Germany*.

Funkhouser was not the only victim of anti-German hysteria that saw careers ruined and lives destroyed. Only one German-American is known to have been lynched during the war (compared with about one hundred African-Americans lynched during the same time, plus several labor union organizers), but foreign-born and second-generation German-Americans were vulnerable to being singled out for other abuse, intimidation, humiliation and violence.

Meanwhile, Hollywood reaped the benefits for its support of the war effort. In selling Liberty Bonds and promoting enlistment and government programs, movie stars were at the same time promoting themselves, wrapped in the flag of patriotism. Leslie M. DeBauche concluded WW1 "provided the film industry with the opportunity to enhance its goodwill with its market— the American public— and to win the goodwill of those in positions of power in the government."

Before the war, the American film industry was a somewhat disreputable business catering to the lower classes. By war's end, Hollywood, as the American film industry became known, was highly influential with extensive government contacts and was declared a vital industry by the government that previously held it in contempt. Directors and produc-

Seven veils and counting. Theda Bara performs 'the Dance of the Seven Veils' in Salome. *(Author's collection)*

ers hobnobbed with presidents and prime ministers. Politicians and military leaders vied to pose for photos with movie stars, who, having helped rally the nation, became national heroes. Hollywood's contribution to the war effort— or arguably, its shameless exploitation of it— had gained it national prominence. Movies became the national entertainment. If the war did not end all war, it did make Hollywood. No wonder screenwriter Anita Loos could say, "I really credit Hollywood on World War One."

The public acclaim of movie stars, the efforts of the movie industry for the war effort, plus the political influence their new wealth could provide, found Hollywood a potent force in America. Cocksure and arrogant, movie executives strutted their newfound power, defying the censors and pressure groups, until the Hollywood scandals of the early 1920s sent them scurrying for cover again.

The whole censorship controversy erupted all over again when Fox released *Salome* in late 1918. John the Baptist was not the only one to lose his head over her dance of the seven veils. Although Theda Bara was mostly cloaked in George James Hopkins bizarre art nouveau costumes,

Salome gave ample opportunities to show ample amounts of Bara's bare skin, which brought the predictable outcry. A St. Louis reviewing committee found Theda's *Salome* 'overbold and underclad.' The Kansas censor board initially banned the movie, but relented by ordering Fox eviscerate all objectionable scenes from the controversial story.

"Eliminate close-up of Salome in opening bathing scene. Shorten scenes and titles of Salome with John in cell, so as to eliminate her sensual advances to him. Shorten to a flash Salome stretched on floor with head on platter."

Although demure and modest in real life, Theda Bara vigorously defended the near-nudity in her films.

"Hypocrisy is to blame for the present-day point which makes it 'sinful' for a woman to expose parts of her body on stage or screen.... Evil to him who evil thinks. I never think of the flesh when I am working in a role such as Salome. I concentrate upon the character and its interpretation, and if proper interpretation of the story calls for a scantily clad creature, the latter is only an incident."

Speaking on the controversy surrounding *Salome*, Bara defended the artistic values of the production, then added, "But as to the matter of seduction appeal, I state that none such was intended in the production, and it is visible only to those who go seeking it." There were plenty who went to seek it.

How nude she actually got for the film is a matter of supposition. The scenario specifies a nude bathing sequence near the start of the film (which Kansas ordered cut) and how many veils she cast off depended on the local censor board, but the veils are nearly transparent in surviving stills. Late in life, Bara assured her young neighbor, Joan Craig, she never appeared nude in movies.

Bara could argue (and did) she had not played a vamp in *Cleopatra*, but in *Salome*, she is definitely a vamp. Her Salome manipulates those around her to eliminate everyone between her and the throne of Judea, then loses her head, sort of speak, over the one person immune to her charms, and in taking revenge, is destroyed. Nor was *Salome* on the epic scale of *Cleopatra*; yes there were the large sets in street scenes in of Jerusalem and Herod's giant palace, but the whole script is a rather claustrophobic tale of palace intrigue. Lacking the scope of the epic *Cleopatra*, *Salome* was merely a big budget vampire movie.

The New York Times gave it a rave review, and *Variety* said, "Miss Bara is in her element as the arch vampire who finds little or no difficulty is luring every male to destruction that strikes her fancy, with the single exception of John the Baptist. The scarcity of her attire, to aid in her allurement, was artistically handled, making it most fascinating and devoid of vulgarity."

Grace Kingsley called *Salome*, "without doubt the greatest Biblical spectacle so far made in the history of films, and one of the greatest photodramas ever made," adding, "*Cleopatra* left us cold, on the human side—and there was raggedness in the spectacle. There was no such raggedness in *Salome*...

"And for me—and probably for thousands of others—Salome, the alluring, the cruel, will always be the colorful intricate characterization of Theda Bara."

Some critics took issue with John the Baptist being depicted as clean-shaven. J. Gordon Edwards argued Renaissance artists had also depicted him without a beard, adding, "We stand by the boyish John visualized by Salome. There's no romance in whiskers."

Most reviews were positive, but there were always the anti-Bara reviewers who hated her no matter what she did.

Calling *Salome* a 'colossal assault on common sense,' critic Julian Johnson declared in *Photoplay*, "Mr. Edwards, the producer, is even more at sea than when he produced *Cleopatra*, truly a new chapter in Alexandrine history; but is it all Mr. Edwards' fault? I have an idea that were Mr. Edwards let alone he would be putting on straightaway, ordinary tales of matter-of-fact life, instead of acting as nominal guide through these bewildering mangles of record and tradition recently affected by Miss Theda Bara. As Salome, Miss Bara does not resemble the tigerish princess of Judea as much as a neurasthenic taking sun-baths. No wonder Herod killed Salome after her dance."

When one critic called her Salome "a fleshy conception and not the mental lady who must have upset the Biblical court," Bara lashed back sarcastically, "How can I portray a mental Salome? Can I show her mind working for the camera? Will I have subtitles tell my brainy sayings? Or will I go through the dance of the seven veils with a finger pressed thoughtfully pressed to my forehead?"

Vanda Krefft notes that in contrast with *Cleopatra*, in which William Fox was very hands-on with the production, Fox showed little interest in *Salome*. Says Krefft, "he didn't champion *Salome* the way he had *Cleopatra*."

When the premiere in New York had to be canceled due to labor issues, Fox moved it to far off Seattle. Instead of roadshow engagements to build up publicity around the movie, Fox gave it widespread release, so it was competing with *Cleopatra*, still in theaters. Fox didn't bother taking legal action against the inevitable censoring of risqué scenes, leaving it to Edwards and Bara to defend the movie. He seemed to have dismissed *Salome* as a failure even before it had been released. According to Krefft, "His heart wasn't in the movie and it showed."

Krefft argues that after the turmoil surrounding *A Daughter of the Gods*, Fox wanted to prove he could make a successful epic on budget, which he did with *Cleopatra*; he finally had his studio working as a factory. He had nothing further to prove with *Salome*.

Nevertheless, *Salome* was another box office hit; Fox's biggest release of the following year. Some sources suggested it outperformed *Cleopatra*. Business logic dictated that another big-budget spectacle be made with Bara in 1919. It was not to be. Was Fox souring on epics—or Theda Bara?

CHAPTER ELEVEN: 'TIE A CAN ON HER'

In 1919, WW1 had ended but there was no peace. Fighting flared up in border skirmishes among new nations being carved out of the fallen empires. Revolutions and rebellions shook the postwar world. The Russian Civil War cost the lives of another seven million people. The Bolshevik revolution alarmed the West, which turned from hating the Hun to hating communists in every shape and form. In the U.S., foreign-born communists were deported, and Red Squads rooted out suspected communists, especially labor leaders. White racists believed Bolsheviks were trying to incite rebellion in African-Americans. They regarded returning Black soldiers as an affront to White supremacy. Violent race riots erupted across America in which hundreds, perhaps thousands of Blacks were murdered. Inspired in part by *The Birth of a Nation*, the Ku Klux Klan revival began. It would exert its influence on American politics throughout the 1920s.

In 1919, the struggle between the star system and the studio system took new form. Chaffing under the thumb of the studios, D.W. Griffith, Charles Chaplin, Mary Pickford, and Douglas Fairbanks formed United Artists. This gave them more creative control and provided them with a greater share of the profits by producing and distributing their own films. On learning of the enterprise, Richard A. Rowland, head of Metro Pictures and opposed to the star system, allegedly coined the phrase, "So the lunatics have taken charge of the asylum."

After completing *Salome*, the Fox Film Company continued to crank out Theda Bara Superproductions with Adrian Johnson, J. Gordon Edwards, and Theda Bara. *When A Woman Sins* (1918) was promoted as 'the greatest woman's story ever filmed.'

For Bara, it had become an unrewarding grind. She knew *Cleopatra* had been her high water mark. She had little interest in making more routine melodramas, especially vamp films.

A nice Jewish girl. Theda Bara as an innocent artist's model posing as the Virgin Mary in The Forbidden Path. *Later, as a fallen woman, she blackmails and then denounces the man that ruined her. (Author's collection)*

Also taxing upon Bara was the strict maintenance of the Vamp mystique. Screenwriter Francis Marion remembered how Bara was presented in public appearances. Actor Milton Sills drove Marion to the Fox studio, where Bara was scheduled to head a luncheon for some distinguished European visitors.

Eager to "catch a glimpse of this man-eating tigress," Marion noted a large crowd "had gathered in front of the studio gates pressed forward when a funereal-looking limousine drove up, its shades drawn. The liveried chauffeur descended. The gates swung wide revealing a red carpet. 'Make way for Bara!' ordered the chauffeur. No one stirred as the well-advertised vampire stepped out of the limousine, heavily veiled, and garbed in what looked like widow's weeds. An awed gasp rose in one breath from the crowd. Suddenly a woman cried out, 'G'wan, let's see your face!' The star raised her veil and gazed at the crowd with haughty contempt, then, lowering her veil, she entered the studio, her walk stealthy, catlike. After we left I remarked to Milton that she made the haunting legends of lycanthropy seem almost believable.

"'Hate to disillusion you but what you have seen is another Pygmalion creation, right out of the head of William Fox. I know Theda. She's a gracious, cultured woman under orders never to let the public know that she is intelligent and unpretentious.'"

"She was so bored, bored, bored by the whole 'woman of mystery' theme," George James Hopkins recalled, "She couldn't go out to nightclubs, couldn't be seen outside of the publicity, because that would have destroyed it all. She wanted company *desperately*, and the company turned out to be me."

Bara enjoyed the company of Hopkins and 'Richard' Ordynski. Having lived in Greenwich Village, she was likely unfazed or at least tolerant of their homosexuality, and they were probably sycophantic enough to feed her ego. Being forced into near isolation by the studio, it made her susceptible to their story ideas. She had already made *The Rose of Blood*, with Ordynski. Now it was Hopkins pitching movie ideas, and so Bara appeared in movies written by her costume designer (which Fox apparently approved). As journalist Celia Brynn noted, "Writing scenarios comes as easy to George as designing costumes, but one always suspects him of doing the costumes first and then fitting a story to them."

The She-Devil (1918) was a vamp comedy with story and Bara's outlandish costumes by Hopkins. *A Woman There Was* (1919) was based on Hopkins' story *Creation's Tears* (under the pseudonym 'Neje Hopkins'). Bara portrays Zara, the daughter of a South Seas island tribal chief, who falls in love with a missionary but dies helping him escape.

Neither movie enhanced Bara's reputation.

America's involvement in the war brought a different tone to the movies, and Bara's vamps sometimes became reformed instead of killed. 1919 saw Bara in *The Light* as the 'wicked woman of Paris,' who atones for her sins by trying to nurse war wounded. In *The Siren's Song*, Bara played a fallen Breton peasant woman who redeems herself by singing to French soldiers. *When Men Desire* 'Womanhood outraged— the Thrilling Adventures of a Woman who Tried to be True' had her as an American woman caught in Germany after war was declared. These movies likely did poorly at the box office, as immediately after the war ended, the American public lost interest in WW1 themed movies. Most of Fox's war propaganda movies lost money. It was a testament to his patriotic zeal that he made them, but there was little propaganda value in a movie nobody wanted to see. He tried to salvage some of his investment by re-editing and re-titling war films: *18 to 45* became *Every Mother's Son*, which Fox released as 'Not a war play,' but "deals chiefly with the tremendous sacrifices of American mothers and with the great economic and social problems which will arise during the period of reconstruction."

Finding audiences weren't interested in Bara playing good girl or redeemed women roles, Fox tried to shove her back into vampire parts. Bara resisted. Conscious of Bara's grousing about the roles she was given, he attempted to assuage her.

"It has always been my one ambition that as long as you are under my direction to add to your fame," Fox wrote to his top star, but since that fateful renegotiation of her contract, Bara did not feel much connection between them.

"Mr. Fox seldom came to the studio— he was busy at the home office. I only saw him a few times a year."

Their relationship had been merely symbiotic; he made her rich and famous, and she had made him very, very rich.

Her vamp movies were no longer making as much money. Vampires, especially her style of overwrought vamping, were becoming passé. The tired formula was wearing thin. Moreover, Bara had her critics; those tired of the vamping, those who never bought into the fantasy, and those who resented the fraud. Some complained that no matter what the character, Carmen, Juliet, or Cleopatra, all were played by her the same way.

"As in all Bara pictures, the picture is all Bara—" a critic said of *The Soul Of Buddha*. "Bara making faces, Bara ogling, Bara wriggling. Bara shoulders— and everything else."

Bara could rely on her fan base, but even this support was limited. In *Motography*, an exhibitor reported about *Her Greatest Love*, "Our patrons were little disappointed as they want Theda Bara as a vampire." In the same issue, another exhibitor opined about *The Tiger Woman*, "Excellent vampire picture but such stories are losing favor."

"Counteracting Theda Bara's vampire reputation is a long and tedious process, and is being indulged in by the Fox Company at enormous financial cost," a reviewer in *The Billboard* observed, "*Heart and Soul* is the latest attempt to make Theda a heroine of a sweet and sacrificing disposition and the result is about convincing as if Charlie Chaplin should essay a Wm. S. Hart role."

"Folks either want to see Miss Bara on the screen, or they don't," commented *Wid's Daily* in 1919, "and in order to attract those numbered among her consistent followers, little is needed beyond a display of the star's name. For those who don't approve of Theda, or the type of photoplay in which she appears, no advertising is effective. A deep-seated prejudice will keep them out of the theater .... it would be unwise for an exhibitor aiming to build up a reputation for showing first class productions of a superior tone to bother with her pictures."

Others, including famed director D.W. Griffith, considered her a skilled actress. Griffith thought it was the terrible scenarios assigned to her that were damaging her career.

"No actress, not even Bernhardt," he declared, "could have saved some of the vehicles handed Miss Bara."

If, as he claimed, William Fox personally approved all the scenarios of the movies he produced and inspected all the movies he released, some of the blame for bad movies must be laid on him. Naturally, Fox did not see it that way. He had become fixated on his studio system of making movies as if on an assembly line. If he promised exhibitors eight Theda Bara movies a year, eight Theda Bara movies would be made, whether they were good or bad was immaterial. If Bara fans buying the tickets wanted her in vamp movies, then she would appear in vamp pictures. If her movies didn't make money, that was her fault. It wasn't just Bara's movies; the majority of Fox films seemed low quality.

"Tell me," an acquaintance dared asked Fox in 1919, "Why don't you some time produce a good picture and not always a bad one? You make the worst pictures of any company I know."

"It's not as if we aren't trying," Fox replied defensively.

Moreover, Fox never really comprehended the appeal of Theda Bara; he was content to crank out repetitive vamp pictures without trying to understand *why* Bara appealed to audiences, especially women. Bara could not shine as an actress if given bad scripts in stereotypical woman roles. Olga Petrova complained about the scripts she herself was given at Metro and the stereotyped roles for women in general.

"The stories and the characters in the stories I had played were unreal or unconvincing. So-called vampire roles were as antipathetic as were those ladies who sold their honor to pay for mother's operation or to put brother Jack through law school. Worst of all were the simple, weak-brained, weak-armed maidens who were led astray in their innocence or in spite of their half-hearted struggles to escape from one or more lascivious gents bent on their undoing . . .

"There was a place for the intelligent, resourceful, self-supporting woman, as there was for the vampire, the magdalene, the betrayed innocent, the sweet and ringleted ingénues."

Bara still received countless letters from an adoring public. Fans across the country sent her newspaper and magazine articles about her along with reviews of her films, which she duly pasted into her scrapbook, even the bad reviews. However, one article sent to her by a fan in March 1918, while she was filming *Salome*, stirred her wrath.

Abraham Carlos gave an interview to the *Cleveland News* claiming credit for discovering Bara at Churchill's, a very fashionable restaurant in Manhattan. That Bara might have been a customer at Churchill's was one thing, but the inference was Bara had been working as a waitress when she had been 'discovered' by Carlos and hired at $30 a week for *A Fool There Was*. The writer of the article commented, "Any young woman who can increase her weekly salary from $30.00 to $5000.00 in the short space of three years is deserving of a modicum of credit— even a vamp."

Carlos also quoted Herbert Brenon making insulting remarks about Bara while directing her in *The Kruetzer Sonata*.

Furious, Bara telegraphed both the *Cleveland News* and Winfield Sheehan, complaining about the 'slanderous interview,' "Most insulting innuendo I ever read," and demanded Carlos retract the statements or deny making them.

Wurtzel also telegraphed Fox, saying that Bara was so angry she was refusing to complete *Salome*. Fox's private secretary wired back that Fox had been ill and wasn't in the office. Having previously been Fox's private secretary, Wurtzel knew Fox's tactic of hiding in his office, refusing to deal with annoying problems. He wired back urging Fox be contacted immediately about the matter.

Bara's ruffled feathers were soon smoothed, and *Salome* completed. Fox would later complain that Bara had become a prima donna, coming in late to work and being difficult on the set. One time, according to Fox, she tripped over an electric cable and demanded the technician who laid it be fired. This was a far cry from the actress who got soaked in a swamped boat and said with a watery grin, "These things happen."

Things were different from Bara's perspective.

"My health was bad and I needed a rest," she later stated, "I had been getting wretched stories and studio life was beginning to get on my nerves. I stopped reporting to work in the morning. Nothing was ever ready. We would wait for hours and hours until some carpenter had corrected a mistake in the setting. And all about you there is a grinding and a pounding. The mechanical staff have a way of blaming all the delays on the star. The star has no come-back because she cannot go and tell tales on men who need their day's wages."

Aside from the fit Bara threw over the Carlos article, Wurtzel's correspondence doesn't indicate trouble from Bara at the Western studio, although there is a gap in the letters during the critical period of late 1918 to early 1919. There can be little doubt that Bara was increasingly unhappy working at Fox, and that William Fox was becoming frustrated with her.

Other stars also caused trouble for Fox. In a continual contest of wills with stars exerting their power, studio heads and producers sought ways of gaining control over their stars by cajoling, bullying, flattering, making promises and other tactics in the fine—or rough and tumble—art of what might be called 'diva wrangling.'

In *Upton Sinclair Presents William Fox*, Fox claimed that Valeska Suratt had a tendency to argue with directors and walk off pictures until her demands were met. Fox outfoxed her by having the end of her pictures shot first. When she walked off one picture, Fox announced the release of

Gladys Brockwell. (Author's collection)

the film anyway, resulting in Suratt demanding to know how they could have completed the picture without her. Fox explained how they had shot the last scene already, so edited the movie that way. Suratt laughed and, according to Fox, "She came back, and from that time on never failed to appear on time at the studio."

It's curious Fox told this story, when after he spent an enormous amount promoting Suratt as the next Theda Bara, she returned to the stage, never to make another movie.

Gladys Brockwell was a seasoned stage and screen performer who played a variety of roles in melodramas. These cost from $25,000 to $30,000, compared with the luxury productions of Bara of averaging $60,000. Brockwell garnered critical praise that Bara could envy. Brockwell, too, campaigned for better roles and complained when she wasn't getting them. She wanted to do more comedy, but Fox insisted she continue in dramatic roles.

"I note what you say about Miss Brockwell," William Fox wrote in response to Sol Wurtzel's letter, "when Miss Brockwell is through with her present picture, if she does not want to work under the terms and conditions of her contract, let her out. She means nothing to the Fox Film Corporation, in fact, in my opinion, she is a detriment to the company... I am not interested in doing Leo Tolstoy's *Resurrections*, or any other story that might suit Miss Brockwell. The company has put up with her pranks long enough, and it is satisfactory to me not to make another picture with her; in other words, 'give her the gate' or 'tie a can to her.'"

Fox said that they needed to find someone to replace her first, and that he was "going to scour the New York market for someone." He instructed Wurtzel to look for someone in Los Angeles, "Notify me by telegraph the lowest possible price any available stars can be hired for."

As they found no one to replace Brockwell, she remained on the Fox roster until 1920, when she was finally 'given the gate.' However, the petty and vindictive William Fox wasn't satisfied with that. Just as he tried to sabotage Herbert Brenon's post-Fox career, it is alleged Fox 'tied a can' onto Brockwell by spreading rumors about her. Notes film historian Anthony Slide, "Producer William Fox certainly branded her [as a prima donna], and his virulent comments, in all probability, limited the star's work in the 1920s."

Instead of starring parts, Brockwell played mostly supporting roles until her untimely death in 1929.

It wasn't just actors who caused problems; directors could fuss and fume about Fox's interference and restrictions. Frank Lloyd had made distinguished epics with William Farnum such as *Les Misérables*, *A Tale of Two Cities* (both 1917) and *Riders of the Purple Sage* (1918). Lloyd wanted to make even bigger movies, trying to leverage Fox by courting other studios. He also threatened to quit if Fox re-edited his films. Wurtzel wrote Fox that he doubted Lloyd would make a reasonable cost film with Farnum again, "before that he was working for the interest of the company now he is working only for himself and for Farnum— he has become arrogant, vain and impossible to talk to— "

"I would be very sorry to see disagreement between Lloyd and the Fox Film Corporation," Fox replied, "for I have a high personal regard for him. I would consider that he is acting dirty and mean if he did anything to disturb the condition of the Fox Film Corporation."

Jewel Carmen. (Author's collection)

In 1919, Lloyd left Fox, and continued his distinguished career, including for Fox again, receiving five Academy Award nominations for directing, garnering two wins, *Divine Lady* (WB, 1929) and *Cavalcade* (Fox, 1930).

The troubles with Bara, Lloyd, Brockwell and Suratt paled in comparison of the headaches caused by Jewel Carmen. Born Florence Lavina Quick in Danville, Kentucky, she made her film debut as Florence La Vinci in *The Will of Destiny* (1912). In 1913, she appeared in several Keystone Comedy shorts, credited as Evelyn Quick. That year, *The Los Angeles Times* reported that two automobile salesmen were released on bail after statutory rape charges made by Quick, who was claiming to be a high school girl. Quick was linked to a prostitution and blackmail ring involving women and underage girls targeting prominent businessmen. When the scandal broke, key Keystone personnel, including Mack Sennett, Henry Lehrman and practically all of the male comedians, fled to Mexico. They filmed a couple of comedies there while waiting out events in Los Angeles.

In preliminary hearings, Minerva Quick, Evelyn's mother, testified her daughter was only 15 years old and produced evidence of her daughter's age by showing her name and date of birth written in the family Bible. A defense attorney proved the date had been altered and further proved Evelyn's real age was 23. All charges were dropped when Evelyn and another witness— Evelyn's sister, Alice—failed to appear.

In 1916, brunette Evelyn Quick resurfaced as blonde Jewel Carmen, being 'discovered' by Douglas Fairbanks. He brought her to Triangle, claiming she had been a convent schoolgirl. She played his leading lady in several of his movies and appeared in *Intolerance* as a harem favorite. Contracted by Fox in 1917, Carmen appeared opposite William Farnum in several prestigious Frank Lloyd pictures before starring in her own films. Although appearing like a Mary Pickfordesque ingénue before the cameras, she proved considerable trouble behind the scenes. Wurtzel reported to Fox that Carmen was spreading rumors that he and his assistant had been making sexual advances on her.

"Of course, I paid no attention to them as it is a very common occurrence for such stories to get around in all Los Angeles studios."

When Wurtzel confronted Carmen, she admitted lying, and he threatened to have her arrested if she made any more accusations.

Next, Carmen presented Wurtzel a doctor's certificate stating she could not work more than two hours a day. He had the studio doctor contact the doctor, and it was revealed Carmen had been operated on for a venereal disease that left her 'very nervous.'

Meanwhile, Wurtzel's private detectives had uncovered Carmen's true identity of Florence Lavina Quick, and her connection to the prostitution and blackmail ring, for which she did jail time. Furthermore, physicians who examined her diagnosed 'a disease' making her believe all men wanted to have sex with her.

Although Wurtzel admitted much of this was hearsay, he called her "an unprincipled, immoral and unmoral creature." He recommended that Carmen should neither appear in another Fox film, nor that she be allowed out of her contract. He wanted her 'humiliated and belittled in every way,' to make sure her screen career was 'forever ruined.' It would destroy studio morale not to punish her, and she should serve as a lesson for everyone else under contract at Fox.

Carmen ran off to sign a contract with the Frank A. Keeney Corporation in 1918. A war of lawsuits ensued. Told of the prior contract with Fox, Keeney canceled his contract with Carmen, who then sued Fox. Carmen also sued to free herself from the Fox contract. She argued that although she was 18 when she signed the contract, legal age in California, in New York, where the contracts were finalized, the legal age was 21 (never mind that Quick was proven to be 23 in 1913).

Fox would have been better off letting her stay at Keeney, as that company folded in 1919. Instead, the legal battle would last a decade, finally decided in Carmen's favor. Her film career would have been wrecked, but she had married director Roland West, who cast her in some of his movies. They divorced after both were linked with actress Thelma Todd at the time of her mysterious death.

There were women willing to use sex to get into the film industry, (Mack Sennett recounted that he asked to see the knees of one prospective Keystone Bathing Beauty, and the woman whipped off her dress, revealing herself completely naked). However, there were men in positions of power at the studios; producers, directors, stars and others, who demanded sexual favors from movie hopefuls in exchange for that tantalizing big break. The same Mack Sennett had in his office what has been called the first casting couch, although the institution predated the invention of movies. Winfield Sheehan was particularly guilty of this 'fringe benefit' of casting young women and sending them to the studio.

Miriam Cooper recalled Raoul Walsh complaining, "Winnie's girls are a pain in the ass." He said they possessed no camera acting skills and he had to train them how to "sit down, or smile, or blow their nose, for Christ's sake."

It wasn't just sexual desire that drove Sheehan. As Glendon Allvine put it, "Sheehan loved to play God, as who with great power does not?"

"On his jaunts to California, Sheehan was known for handing out jobs 'like Rockefeller handing out dimes' in a calculated effort to be well liked in Hollywood," noted Robert S. Birchard. Once back East, Sheehan would "wire to Wurtzel to fire all the new employees, making Wurtzel take the rap for his own ruthlessness."

Dealing with the tyrannical Fox and the conniving Sheehan on one end and troublesome stars, egotistical directors and thieving employees on the other, it is no wonder that the stress gave Sol Wurtzel chronic constipation and a severe facial tic. He reportedly suffered a nervous breakdown.

If Theda Bara was ever a victim of sexual harassment, she took that secret with her to the grave, as did thousands of other Hollywood stars and hopefuls who were propositioned, exploited or even raped, for it was an era when nobody was supposed to talk about such things, and until recently, they didn't.

Bara considered herself exploited in a different way she did talk about. She felt overworked and underpaid in comparison with other stars of her stature, that she was typecast as a vampire and that she was being forced to make bad movies. Lingering resentment over all this came to a head as negotiations began for renewing her contract, and it led to a showdown. She had been loyal to Fox, compared with other big stars, like Pickford and Chaplin, who had jumped to any studio which offered more money and creative control. Not all stars had that kind of clout—or respect.

James R. Quick, in his column 'Star Dust' for *Photoplay*, commented, "personality will often triumph over the most depressing conditions, just as William Farnum has made himself a great star in spite of the sordid fact that he works for William Fox, the vampire producer, it requires remarkable inward power to accomplish this end. Mr. Farnum is the only Fox star of any importance, probably for this very reason . . . .

"Theda Bara is in a class by herself, and not to be considered among the stars of healthier growth, since her success has been based upon a constant appeal to low sensationalism and morbidity. I believe this appetite has been, to a great degree, satiated. I believe the Theda Bara star is on the wane."

Dubbed a 'falling star' in Hollywood, Bara could guess her contract might not be renewed. Despite this (or because of this), Bara demanded her salary be raised from $4,000 a week to $5,000 a week. Other stars of her stature were making as much or more. Although his pictures made less money than Bara's did, William Farnum was paid about $10,000 a week. For Bara, it wasn't about the money, but she wanted to be paid what she thought was due to her.

To Fox, her demands were unreasonable. Bara refused any more vamp roles—but her vamp films made the most money. She wanted a vacation; she had been working virtually non-stop for four years. Fox, who had been working almost daily since he was nine years old, was unsympathetic. He drove himself to exhaustion and beyond, and he didn't understand why she wouldn't do the same for him.

Bara was still his top draw, but revenues were falling. Times were tough in Hollywood. The deadly influenza pandemic that had kept people away from theaters, plus the postwar financial slump, resulted in poor business at the box office. Moreover, Fox's Tom Mix westerns, which were much cheaper to produce than the average $60,000 six-reel 'Theda Bara Super-production,' were gaining popularity, and Fox only paid Mix $400 a week. Yet Mix appealed to boys, Fox was aware that Bara's films drew women, which were the main bulk of the audience.

Fox hunkered down in businessman mode, but more was influencing him than that. There were Robert Hilliard's prophetic words about replacing the actress on the stage version of *A Fool There Was* as soon as she regarded herself as another Sarah Bernhardt, (never mind Fox publicity called Bara 'The Divine Theda' in imitation of 'The Divine Sarah.') Fox was still smarting over the 'legal loophole' Bara had pulled on him two years earlier. He regarded her current intransigence as another betrayal. Coldly, he told her he would not even renew her contract for $4,000 a week; she wasn't worth it.

Fox did have a very big carrot to offer. J. Gordon Edwards was preparing another epic, based on the Biblical story of the Queen of Sheba. Naturally, the role would go to Bara—if she stayed without a pay increase or vacation. This time, Bara wouldn't bite.

Both were stubborn. Fox, who had quit his job at the garment factory when he didn't get the $3 raise he wanted, and Bara, who had quit a touring company when her salary was reduced from $25 a week to $18, were in vastly different circumstances, but both dug in their heels and refused to give in.

Meanwhile, in apparent ignorance of the breakdown in negotiations, Fox publicity assured exhibitors, "Theda Bara has been felicitously styled 'the Bernhardt of the Screen.' Her name suggests the weirdly alluring in dramatic expression, and her fame is limited only by the circumference of the earth. She is a Fox star for who the claim is consistently made that the exhibitor who books her takes no chance."

Bara had several more pictures to make before her contract expired.

Fox vindictively relegated Bara to secondary status at the studio. He removed Edwards as her director and Johnson as her screenwriter, and he assigned lesser directors and writers to her final films for his studio. Yet, in something of a concession, Fox gave Bara the role of a sweet Irish lass in *Kathleen Mavourneen*.

"This is the best role I ever had," Bara announced, "There isn't the slightest trace of the Vampire in Kathleen."

It was a role suitable for Mary Pickford, Mabel Normand or June Caprice, already typecast in such parts, but burdened by her vamp image, wholly unsuitable for Theda Bara. Had she played this role at the start of her film career, she might have been accepted, but as it was, reviewers merely sneered.

Fox gave it very little publicity and not much of a release, only as the secondary picture released with *Evangeline*, which starred Bara's rival Miriam Cooper. The attention it did get was the worst kind. Irish groups were outraged that the colleen Kathleen had been played by a Jew, and the 'Queen of the Vamps' at that. In San Francisco, a rowdy gang of youths disrupted showings by throwing stink bombs at one theater. The row did not help the picture this time, and it died at the box office, further embittering Fox against Bara's insistence at playing non-vamp roles. Just as audiences refused to see Mary Pickford's films unless she was playing the part of a sweet teenage girl, forcing Pickford to continue to play ingénues even into her thirties, they refused to see Bara in anything but vampire roles.

Next was *La Belle Russe* (1919), with Bara both as the good girl Fleurette and her evil twin, the titular La Belle Russe. Edmund Lawrence, who had been directing Virginia Pearson pictures, directed Bara in her final film for Fox, *The Lure of Ambition* (1919), about a conniving Englishwoman setting her sights on a married duke. Fox publicity called it, "truly one of the greatest pictures Theda Bara ever made." Bara got some good reviews, but one critic said, "It is a picture of the regular Theda Bara style, of the age of 1915, the kind that should be dead and buried deep into the ground, with no cross to mark its grave."

After this, Bara left Fox for good. Fox continued making money on Bara's films, which were in continual circulation or being re-issued. *Cleopatra* was reissued in 1920, for which Bara saw not a dime.

Perhaps she pressed the issue to get free of Fox.

"Five practically uninterrupted years of vamping had drawn my nerves pretty taut," Bara said, "I have seldom had longer than a week between pictures, and even this was not my own. It was replete with dressmakers

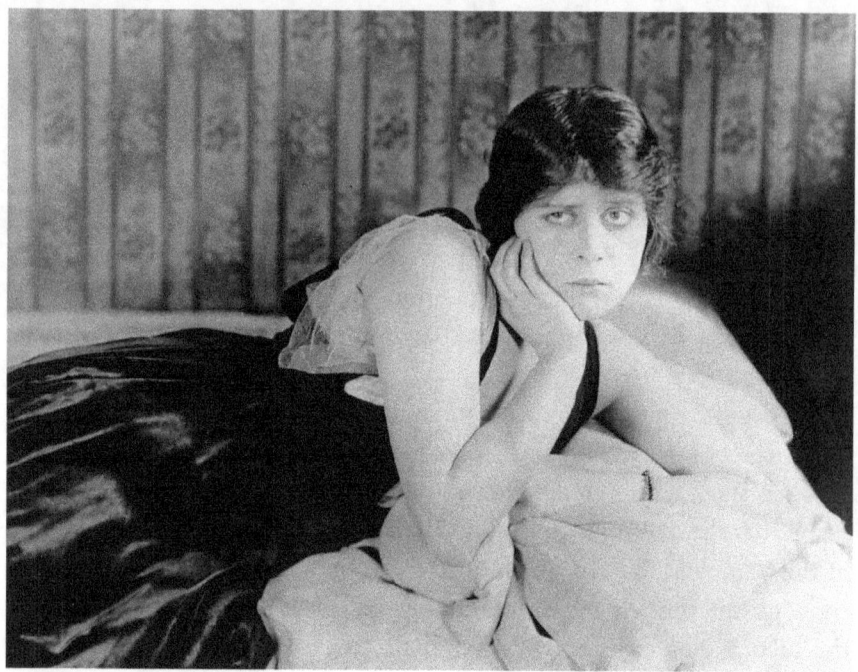

Theda Bara in The Lure of Ambition, *her last film for Fox. (Author's collection)*

and costumers and period experts, days of intensive preparation for work to come. And gradually those vampire emotions began to weigh me down. I felt heavy, depressed. There were not enough laughs in my life, and I do so love to laugh..."

Postwar Hollywood saw a lot of changes; it wasn't just Bara leaving the Fox lot. So did Henry 'Pathe' Lehrman, Frank Lloyd, Dustin Farnum, Gladys Brockwell, Madlaine Traverse, Peggy Hyland, Pearl White, Virginia Pearson, June Caprice, Evelyn Nesbit, Miriam Cooper, Raoul Walsh, and George Walsh, who claimed he turned down an offer from Fox for $4,000 a week. Even Fox's favorite star, William Farnum, left in 1923, being told he was 'too old' for leading man roles. Some went for bigger pay at another studio, some just wanted to be free of Fox, and others Fox had simply let their contracts lapse or fired them when he considered them disposable. A few, like Raoul Walsh, would return to Fox (even Herbert Brenon returned to Fox to direct a few films, for chrissakes). Not Theda Bara.

When in 1920, Geraldine Farrar's pictures were no longer financially successful, she and producer Samuel Goldwyn mutually agreed to tear up her contract. Close collaborators D.W. Griffith and actress Lillian Gish parted ways after making *Way Down East* (UA, 1920). Gish told him she was thinking of leaving his company and Griffith assured her she could make better money at another studio, "I can't afford to pay you what you are worth." Gish opined to Adela Rogers St. John, "I think he just got tired of seeing me around."

If Farrar and Goldwyn parted amicably, as did Gish and Griffith, Bara and Fox did not; both were bitter and resentful of the other's intransigence and perceived ingratitude. Each harbored a grudge against the other that lasted the remainder of their lives. Fox tried to bar Bara from using the Theda Bara name, claiming it was Fox intellectual property, but Bara had outfoxed Fox when she had her name legally changed to Theda Bara back in 1917.

Not mentioning her in public, Fox spoke derogatorily about Bara in private, belittling her talents, calling her a prima donna and difficult to work with. He emphasized the money lavished on her productions, and he claimed Bara became a star only because of Fox publicity. It can only be guessed at how effective was this 'whisper' campaign.

At least, Bara probably never sneered at Fox as a 'pants presser' as others did; after all, her father had been a tailor and she herself cut fabric for him. If she did not denigrate Fox publicly, privately she spoke bitterly of how he had treated her. Vanda Krefft states one time they chanced to meet on the sidewalk in New York, and she simply ignored him.

Before she had left Fox, a rumor circulated that Bara was dead—that she had, in fact, died a year earlier, and that she had been replaced in her final movies by a lookalike named Esther Bara. (Esther, of course, was the original name of Theda's sister, Lori.) Despite looking like her and having the same last name, she was unable to re-capture that old Bara magic, which accounted for the failures of final films. Rumor said that William Fox had reluctantly given up the idea of using an impostor, and stopped making Bara movies. Certainly, there were few people who had seen her last films to contradict the rumor, but this urban myth indicates how the Fox publicity machine had kept Bara in the public mind. So when it ceased stamping out wild stories about the great star, her adoring fans noticed, and started concocting their own— unless it was a ploy of Fox publicity, wringing out the last bit of money from the Bara mystique. After all, it worked for Carl Laemmle when he claimed Florence Lawrence was dead—and then that she wasn't.

Theda Bara and her sister Lori in Italy—not Russia. (Courtesy of Robert S. Birchard)

"Theda Bara is not dead," stated Fox press releases in promotion of Bara films, adding, "The great Russian Jewish vampire of the screen is not dead, but very much alive, retired and living in her native land, Russia, where she has purchased an estate with a comfortable fortune made under the banner of William Fox. Just before sailing for Europe, Theda Bara finished the last picture she will ever make, entitled *La Belle Russe*."

Of course, *La Belle Russe* wasn't her last film, even for Fox, nor was she Russian, nor had she retired to Russia—an unlikely place to which to retire when one considers the brutal civil war still being waged. Bara had sailed to Europe with her sister Lori, but to peacetime Western Europe for the long vacation she wanted. When she returned, she did not resume making movies. Were there no offers from other studios? Did the vindictive William Fox spread rumors about her, 'tied a can to her' with tales she was a temperamental and untalented actress? Or was it believed she was dead or in Russia?

Free of Fox restrictions, Bara took control of her public image. She sought to set the record straight in a series of interviews for fan magazines and articles purportedly written by her, but perhaps ghostwritten, dispelling the 'born in the shadow of the Sphinx' myth. Bara blamed William Fox, not for rumormongering, but for typecasting her as a vamp and forcing her to do bad scripts, and she blamed Goldfrap.

"I am the victim of overzealous press agents," Bara sighed, disingenuously if it was all her idea in the first place, "This vampire stuff was started by a press agent named Goldfrap, when I made my first appearance, in *A Fool There Was*. He called me a 'Soulmate of the devil' and started a pack of lies, which I'll never be able to live down. Why, he even said I was born two blocks from the Sphinx . . . I was born in Cincinnati, and I have a perfectly good Jewish father. His name was Goodman. But I read so many lies about myself that I hardly know what is the truth anymore . . ."

Theda Bara may not have been the man-devouring *femme fatale* of legend, but she was no Mary Pickford—neither was Mary Pickford, for that matter. Bara claimed she was really Theodosia Goodman, a nice Jewish girl from Cincinnati, Ohio, and yet for more than a decade, she wanted to be anybody but Theodosia Goodman. She had been struggling actress Theodosia de Coppett and then superstar Theda Bara. She could not go back to being Theodosia Goodman any more than Marilyn Monroe could go back to being Norma Jean Baker.

Bara thought that coming clean about her origins would win over those who hated the vamp. It didn't. The 'vamp' image and the humbug about her origins that had helped make her a superstar, also ruined her career. Cynical and sophisticated postwar audiences sneered and laughed at the vamping antics in re-releases of Bara's films. She had become a joke, and few stars survive becoming a joke. Although she did not know it yet, her acting career was virtually over. Her reign as Queen of the Vampires had lasted less than five years.

"It was an original idea, the designing of exotic fables," she sighed, "but unfortunately the over-efficient public carried it to an incredible point—and the mystery which we had created aroused ridicule."

Many people believed her when she said she was the innocent victim of press agents. Even many of her biographers seem to have been hoodwinked. Her personal life seemed so free of scandal that in the book *Hollywood Babylon*, that tome of character assassination, Kenneth Anger dubbed her a 'goody-two-shoes.' She may or may not have been innocent, but she was very adept at being discreet.

Bara might have been getting film offers, but the actress who never wanted to appear in movies and hated the moviemaking process might have turned all offers down, especially if they were vampire pictures.

"I will not slink and writhe and wriggle day in and out. I demand to bob my curls and climb trees and love for love's sake. I want to be— well, natural."

Natural was not enough. Times had changed in postwar America. Women had the vote—civilization did not collapse as a result— and they were making gains socially. They bobbed their hair to demonstrate their new status in society. Neither dignified matron nor innocent ingénue, the flapper, sexually liberated, but free-spirited instead of menacing, took over the movie screens. Although the voluptuous and evil vamp would make re-appearances, the golden age of the Vampire were over. Nevertheless, it was the crude, overblown image of the Vampire that had exploded the wall of sexual repression to allow the flapper to shimmy through.

Yet another shift was taking place. Hollywood pursued the young and slender ingénue and flapper at the expense of the matron, who was increasingly perceived as old fashioned and no longer a symbol of beauty. Changes in fashion demanded changes in public tastes regarding what was thought of as the beautiful female figure (or at least what movie producers and the fashion industry thought were changes in the public tastes). Increasingly, the ideal beauty was that of a slender young woman. Actresses struggled to maintain their youth in a losing battle against the march of time. Movie moguls searched for new stars among young actresses who were cheap, pliable and easily replaced.

It seemed vamp actresses Theda Bara and Olga Petrova were out of style. When Petrova interviewed Bara on the abrupt change in her career, she asked, "Why did you leave Fox?" Theda countered with, "Why did you leave Metro?"

Nevertheless, Bara completely charmed Petrova, as she charmed so many.

"In person she had for me little in common with her screen portrayals," wrote Petrova, "Not that she was less attractive. She was much more so, and in a very different way. I had expected to greet a tall, statuesque, opulent siren. I found, instead, a soft little blue mouse whose gentle ears I hesitated to shock with even an allusion to some of the fabulously sinful women her celluloid heroines were said to be . . . .

"I don't know when I found a safer or saner person than Miss Bara proved to be. She hadn't an unkind word to say about anyone, and when I put words into her mouth they emerged honey-coated."

"Vampires, poor things, are not cinematic vogue just now," noted Louise Glaum at the time. "Their era is waning. They will come back— perhaps!"

In fact, although 'vampire' pictures were in momentary eclipse, they did not disappear. Glaum herself made her most famous 'vamp' picture, *Sex* (1920). Barbara La Marr was gaining fame in *femme fatale* roles. Showgirl Nita Naldi was just starting her rise to stardom in *Dr. Jekyll And Mr. Hyde* (1920), going on to vamp Richard Barthelmess in *Experience* (Paramount, 1921) and Rudolph Valentino in a number of movies, not to mention her portrayal of the slinky Eurasian Sally Lung in Cecil B. DeMille's *The Ten Commandments*.

Nor were foreign vampires out of fashion. In contrast to Naldi's phony biographies, dubbing her as a Spaniard or as an Italian, there arrived in the Hollywood the real thing. Polish actress Pola Negri had gained success in German films in the same kind of roles that made Bara famous, such as Carmen and Madame Du Barry. Once in America, Negri could be as bizarre in interviews as anything cooked up by Goldfrap and Selig for Bara. That didn't prevent Paramount from creating a fictitious rivalry between her and its other movie diva Gloria Swanson to captivate fans.

Notably, Negri, Naldi and La Marr all bore a striking resemblance to Bara in face and form, and their success in *femme fatale* roles suggests audiences hadn't completely tired of Bara and vampire movies. So Bara could have continued at Fox making vamp pics, had she and Fox been less stubborn.

Bara still had star status, and it landed her a role, (with a hefty share of the profits) in a science-fiction stage melodrama called *The Blue Flame*.

Bara told the *Boston Sunday Post*, "During my career as a screen star I have felt the limitations of the camera, as all must have felt then who worked in the silent drama. It is, therefore, for the purpose of gratifying my own ambition to meet the public on a more personal basis that I accepted Mr. Woods' offer to present me in the spoken drama."

'The Sphinx will speak!' it was announced in the press.

The plot was a rip-off of 'Frankenstein' and concerned a scientist who invents a ray that can re-animate the dead, and therefore denies God. Bara played the role of his religiously devout fiancee. After she is killed by

Theda Bara and Alan Dinehart in The Blue Flame. *(Author's collection)*

lightning, the scientist uses the ray to bring her back to life, but without her soul— making her reborn an evil woman. It was another vamp role; another wicked, immoral woman who manipulates and murders until the end of the play, when it is revealed it has all been a dream of the scientist, who abandons his experiments and agnostic ways. Ominously, none of the writers attended the rehearsals. They took the money and ran.

"I chose it because it gave me an opportunity to play the sort of part the public wants to see me play," Bara explained, even more ominously.

The play opened in Boston to sold-out audiences for two weeks, then played in Pittsburgh and Washington to large audiences. The producer, A.H. Woods, wanted to continue on the road, but Bara insisted the show must go to New York to fulfill her long-time wish, to star in a play on Broadway. Reluctantly, Woods agreed, and the play opened in New York to the derision of the critics. They had been sharpening their knives, eager to slice up any Hollywood movie star that came their way, but this appalling melodrama handed them must have been a delight to rip apart.

Alexander Woollcott, writing for *The New York Times*, said of Bara, "She is pretty bad, but not bad enough to be remembered always. Indeed, she has a very pleasant voice. She speaks her lines distinctly . . . And she displays a fine self-possession which enabled her to proceed last evening with unflinching gravity even when the audience lost control of itself and shook with laughter."

Critic Louis DeFoe sniffed, "It shows what very slight attainments are needed for a successful career as a movie actress. With sufficient self-assurance it is plain that anyone can become queen of the screens."

"Perhaps *The Blue Flame* is not a perfect title for Miss Bara's play," another critic summarized. "Why not: Tenting on the Old Vamp Ground?"

"I really don't know what the critics said about me. I haven't read them at all. They might disturb me," Bara said. "I do not play to Broadway. Broadway is the workshop of theatrical people. I play to the ordinary people who go to theaters or the movies to be entertained, not to compete."

Despite the bad reviews, *The Blue Flame* sold out its first few weeks. A month later, however, the show was selling seats at a discount. Back on the road, it continued to tour successfully in eastern cities for a few more months. Its appeal was pure camp, and Theda Bara was high mistress of camp at this point. Curiously, *The Blue Flame* echoed her life. A 'demure and circumspect' woman magically transformed into an evil temptress—only to be discovered to have been a mere illusion, and nobody cared.

"I shall go back to the stage after a few pictures," Bara reported, "but not in the same sort of horrid role I had in *The Blue Flame*."

Regarding her acting ability, Bara didn't like her performances in many of her 'vamp' pictures either. Nevertheless, she was proud of some of her performances.

"Not all of my screen work was bad. I can look over some of the old films and find scenes that were good. I know when I have done good work. There is a little bell inside of me that rings when I hit my mark.

"My most interesting character, to my mind, has been Cleopatra," Bara said in 1919. "She was a woman of immortal pride. She, too, must be the victim of moving-picture demoralization; she, too, must be labeled a vampire, on that account. I do not think she was, in spite of the opinion of movie fans."

British-born Charles Brabin had been directing movies since 1911; at Edison, Vitagraph, Essanay and other companies. He had directed Bara in *Kathleen Mavourneen* and *La Belle Russe*. Still at Fox, he re-entered Bara's life, interested in the off-camera Theda Bara, of whom nearly everyone said was 'charming and intelligent' and possessed a 'delightful sense of humor.' Although Bara had said, "I didn't want to get married. I hadn't ever cared about getting married," Brabin proved how charming, intelligent and witty he could be.

That would be enough for some women, but of course, Bara was different, noting, "His mental brilliance was not the first attractive quality I noticed about him. It was the way he walked. Like an Indian... He stalked in and in two strides crossed the room. It still fascinates me to sit and watch him approach me."

In 1921, Bara drove with Brabin to Connecticut and they were married in a simple ceremony. "Neither of us had ever been on time in our lives," reminisced Bara. "So I thought, 'I'll shampoo my hair.' I did. And then bless you if the man wasn't actually punctual. I had to stick up my wet hair under my picture hat, and sneezed throughout the ceremony."

They honeymooned in Nova Scotia by the Bay of Fundy. After years of hoopla all about Theda Bara, Fox publicity barely noted the marriage in their press releases, and only because Brabin still worked at Fox. Other Fox press releases still insisted Bara was not dead and living on her estate in Russia.

"I would tell every girl... that the glamour of a career fades beside that of a happy marriage," the former home-wrecker told a reporter. "That is the most supreme happiness given us mortals. I was a long time finding mine, but I did, you know."

Theda Bara and Charles Brabin caught by a photographer at the train station in 1923. (Author's collection)

J. Gordon Edwards had been working on *The Queen of Sheba* scenario with Bara in mind. With her no longer at Fox, Edwards looked for another actress to play the Biblical queen.

"J. Gordon Edwards intends to make a special production without a star," Fox wrote to Sol Wurtzel in 1920, comparing it with earlier epics. "Both *Salome* and *Cleopatra* could have been made without stars and would have been successful—more successful than they were with the stars."

Both productions starred, of course, Theda Bara. Fox could not forgive her for leaving him.

Betty Blythe, an actress who had found modest success in roles in Vitagraph films, told of her audition for the role of the Queen of Sheba to film historian Kevin Brownlow for his admirable book, *The Parade's Gone By*.

"Mr. Edwards made an immediate impression on me. He looked at me so keenly, so alertly."

He asked her to comment on a painting of Solomon's Temple he had in his otherwise bare office.

"I don't remember exactly what I said, but something about how its greatness and expansiveness were quite overwhelming, emotionally and historically. 'They must then have been great lovers of the arts to have lived in that style.'"

Blythe heard nothing from Edwards for a long time. After greenlighting the big-budget spectacle, Fox said to Edwards, "Well, we've got to find Sheba now, haven't we?"

"No," replied Edwards, "I've found her in California."

Decades later, Blythe was still amazed by Edwards' confidence.

"I don't suppose I was in his office for half an hour— but the discernment of that man! A feeling, I suppose, that I had been a student of the arts ..."

Doubtful, Fox viewed some of Blythe's movies she made at Vitagraph.

"Oh, she's terrible," said Fox. "Look at this... look at that... that could never play a queen! What are you talking about, Jack?"

"Never mind," replied Edwards. "That's my Sheba."

"Fox saw more films, brought over thousands of stills of me from Vitagraph," Blythe recalled. "He was still completely opposed to having me."

Then Edwards summoned Blythe for a screen test.

"The actor who played Solomon was there— Fritz Leiber. Fritz Leiber escorted me to the throne. 'Ad lib this,' said Mr. Edwards. Since Leiber was a marvelous Shakespearean actor, he read a Shakespearean phrase to me. I received it in silence, and then replied in some sort of poetry which sufficed for expression, for the contact that was so important between players."

Blythe won the role, but she was in for a shock when production started. The costumes she had to wear were even skimpier than Bara's in *Cleopatra*. Costume designer Margaret Wheeler "showed me a real cute little lampshade with a few beads on it..."

"'What's that?' says I.

"'That's your first costume,' says she.

"When I came to she was trying to decide where she could put a hook without having it show."

"Twenty-eight costumes," Blythe marveled, "and if I put 'em all on at once I couldn't keep warm!"

While the scantiness of Sheba's costumes attracted a lot of attention, Edwards having Leiber's Solomon clean-shaven drew criticism the same

Betty Blythe and Fritz Leiber in The Queen of Sheba *(Author's collection)*

way as his beardless John the Baptist had in *Salome*. Edwards responded, "No motion picture audience would stand for Sheba falling for a set of whiskers."

Released in 1921, *The Queen Of Sheba* was a great critical and financial success, which catapulted Blythe to international stardom. Contrary to what some sources say, this queen of Sheba was a virtuous woman and not a vamp, but Blythe's regal beauty and scanty attire positioned her as the next Hollywood sex symbol.

"I was to have gone right on as Theda Bara had done," Betty Blythe remembered, "with one great production after the other."

Then one day, according to Larry Lee Holland, citing 'some sources,' William Fox called Blythe into his office, informing her he wanted to make her the main star on the Fox lot. He also wanted her to be his mistress. Blythe told him she loved her husband, director Paul Scardon, and would not cheat on him. She continued to refuse as he offered her money and film opportunities, then she walked out of his office after he threatened to ruin her career.

Fox biographers doubt this story. Whatever his other faults, Fox was known for being faithful to his wife and a dedicated family man, unlike many other movie producers who were notorious philanderers. Another problem (admittedly, not insurmountable) was that Blythe was based in Los Angeles and Fox rarely left New York. Some have suggested Winfield Sheehan a more likely culprit. Since it was a time when nobody spoke publicly about sexual harassment, Blythe was vague on the matter, but

Scene from Nero, *directed by J. Gordon Edwards. (Author's collection)*

she blamed Fox for damaging her career and that of J. Gordon Edwards. Blythe's American film career certainly seems lackluster after *The Queen of Sheba*, although she had considerable success in exotic starring roles in Britain, possibly out of reach of William Fox's 'tying a can to her.' It's possible that she and her husband tried to capitalize on her Sheba fame with independent productions that failed at the box office. Others have suggested Blythe was a so-so actress, whose main talents lay in wearing fancy gowns or in wearing hardly anything at all. In any case, her career at Fox abruptly ceased and her Hollywood career suffered.

"We were to go over to Italy to make *Pelleas and Melisande* and *Pygmalion*," Blythe remembered years later, "Mr. Edwards had five [pictures] all laid out to follow *Sheba*. He went over and had all these great sets made and then that man Fox did him in about me. He ruined his career and he ruined mine."

Edwards went to Europe to establish Fox studios in Britain, Italy and possibly elsewhere. A project to be filmed in England, *Mary, Queen of Scots*, with Blythe in the title role, was abandoned. In Italy, he made the epic *Nero* (1922), about the notorious Roman emperor. His next epic,

Scene from The Shepherd King. *(Author's collection)*

The Shepherd King (1923) about the Biblical King David, was filmed in Italy, Egypt and Palestine. Filming overseas was supposed to save money through lower labor costs, but Edwards encountered red tape entangled bureaucracy, logistical inefficiency and a poor work ethic among laborers, who resented the foreign intruders even while accepting their money.

"Anyone who tries to make pictures in Italy must console themselves to their methods," Edwards later commented ruefully, "It takes three Italians to do what one American can do."

"I had some very fine talks with Mr. Fox," Sol Wurtzel wrote Edwards in June, 1922, "Mr. Fox took great pride in telling me he felt sure (*Nero*) was going to be a wonderful picture, made at half the cost of *Queen of Sheba*. This last was said with special emphasis . . ."

He also wrote that Tom Mix offered to manage chariot races or 'slaughter some gladiators' or even fiddle while Rome burned in Edwards' next production. Wurtzel finished with, "Here's hoping your new picture, *Shepard King* will knock 'em dead."

Both *Nero* and *The Shepherd King* were costly flops. *Nero* received good reviews, but audiences ignored it. *The Shepherd King* was reportedly an unsalvageable mess, but some have blamed William Fox's damaging edits and his insertions of ponderous Biblical text.

Other directors hailed as geniuses just a few years earlier had difficulty coping during the 1920s. The most notable of these was D.W. Griffith, who, after he made *America* in 1924, seemed increasingly out of touch with audiences. Perhaps the same might be said of Edwards; film techniques and style had changed so much since the end of the war that his work may have seemed dated and stale. He may have also have been dependent on the star appeal of his actors. The movies he made with Theda Bara and William Farnum were mostly successful, and he pulled off a coup with *The Queen of Sheba*, making a minor player like Blythe into a big star. However, *Nero* and *The Shepherd King* featured Italian actors with no name recognition in the States. Despite William Fox's insistence that epics would sell themselves, it was Theda Bara in the title roles that 'sold' epics like *Cleopatra* and *Salome*. It was Edwards who caught the brunt of Fox's wrath for his failed epics.

"Mr. Edwards returned to this country and his whole flash of genius as a director just went to ashes," recalled Blythe. "I don't know the details, except that the blame lay with Fox."

Assigned the administrative job of director general, Edwards oversaw other Fox productions, but was allowed to direct only three more minor films between 1922 and 1924, compared with eight movies a year in his glory days. Fox laid him off in April 1924. Edwards, who had once rivaled D.W. Griffith, Thomas Ince, Herbert Brenon and Cecil B. DeMille as a maker of epic movies, was unable to get work. As Fox's modest and loyal lieutenant, he had only worked for Fox and had not built up contacts with other studios. He was still trying to find a job when he became ill on

Left to right: Dustin Farnum, unknown woman, William Farnum and J. Gordon Edwards on a Fox studio set. (Author's collection)

Christmas Day, 1925. He died five days later, at the age of 58. The coroner gave the cause of death as pneumonia. Others said it was due to a 'broken heart.'

Ignored by Hollywood toward the end of his life, Edwards was virtually ignored upon his death. There were only brief obituaries in the trade papers, but *Film Daily* gave a front-page two-paragraph death notice, followed a week later adding that Edwards had been, "A prince among men; one of the finest who ever entered into this business of motion pictures."

From the Fox Film organization that he was instrumental in helping to build, there was not one word of acknowledgment of his passing or of his contributions to the company.

CHAPTER TWELVE: 'THE GRAND ILLUSION'

In 1921, Theda Bara went on a twelve-week cross-country speaking tour, sharing the stage one time, oddly enough, with baseball star-turned evangelist Billy Sunday, who had previously denounced her films and hedonistic Hollywood in general. Bara received the more enthusiastic response. In the speeches she made to audiences, she repeated the Fox organization's statements that her vampire roles had strengthened 'family values' by showing its contrast.

"Will you all wish me to play the Vampire again?" she asked the audience, and they shouted their approval.

Then she asked, "Would you also like to see me in the role of a good girl?"

The response was more polite than enthusiastic.

"Well, there you are," she sighed, "It just looks as though you will not let me play anything but vampire parts. So I suppose I shall have to continue in parts somewhat similar to those I have played in the past."

Yet Bara's acting career was like a car whose engine would turn over but not start. An announced film version of *The Blue Flame* never materialized. Bara's plan to start her own film company went nowhere. Bara and Brabin said they would film a version of Longfellow's *Evangeline*, but nothing came of it. David O. Selznick signed her in another vampire role in *The Easiest Way*, but it was never filmed. It was announced she would make *Restless Wives*, but the project fizzled. She wrote her memoirs, *What Women Never Tell*, but it was never published.

Did Fox, with his petty vindictiveness, sabotage Bara's career after she left the studio, bad mouthing her as a prima donna, as he had done to Herbert Brenon, as he reportedly had done to Gladys Brockwell, and possibly Betty Blythe?

If it suited Theda Bara to cast herself as the victim of press agents, that suited William Fox as well. He repeated this fable to Upton Sinclair for the biography of himself he commissioned. Bara was a nobody he made her into a star through his publicity campaign. There is no further men-

the Vampire

A Fool there was, and he paid his Coin
To a dark-eyed Dame, from the Ten-der-loin.
He took her out to a West Coast Town,
Dressed her up in a Form-fit Gown,
Filled her Eyes with Bel-la-Don-na,
And said, "Now, Kid, for-get your Hon-na,
For, Hence-forth, you're a scar-let Scamp—
A reg-u-lar, red-lipped, black-souled Vamp."
She signed his Con-tract, for she was Meek,
He made her Fa-mous with-in a Week;
And when I tell you his Pro-fits, you'll
A-gree that, per-haps, he wasn't a Fool.

From Life Magazine, April 14, 1921.

tion of her in Sinclair's biography. Fox even denied knowledge she had a theatrical career before she came to Fox studios.

If Fox wanted Bara forgotten, many people wanted their Theda Bara back.

"Come home — all is forgiven," *Photoplay* in 1923 begged Bara in an open letter. "Theda Bara, welcome back! The flapper died with short skirts. You may return to the screens and be received with open arms. We've missed you!

"The first lady of the purplish photoplays, La Bara, is now making a new picture for Selznick studios. She was on the stage for many months; then she found a screen story which suited her, and soon you'll be seeing her again."

As noted, the Selznick film was never made.

In 1925, Bara made what she hoped would be a comeback movie for Chadwick Studios, appropriately titled *The Unchastened Woman*. Upon seeing it, screenwriter Sally Benson commented, "When I realized that this was Theda Bara's comeback picture, and not just one of her old releases, I could hardly believe my eyes."

This hardly seems fair. Bara played a matron, the defender of hearth, home and family. Her character was like the wife of John Schuyler in *A*

The Unchastened Woman *with Theda Bara. (Author's collection)*

Fool There Was, except she vamps to save her marriage. A mother-to-be who discovers her husband is cheating on her, she pretends to be a woman of the world to make him jealous, and only then reveals to him their baby son. Its plot imitated Cecil B. DeMille's popular sex comedies, such as *Why Change Your Wife?* It was, in fact, typical of a number of women's movies of the 1920s. However, with Bara in the lead, most viewers saw it only as a revamped version of the vamp picture.

The Unchastened Woman wasn't a throwback to the movies Bara made at Fox—that was the problem. Her audience wanted their vamp back. They

Theda Bara in costume for Madam Mystery. *(Author's collection)*

wanted their vamp back. The box office failure may have chastened Bara somewhat.

Which may have been why she was so enthusiastic about being signed to play in a Hal Roach comedy short, *Madame Mystery*, in 1926. His 'All-star' comedy series made use of has-been stars for their name value and low price. Bara was nevertheless pleased.

"Vamping requires no artistry whatever," she told the press. "For me, henceforth, high comedy!"

Madame Mystery was hardly high comedy. Bara appeared as an exotic Mata Hari-type spy, spoofing her former vamp roles, but mostly played straight woman to the antics of klutzy slapstick comedians. Otherwise, *Madame Mystery* is notable only for the appearance of Oliver Hardy as a bumbling ocean liner captain, with his future comedy partner Stan Laurel as one of the film's co-directors.

Bara apparently balked at appearing in a second such film. In a compromise to complete the terms of her contract, an outtake of Bara from *Madam Mystery* was used in another Roach film, *45 Minutes From Hollywood*; ironically, in a scene in which a Hollywood tour guide points out the famous star Theda Bara creeping about in spy fashion. After this, she left the screen, never to return.

It is often said that she couldn't get any additional film roles. However, there is an alternative—in fact, two alternatives. She could have resumed her movie career had she wanted. The woman who claimed she didn't want to get into movies, was forced by economic necessity to go into movies, and complained and rebelled against the 'sausage factory' of making movies—how anxious was she to return to being in film?

"Do you think ditch-diggers like digging ditches?" Bara had retorted to Olga Petrova when the latter asked if she missed moviemaking.

Maybe this is why she made so few movies in the Twenties, and the ones she did were one-shot deals. She was unwilling to subject herself again to the studio system grinding out movie after movie. She did not want to be just another star in the stable of one studio's system. She was rich, so she didn't have to return to the screen to pay bills. So why should she?

Alternatively, she may have been a prima donna, so full of herself as a top box office star she couldn't bear being anything less. She started as a star, she left as a star; why should she play second fiddle to anyone else? It could be that negotiations for film comebacks fell through when she began making unreasonable demands.

Unlike Theda Bara, those playing supporting roles in *Cleopatra* still had film careers. Fritz Leiber continued to work in films and on stage. He worked again with J. Gordon Edwards, appearing as Louis XI in *If I Were King* (1920) as well as Solomon in *The Queen Of Sheba*. This provided the capital with which he founded his own Shakespearean company. After his company folded in the early 1930s, done in by the Depression, he returned to Hollywood as a character actor in supporting roles, notably as

Fritz Leiber (Author's collection)

Gaspard in *A Tale Of Two Cities* (1935). Other films include *The Story Of Louis Pasteur*, *Anthony Adverse* (both 1936), *The Hunchback Of Notre Dame* (1939), *All This And Heaven Too*, *The Sea Hawk* (both 1940), *The Phantom Of The Opera* (1943), *The Spanish Main* (1945), *Humoresque*, *Angel On My Shoulder* (both 1946), *Monsieur Verdoux* (1947), and *Samson And Delilah* (1949). When Leiber died in 1949, his son Fritz inherited the more than 200 portraits in oil, charcoal, clay and other media of his lookalike father in his many roles, which surrounded him in his cramped home. Becoming

Thurston Hall (Author's collection)

a writer of fantasy and science fiction, Fritz Jr. adapted this disconcerting situation in his 1963 story, '237 Talking Statues, Etc.'

After *Cleopatra*, Thurston Hall continued in movies, getting typecast as a heavy.

"Say, I haven't always been a villain," Hall objected in a 1923 interview, "My stage career was above reproach until now."

"My hobby's acting, I think," Hall added, "I like the quiet little game of cards with Cecil and Bill Farnum when I'm in California. And I'm a model youth off the screen. Don't drink, don't smoke—much. My only fault is a tendency to grow unromantically solid."

Hall had formed his own theatre company in London and toured Africa, Australia and New Zealand, and appeared on Broadway before returning to Hollywood in the 1930s to be a busy character actor. Again, he was typecast in the role of a heavy, usually a crooked politician or businessman. Late in his career, he made the transition to television, appearing in *Maverick* and as Cosmo Topper's boss in *Topper*. He continued acting until his death at the age of 75 in 1958.

J. Gordon Edwards made further use of the actor Herschel Mayall, who appeared with Bara in *The Rose of Blood* and *Madame Du Barry*, as well as Edwards' *Wings of the Morning* (1919), *Drag Harlan*, and *The Scuttlers* (both 1920). Mayall also appeared in *The Queen of Sheba*. He remained a busy character actor, with more than one hundred screen credits, going into the Talkie era. As he got older, his roles got smaller. His last known role as a 'dinner guest' in a 1934 comedy short. Mayall died in 1941.

After *Cleopatra*, Henri De Vries returned to Europe to make movies there and in Britain. Genevieve Blinn appeared in *When A Woman Sins* and *Salome* with Bara and *Queen Of Sheba* with Betty Blythe, as well as a few other films spanning the remainder of the silent era. Dorothy Drake also made more movies, at least two in the sound era. Dell (or Delle) Duncan appeared in a couple more films then disappears. After being Cleopatra's battered messenger, Hector V. Sarno continued in movies as a character actor. His credits include *Cobra* (1924) with Rudolph Valentino, DeMille's *King Of Kings* (1927), *Death Takes A Holiday*, *The Merry Widow*, *Viva Villa!* (all 1934), *The Mark Of Zorro* (1940), and *The Egg And I* (1947).

Albert Roscoe continued in Fox films, occasionally with Theda Bara. One of his most acclaimed roles was that of Uncas in *The Last Of The Mohicans* (1920), with his pal Wallace Beery. It also starred Barbara Bedford as Cora Monroe. Bedford was a fan of Roscoe's, and he became one of hers. They married, later divorced, and, in Hollywood tradition, remarried. In the late 1920s, he changed his name to Alan Roscoe, causing confusion to some film historians, who look at the different names and birthdates and conclude that he was his own brother. Never managing to break through to stardom, Roscoe worked in supporting roles until his untimely death in 1933 (though not as untimely as the reference book that listed Albert dying in 1925, and Alan in 1933). After his death, widow Bedford battled

Art Acord (Author's collection)

Beery in court over Roscoe's insurance policy. Beery claimed to have paid Roscoe's debts and set up a trust fund for his daughter.

Also tragic was the fate of Art Acord, who played Cleopatra's captain of the guard, Kephren. After making *Cleopatra*, he joined the Army. His experience with horses made him an asset to the 144th Field Artillery. Press reports he earned the *Croix de Guerre* for his bravery at the front are false; he probably saw no action. Honorably discharged with no special awards, Acord returned to movies, notably working for Universal. He had found stardom in playing Buffalo Bill in low-budget Westerns. However, his squeaky, high-pitched voice rendered him unemployable in Talkies. His drinking got worse, and his third marriage (to serial queen Louise Lorraine) disintegrated. After an arrest for bootlegging, Acord joined a rodeo in Mexico, where his movies had been especially popular, but he squandered his money on booze and gambling. He ended his days working as a miner, and he was found dead in a Mexican flophouse in January 1931. Rumors circulated that he had been stabbed or died of complications of chronic alcoholism. The cause of death was a massive dose of cyanide ('enough to kill 2500 men... dead before he hit the floor...') and was thought a suicide, but suspicions of murder were never completely eliminated. As suicide was considered shameful, friends likely concocted a story that his involvement with a Mexican official's wife led to him being poisoned or stabbed.

Hollywood had forgotten Acord, but his comrades in arms had not. Los Angeles war veterans and the Legionnaires of El Paso, Texas, chipped in to have his body brought back to be buried with military honors.

Adrian Johnson continued screenwriting, but in 1919, he abruptly left Fox. He wrote for different companies, including for Marion Davies in *April Folly* (1920). In 1920, he was hired by Alliance Studios in London to write scenarios. While in Britain, he advertised his 'how to' books for writing scenarios in *Variety* and other American trade publications.

In 1923, a short article in the *Los Angeles Times* asserted that 'Miss' Johnson "who wrote almost all of Theda Bara's scripts," had "returned to Los Angeles" after more than three years in Europe, where "Miss Johnson wrote scenarios for European productions."

Gender confusion aside, as well as other errors, Johnson had indeed scripted several British and Italian films, three for cinema diva Francesca Bertini. After a few films at Universal, Johnson wrote for smaller production companies. There were various announcements into the 1940s of his stories or scripts being sold, but his days as a major screenwriter ended when he left Fox. On the plus side, in 1926, he wed Margaret Cloud, a Mack Sennett comedienne. Their marriage lasted until Adrian's death in Los Angeles in 1964.

In 1919, Clare West started working for Cecil B. DeMille, notably designing stunning gowns for Gloria Swanson on *Male and Female*, *Why Change your Wife* and *The Affairs of Anatol*.

West noted, "Gloria was wearing the most exotic gowns and wraps she had ever worn. And I'm sure that she could make the most far-fetched creation in the world seem entirely logical."

Knowing movie fans were as fascinated by film fashions as the stars that wore them, DeMille actively promoted West in publicity for his films. Film historians consider her to the first costume designer to gain screen credit, including on epics like DeMille's *The Ten Commandments* and *Manslaughter*. West also designed costumes for *Blood and Sand*, with Rudolph Valentino and Nita Naldi.

Going to Paris to purchase fabric, West returned saying, "The American motion picture has become virtually the dictator of the world's fashions ... Our designers, especially those whose work is reflected on the screen, are months ahead of those of Paris and London."

West even had a cameo as herself in the celebrity-studded comedy *Hollywood* (1923).

Mitchell Leisen, later a costume designer and art director before becoming a noted film director in the 1930s, recalled being a costume assistant under West. Leisen and others found West very difficult to work with and prone to temper tantrums.

"Clare West was the head of wardrobe at the Lasky studio and she wasn't about to have me making anything in her workroom. She stuck me in a little room about 4' by 6' with six seamstresses, and I sweated the whole thing out myself."

When DeMille left Lasky to independently produce, West went to First National, where she was kept busy designing costumes in numerous productions from 1923 to 1925. Among the stars she designed costumes for was Norma Talmadge in *Ashes of Vengeance*, *Song of Love* and *Secrets*, 'The Too Beautiful Girl' Barbara La Marr in *The White Moth*, Colleen Moore in *Flirting with Love* and Constance Talmadge in *The Goldfish*, about which Constance quipped, "They've got me all dolled up like a Christmas Tree."

West also designed for Buster Keaton's *Sherlock Jr.*, most likely creating Kathryn McGuire's gowns in *Hearts and Pearls*, the film within the film. In 1925, West went back to work for DeMille, designing for his *The Golden Bed* and *The Road to Yesterday*. After that, her screen credits end.

In December of that year, *Variety* reported that West was opening her own *modiste* shop in downtown Los Angeles. This apparently did not succeed, as she is listed as a dress designer for a department store in the 1930 census. A decade later, the Los Angeles City Directory listed her as a designer of Patricia Perkins, Inc., which made ladies' evening wear. Then she disappeared.

"I was intrigued by the abrupt end in 1926 to the career of Clare West," wrote Jay Jorgensen, researching a book on fashion in film with co-author Donald L. Scoggins. "It took a lot of detective work, ... but we discovered that she had a rather inglorious end." Most of West's family had died, but Jorgensen and Scroggins tracked down two of her grandchildren.

"With their help, we learned that West was bi-polar and that it wreaked havoc in both her professional and personal lives."

Living in seclusion in a trailer park in Ontario, California, West died of natural causes in 1961.

Film historians have neglected West. Her work on *Cleopatra* was forgotten, and her creations have sometimes been credited to other designers such as Mitchell Leisen and George James Hopkins. Having fallen into obscurity in her lifetime, Clare West, the first Hollywood costume designer to receive screen credit, was inducted into the Costume Designers Guild Hall of Fame in 2003.

George James Hopkins' friendship with Bara helped launched him on a very successful career as a designer. He eventually abandoning costuming to focus on set design and interior decorating, becoming top in the field. Nominated thirteen times for Academy Awards for Art Direction (today designated Production Design), Hopkins won for *A Streetcar Named Desire* (1951), *My Fair Lady* (1964), *Who's Afraid of Virginia Woolf?* (1966) and *Hello, Dolly!* (1969). He died in 1985, and his 1981 autobiography, *Caught in the Act*, remains unpublished.

After his promotional work on *Cleopatra*, Edward Bernays joined the CPI, promoting the American war effort. Like George Creel, Bernays disliked the term 'propaganda', preferring 'public relations.' Postwar, he "had a professional encounter with Samuel Goldwyn, who reminded me of a salesman in a perpetual rush, never stopping to resolve the situation at hand."

"Several months' work with the movies thoroughly disillusioned me," Bernays concluded, "I decided this was no world I wanted to associate myself with permanently. It was a crude, crass, manufacturing business, run by crude, crass men. I have continued to enjoy the movies occasionally as a spectator only."

In the 1920s, Bernays published a book, *Crystallizing Public Opinion* and styled himself as a 'public relations counsel', serving corporations in various promotional activities. Wanting to increase their customer base by increasing the number of women smokers, the American Tobacco Company hired Bernays to eliminate the taboo against women smoking cigarettes in public. As part of his campaign, Bernays hired models to smoke in a women's rights parade in 1929, lighting their 'torches of freedom.'

When the 20th Century-Fox version of *Cleopatra* came out in 1963, Bernays noted nothing had changed "in the motion picture field since I handled Theda Bara in *Cleopatra* . . .

"I don't think the attitude of the motion-picture companies toward the exploitation of sex has changed since that time. They still seem to be just as ready to exploit lust, voluptuousness and sensuousness; only their methods have changed."

Today, Bernays is called 'the father of public relations.'

In October 1917, Fox studios donated four camels it had bought for *Cleopatra* to the Los Angeles Griffith Park Zoo, with the proviso the studio could borrow the camels back for future pictures. This gave the underfunded, animal-sparse zoo some valuable creatures while relieving Fox of the responsibility of caring for the beasts. One of the camels was Topsy, who was borrowed back occasionally to do film work at Fox and other studios. She may have been the Bactrian that bore Theda Bara on her back in *Salome* and Betty Blythe in *The Queen of Sheba*. As she got older, Topsy was hired out less often, but maintained her queenly dignity as an army veteran, western pioneer, former circus performer, fading movie star, and the zoo's most popular resident throughout the 1920s.

"From comfortable quarters in old Griffith Park . . . old Topsy, a veteran Bactrian, watches the visitors go by," wrote the *Baltimore Sun* in 1931. "She observes them with an eye of tolerance, having seen much and traveled far in a colorful and eventful career."

Finally, having lost all her teeth and being crippled from arthritis, Topsy was put down by zoo officials in 1934. In an unusual move, her ashes were sent to Quartzsite, Arizona, where they were interred alongside her old acquaintance, 'Hi Jolly,' who had died there in 1902. In 1955, the Arizona Highway Department put up a monument honoring their service in the

Camel Corps. Estimates of Topsy's age at the time of death range from 81 to more than 100 years; unusual, but camels can be long-lived in captivity. Then again, it is possible she had been born to one of the original Army camels after they had arrived in America, or had been one of a contingent of Bactrians that had been imported from Siberia in the 1870s. Like most Hollywood celebrities, Topsy never revealed her real age and publicists weren't above embellishing her resume.

***

"For more than thirty years, I avoided carrying a watch," William Fox once said. "I never wanted to know what time it was. My day ended when my day's work was completed. Again and again I did not go to bed at all during the twenty-four hours."

He went on to say, "I have always bragged of the fact that no second of those contained in the twenty-four hours ever passed but that the name of William Fox was on the screen, being exhibited in some theatre in some part of the world."

While Fox was a slave-driver, he drove no one harder than himself, ending up twice a year in a sanitarium for a 'rest cure.' Even golfing, he was driven to compete, placing bets on each hole. Gripped by a kind of siege mentality, he preferred to remain locked in his office with the shades drawn and plainclothes guards outside the door. He liked people to refer to him as 'The Fox' (he also referred to himself in the third person as the Fox) while insisting all, including his family, call him 'W.F.' to his face. He was quick to take offense at the smallest slight, and the only person he trusted was his wife Eva.

"The only way I could ever be with my husband was to go and be a slave with him," she recalled. "We hardly ever got home from the studio before three o'clock in the morning, and the canary bird in our home adjusted its hours and sang for us at whatever hour we returned."

In revenge against the poverty of his youth, he never carried anything smaller than a one hundred dollar bill in his wallet. He put together a priceless art collection, which included works of Reubens, Gainsborough, Van Dyck and Tintoretto to decorate his Park Avenue apartment and his Long Island mansion, grandly named Fox Hall.

He wanted his name, even one tabbed on him by immigration authorities, to live on in other ways. His wife bore daughters, but no sons, but that did not deter Fox. He married his daughters off to husbands of his choosing (both Fox employees) bided his time until they gave birth to grandsons. The fathers of his grandsons were then dumped via quickie divorces, and the grandsons, brought into the Fox household, were re-named Fox. Legend (false of course) had it one unfortunate victim was so shocked at arriving home and finding wife and children gone that he dropped dead of a heart attack.

"William Fox?" Martin Quigley Jr. former publisher of the *Motion Picture Herald* recalled, "He was the one no one liked."

Others were stronger in the statements, such as actor John Gilbert, who reluctantly signed a contract with Fox in 1921.

"Fox doesn't have a friend in the world, because he's mean, cheap, vulgar and he's notorious for breaking his word. He's a fifth-grade dropout with an absolute contempt for education ... He said, 'Why should I read a book when I can buy the bum who wrote it?' To him, a man like Gouverneur Morris is a bum, who can be bought and then discarded. I don't know how I am going to stand it."

At a Jewish charity fundraiser at the Waldorf-Astoria Hotel, "one of those hundred-dollar-plate dinners" according to Glendon Allvine, Fox was 'trapped' into making an exorbitant pledge. As the campaign manager appealed for pledges, a spotlight was focused on Fox. Although he hated being singled out, he rose and promised $150,000, receiving an ovation. Afterwards, he reneged.

"If your word is no good, how can you expect people to trust you?" someone dared to ask him, "Outside of your family and your golfing companions, you have very few friends."

"What do I need friends for when I am sitting on my money bags?" Fox retorted.

Fox didn't care if he was widely disliked. He carried life insurance policies totaling $6,400,000, saying, "I think I can say that if nobody else grieves my passing I can at least depend upon the president of every large insurance company in the world."

"William Fox was dour and pugnacious, and many think he was the most greedily ambitious of all the moguls," observed Norman Zierold, "And yet Adolph Zukor, the Warners, Nicholas Schenck, and others all played the power game with equal savagery ...[Fox] was poor at public relations, hating to be interviewed or have his picture taken ...

"Few knew of his lavish bequests to artistic and charitable organizations, or of the fact that he dearly loved his many employees and readily gave expensive watches as gifts. Forgotten were his pioneering contributions to the film industry."

Fox preferred being a loner and worked in self-imposed isolation. Aside from golf, the only game he played was hardball. When a critic gave a bad review to a prestigious Fox picture, Fox pulled all advertising from the critic's newspaper. Other studios followed his example, and the loss of advertising helped push the paper into being sold off. When the *Dearborn Independent*, an antisemitic newspaper owned by automobile tycoon Henry Ford, began to run a series of articles critical of Fox, Fox responded by threatening to produce newsreels questioning the safety of Ford cars, and with the massive Fox theater chain and distribution, he could make sure millions saw the films. The articles were dropped and the antisemitism of the paper toned down temporarily. When his niece Angela was sent before him to get stern lecture after beating up a schoolmate in a schoolyard brawl, he looked at her, gave her a $100 bill and told her, "Don't let anybody push you around."

His original success had been based on Theda Bara's vamping, so William Fox tried to grab the public's attention with other 'vamp' stars, but never could find a replacement for Theda Bara. In 1922, Fox remade *A Fool There Was* starring Estelle Taylor, but it flopped. Despite tight finances, Fox kept expanding. In 1923, he bought up 450 acres on the west side of Los Angeles, which he named Fox Hills, and began building new studios. On August 29, 1926, the public was invited to the grand opening of the 'Greatest Outdoor Studio' on the developed 150 acres.

After operating the first few years in the red, Fox newsreels had forged ahead and become a regular part of the moviegoing fare. By 1922, Fox newsreel cameramen were filming around the globe, from Paris to Tibet, Moscow to New Guinea. The advertising claim 'The Mightiest of All' was on the mark, for by 1924, William Fox was the foremost producer of newsreels in the world.

Although he could pick directors, Fox never developed a knack for picking stars. He never had again another superstar like Theda Bara. Nor did he have as many prestigious productions of his more illustrious rivals MGM or Paramount. In spite of his success with epics *Cleopatra* and *The Queen Of Sheba*, he favored routine but reliable moneymakers like Tom

Mix westerns, and what Glendon Allvine called, "a steady flow of unpretentious, sentimental and folksy pictures ..."

One of his biggest successes was his favorite film, the sentimental tearjerker *Over the Hill to the Poorhouse* (1920), about a humble mother with a ne'er-do-well husband and her grown children who abandon her to poverty. Nevertheless, his studios did produce motion picture classics, including John Ford's Western epic, *The Iron Horse* (1924) and Raoul Walsh's war-pic, *What Price Glory?* (1926). F.W. Murnau's beautiful *Sunrise* (1927) earned the first Oscars for both Outstanding Production and Cinematography, and *Seventh Heaven* (1927), which won the first Photoplay Award, along with the first Academy Awards for Best Director Frank Borzage, Best Actress Janet Gaynor and the Writing Achievement Award to Benjamin Glazer. Winfield Sheehan claimed credit for discovering Gaynor—but he also boasted he discovered Theda Bara, as apparently did everybody at Fox.

"The business of making pictures is unlike anything else, for it is at once an industry and an art," Fox once commented, "Directors are becoming geniuses— players are realizing their art more and more— the public is fully able now to discriminate. It is our hope in our organization to push on, improving as we go. We intend to take advantage of every invention and every idea that will make for better pictures."

William Fox was one of the first to recognize the advantage of sound film while others were dismissing it, refusing to join in the informal agreement among the major studios not to pursue talking pictures. He pushed forward with experiments using synchronized-sound film. He held back until his system was perfected, so Warner Brothers beat him in the history books out by releasing the first major sound feature films, *Don Juan* (1926) and *The Jazz Singer* (1927). Their Vitaphone sound-on-disc system was unreliable and frequently fell out of sync. It was Fox's Movietone, with its sound-on-film system, which proved reliable; so reliable a version of it is still used today.

While Warner Brothers issued their Vitaphone shorts of vaudeville acts (dubbed 'canned Vaudeville' by *Variety*), Fox not only released similar shorts but also brought out Movietone News, the first sound newsreel. Fox believed that sound newsreels would pave the way to public acceptance of sound, help promote his Movietone system, along with promoting William Fox. He scored a coup when he had Charles Lindbergh's takeoff for Paris filmed with sound. That same night (May 20, 1927) Fox had the newsreel projected at the packed Roxy movie palace. When the six thousand people in the audience not only saw but also heard the *Spirit of St. Louis* going up the runway, they 'stood and cheered for ten minutes.' No doubt many of the cheers were for Lindbergh himself, who was still flying across the Atlantic at the moment.

For sound to take hold, it would have to be in feature films, and Fox charged ahead where much of reluctant Hollywood hesitated. After Fox's prestige piece, *Sunrise*, was released with a synchronized music track, he decided all Fox pictures, 'Talker' or silent, would be released with a soundtrack, silent movies with synchronized music. Theaters not wired for sound would as usual provide their own music, but as time went on, this applied to fewer theaters. Fox had already ordered all theaters in his chain switched over to sound. He tore down the glass-roofed silent movie studios and built the largest sound stage called the 'Fox Movietone Studio.' Fox's *In Old Arizona* (1929) was the first feature Talkie produced outdoors and on location. After this success, other studios and exhibitors abandoned sound-on-disc and adopted Movietone.

Fox also experimented with the possibilities of widescreen formats, making *The Big Trail* (1930) in 70mm 'Grandeur Screen.' It was a success, but because of the costly changeover to sound and other reasons, other exhibitors and studios did not adopt the widescreen format. It would take the competition of television two decades later to revive the concept. The young star of *The Big Trail*, a former property man named Marion Morrison, re-named John Wayne, had to wade through a decade of B-Westerns before he finally caught the public's attention in *Stagecoach*.

Television was in its infancy, but Fox saw it as the future.

"The new medium will put a stadium, amusement park, theater and university into every home. The modern home will be built around the television room. Rooms designed by interior decorators will arrange the family in concentric half-circles in front of the television screen."

In 1929, William Fox was head of the largest singly-controlled motion picture organization in the world, owning an international chain of 1,500 theaters, a magnificent distributing system, and he had anticipated the rise of sound film and built giant sound stages on his expanding Hollywood studio lots. His empire was worth $300 million, which he claimed was due to the magical 'three' multiplying his original investment of $16,666.

A combination of events dashed his empire to pieces. It started by a spending spree, buying up Poli theatre chain in New England and half-controlling interest in Britain-Gaumont, an Anglo-French movie concern. He bought Mitchell Cameras, which was the leading camera for the motion picture industry, and he attempted to buy CBS, the leading radio broadcasting network in America, but was rebuffed.

It was his attempt to buy Metro-Goldwyn-Mayer that would be his high-water mark, and fatal misstep. After the death of Marcus Loew, his empire, Loew's Incorporated, which included MGM, seemed up for grabs. There were other sharks circling, such as Adolph Zukor at Paramount and the Warner Brothers, but it was William Fox who successfully cajoled Nicholas Schenck, president of Loew, Inc. into selling. Still believing in the number three, he chose the third day of the third month, March 3, 1929, to announce his acquisition of MGM. Fox also said that his marriage to Eva (maiden name Leo) had been a propitious omen of the Fox joining with the Lion, referring to the mascot of the MGM logo.

'The Fox swallows the Lion,' was how the press put it.

In the April 8, 1929 issue, *Time Magazine* observed, "To the cinema world there came the announcement, last week, that henceforth William Fox, head of Fox Film Corp., would produce only talking pictures. Inasmuch as Talker Fox, through his recent acquisition of Loew's, Inc., had become the Greatest Film Man (succeeding Adolph Zukor, head of Paramount-Famous-Players-Lasky-Corp.) his announcement was widely interpreted as 'dooming' the silent picture. Furthermore, as Mr. Fox also announced that he had secured the services of some 200 'legitimate' actors, stage-directors, dialog writers and dramatists, singers, dancers and musical comedy producers and composers, it was also felt that the entire theatrical world was about to undertake a Hollywood migration. Given tongue, the cinema appeared also to have been given teeth. It had seemingly cast itself for the role of the Wolf, with the silent cinema as the Old Grandmother and the speaking stage as Little Red Riding Hood . . ."

It turned out that the Fox had bitten off more than he could chew. The production head of MGM, Louis B. Mayer, was going to bite back. Mayer had a life history nearly identical to Fox. He had immigrated as a child from Eastern Europe with his Jewish parents, suffered a hard childhood, and quit school at an early age to work. Like Fox, he had bought a run-down movie theater and renovated it into a profitable one, making his fortune in exhibition and distribution before entering film production. He also had a nearly identical personality; work-obsessed, hard-driven, dictatorial, poorly read and anti-intellectual, ruthless and quick-tempered.

"A daughter of mine go to college?" he roared at someone who dared suggest the idea, "Become an *intellectual?*"

When Mayer read about the Loew acquisition, he hit the ceiling. Cursing Schenck as 'Mr. Skunk,' Mayer acted quickly, using his close connections with the Republican administration of President Herbert Hoover to break the deal as an unfair restraint of trade. The anti-trust laws Fox once used to defeat the Patents Company now were being used against him. Fox also tried to court the Hoover administration, but his influence was decidedly ineffective compared with Mayer's. In fact, Fox found himself referred by the White House back to Mayer.

The loner who preferred moneybags to friends invited Mayer over to Fox Hall to talk things out. "It was my job to make him my friend if I could."

Friendship was not on the minds of either of the two ruthless, suspicious movie moguls involved in the high stakes maneuvering on which their very futures in motion pictures depended. Mayer accused Fox of treachery and underhandedness in trying to buy MGM without including him on the deal. Fox admitted that Mayer had not been 'treated properly,' but Mayer refused to get chummy, rebuffing Fox's invitation to call him 'Bill.'

"You must have known that I have moved heaven and earth to prevent this consolidation," Mayer told Fox. "Surely you felt that someone used his influence to have the government change its opinion with reference to these shares. I was responsible."

Fox bought off Mayer with two million dollars and a new contract. Only then did Mayer give the green light, but the damage had been done.

"Now you have given me a difficult task," Mayer said, saying he didn't know how to get the government to reverse its position.

Marcus Loew's son marrying Adolf Zukor's daughter further complicated the deal. To the government, it seemed too much like a political marriage between royal families of allied kingdoms or between mafioso clans; that William Fox was pulling the strings for a takeover of Paramount as well.

Confident he would overcome the remaining obstacles, Fox was on his way to a golf game with Nick Schenck to sew up the deal when his Rolls

Royce collided with a Ford and rolled over, instantly killing his chauffer. Fox was badly injured and bleeding profusely from a head wound, but he crawled out of the car and stood up to test his good right arm, to make sure his golf swing was unimpaired.

His injuries required hospitalization. Legend has it a character actor provided transfusions of Fox's rare blood type, and he was rewarded with a lifetime contract at Fox. While he was in the hospital recuperating, Fox was hit in a crash of a different sort: the Wall Street crash of 1929. It left him dangerously over-extended at a dangerous time. The Loew stock he bought was reduced to half its original value. Fox stock dropped from $119 a share to $1 a share in two days. The millions of dollars worth in loans came due, and the banks refused his pleas for extensions.

The Crash and Depression did enormous damage to the other studios as well, and exhibitors, having just invested heavily in wiring their theaters for sound, were especially hard hit. Thousands of theaters closed. Few were hit as hard as William Fox.

The blows came in rapid succession. A month after the Crash, the United States government moved against both Fox and Warner Brothers, filing suit for restraint of trade. In July of 1931, Judge John C. Knox, in United States District Court, ordered Fox Film Corporation to divest itself of the Loew stock. In 1932, the Chicago Title and Trust Company took over the Fox Theatre Corporation in an equity receivership. Already, William Fox, one of the original movie moguls, had lost his film company. In 1930, he had been teetering on the edge of the abyss when the push came from behind; a palace coup unseated Fox, aided by Winfield Sheehan. (Et tu, Winfield?). Bitter, Fox claimed he had rescued Sheehan from a murder charge.

"In July, 1931, the use of the text 'William Fox Presents' was discontinued on main titles," recalled Glendon Allvine, "and I received word, as director of advertising and publicity, to eliminate William Fox in all copy."

Fox approached Socialist author Upton Sinclair to write the story of his spectacular downfall, promising Sinclair $25,000 for the complete manuscript. It turned out Fox had only wanted to use the threat of publication as a bargaining tool against his enemies. Sinclair published the book anyway, *Upton Sinclair Presents William Fox*, despite Fox's orders to desist presenting him.

"I do not know whether foxes ever run in packs, but I have read about wolves," Sinclair wrote in his book, "and have learned that a wolf is not attacked so long as he is well and strong, and is running at the head of the pack. It is only when something happens to him, that he stumbles and falls, that the other wolves fall upon him and 'merge' him."

Employees at Fox studios were threatened with being fired if caught with Sinclair's book in their possession.

The Fox was down, but not out, and he came up swinging. Since he was contractually bound for five years not to produce any feature films, Fox announced he would make educational movies instead, using the German Tri-Ergon sound-on-film process to which he still owned the American rights. But to the menagerie of 'reptile' lawyers and 'vultures' of Wall Street he believed persecuted him was added a third, the 'octopus' of AT&T, disputing the validity of his Tri-Ergon patents. Fox sued it and the major studios using his system.

Winning his suit in the U.S Supreme Court, publicly Fox assured all he would use the patents 'as an influence for the good.'

In the privacy of his office, he declared, "Now I've got the sonsabitches by the balls, and don't think I won't twist them." He immediately sent out 14,000 warning letters, one to every exhibitor in North America, in an attempt to force his way back into the industry. Alarmed by this, twenty-two weeks after its original decision, the court reversed itself 'in the public interest,' declaring Fox's patents invalid. Fox was out a million dollars in legal fees, and to top it off, the federal government demanded three and a half million in back taxes. The Fox was at last brought down.

Without William Fox at the wheel, the Fox Film Corporation struggled under indecisive and continually changing management, its expensive studio cranking out box office duds, the Academy Award-winning *Cavalcade* being an exception. The studio kept afloat mainly through the homespun movies of Will Rogers and the antics of an adorable moppet named Shirley Temple. Fox Film was on the verge of bankruptcy and ripe for takeover. The latter came in 1935, when it was merged with the vibrant newcomer, Twentieth Century Pictures, started in 1933 by Darryl Zanuck and Joseph Schenck (brother of Mr. Skunk).

"It was a lopsided merger," commented Glendon Allvine, "like Mickey Mouse swallowing Dumbo, for Twentieth Century Productions had only the residual value of about twenty pictures produced in two years, no studio, no theatres and no film exchanges at home or abroad, in contrast with the Fox Film world-wide empire worth more than two hundred million dollars. Indeed, practically its only assets weighed in at about 300 pounds on four feet."

Milton Sperling, Winfield Sheehan's executive assistant, witnessed Zanuck's arrival on the Fox studio lot, and compared it with Adolf Hitler's entry into Prague after Germany had seized Czechoslovakia.

"The whole studio was shuddering behind drawn blinds and peering out at the main street of the lot," Sperling recalled. "A cavalcade of black cars came through the main gate and drove slowly around the studio, examining the premises, and we watched those sinister cars, with Zanuck in the leading vehicle, and we said: 'Boom! Now he's going to fire everybody!'"

A lot of heads did roll and many pictures were canceled. Winfield Sheehan, meanwhile, glided away with a 'golden parachute' of half a million dollars. Remaining Fox executive Sidney Kent urged the name of the new company be Fox Twentieth Century Films, but Schenck and Zanuck insisted it be called Twentieth Century-Fox.

For William Fox, the blows kept coming. He had been helpless as he vainly tried to stop the takeover of Fox films by Twentieth Century. In the end, he could not even save himself as he was swept under by litigation. Before the fall, his personal worth had been estimated at $100 million, ruling an empire worth $300 million. Filing for personal bankruptcy, William Fox listed his assets at $100, and his liabilities at $9,935,261. It was June 1936. The number 'three' had turned against him.

His shady dealings caught up with him when he tried to rely on his old Tammany Hall connections. He was caught giving a bribe of $27,500 to U.S. District Court Judge J. Warren Davis presiding over the bankruptcy hearings. Davis and the lawyer acting as go-between got off after two hung juries. However, Fox was found guilty of obstructing justice and defrauding the United States. He was fined $3,000 and sentenced to a year and a day (that's 366 days) in the federal pen.

On May 3, 1943, after serving five months of his sentence, William Fox was released from prison. His loyal wife and daughters welcomed him home, although their Park Avenue apartment was now denuded of its proud art collection, which had been sold off at bargain prices to pay the bills. Fox was 64 and diabetic.

With the spunk of the William Fox of 24, he opened an office in New York, optioned 1,500 acres of land in Los Angeles, and announced he would start a new movie studio. In April 1944, *New York Times* reporter Thomas M. Pryor interviewed Fox, observing that the unfurnished office with a battered telephone table serving as desk was "a far cry from the regal surroundings in which he used to hold press conferences as czar of the world's largest amusement enterprises."

Fox was determined. "I started with nothing and I'm not afraid to try again."

"First," Fox told Pryor, "I think the most important step is to prepare the physical set up of the company."

Innovative as ever, and declaring his film company would be "unique in film history," Fox planned to attract talent with a profit-sharing arrangement.

"Everything in the pictures is on the shoulders of the directors, stars and writers. It is my intention to make pictures on a cooperative basis with each of the integral creative parts participating in the profits of their creations."

Pryor noted that, "This is an arrangement which has been widely talked about in recent years as the coming thing in Hollywood, but only a few top-notch artists hold such contracts."

"Who knows what kind of entertainment people will want next year or two years from now?" pondered Fox. "Personally, I anticipate great changes, not only in subject matter but in production technique."

Fox said he "anticipated no difficulty either from within or without the industry."

No investors responded to his rallying call. In shades of Theda Bara's rumored demise, *The New York Times* printed a retraction after calling him 'the late William Fox.'

"Mr. Fox, former theatrical man, is alive."

Finally broken in spirit and health, Fox entered New York's Doctors Hospital in 1950, besieged by a host of ailments. He lived long enough to see Louis B. Mayer ousted as head of MGM in 1951, if that provided any satisfaction.

One can only wonder how the history of entertainment, of American film, television and the fortunes of Fox Films and MGM would have changed had Fox been successful in his bid to 'swallow the Lion'. His far-sightedness in anticipating television as the future was vastly different from the attitude of the movie moguls of the late 1940s and 1950s. His niece Angela Fox Dunn recalled he spent his lasts days "a frail, diabetic and stroke victim, semi paralyzed for the last year of his life, still grieving over the loss of his dream."

Fox was to linger for more than a year before dying in 1952 at the age of 73 from complications of diabetes and a stroke. On his deathbed, he told his young niece, "Don't ever marry a gentile. Someday he will turn on you and call you a 'dirty Jew.'"

William Fox had risen from the ghetto slum, yet he never completely escaped it.

Not a single representative of the film industry he helped establish bothered to show up at his funeral, but Twentieth Century-Fox did place a trade ad in *Variety* that read in part "His daring, initiative, and courage abled him to make a signal contribution to the growth and development of the motion picture industry …. From the beginnings of his career he engaged in the production of films of magnitude and scope and blazed a trail for the industry in providing box-office attractions of wide popular appeal. He was truly a pioneer in foreseeing the present status of the screen as a medium of popular entertainment."

***

"There is something in the click of the camera as it registers the emotions, foot by foot, that demoralizes artistic expression," a somber Theda Bara had written in 1919.

"One becomes a species of human mechanism, speeding up all the deep sources of feeling, chopping them in bits to fit the inexorable ribbon of reel. It is an art of lies because it is limited to primitive impulses, to barren emotions; because it is a record of the feverish pulse of life, instead of the normal pulse. Everything must be told quickly, briefly, without a fair chance to develop artistic wants.

"These are confessions of intimate disappointment in the work that I have never overcome. It is no one's fault. It is because the movie-actress is a bit of machine-made, not hand-made, art …

"What is any movie studio but a chamber of torture to the girl whose imagination is tainted with the flavor of artistic ideals?" she continued, "I am one of the women who like a great poem better than a poor one; Browning is more comforting to me than the philosophy of George M.

The perfect Hollywood couple. (Courtesy of Robert S. Birchard)

Cohan . . . With the success of *A Fool There Was* I renounced all former expectations of the art of acting. I cut my soul in two. One-half I kept for myself; the other half I gave to movies. I kept the better half."

A superstar at thirty, a has-been at forty, Theda Bara did not suffer the fate of other media meteors unable to cope with the loss of stardom. She did not hit the bottle or end up impoverished. In contrast with other sex symbols, like Clara Bow or Marilyn Monroe, Bara had a very stable childhood and eased into a very stable retirement. Her hubby Brabin continued to work as a successful director until his retirement in 1938. They were a respected Hollywood couple, attending the first Academy Awards dinner. Having once played the role of the notorious Theda Bara, she seemed content to play the role of Mrs. Charles Brabin.

In 1929, Grace Kingsley was at the horse races with friends when they "heard Mr. Brabin call the remote and dignified Theda, 'Tootie,' which made her seem entirely human."

One friend said that she "should never feel the same way about Miss Bara."

"'Imagine calling the incarnation of Cleopatra and Mme. DuBarry 'Tootie'!' another exclaimed, "Well, I've always loved Theda, but I like her even better now. After all, I suppose that maybe Julius Caesar called Cleopatra "Cleo" for short...'"

The Brabins enjoyed traveling extensively in Europe. Once on their return. She responded, "I don't plan to do anything. I only live twenty-four hours a day, getting such happy fragments from life as I can. In this life we suffer so much, we try to find happiness when we can."

"She lives in Beverly Hills and doesn't do anything but luncheons and dinners and that sort of thing," said her sister Lori, who found modest success screenwriting jungle pictures. "Her retirement was on account of her husband, Charles Brabin, the famous director. He's English, you see. You know how they are?"

"The real reason why I left pictures, if you must know, is that I married an Englishman," Theda once said, "Need I say more?"

It was convenient enough as an excuse, but it is likely he discouraged her from seeking movie employment. Biographer Eve Golden suggests he was old-fashioned enough not to want his wife working and she was old-fashioned enough to comply with her husband's wishes. Aside from an occasional stage or radio appearance, she never acted again. It was an advantage female actors had over their male counterparts. Women could get married and retire from the stage or screen no questions asked; men had to keep working or explain why they weren't.

Bara became noted for the superb cuisine at the dinners she hosted. Once, when a star in a play was ordering a mouthwatering gourmet dinner, in the audience film director King Vidor whispered to Ethel Barrymore, "Ah, potluck at Theda Bara's!"

"If you were invited to her home, as I was frequently," wrote Adela Rogers St. Johns, "you would find a hostess who talks wittily, wisely, of music

Mr. and Mrs. Charles Brabin. (Courtesy of Robert S. Birchard)

at the Hollywood Bowl, of new pictures acquired by the Museum, of European capitals and celebrities in every field who are her close friends."

Was this all another façade? Was she simply playing the role of Mrs. Charles Brabin, cultured, refined, a great hostess—in antithesis to her playing the notorious vamp Theda Bara? Or had she really assimilated like her parents had, and become a respectable matron?

And yet—and yet, she couldn't resist playing Theda Bara every now and then. When actress Leatrice Joy naively sought her advice to attract potential boyfriend actor John Gilbert, Bara carefully applied make-up to her face, and then went into full vamp mode, in a parody of her screen persona, adding rouge on Joy's earlobes with a dipped rabbit's foot, purring, "Zis is for the earlobes pulsing vit ze blood of love. Zis means passion. Seething passion."

Joy's horrified mother scrubbed off most of the make-up before her big date, but Gilbert noticed something strange about her ears.

"That's my seething passion!" Joy explained. Gilbert replied that he thought she had an ear infection. They both laughed, and while one hesitates to ascribe Bara's magic to the result, the pair later married.

Screenwriter DeWitt Bodeen remembered one time Bara "visited a Hollywood friend of mine for cocktails. Her chauffeur brought her in the Brabin town car, and was instructed to call for her one hour hence. Promptly, at half past the hour, she peered at her diamond-studded wrist watch through her diamond-rimmed *lorgnette*, and said, 'Theda Bara waits for no man.' A taxi was called, and it arrived simultaneously with her chauffeur tardily at the wheel of her town car. Miss Bara brushed past the chauffeur without so much of a glance, got into the cab and the town car followed that taxi to her home in Beverly Hills."

The childless Brabins had befriended a neighbor, a little girl named Joan Craig, who they invited into their home, which was decorated with various exotic artifacts. Bara went into full mystical character mode, as she had enchanted the future Preston Sturges. Upon learning that Joan's grandfather had recently died, she pulled a purple coverlet from a crystal ball and said, "Let's see if we can find your grandpa here. There are spirits and sometimes they appear there."

Bara explained, "There are all kinds of spirits and sometimes called fairies. There are also guardian angels. Your grandpa may be one of them!"

On other visits Bara would talk about spirits and fairies, assuring Joan that she was the daughter of an artist and a princess, 'born in the shadow of the Sphinx,' and she had been 'weaned on serpent's blood,' even as Joan saw Charles stifling a smile as he stole from the room.

If these astrological charts and other occult paraphernalia were nothing but props from the Fox studios for her vamp image, then what were they doing in her house decades after she left Fox? Although she may have assumed the mantle of American respectability, deep down, Bara remained exotically weird.

Some profiles of the former 'wickedest woman in the world' said she devoted herself to committees of charitable organizations and with being a prominent member in Los Angeles society—the society that had once been so appalled by her presence in their exclusive neighborhood. However, Eve Golden could find no evidence of this. More of Bara's smoke and mirrors?

"What goes on behind those eyes, so unusual in color that I cant tell you myself what color they really are, it is impossible to say," Bara's mother had written, "She lives in a world of her own—imaginary, often filled with strange fantasies, I have no doubt. The soul of any individual is the resting

Theda Bara on Valentine's Day, 1939. (Author's collection)

place of many and varied thoughts—visitors, each one impenetrable and unknowable, except to itself, some of them transients, others life residents."

Bara sold the rights to her life story to Columbia Pictures, but the proposed movie musical, called *The Great Vamp*, with Betty Hutton, was never made. Right up to the time of her death, she advertised herself as being available for movie work, but little suggests that she really wanted to return to the grind of making movies. Poverty forced her into the movies, and she was wealthy enough she never had to go back.

Besides, Bara and Brabin had that rarity in Hollywood; a happy marriage. It lasted the remainder of their lives, and it was so close that she eventually acquired some of his English accent. On birthday cards to Brabin, Bara wrote such endearments as 'To my darling Mouchey-Mou— from your Wiffle Tree.' If a marriage could survive this, it could survive anything. (At least it's unlikely that Brabin ever called Bara 'a dirty Jew.') One can honestly say that they lived happily ever after— or at least until death did them part; Bara first, of stomach cancer in 1955, with loyal Brabin following her two years later.

Late in her life, Theda Bara was philosophical about her career as the original movie vamp.

"To understand those grand days, with the world of movies so new and all, you must consider that people believed what they saw on the screen. Nobody had then destroyed the grand illusion. They thought the stars of the screen were the way they saw them. . . . Now they know it's all just make believe."

When Marilyn Monroe, posed for *LIFE* magazine in a pictorial depicting movie sex goddesses of the past, one set-up included a Bara-esque pose with Monroe wearing a coiled snake bra amid faux-Egyptian splendor, directly touching on Bara's biggest film, *Cleopatra*.

"What am I supposed to be thinking of?" Monroe giggled, bemused, possibly as Bara herself had wondered four decades earlier when posing for her publicity photos.

Nowadays, Theda Bara is mostly regarded as a kind of joke. People stare at her pictures and cannot conceive that a woman of her face and physique could have ever been considered a sex goddess. The phony publicity statements amuse, the few surviving films bewilder rather than beguile. However, late in life, rival Betty Blythe summed up Bara's career with greater appreciation, "She had a world public. She filled a marvelous niche in our business, in her style. The world took it— and demanded her."

If Bara was not the evil woman who vamped in real life, nor the nice girl from Cincinnati victimized by press agents, she remains something of an enigma. Perhaps there was some truth in those sphinx-like photos that depicted her as 'the most mysterious woman living.'

Although the 'Vampire' phenomenon was short-lived, the 'vamp' legacy lives on. The man-devouring temptress-as-destroyer makes an occasional reoccurrence in movies, from Marlene Dietrich in *The Blue Angel* to Sharon Stone in *Basic Instinct*. Mae West's character was very much a satirical version of the silent screen vampire. ("Mae West," Theda Bara once observed, "Ah, there's a real vamp.") The soap opera 'bitch-queen' is a direct descendant of the silent screen vampire. And those notorious publicity photos spawned the idea of what a vampiric *femme fatale* should look like; long dark hair, slinky black dress, exotic eyed— all can be seen in such pseudo-vampires as Vampira, Elvira, Evila and Morticia, right to Hela, the Goddess of Death in *Thor: Ragnarok* (2017). *Femmes fatales* continued to be called 'vampires' until Bela Lugosi in *Dracula* returned the word's meaning to its original nosferatu definition, but 'vamp' remains in the dictionary as both a noun and verb.

Bara was honored for her contribution to motion pictures with a star on the Hollywood's Walk of Fame. In 1993, the US Postal Service issued stamps commemorating silent movie stars with illustrations by Al Hirschfeld. Among those remembered was Bara, hand clasped to brow, emoting again.

It is something of a curiosity that Bara is remembered at all. Hundreds of other stars achieved fame equal to hers but are now almost entirely forgotten. Yet while William Fox is only briefly mentioned, Theda Bara remains in the film history books, and those writing on silent films can barely avoid mentioning her in one way or another, however dismissingly. Her movies made her immortal; somewhat ironically, as few of them managed to survive after her.

CHAPTER THIRTEEN: THE END

Bitten by the asp, Cleopatra goes to her throne to await death. (Author's Collection)

It would be difficult to conduct a tour in southern California of important sites related to the making of the Fox *Cleopatra*. During the century that has passed, Southern California has been engulfed by suburbs, skyscrapers, fast food restaurants and malls.

The Moorish-inspired architecture of Atchison, Topeka & Santa Fe La Grande Station, where Theda Bara first arrived in Los Angeles, was severely damaged in the 1933 Long Beach earthquake. The station's copula was removed and rest of the station was closed in 1939, its services being replaced by the new art deco style Union Station. La Grande station was torn down in 1946.

Once the most luxurious hotel in Los Angeles, the Hotel Alexandria fell on hard times as the downtown was abandoned. It became the haven of prostitutes, drug addicts and others just a step away from Skid Row. Saved from demolition as part of the downtown revival, the Hotel Alexandria now houses apartments.

The mammoth glass studio on the Western Fox lot soldiered on into the 1920s, its glass panes painted over as lighting technology improved. It would serve as a studio until the coming of Talkies, and then it was converted into a storeroom, finally being torn down in June 1943, the metal being scrapped for conversion into "ribs and plates for a Victory ship," or so noted its obituary notice in the *Hollywood Reporter*. The Fox studio at Western and Hollywood did not long survive it. Production had already shifted to the new Fox studio in Culver City in 1924, and by the 1950s, the Western Street studio was gone.

Henry T. Hazard's beautiful gardens, used in the Roman scenes in *Cleopatra*, were bulldozed to oblivion and replaced with housing in what is now called Koreatown. 'Nigger Slough,' which *Motion Picture News* dubbed 'the Nile of California,' became Laguna Dominguez when the Los Angeles Board of Supervisors officially changed its name in 1938. Dominguez channel was dug to drain the wetlands, which become housing tracts in Torrance and Gardenia. The name 'Nigger Slough' was quietly forgotten, though it survives in old maps of Los Angeles.

One would expect the sand dunes of Oxnard, where the desert scenes for *Cleopatra* were filmed, to still exist, but they fell victim of their own notoriety. More desert scenes were filmed there, including *The Sheik* (Paramount, 1921), starring Rudolph Valentino. Consequently, the area became popular with tourists, and then with real estate speculators, who divided up the land for vacation homes. The dunes, which originally drew people there, were swept away as 'Hollywood Beach' and 'the Silver Strand' properties took over. The final blow was the dredging of Channel Islands Harbor, and the dunes are but a memory.

There is no longer any Balboa Bay—no, it wasn't drained or paved over, but the land around it was bought up and built up by progressively wealthier folk, who thought 'Newport Bay' sounded ritzier than Balboa Bay, and

Cartoon showing the spirit of Theda Bara, clad in her infamous Cleopatra outfit, attempting to guide Fatty Arbuckle toward culture and sophistication after he moves into the West Adams home vacated by her. (From the Los Angeles Times, June 16, 1919)

thus more exclusive. All that remains of the original bay where the battle of Actium was fought is a wildlife refuge in the upper bay, visited only by waterfowl and kayakers, possibly gliding over the ghostly timbers of lost war galleys entombed in the mud below.

The Tudor-style house Theda Bara lived in during the filming of *Cleopatra* still exists, a rarity in bulldoze-and-build LA. Bara moved out in 1919 after her contract had expired with Fox (suggesting Fox had rented it for her). At first relieved, her neighbors were appalled when slapstick comedian and party animal Roscoe 'Fatty' Arbuckle next rented the house. He later bought it, saying he needed a reliable place to store his booze during Prohibition. He was obliged to rent out the house amid the scandal and trials related to the death of Virginia Rappe. Next to rent the house was, of all people, Miriam Cooper and Raoul Walsh, and then Joe Schenck and his wife, Norma Talmadge, before the property was finally sold. Today, the house is a residence for seminarians.

There have been a number of 'Cleos' over the years, in a strange progression linked with the major *Cleopatra* films made during the history of film. There was (and still is) the pre-Hollywood Helen Gardner version. The Fox *Cleopatra* was made at the beginning of the rise of the major motion picture studios. The Paramount *Cleopatra* (1934), starring Claudette Colbert, was released at the height of the studio era, and was pure Cecil B. DeMille. Yet DeMille sought inspiration from the Bara version, screening it as he prepared his production (The Fox company lent him the print on the condition it be returned immediately after viewing, belaying hope the print might be lurking about the remaining Paramount archives.) The 1963 Elizabeth Taylor-Richard Burton *Cleopatra* was released during the decline of the major studios—in fact, it was such a financial disaster, it nearly finished off its studio: Twentieth Century-Fox. Contrary to popular belief, it wasn't a box-office bomb; in fact, it was the number one grossing movie release of its year, and one of the top box office movies of the 1960s. Due to studio mismanagement and cost overruns, it simply couldn't possibly earn back the cost of the production. The one chance to make it profitable was to divide it into two movies that could separately earn back the costs; an idea nixed by studio head Darryl F. Zanuck.

Ironically, part of the inspiration for re-making the film had been the fabulous success of the earlier version. The old Adrian Johnson scenario had been carefully pulled out of the files and carefully perused before it was carefully put back in the archives. A whole new script was written from scratch, which was probably for the best. On the other hand, Glendon Allvine commented, "who shall say that Theda Bara's 1917 *Cleopatra*, the script of which President Spyros Skouras commended to Producer Walter Wanger, was not a better commercial venture for Fox than the Elizabeth Taylor fiasco. These *Cleopatra* troubles came after the death of the nineteenth century Fox."

The name 'Fox' continues to live on TV and movie screens around the world in the 21st century, something might have given William Fox in the grave some satisfaction. Fox might be less satisfied with the fate of many of the movies he made during his reign as movie mogul.

After the dawn of the Talkie era, silent films had to endure numerous indignities heaped upon them by Hollywood and the rest of the world. Everything associated with silent films became considered old fashioned and obsolete.

Movies such as *Sunset Boulevard* (Paramount, 1950) and *Singin' In The Rain* (MGM, 1952) ridiculed the silent period. There were TV series called *Fractured Flickers* (1963) and *Silents Please* (1960-61) showed silent features edited down in length to a half an hour (with commercials) bookings on television. The result may have introduced silent films to new audiences, but the narration tacked on was sardonic, dismissive, and ultimately contemptuous.

One problem of exhibition is that silent films were often filmed at least 16 to 18 frames per second (fps) to save on film. That was the minimum speed to run films and avoid the annoying flicker effect. When sound came in, the speed had to be increased to 24 fps necessary for the optical soundtrack to be read smoothly, and this speed became standardized throughout the industry. But when silent films shot at 16 fps were shown on projectors permanently set at 24, the movements of the actors became jerky and sped up— okay for comedies, but took a certain amount of seriousness away from dramas. Some, including Theda Bara, who should have known better, could be fooled into thinking that was how movies originally appeared in theaters in the silent era.

Nowadays, there is a greater effort to run silent films at their proper speed, if the proper speed is known—silent films were shot at anywhere from sixteen to thirty fps. Trying for 'normal' speed can be overdone, as in the case with the comedy, *Tillie's Punctured Romance*, a slapstick farce obviously meant to be projected at a fast speed gets run at slow to its 'natural' pace, effectively killing the comedy. Modern audiences found Mary Pickford's *Dorothy Vernon Of Haddon Hall* (UA, 1924) dull and slow paced when projected at 16 fps, and no wonder: It was filmed at 28 fps.

There came the rise of cable television with a virtually unlimited number of channels, including some dedicated to showcasing old movies, along with the emergence of home video. Studios realized there was money to be made in old films otherwise moldering neglected on archive shelves. However, for many movies made before 1950, and the vast majority of silent films, revival is out of the question. A worse fate than disrespect befell silent films: Most of them have ceased to exist.

So much of human heritage has been lost or exists in fragments. The loss of the libraries of Alexandria, Bagdad and Persepolis wiped out ancient knowledge and literature. That which survived was whatever medieval monks or Arab scholars thought worth copying. Works of art have also been destroyed over the centuries of wars, fires and neglect. Even the Philip Burne-Jones painting that inspired Kipling's poem *The Vampire* is lost, existing only in photos. Motion pictures being a modern art form, little more than a century old, one might ordinarily believe nearly all movies would still be with us today.

A motion picture is something akin to a magical being. A creature of illusion, it is no more than a trick of light and shadow, yet it has the power to capture imaginations and emotions of humans, to make people laugh, weep, tremble in excitement, scream in fear or, for that matter, bore them into slumber. Part of cinematic sorcery was that movies had the power to defy time, to capture a performance for repeat viewing through the years. It was boasted that movie made gave a kind of immortality to those who appeared in them, which would last forever. Instead of movies making them immortal, many motion picture stars outlived the movies in which they had appeared.

Just as magical spirits of legend, motion pictures proved very susceptible to fatal flaws in their creation. Like vampires or fairies that perish when exposed to the sun's rays at dawn, many of these vulnerable entities of light and shadow simply disintegrated. They melted away to nothingness, crumbled to dust, or exploded into flames; all cruelly cheated of the immortality that should have been their birthright.

Prior to the 1950s, motion picture film was composed of cellulose nitrate, more commonly referred to as silver nitrate stock. There were benefits to using this type of stock, but it was highly vulnerable to decomposition if not properly stored. Moreover, silver nitrate is highly flammable under the right conditions, say, while running through a hot projector. The early days of cinema had many instances of projection booth fires. Considering the cramped nickelodeons of the era, it is surprising there weren't more disasters involving loss of life than there were. Once ignited, burning silver nitrate film is almost impossible to extinguish, as it carries its own oxygen supply. The U.S. Navy produced an instructional film showing the hazards of silver nitrate stock. It included a scene depicting a reel of nitrate film burning while underwater. Worse, nitrate stock, while decomposing to goo and then powder, releases gasses susceptible to spontaneous combustion. Improper storage of nitrate film in which inflammable gasses were not vented away led to whole archives being wiped out.

Alla Nazimova as woman threatened by brutish soldiers in Herbert Brenon's acclaimed antiwar movie, War Brides *(1916). Lost film. (Author's collection)*

Fire has been a major destroyer of film since the invention of cinema. In June 1914, fire destroyed practically all of Lubin Manufacturing Company's films stored on its lot in Philadelphia. Among the films wiped out in the blaze was footage of President McKinley and his cabinet at Camp Alger during the Spanish American War, as well as footage of McKinley's ambulance leaving the Expo after he was shot, the funeral of McKinley, as well as other newsreel footage. Also gone were Lubin's early dramatic films, including a production of *Uncle Tom's Cabin*, (1903) directed by Siegmund Lubin, with Lubin himself as Simon Legree. Also gone, Oliver Hardy's film debut, *Outwitting Dad* (1914), and Hobart Bosworth's 1913 version of *The Sea Wolf* (with author Jack London appearing as a sailor). Destroyed as well were the negatives for a number of unreleased new films, which severely hurt the company.

Aside from the financial loss, the loss of the footage "caused Siegmund Lubin many a heart ache which even this stoical business man could not well conceal." according to *Motography*.

Another fire later that year destroyed the Thomas Edison laboratory complex in New Jersey. The New York studio of the Famous Players Film Company burned in September 1915. In July 1920, a fire destroyed a shipping facility containing films of Famous Players-Lasky. In 1922, more than 185,000 feet of film burned on the Universal lot, and in 1924, a vault fire destroyed many Universal negatives. More vault fires occurred in 1928 and 1929. In 1933, a vault fire at Warner Brothers/First National wiped out most of the studio's Vitaphone talkies. Many of these exist only as soundtracks, as the Vitaphone discs were stored separately.

Although spontaneous combustion had not been proven in these early fires, by 1933, the potential of nitrate film to self-ignite was at last understood, and that improperly stored film in under-ventilated vaults could burst in flames.

The new Twentieth Century-Fox organization was looking for a place to store all the Fox films acquired in the merger. Contrary to some reports, these films were not shoved into an old warehouse. In 1934, DeLuxe Laboratories built a supposedly fireproof film storage facility in Little Ferry, New Jersey. It was a massive concrete and brick structure, equipped with steel doors to keep fire out of the forty-two individual film vaults. However, it had no sprinkler system to stop the spread of fire. Most ominous of all, there was no mechanical ventilating system to reduce the possibility of explosive gasses accumulating around decomposing film. In a policy akin to keeping all of one's eggs in one basket, all of the original camera negatives, the fine grain prints; in fact, most of the films produced by the Fox Film Company were stored there and forgotten as the lords of Twentieth Century-Fox pursued making their own legacy. The building was less a protective vault than a bomb waiting to go off.

In the summer of 1937, New Jersey experienced a heat wave with temperatures rising into the triple digits. The stifling heat contributed to the decomposition of the stored film and the build-up of combustible gasses. On July 27, between 2 and 3 AM, the gasses self-ignited and film vaults exploded into an inferno. One nearby resident was killed and others were injured. Firefighters were able to contain the blaze, but the fire incinerated all the film in the building, wiping out the cinema legacy of the Fox Film Company. Nothing was left of more than 40,000 reels of negatives and film prints besides ashes inside the film cans. Twentieth Century-Fox valued the ashes more than it had the films; the ashes in each reel can were worth 5¢ of silver that could be salvaged. The company recouped about $2,000 from the fifty-seven truckloads of incinerated movies.

That was not the end of *Cleopatra*. Some Fox films found a refuge. In a press release dated December 3, 1935, the Museum of Modern Art (MOMA) in New York announced "The 'Vamp' and Mickey Mouse" would be added to its new collection of films. Walt Disney contributed a number of his pioneering animated shorts, including the first Mickey

Valeska Suratt as Ayesha, She-Who-Must-Be-Obeyed in the Fox 1917 version of She. *None of the eleven movies Suratt made still exist. (Author's collection)*

Mouse cartoons. MOMA also received the LeRoy Collection of photos, documents and manuscripts related to the earliest days of cinema. Included were more than 350 films, both American and foreign, "all of them rare and many extremely important as landmarks in the development of motion pictures." Included were films of Georges Méliès and *The Execution of Mary, Queen of Scots* (Edison, 1895).

From its acquisition of the Fox archive, Twentieth Century-Fox donated to the MOMA film library thirteen films made between 1916 and 1933. Among them were three starring Theda Bara; *A Fool There Was*, *Carmen*, and *Cleopatra*. Other donated films included *A Daughter of the Gods*,

Sunrise, and a number of Westerns, *Riders of the Purple Sage* (1918), *Sky High* (1921) with Tom Mix, John Ford's *The Iron Horse* and *Three Bad Men* (1926). There was also a Fox Movietone newsreel featuring Benito Mussolini and George Bernard Shaw, a comedy short, *The Sex Life of the Polyp* (1928), written and performed by Robert Benchley, and prints of not only *Cavalcade* but a filmed version of the original London stage production of *Cavalcade*. Twentieth Century-Fox followed up with more donations of Fox films, including the Bara version of *Salome*. Additional movies promised to MOMA perished in the Little Ferry blaze. So the films at MOMA should have survived.

However, even at a film library dedicated to preserving motion pictures there can be negligence. In the 1940s and 1950s, vault fires destroyed at least some of these films; others were lost due to decomposition. One source suggests that two-thirds of the collection ended up destroyed. This included the Theda Bara movies stored there, including *Cleopatra*.

Even that might not have been the end of *Cleopatra*. Often movie stars had enough pull to get prints of their films from their studios, and Bara owned prints of at least some of her movies.

"Theda described to us the filming of *Cleopatra*," Joan Craig, Bara's young neighbor, recalled in her memoir about Bara, "I was invited into Theda's house to view the movie *Cleopatra*."

Bara and Charles Brabin stored their film collection in the basement of their Beverly Hills house.

"This was to be a big moment, and Theda was very excited," Joan remembered, "She wanted this to be the very first movie I would see. Uncle Charlie carefully removed the reel from its canister, placed it on the projector, and flipped the switch. Very quickly there was a puff of smoke! On the screen was a blotch that kept getting bigger and bigger. The projector kept turning and Uncle Charlie immediately turned off the switch."

The reels of *Cleopatra* had deteriorated to the point they could not run through the projector.

"Theda screamed in despair, 'This is karma! There is nothing left of my work!'" Joan remembered, "She went to her room and would not come out for days. Uncle Charlie was very sad and concerned. He brought up the other reels from the basement. One by one he opened them and he said that they were all unusable."

Serial queen Ruth Roland was the heroine of many movie adventures. Few survive. (Author's collection)

Brabin conducted a search for any other prints of the films, but none could be found.

"Theda would lament the loss of her films for the rest of her life."

Such was the case of many other stars and their film archives. Ruth Roland was a serial queen whose popularity nearly equaled Pearl White's. She kept copies of her films in an underground vault at on her property.

However, after the plucky heroine succumbed to cancer, no one stepped forward to preserve her films. When the vault was finally discovered, it was too late for the rolls of film that had simply disintegrated on the shelves.

As one of the most successful film comedians, Harold Lloyd was rich enough to have copies of all his films. In 1943, a fire tore through his personal vault, wiping out his collection, including his Lonesome Luke series and the original camera negative of *Safety Last!* Fortunately, his films from the 1920s had back up prints, but much of his work in the 1910s remains lost.

Sometimes movie stars knew they could not properly care for the films themselves and donated their movies to archives. As seen, archives were often no safer that Beverly Hills basements. Colleen Moore started in movies at the age of 17, appeared as leading lady in a number of Tom Mix oaters. Her career zoomed into superstardom when she bobbed her hair and became the quintessential flapper, starting with *Flaming Youth* (1923), the movie that virtually started the flapper craze in the movies. For the rest of the Twenties, she was a top box office star in Hollywood. Charles Brabin directed her personal favorite of her films, *So Big* (1924).

"*Flaming Youth* proved that Colleen Moore is an actress of talent," noted one reviewer, "*So Big* confirms the fact."

About half of her films are now lost. Only fragments of *Flaming Youth* survive, and only a trailer of *So Big*. Moore donated prints of movies she had made for First National to MOMA, where, neglected, they decomposed.

It wasn't just MOMA; other archives were equally negligent.

Hollywood is awash in dough; there should have been enough money to preserve movies at the studios, right? The studios maintained a callous disregard for their film vaults. In the 1950s, a vault fire at RKO destroyed the original negatives for *Citizen Kane* and *King Kong*. Fortunately, prints survive of these films, but other RKO titles are believed to be completely lost. These include Herbert Brenon's antiwar talkie, *Case of the Sgt. Grischa* (1930), *Freckles* (1935), pre-code sex comedy drama *White Shoulders* (1931), the Western *West of the Pecos* (1934) and some early musicals, such as *Leathernecking*, *Hit the Deck* (both 1930), and the Technicolor *The Runaround* (1931). The last survives in a black and white version with the musical numbers removed. RKO's pre-Code horror film *The Monkey's Paw* (1933), directed by Ernest B. Schoedsack, survives only in a French dubbed version, found in 2016.

Goldwyn's The Slim Princess *(1920) with Mabel Normand (on floor). Lost film. (Author's collection)*

Another devastating fire struck in 1965, when an electrical fire ignited gasses in MGM's Vault #7. One person was killed, and the blaze annihilated 1,912 pre-1924 films, made by Metro Pictures, Goldwyn Pictures, and Louis B. Mayer Productions before the merger creating MGM. The destroyed included nearly all the Metro films starring Olga Petrova, four of the six movies Mabel Normand made for the Goldwyn Company, *The Glorious Adventure* (1918) starring Mae Marsh, and *The Divorcee* (1919), starring Ethel Barrymore in her last silent film appearance. Also burned were *The Divine Woman,* starring Greta Garbo, *The Actress* (1928) starring Norma Shearer, and the part-Technicolor *So This Is Marriage?* (1924). The fire also claimed the Lon Chaney films *A Blind Bargain* (1922), *London After Midnight* (1927) and *The Big City* (1928). Among others that perished was the last known print of the all-Technicolor musical-drama *The Rogue Song* (1930). Also destroyed were numerous cartoons, shorts and other films, pre-1951 MGM cartoons, most notably the *Tom and Jerry* series and Tex Avery shorts, some of which only survive in edited down re-issue prints. Also lost are a complete version of a Laurel and Hardy short, *Blotto* (1930), and *Jail Birds of Paradise* (1934), a comedy short featuring two of the Three Stooges.

Although incredibly negligent, MGM and Twentieth Century–Fox weren't as ruthless as Universal Studios. After its founder Carl Laemmle was ousted, the new overlords of Universal concluded in 1948 to skip the middleman of an accidental fire. With only an eye at the bottom line, the studio sold nearly its entire inventory of pre-1928 films, prints and negatives, for the few dollars worth of silver that could be recovered scrapping the film. Frances Goldwyn ordered her husband Samuel's silent films destroyed because she believed they had no value. She kept *The Winning of Barbara Worth* (1926) because it starred Gary Cooper.

Most losses weren't deliberate. Some studios, like Paramount and MGM, where prints and negatives of some classic films disappeared in a few vaults fires or were allowed to disintegrate, still had many films surviving in their vaults. For these studios, it could be asked what has gone missing. In contrast, in the case of Fox and Universal, where the destruction of everything in the vaults was almost total, the question was what, if anything, has survived. The answer is whatever few prints of film that happened not to be in studio vaults when the destruction occurred. The fire at Little Ferry did not spur preservation at Twentieth-Century Fox; instead old films suffered neglect. When they did act to preserve, it was often too late. Twentieth Century-Fox turned a warehouse full of surviving old films over to an archive. The archivist sent to examine the contents found the warehouse walls cracked open, the roof falling in, and shelves of film rotting beyond salvation. Furthermore, there were not enough funds available to preserve what little remained intact.

Sometimes the destruction was deliberate. When Dennis Stanfill became chairman of the board of Twentieth Century-Fox and closed its New York headquarters, he had its story files burned, including those dating back to the William Fox era. He ignored the pleas of subordinates that the files be donated to some university or library. It is likely that among the papers destroyed were those relating to the films of J. Gordon Edwards and Theda Bara.

The cinema legacy of William Fox (and Fox Film after Fox) has been nearly obliterated. William Fox produced about 1200 silent features and only about 120 are thought to still survive, most of these from the 1920s. The few remaining Fox films seem like the dazed survivors of a shipwreck straggling in on a lonely beach, looking back for additional survivors and seeing only empty ocean.

The massive loss of his films prevents a proper evaluation of the reign of Fox. That, and the disregard of silent films in general, those writing on Hollywood tend to be dismissive of the William Fox era, even treating it with contempt. They find only the films of Twentieth Century-Fox are worth discussing. Ethan Mordden, in his book *The Hollywood Studios*, gives a glowing appraisal of the Zanuck era, but disdains "Fox Film, an Old Hollywood firm run by mogul William Fox on a medium-size budget with mostly second-rank stars and a conservative aesthetic. A successful studio: not an important one."

As film historian Aubrey Solomon noted, "The majority of surviving pre-merger Fox films, with the exception of *Sunrise*, is rarely exhibited in any format and is seldom re-evaluated."

Gone were all the Fox films made by Betty Nansen, Nance O'Neil, George Walsh, Evelyn Nesbit, and Pearl White. All of the films Valeska Suratt ever made, eleven in all, were destroyed. June Caprice made sixteen films for Fox; none survive. Virginia Pearson's Fox films were wiped out, save for *When False Tongues Speak* (1918), hiding in a foreign archive. *The Stain* and *Impossible Catherine* (1919) she made for Pathé, also survive, as well as her some non-starring roles in films made in the 1920s. None of Madlaine Traverse's Fox films survive, but some of her non-Fox (and non-starring) films exist. Only twelve of Tom Mix's eighty-five westerns made for Fox survive in their original-release versions. Anthony Slide considers Gladys Brockwell to have been an excellent actress who was underappreciated at Fox. Only one of her starring films at Fox, *The Devil's Wheel* (1918), survives for evaluation.

Most of William Farnum's Fox films are lost, yet he is reasonably represented in extant films. In addition to three movies he made with J. Gordon Edwards, there is Frank Lloyd's *A Tale of Two Cities*, as well as their *Les Misérables*, which has two surviving prints in foreign archives. Whether the money can be raised to restore them before they disintegrate is unknown. A Brazilian archive has Farnum's *Samson* (1915).

Gone too are the Balboa Films which Fox had distributed. Also destroyed was the original negative for D.W. Griffith's *Way Down East*, which Fox had purchased, along with the rights to remake the film, a number of negatives for Buster Keaton's early films and a number of Educational comedies Fox distributed. Gone are most of the Fox comedies, only a random few survive. A smattering of Fox's Mutt and Jeff cartoons survive.

Of the more than forty movies Theda Bara made, few survive. All of her non-Fox films survive in one form or another: Pathé's *The Stain*, Chadwick's *The Unchastened Woman* and the two Hal Roach shorts. Only two of her films at Fox still exist. One is a heavily censored version of *A Fool There Was*, missing several scenes, including the initial seduction of Schuyler and other incidents described by reviewers, along with whatever shots existed of Bara in the one-piece swimsuit. No other of her Fox films were known to survive until a 16mm print of the non-vamp tearjerker *East Lynne* was discovered in 1971, somewhat ironically, because if anyone generated a list of some forty sought-after Bara films in order of desirability, *East Lynne* would have been at the bottom of the list.

"Though *East Lynne* received good reviews at the time," observed Merrill T. McCord, "viewing the surviving print of the picture today leads to the conclusion that it is one of the worst, if not the worst, of Miss Bara's Fox productions. The depressing, illogical, confusing story by Fox Film with numerous night exterior and dark interior scenes, poor editing, and the lack of badly needed intertitles to explain what was going on at times . . ."

The discovery of *East Lynne* did not enhance Bara's reputation, save that her performance in a non-vamp role did not seem any better or worse than most movie actresses of the time. Aside from these two films and her non-Fox films, plus a few clips of newsreel, the film record of Theda Bara, one of the biggest silent movie stars, has been virtually obliterated. Neither separately nor all together can the surviving films be said to represent Bara's work at the height of her career. Even though they had helped build the foundation of the Fox film empire, all else that remains of Bara's life's work are tantalizing production stills, hinting of the glorious films that once were, and those notorious publicity photos of her posed with deadly intent.

Having worked solely at Fox, J. Gordon Edwards also has suffered from the holocaust at Little Ferry. Of the fifty-four movies Edwards made, four survive. Three are William Farnum films, *If I Were King*, *Drag Harlan* (both 1920) and *His Greatest Sacrifice* (1921). One of Edwards' last films, (and first American film of Bela Lugosi), *The Silent Command* (1923), exists. Not one of the movies Edwards made with Theda Bara survives. Also lost is *The Queen Of Sheba*, with little hope for it ever being found.

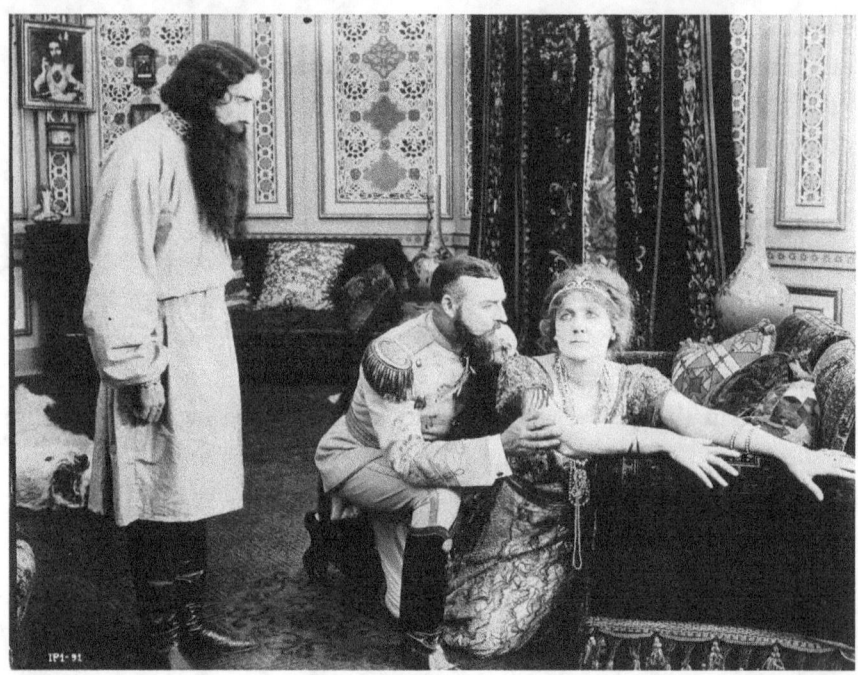

Herbert Brenon's The Fall of the Romanoffs *(1917), made just after the Tsar's abdication. With Alfred Hickman as Tsar Nicholas II, Nance O'Neil as Empress Alexandra and Edward Connelly as Rasputin. Lost Film. (Author's collection)*

Betty Blythe told Kevin Brownlow, "Now I just carry in my heart the love of this beautiful thing— *The Queen Of Sheba*."

Edwards' only other legacy is that he was the father of stage director and film production manager Jack McEdwards, who was the stepfather of writer-producer-director Blake Edwards.

Herbert Brenon, a director once as influential as Griffith, Ince and DeMille, also has few films to demonstrate his work, mostly from the 1920s. Of his four Theda Bara movies, in which he also appeared as an actor, none survive, and the loss of much of his early film work makes it hard to put his career and artistry in perspective.

Raoul Walsh, whose directing career lasted into the 1960s, made two Bara movies. Neither *The Serpent* nor *Carmen* survive. Most of his silent output has also been lost, but his first film for Fox, *Regeneration*, has been found, though some scenes are severely decayed. Other films for Fox in the 1910s including his acclaimed *The Honor System* and his controversial *The Prussian Cur*, remain missing. Some of the films he made for Fox in the 1920s survive, but not all.

Other studios also suffered serious losses. Paramount produced some 1200 silent features, but neglectfully allowed much of these to rot away on their vault shelves. By the late 1960s, only about 250 survived. For a time, Marguerite Clark was second only to Mary Pickford in popularity. Of the movies she made, only four survive, including *Silks and Satins* and *Snow White* (both 1916), the latter inspired Walt Disney to make his version of the tale. The library of Warner Brothers silents is just as depressing.

Things were even worse at production companies that went out of business. Their films were scrapped, thrown away or left to decay in whatever storage was given to them. Thanhouser Company and its succeeding company, Mutual's Thanhouser Film Corporation, was a leading film producer from 1909 to 1918. Shaken by the death of their chief drawing star Florence LaBadie in a car accident and by declining box office revenues, the company closed shop. Of the more than one thousand movies Thanhouser produced, only 187 are known to survive.

The films of such major companies such as Vitagraph, Kalem, Lubin and Selig, four members of the Trust, are represented by a scant list of surviving films. Essanay is best known for the comedies Chaplin made while with that company— and that will likely be all it is known for, for besides the Chaplin shorts, few other films it produced still survive.

Overseas, the news is no better. Unable to compete with the output of other studios, Georges Méliès ceased production by the start of WWI, and the French government appropriated his main studio as a military hospital. The army confiscated over four hundred Méliès original film prints, melting them down to recover the silver content, and used the celluloid to make boot heels for the troops. Financially ruined, his studio taken over by Pathé, Méliès in a fit of pique burned all of the negatives of his films, along with costumes and props. Of Méliès' five hundred productions, only about two hundred survive in one form or another.

Producer Leon Popescu, one of the pioneers of Romanian cinema, despondent over the financial failure of his movies, reportedly burned all his films and then committed suicide in 1918. (Another version of the story says he died of shock after the studio accidentally burned.) In either case, only an incomplete print of his *Independenţa României / The Independence of Romania* (1912) survives as a cultural and national treasure.

Sources differ over how much has been lost. It is commonly stated that fifty percent of all movies made before 1950 and three-quarters of movies made before 1920 no longer exist. Some say that nearly ninety percent of the silent movies are gone. No one knows for certain. That would require knowledge of how many films were made, and how many survive, then do the math. Nobody knows a movie is lost until a search for a particular title yields nothing in the many film archives around the world. They have been lost forever; burned, discarded, scrapped for their silver content, or simply disintegrated in warehouse vaults as the unstable cellulose silver nitrate film decayed the images that once awed and thrilled.

Theda Bara is not the only star whose film works have suffered. King Baggot was one of the first movie stars known to the public by name. He appeared in more than 300 films and directed dozens more; most of these films no longer exist. 'Broncho Billy' Anderson was the first cowboy movie hero, but 'pitifully few' of his films survive to thrill moviegoers of today. Norma Talmadge was one of the most popular leading ladies of the silent era, but few of her movies survive to be seen.

Films with big stars and famous directors are more eagerly sought after than other films. Admirers of Blanche Sweet and Dorothy Gish must grapple with the knowledge that most of their films have been lost. Fans of Clara Bow, of course, want to find some of her missing films, such as *Ladies Of The Mob* (Paramount, 1928), with Bow typed against flapper mode as a gangster's moll. Lon Chaney fans mourn the eradication of his early Universal films and the loss of his MGM films.

Many stars faded into obscurity along with their films, but having famous names associated with a movie did not prove much protection. Such was Rudolph Valentino's appeal and drawing power that several of his silent films continued to be re-released into the sound era, long after his death. Missing are Valentino's performances in *The Sainted Devil* with Nita Naldi and *The Young Rajah*. Most of Naldi's films are also missing, including *What Price Beauty?* (Pathé, 1928) which featured a young Myrna Loy during her 'vamp' period. Film historians probably regret more the loss of one of Naldi's European movies, *The Mountain Eagle* AKA *Fear O'God* (UK, 1925), which was Alfred Hitchcock's second directorial effort. The works of acclaimed directors to have suffered. George Loane Tucker directed *Traffic In Souls*, which survives, but none of his other American films survive, including the now-sought-after *The Miracle Man* (Paramount, 1919).

The Sainted Devil *(Paramount, 1924) with Rudolph Valentino and Nita Naldi. Lost film. (Author's collection)*

Critical acclaim is also no guarantee of preservation. Emil Jannings won the first Academy Award for Best Actor for his performances in two Paramount films, *The Last Command* (1928), which still exists, and *The Way Of All Flesh* (1927), which does not. Also gone is another of his great films, *The Patriot* (Paramount, 1928), which was directed by Ernst Lubitsch and received Oscar nominations for Best Picture and Best Director, but this highly praised film exists only in fragments.

If studios made no special effort to preserve movies that were critically praised and financially successful, there seemed even less reason to save box office duds. *The Courtship Of Miles Standish* (Charles Ray, 1923) which had been such a costly flop in its day, it destroyed the career of producer and star Charles Ray. It no longer exists to be given a second opinion. Bad reviews and financial failure can't be the only measure of a film. Some movies that were box office bombs when first released are now considered classics and are virtually required viewing for film students and buffs. What other films, had they survived, would be hailed as masterpieces of cinema by film historians?

Emil Jannings as the mad Tsar Paul trying to hide from assassins in The Patriot. *Lost film. (Author's collection)*

Most lost films weren't masterpieces, of course. *Janice Meredith* (Metro-Goldwyn, 1924), which starred Marion Davies with the comic support of W.C. Fields, was long thought lost when a print was discovered. At the conclusion of one screening, an audience member commented that the film hadn't been lost; it had been in hiding. Yet sometimes films resurface do prove to be treasures. Reginald Barker's *The Italian* (Ince, 1915) and Maurice Tourneur's *The Wishing Ring* (World, 1914), give us a greater appreciation of their work.

Lon Chaney and Edna Tichenor play vampires—that is, the blooddrinking kind, in the highly sought after London After Midnight *(Author's collection)*

Ironies abound. F.W. Murnau, unable to obtain filming rights for *Dracula*, went ahead and filmed *Nosferatu* (Germany, 1922), changing the names of the characters but maintaining the major plot themes of the novel. Bram Stoker's widow sued for copyright infringement and Murnau was ordered to destroy all prints of *Nosferatu*. At least one print escaped, and *Nosferatu* is the most watched of Murnau's films. Of his acclaimed American film, *The Four Devils* (Fox, 1929) both silent and sound versions, nothing remains, incinerated in the Little Ferry fire.

The 1911 version of *Vanity Fair* starring Helen Gardner survives, but not the 1923 version starring Mabel Ballin. Most of D.W. Griffith's 457 Biograph shorts exist in archives in one form or another, but some of the last movies he directed, such as *That Royle Girl* (1926), starring W.C. Fields, no longer exists. The original 1914 *Tillie's Punctured Romance* survives, but the 1928 remake does not.

Not only silent movies were lost. Many early sound features are also missing. *Beggars Of Life* (1928), starring Wallace Beery, Louise Brooks and Richard Arlen and directed by William Wellman, was made in both silent and sound versions, and only the former survives.

When it was understood how much of the cinema legacy was gone, efforts were started to find lost films. In 1980, the American Film Institute announced its 'Ten Most Wanted' list of historically and culturally significant lost films. The Fox *Cleopatra* headed the list that also included *That Royle Girl*, *The Rogue Song*, the Hate-the-Hun film, *The Kaiser: The Beast Of Berlin* (Universal, 1918), an early Walt Disney film, *Little Red Riding Hood* (1922), and the first movie version of *Frankenstein*, made in 1910 by the Thomas Edison Company. Also on the list are Tod Browning's *London After Midnight*, with Lon Chaney in his 'vampire' role, Norma Talmadge in the 1927 version of *Camille*, and Greta Garbo's *The Divine Woman*. Added to the list is the forlorn wish to find an uncut copy of *McTeague* (MGM, 1925), also known as *Greed*, the magnum opus of director Erich von Stroheim—all forty reels of it; eight hours worth. It currently survives only in a severely truncated release version of ten reels at about two hours.

Since the release of AFI's 'wanted list,' two film fugitives have been found; *Little Red Riding Hood* and *Frankenstein*. One reel of *The Divine Woman* turned up in a Moscow film archive, along with three reels of the Talmadge *Camille*, of which an incomplete print reportedly exists. Rumor had it that an uncut version of *McTeague* existed in an Argentine archive. A nearly complete print of Fritz Lang's *Metropolis* (Germany, 1927) was found instead, leading to the near full restoration of that film.

In 2010, the British Film Institute came up with an even more ambitious list of seventy-five titles of 'Most Wanted of missing British films,' which includes not only silent films, but also a substantial number of sound movies. A number of these have been found in complete or semi-complete versions.

Footage missing in one print of a film may be located in another print at another archive. Kevin Brownlow restored Abel Gance's epic *Napoleon* (France, 1927) and Lon Chaney's *The Phantom Of The Opera* (Universal, 1925) by searching archives, movie vaults and private collections to obtain the best available snippets of film to re-assemble these masterpieces. The discovery of a 35mm print of one of Mabel Normand's feature films for Mack Sennett, *Molly O* (1921), in the Russian archive Gosfilmofond, allowed an attempt at a restoration. The third reel and both the opening and closing credits were missing, and the Russians had inexplicably cut out many of the slapstick comedy segments. The missing footage could be replaced with clips from an American 16mm print. *When A Man*

Loves (Warner Brothers, 1927) starring John Barrymore, long considered lost, was also reconstructed using footage from surviving reels at different archives and collections. Even the original Vitaphone musical soundtrack was restored.

In the case of one Mary Pickford feature thought to be lost, the elements, which had been disassembled for the tinting process, were discovered in a film laboratory, along with the title cards. Everything was out of order, and it was the American Film Institute's task to reassemble the elements into a cohesive story— and hopefully close to the original continuity. A lot of detective work is sometimes needed to determine what is missing and how it can be replaced.

The 1922 version of *Oliver Twist*, starring Lon Chaney and child star Jackie Coogan, was found in Yugoslavia, but lacking the intertitles. Coogan himself aided in the reconstruction of the lost titles, and again audiences thrilled to a lost treasure. *Anna Christie* (1923) starring Blanche Sweet, was also found in a Yugoslavian archive in the 1970s, and Sweet was still around to help reconstruct the intertitles. As the few veterans of the silent era became even fewer, film restorers must rely increasingly on their own research.

New tools have been employed in the effort to save films. A print of *The Matinee Idol* (1928), one of director Frank Capra's early efforts, was found in the vaults of Cinémathèque Française. It became the first live-action film restored and repaired using a digital process, eliminating scratches and wear marks. Such technical fixes are expensive, and there is little funding for preserving known surviving films, let alone attempting to restore them. Also, for a movie to be restored, there must be some film to start with. Such restorations are harder when movies survive only in fragments, such as only one or two reels out of a six-reel feature. Only three odd reels are known to survive of the 1921 Fox version of *A Connecticut Yankee In King Arthur's Court* starring Harry Myers. It was a hit film in its time. Now Myers is remembered only for his performance as the besotted millionaire in Chaplin's City Lights (United Artists, 1931).

Sadie Thompson (United Artists, 1928), directed by Raoul Walsh and starring Gloria Swanson. existed in nearly complete form, but the last reel was damaged. This last reel was 'reconstructed' using all the available stills and the titles drawn from the continuity script. An attempted restoration of a truncated Laurel and Hardy short using still photographs for the missing scenes lets the viewer know what used to be there, but the experience is more one of regret and sadness than of enjoyment. *London After Midnight* underwent a reconstruction, using nothing but stills and the original script. For my part, I have reconstructed *Cleopatra* on video using more than five hundred surviving stills and a few feet of surviving footage. Outside of one scrap of footage lasting a dozen seconds or so, nothing of *Cleopatra* is known to survive.

This clip has its own tortured history. Discovered by Anthony Slide, he passed it along to James Card, a film preservationist at the George Eastman House film archive. Instead of preserving it as part of the Eastman collection, Card sold it to a film collector, Harold 'Rusty' Casselton. Casselton allowed a video transfer of the clip for the use in the documentary about Theda Bara, *The Woman with the Hungry Eyes* (Timeline, 2006). After Casselton's death, his film collection was broken up, and the fate of the clip is unknown.

In 1978, in Dawson City, Yukon Territory, Canada, a treasure trove of silent movies was discovered in what had been an abandoned swimming pool. They hadn't been stored there, but dumped in the pool in place of more valuable fill dirt after the town's movie theater cleared out its basement; the rest had been thrown in the Yukon River. 533 reels of film were recovered from the pool, but most were too heavily damaged to restore. A few could be preserved and some proved to be lost films, such as *Bliss* (Pathé, 1917), starring Harold Lloyd, and *Polly of the Circus* (Goldwyn, 1917). Along recovered were newsreels with rare footage of historical events, including the infamous 1919 World Series, W.E.B. DuBois at a 1917 civil rights rally, and the destruction caused by the terrorist bombing of the New York Stock Exchange in 1920. In most cases, even when good enough quality reels of were found, the movies were incomplete, as the other reels long since vanished in the river.

A better source of lost films than Klondike swimming pools are foreign film archives. Yet foreign archives were not necessarily safer than American ones. French film preservationist and historian Henri Langlois, co-founder of the Cinémathèque Française, wanted only 'classics' while collecting films for its film library. Thus, he rejected a print of the Bara *Salome*; he didn't regard it as a classic. Although he later regretted his decision, that print of *Salome* had long since vanished. Even if he had taken it, many pre-1937 films were ordered destroyed at Cinémathèque Française by the occupying Nazis, and a 1959 vault fire destroyed a number of films, including the last known print of Erich von Stroheim's The Honeymoon (Paramount, 1930), sequel to The Wedding March (1928).

However, a search at the New Zealand Film Archive turned up many films previously thought lost, including a Fox feature, *Upstream* (1927), directed by John Ford. Also found was a Fox Sunshine comedy short, *Her First Kiss* (1919). A number of other 'missing' Fox films are reportedly at foreign archives, awaiting a benefactor to restore them, hopefully before they disintegrate, as the clock is ticking on that unstable silver nitrate. Most linger neglected because no one is interested in them.

One difficulty in searching for movies is that they were sometimes renamed when being shipped to foreign markets; Bara's *The Vixen* was retitled *The Love Pirate* in the UK and *Il Pirata Dell'Amore* in Italy. In France, *When a Woman Sins* became P*oppéa*, *The Serpent* became *La bête à misère / The Misery Beast*, and *Destruction* became *La ravageuse / The Ravaging*. *Cleopatra* was released in France as *La Reine des Césars / Queen of the Caesars*. What other titles may exist for it in foreign lands?

Another possible source of lost films are movie collectors. Driven by the love of old cinema, they collected movies from various sources. Sometimes, they illegally duplicated and sold copyrighted films. Although indifferent about preserving their films, companies owning the copyrights didn't want anyone else profiting from them, and they relentlessly harried the collectors with legal action. In a raid on actor Roddy McDowall's home, the FBI seized his movie collection, although McDowall merely used the films for private screenings. Yet some of these private archives have yielded up lost films. Film collector and archivist Murray Glass of EM GEE Films saved the sole surviving print of the Kalem *Ben-Hur* among footage being sold for scrap.

Sometimes, the collectors would be like dragons guarding their hoard, refusing to allow films in their vaults to be screened. A collector who owned the only known copy of the Edison *Frankenstein* reportedly wanted a million dollars to sell it. While it was certainly of cultural significance, no one was willing to pony up that amount of dough for it. The film was eventually recovered after the collector's death. Another case is *Beyond the Rocks* (Paramount, 1922), the only film screen legends Gloria Swanson and Rudolph Valentino appeared in together. The film was long lost and Swanson hoped it would one day be found. Long after Swanson's death, a print was discovered in the archive of a private collector in the Netherlands.

Film collectors and film societies often come up against studios heavy-handedly asserting their copyrights, unwilling to share with the general public, because there was no profit in it. Movie buffs were denied screenings, and collectors were subject to criminal charges and FBI raids for their owning copyrighted material such as movie prints. With new technologies allowing for copyright owners to profit from old movies with little expense, the tragedy of lost film has finally hit Hollywood.

While fire has been a major destroyer of film, the main culprit was undoubtedly neglect. Before too much blame is put on the studios for the loss of our film heritage, it must be remembered that audiences themselves rejected silent movies when sound came in. Obsessed with the newfangled innovation, filmgoers ignored silents and ran to the nearest talkie instead. The message to the studios was clear: Silents were not only out; they were never coming back. Film companies, after all, operated for profit. If no one was interested in seeing old movies, how much studio capital was to be expended preserving movies that had little chance of making any return on the investment? Considered worthless, shoving old movies into unventilated warehouses seemed good enough. That these films would later be considered part of our cultural heritage was hardly ever considered. Way back in the 1910s, who would have thought it a good idea that great movies needed to be saved for future generations?

William Fox did. The William Fox so many dismissed as a crass, penny-pinching and greedy businessman with no concern for art.

In December 1916, Fox proposed building a film archive-museum to house the best of American cinema, pledging a million dollars to the project. Vanda Krefft notes, "At personal expense, he commissioned prominent Philadelphia architect John Frederick Harbeson, who drew up plans for a large fortress-like structure made of New England granite and ornamented with huge bronze doors, a sculpted frieze depicting historic events around the world, and broad steps flanked by two giant sphinxes.

"Fox planned that any producer would be able to submit movies with historic value, and each year an expert board of trustees—scientists, historians, and various public leaders—would choose ten for inclusion in the museum's collection. To prevent decomposition, movies would be stored in airtight containers in fireproof vaults. A sixty-by-one hundred-foot

Artist's rendering of William Fox based on photo, making him less stern for a magazine illustration (Author's collection)

projection room would host public screenings, and a library would collect world literature. This would have been the first American institution to recognize the artistic value of film and it would have ensured the preservation of early American movies..."

Fox wanted to build this temple to the muse of cinema in New York's Central Park, but Park Commissioner George Cabot Wood nixed the idea, saying there was no room for it. Nor was there any interest in Congress in establishing the museum in Washington DC. No other producers rallied behind Fox's plan, which *The New York Times* ridiculed as 'preposterous.' So Fox abandoned the idea, never to return to it.

Art Acord as Kephren carrying Theda Bara's Cleopatra. (Courtesy of Academy of Motion Picture Arts and Sciences)

Notes Merrill T. McCord, "if William Fox had built such a place, today he would be one of the most revered individuals in the history of motion pictures."

It's possible Fox's film museum would have suffered the same fate as other archives with their 'airtight vaults' and gone up in flames. It is also possible that a museum dedicated to the idea of motion pictures as cultural treasures, backed by resources dedicated to the preservation of those films might have staved off the destruction of many important films. Fox, the visionary, was not ahead of his time; his idea was simply unappreciated. It was not until 1935, when MOMA founded its film library, that film would gain its official recognition as an art form. By then, it was too late for many films, and many more have been destroyed since then.

There is always hope that somehow, somewhere, there sits a copy of *Cleopatra* waiting to be discovered. Unless a copy of it remains intact, all eleven reels of it, despite the ravages of years on some forgotten shelf, *Cleopatra* is as vanished from the Earth as the Colossus of Rhodes and the many volumes of the library at Alexandria. Murray Glass once excitedly opened a film can marked *Cleopatra*, only to find it as empty as the plundered tomb of an Egyptian pharaoh.

Cleopatra will likely remain a ghostly reminder of what can happen when we take it for granted that somebody somewhere is preserving our cultural heritage. The great tragedy of cinema history is not just that so many films have been lost; it is also that they are still being lost. Preservation is tremendously expensive. The staggering costs of restoration are prohibitive for all but a handful of films. With the funding needed to maintain films in short supply, archivists find they must choose which films will be preserved and which are to be allowed to decompose on the shelves. To appreciate William Fox, Theda Bara, and the many others who toiled in cinema for the love of their professions, it is necessary to make an effort to find and preserve their movies. To justify the effort, more people must want to see those movies.

Movies are magical beings akin to fairies; they can be immortal, but they also can wither and die from the casual cruelty of mortal humans. To survive, they need more than to be put on a shelf in a film vault and be forgotten. To survive, they need to be loved.

NOTES

INTRODUCTION

"... suspect they were ghosted or the effusions of the publicity department." [Robert Hamilton Ball, *Shakespeare on Silent Film*, Theatre Arts Books, 1968, pp. 364-365]

"Almost everything in print on the Bara name is wrong," [Ibid., pg. 365]

CHAPTER ONE: A FOX THERE WAS

"Every section of the city was represented . . . " [David Nasaw, *Going Out: The Rise and Fall of Public Amusements*, Basic Books, 1993, pg. 161]

"My father . . . was just as happy when he worked as when he didn't work." [Upton Sinclair, *Upton Sinclair Present William Fox*, published by the author, 1933, pg. 18]

"You son of a bitch." [Vanda Krefft, *The Man Who Made the Movies: The Meteoric Rise and Tragic Fall of William Fox*, Harper Collins, 2017, pg. 11]

"Every penny was something I denied myself . . . Capital was what I needed." [Sinclair, pg. 25]

"Long years of poverty made him join the Socialist Party . . . which ranked him among the capitalists." [*Theatre Arts*, Vol. 35, 1951, pg. 113]

"It was a strictly commercial proposition . . . sufficient expression in the cloth examining and shrinking business." [Sinclair, pg. 51]

"The sword swallower did swallow a sword. . . . the crowd followed him up." [Kennedy, Edgar J., *The Story of the Films*, A.W. Shaw, Chicago & New York, 1927, pp. 310-311]

"I remember distinctly, . . . I know some one is shaking the screen.'" [Ibid., pg. 311]

". . . ten thousand people marched down Grand Street . . . It has been a family theatre ever since." [Neal Gabler, *An Empire of Their Own: How the Jews Invented Hollywood*, Crown Publishers, Inc. 1988, pg. 68]

"I would not allow anything on the stage and screen that I was unwilling to have my wife and daughters see." [Sinclair, pg. 52]

"I catered to the family trade . . . unwittingly, I became a reformer." [Glendon Allvine, *The Greatest Fox of Them All*, Lyle Stuart, Inc. 1969, pg. 42]

"By the afternoon the place smelt like a menagerie. . . . spraying a pump gun filled with odor of magnolia or rose blossoms." [Betty Harper Fussell, *Mabel*, Limelight Editions, 1992, pg. 61]

". . . foul air laden with death-dealing germs," [Nasaw, pg. 183]

"...moving picture places . . . foci for the dissemination of the tubercle bacilli." [Robert James Maddox, *American History: Reconstruction through the Present*, Dushkin Pub. Group, 1997, pg. 59]

"Movies are schools of vice and crime offering trips to hell for a nickel." [Nancy Day, *Censorship, Or Freedom of Expression?* Lerner Pub Group, 2000 pg. 47]

"We elected Bill Fox because he could holler the loudest." [Terry Ramsaye, *A Million and One Nights: A History of the Motion Picture*, Simon & Schuster, 1986, pg. 478]

"Everywhere it is the pictures, more than the vaudeville acts . . . realize the American idea of speed and activity." [Gabler, pg. 67]

"My one task. . . Was to get there ahead of the others." [Ibid.]

"They regulated the wages paid in every branch of the industry. . . . it was a mechanical occupation and that it required no brains." [Kennedy, pg. 304]

"They controlled the majority of the theatres of the country. . . They either bought him out or drove him out." [Ibid.]

"We are a great, gigantic wheel and you are a little splinter. . . .because you are a stumbling block." [Merrill T. McCord, *William Fox and the Fox Film Corporation*, Alhambra Publishers, 2016, pg. 4]

"Bill Fox needed a standing army and he came to me to raise it," [Terry Ramsaye, 'WINFIELD R. SHEEHAN, FAMED PRODUCER, DIES ON COAST,' *Motion Picture Herald*, July 28, 1945, pg. 21]

"Like a warrior who had stepped out of the pages of Homer . . . But even the most optimistic feared for the final fate of Fox." [W. Stephen Bush, 'Stories of the Builders,' *Moving Picture World*, January 3, 1925, pg. 18]

". . . refused to accede to the demands of the Film Trust. . . . But in the end, the bulldog won." [*The New York Times*, Jan. 2, 1916, pg. 68]

"Burn the damn thing," . . . "No, let's run it. . ." [Ramsaye, *A Million and One Nights*, pg. 701]

"This mug of mine won't sell tickets so just forget about me. . . ." [Allvine, pg. 61]

"In his heyday he let his dark moustache grow thick . . . the mustache." [Norman J. Zierold, *The Moguls*, Coward-McCann, 1969, pg. 233]

"Don't tell your friends your father is in the cinema business. It isn't quite respectable." [Angela Fox Dunn, interview with the author]

"William Fox was president of all these entities, wife Eva secretary of at least nine, and treasurer of one." [McCord, pg. 15]

"Mr. Fox is one of our notorious offenders . . . matter in connection with all of his pictures." [McCord, pg. 15]

"To be regarded as the 'Tiffany' of the moving pictures business . . . the leading theater owners in the country." [Mabel Condon, "Film Men's New Year Resolutions," *Motography*, Vol. XII #26, Dec. 26, 1914, pg. 888]

"FOX USES EVERY HOUR . . . William Fox has finished his day's task." ["FOX USES EVERY HOUR," *Motography*, Vol. XV #4, Jan. 22, 1916, pg. 174]

"A careful computation . . . William Fox works twenty-six hours out of every twenty-four." [McCord, pg. 17]

"It has always been a charge that the Fox Film organization was a one-man organization. . . . They were right when they said that." [Sinclair, pg. 29]

". . . his own most exacting critic. . . . 'better than the best' before he will permit it to be released." [McCord, pg. 17]

"Among the early pioneers, William Fox was not a lovable character, like Uncle Carl Laemmle or Joe Schenck." [Allvine, pg. 35]

"William Fox was a tough man. . . . He was strictly business." [Anthony Slide, "George Walsh in an interview with Anthony Slide," *The Silent Picture*, Autumn 1972, Issue 16, pg. 14]

"Although William Fox was relentless ... He had a good word for some, and some had a good word for him." [McCord, pg. 112]

'Greatest Tragedienne in the World.' [Ibid., pg. 11]

"Cameras were everywhere, grinding out dramas.... Kindly old ladies didn't blink an eyelid when three galloping Mexicans were shot and killed at their very door." [Channing Pollock, 'The Discovery of Fort Lee,' *Photoplay*, Vol. IX #1, December 15, pg. 67]

"... that any clergyman may have any Fox film free of charge ... or home for the aged." [Sinclair, pg. 13]

"... so long as they don't do it in the streets and frighten the horses." [Alan Dent, *Mrs. Patrick Campbell*, Museum Press, 1961, pg. 78]

"... picture dramatization from Sir Ed Burne-Jones' famous painting ... This great subject handles deftly the realms of the imaginary inner circle of society." ["Comments on the Film," Review of 'The Vampire', *The Moving Picture World*, Nov. 26, 1910, pg. 1236]

"In my experience, I have had to change my leading lady six times.... and the part will make her." [Sinclair, pg. 56]

CHAPTER TWO: DESTINY'S DARK ANGEL

"She has the science of silent seduction ... all the gallants in the neighborhood trotting Baraward." [Norman J. Zierold, *Sex Goddesses of the Silent Screen*, H. Regency Co., 1973, pg. 22]

"... descended into the sea with graceful composure, as if she had been alighting from a carriage." [Mary Caroline Crawford, Romantic *Days In The Early Republic*, Grosset & Dunlap, 1912, pg. 333]

"And you could not remain angry with her very long—... I'm going to have you stuffed.'" [Pauline Bara, "My Theda Bara," *Motion Picture Classic*, Vol. 11 # 5, Jan. 1921, pg. 79]

"I always had the instincts of an actress.... I needed advertising, no one knew what an actress I was." [Theda Bara, 'How I became a Film Vampire,' *The Forum*, Vol. 61, June 1919, pg. 719]

"... was almost as good as the average motion-picture theater.... I knew that hundreds of thousands of people would some day come to see me as an actress." [Ibid., pp. 718-719]

"Through all the usual little obligations and home duties of an average school girl.... Like many children I lived in a world of incomprehensible imagination." [Ibid., pg. 729]

"I believed in fairies, I still believe in them." [Ibid.]

"Often I did not understand her ... she is so remote and even to me, her mother, strange." [Pauline Bara, 'My Theda Bara,' *Motion Picture Classic*, Vol. 11 #5, Jan. 1921, pg. 79]

"Theo excels in the literary art... She is an entertaining conversationalist." [Eve Golden, Vamp: *The Rise and Fall of Theda Bara*, Emprise Publishing, Inc. Vestal, 1996, pg. 17]

"She loved to act ... desire the very thing we were trying to avoid." [Pauline Bara, 'My Theda Bara,' *Motion Picture Classic*, Vol. 11 #5, Jan. 1921, pg. 79]

"With heart and fancy all on fire, To climb the hill of fame." [Golden, pg. 17]

"... a modern celebrity who practiced conspicuous self-display and deliberately sought sensation.... Exoticism and eccentricity were her hallmarks..."[Stephen Gundle, *Glamour: A History*, pg.126]

"Her performances and offstage publicity stunts blended seamlessly ... a symbol and ideal more than a woman." [Ibid.]

"... in so doing they only increased the public's fascination.... her capacity to merge her personality with the roles she played." [Ibid., pg. 127]

"Bernhardt's performances ... women were primarily spiritual rather than sexual or physical beings." [Anne Helen Petersen, 'Scandals of Classic Hollywood: The Most Wicked Face of Theda Bara', *The Hairpin*, Jan. 8, 2013]

"Nothing happens without a cause ... into strange channels and dangerous harbors, and oft go far, far adrift. [Theda Bara, manuscript, University of Cincinnati, pg. 34]

"Call them good fairies ... when we submit out own will to a greater will, that power never fails." [Ibid., pg. 35]

"I absolutely declined to have my salary cut ... I was a real actress." [Bara, Theda, 'How I became a Film Vampire,' *The Forum*, pg. 724]

"However, my fairies stayed with me ... and sustained me." [Ibid., pg. 725]

"... his only salvation was in getting away.... What about my child?'" [Mary Desti, *The Brooklyn Daily Eagle*, Oct. 6, 1929, pg. 69]

"I curse you. The gods of my fathers curse you and your children forever." [Ibid.]

"... first adventure with a movie star.... I put her on the boat train." [Preston Sturges, *Preston Sturges by Preston Sturges: His Life in His Words*, pg. 65]

"Isadora Duncan could have been known as *La Grande Horizontale* ... living life to the hilt." [Valerie Lawson, online review of *Isadora: The Sensational Life of Isadora Duncan* by Peter Kurth]

"... a year or two of weird incomprehensible experiences which are too intimate for the public eye.... They flourished for a time in that beautiful twilight called love." [Theda Bara, 'How I Became a Film Vampire,' *The Forum*, Vol. 61, June 1919, pg. 724]

"I returned to New York a slender, pale, sad-eyed girl.... I couldn't have looked it by any stretch of the imagination." [Ibid., pg. 725]

"Theodosia played a Frenchwoman with an accent ... tappings on the wall behind my bed." [Hopper, Hedda, *From Under my Hat,* Doubleday & Co, 1952 pg. 38]

'Theodosia de Coppet, New York,' [*Dramatic Compositions Copyrighted in the United States, 1870 to 1916*, US Library of Congress, pg. 2992]

"The theatrical engagement that I expected to last a whole season ... so I went over to the studio to find out what it was all about." [Olga Petrova, 'Mme. Interviews Theda Bara,' *Shadowland*, March-April 1920, pg. 44]

"Being accustomed to the more or less orderly procedure of the theater, ... but not badly enough yet to get it in that way." [Ibid.]

"... nothing would induce me to become a moving picture actress." [Theda Bara, 'How I became a Film Vampire,' *The Forum*, Vol. 61, June 1919, pg. 725]

"It seemed to me that the fairies interfered in my favor again ... set out once again for the picture studio." [Ibid., pg. 726]

"...failing to take much notice of Theodosia Goodman although she used to come to our office hopefully when she heard we might be casting." [Golden, pg. 23]

"I'll be very glad to go into pictures ... Next day I reported with the one-piece bathing suit." [Petrova, 'Mme. Petrova interviews Theda Bara,' *Shadowland,* pg. 44]

"It's all well to say noble things about rather starving than debase . . . Your flights of fancy won't bring you three meals a day." [Ibid.]

"I was never an extra player, . . . for there is nothing so important as being with an organization and climbing up from the ranks." [James Robert Parish, *The Fox Girls*, Arlington House, 1971. pg. 24]

". . . a rancher, an advance man, a reporter . . . and Annette Kellermann." ['Goldfrap goes to World,' *Motography*, Jan. 1, 1916, Vol. XV #1, pg. 26]

"Prominent actress imported from Paris . . . an actress who fulfilled absolutely the type he required." [Zierold, *Sex Goddesses of the Silent Screen*, pg. 11]

"Theda Bara is the daughter of Giuseppe Bara . . . who remembered her when casting *A Fool There Wa*s." [Ibid, pg. 12]

"I shall never forget the terrible experience. . . there on the dock." [Theda Bara 'How I became a Film Vampire,' *The Forum*, Vol. 61, June 1919, pg. 727]

"Well, any girl who does that is ambitious." [Krefft, pg. 147]

"In playing this fascinating but despicable character . . . trains himself in the business of the deft extraction of purses." [Zierold, *Sex Goddesses of the Silent Screen*, pg. 51]

"As the Vampire, Theda Bara gives the woman not one redeeming feature, . . . add greatly to the forcefulness of Miss Bara's work." [Ibid, pg. 6]

"Miss Bara misses no chance for sensuous appeal in her portrayal of the Vampire. . . irrespective of less enjoyable ones to follow." ['Reviews of Feature Films,' *The New York Dramatic Mirror*, Vol. 73, # 1883, Jan. 20, 1915, p. 51]

"I was assigned to support of a well known star . . . Again I was a 'vampire,' and I was not particularly happy in the role." [Golden, pg. 47]

"When I found myself cast in my second picture. . . I felt only an ambition to do as well as she did." [Theda Bara, 'Curse on a Moving Picture Actress,' *The Forum*, Vol. 62, July, 1919, pg. 87]

"Startling and remarkable, their acting is splendidly realistic and emotionally powerful." [Golden, pg. 47]

"When the picture was released there were. . . which romance is a food all hearts crave." [Theda Bara, 'Curse on a Moving Picture Actress' *The Forum*, Vol. 62, July, 1919, pg. 87]

"Sergeant, send up your man. I have just killed my wife." [Zierold, *Sex Goddesses of the Silent Screen*, pg. 9]

". . . giant king python . . . she clutches the toy to her in an attempt to keep it from falling to the ground with a thud." [Golden, pg. 48]

"Were The National Board of Censorship possessed of any judgment. . . were too good to be engaged in a picture production of this kind." [Ibid., pg. 49]

"I first met D'Annunzio when he came to Paris to put on a playlet of his at the Théâtre Antoine. . . . He declared that if I did not take the part, he would not put on the playlet . . ." [Zierold, *Sex Goddesses of the Silent Screen*, pg. 16]

"There is no one else on earth who is half serpent and half woman like my Gioconda, except Mlle. Bara." [*The San Bernardino County Sun*, Sept. 16, 1915, pg. 8]

"As this man has done to me, so will I do henceforth to all men . . . Let all men beware." [*The Danville Morning News*, Oct. 26, 1915, pg. 3]

"Mlle. Bara's facial expression is wonderfully brutal and fiendish, but every movement shows grace and charm." [Zierold, *Sex Goddesses of the Silent Screen*, pg. 17]

"To turn from a sinuous vampire . . . The result shows what a powerful versatile actress can accomplish." [Golden, pg. 52]

"Tender, bewitching and passionate in turn . . . undeniable proof of her extraordinary versatility." [*Pittsburgh Daily Post*, September 26, 1915, pg. 26]

'. . . the wickedest face in the world, dark, brooding, beautiful and heartless,' [Parish, pg. 23]

"I sat up all night deciding what pin-point on the globe to select as my birthplace. . . . Suppose we say I was born in Egypt." [Adela Rogers St. Johns, *Love, Laughter and Tears: My Hollywood Story,* Doubleday 1978, pg. 22]

"Oh, very well, make it two blocks from the Sphinx," [Krefft, 141]

"Theda Bara was born in 1891 in Egypt . . . who had eloped to an oasis in the Sahara." [*The San Francisco Examiner*, October 15, 1950, pg. 119]

"Half-Arabian embodiment of wicked delight . . . the Théâtre Antoine." [DeWitt Bodeen, *From Hollywood: The Careers of 15 Great American Stars*, A. S. Barnes, pg. 13]

". . . a young man killed himself in her dressing room because she had spurned his love . . . died at her feet!" [Nixola Greeley-Smith, 'Fat Women Can't Become Vampires, Asserts Theda,' *The Seattle Star* Vol. 17 #305, February 19, 1915, pg. 1]

"Anyway, some of them were so wild that we didn't think they would be printed, . . . I think I kept a whole publicity staff working nights." [Agnes Smith, 'Confessions of Theda Bara,' *Photoplay*, Vol. 17 #1, June 1920, pg. 58]

"My conception of the vampire character . . . Such is my conception of the woman who wrought the fool's undoing." [Zierold, *Sex Goddesses of the Silent Screen*, pg. 8]

". . . deceived fifty men with her wiles, made one hundred families suffer, caused fifty children and one hundred wives to beg her to give back to them their daddies and their husbands." [Ibid., pg. 28]

". . . shop girls read it and swallowed their gum with excitement." [Ramsaye, pg. 703]

"What mid-country wife . . . arch-torpedo of domesticity?" [Wallace Franklin, 'Purgatory's Ivory Angel,' *Photoplay*, Vol. VIII #4, Sept. 1915, pg. 70]

". . . she was sex, blatant and overt and so far removed from reality . . . gave her amazing license." [Rosen, Marjorie: *Popcorn Venus : Women, Movies and the American Dream*, New York : Ward, McCann & Geoghegan, 1973, pg. 6]

"Is this the wickedest face in the world? . . . with others to form the soul of Mlle. Theda Bara?" ['Is This the Wickedest Face in the World?' *Atlanta Constitution*. August 1, 1915.]

"Fox didn't just give Bara a new name or a new ethnicity . . . simultaneously disavowing it in oneself . . ." [Anne Helen Petersen, 'Scandals of Classic Hollywood: The Most Wicked Face of Theda Bara', *The Hairpin*, Jan. 8, 2013]

CHAPTER THREE: 'THE FLAMING COMET IN THE CINEMA FIRMAMENT'

"Do you consider the word 'movie' . . . it is short and popular." ['The Question is Settled,' *Photoplay*, April 1915, pp. 129-130]

"I have frequently expressed my profound admiration . . . greatest living motion picture actor . . ." ['How Fox, the Exhibitor, Decided Upon "Standard Pictures,"' *Motion Picture News*, August 4, 1917, pg. 819]

"... like an electric current ... given orthodox pronunciation of the word." [Krefft, pg. 147]

"... as enigmatic as the proverbial noncommittal demeanor of the Sphinx." [Ibid., pg. 149]

"The 'comedy' certainly did not seem funny to me ... We had a good laugh." [Ibid., pg. 148]

"No rumor would ever surface about any flirtation between them ... An affair would not have been out of the question." [Ibid., pg. 146]

"Was Bara sexually exploited by William Fox? ... know how many of the old stars were sexually involved with a studio chief." [Ronald Genini, *Theda Bara: A Biography of the Silent Screen Vamp, with a Filmography*, McFarland, 1996, pg. 82]

"... a complex character: affable, sentimental, suspicious, cynical, ruthless, and a squat dynamo of energy." [Allvine, pg. 61]

"... her looks are considered rather plain and bovine.... Even in her day she was thought a few pounds overweight." [Golden, pg. 57]

"... a broad, flat face, asymmetrical features.... Jewish tailor's daughter from Cincinnati, Ohio." [Krefft, 133]

"The lustrous beauty of the screen apparition ... catching Miss Bara in an unbecoming pose." [Zierold, *Sex Goddesses of the Silent Screen*, pg. 23]

"... lovely to look upon ... she has adapted her fine skill to the new medium." [*The New York Times*, Jan. 15, 1917]

"From this naïve kindly girl ... Stoker were hovering around." [Rex Ingram, *Long way to Tipperary*, unpublished manuscript, Trinity College Dublin, pg. 273]

"Theda a docile mannequin whom he could dress up to convey his idea of sexual allure..." [Krefft, pg. 147]

"Mr. Fox urged me ... a loss of $30,000 to $40,000." [Ibid., pp. 148-149]

"Mr. Griffith told me to hold onto you ... but you know these fly by night companies." [James Childs, 'An Interview with Raoul Walsh,' *Sight and Sound: International film quarterly*, Winter, 1972-73 pg. 10]

"Who's backing them—God?" [Raoul Walsh, *Each Man in his Time*, Farrar, Strauss, & Giroux, 1972, pg. 113]

"He was a dynamic character ... He believed in getting the best of everything." [Richard Schickel, *Men Who Made The Movies*, Atheneum, 1975, p. 29]

"So I got an idea and I went down... but she was a great girl off." [Ibid., pg. 31]

"*The Serpent*, ... got a good press and made money." [Walsh, pg. 126]

"And the picture turned out pretty good as a Russian picture." [Schickel, pg. 31]

"... it is an unwholesome offering and a vulgar one." ['Review of "The Serpent"' *The Moving Picture World*, Feb. 12, 1916, pg. 978]

"... tractable, even humble, rare qualities in a rising star of her magnitude." [Walsh, pg. 124]

"Sopping wet ... 'These things happen.'" [Ibid., pg. 129]

"In all my directing career ... one of the nicest actresses I had ever met." [Ibid.]

"I thought she was terrible ... But in stage makeup she looked exotic and sultry..." [Miriam Cooper, with Bonnie Herndon, *Dark Lady of the Silents: My Life in Early Hollywood*, Bobbs-Merrill Company, 1973, pp. 101-102]

"Raoul and I were very much in love … she was driving him nuts." [Ibid., pp. 101-102]

"… really a nice man, kind and considerate.… you compared everybody with him." [Ibid., pg. 117]

"'What are you trying to do, Raoul?'.… They'd have made Jesus Christ Greek if it would make money." [Ibid., pg. 102]

"Audiences loved to see her die in her films … and she did it very well." [Eve Golden, Interview with the author]

"DeMille's production was marvelous, … that was the big moneymaker." [Cooper, pg. 103]

"Her picture on a poster outside is a guarantee of a crowd inside." [Golden, pg. 39]

"… to suggest, as film historians tend to … Fox displayed considerable ambivalence." [Krefft, pg. 142]

"All eighteen Theda movies that Fox released during 1915 and 1916 had pedigreed source material …" [Ibid.]

"The most famous vampire in her most daring role, bringing ruin and disaster to thousands . . ." [Parish, pg. 25]

"It proves what her film friends have long feared … and go up in smoke." [Zierold, *Sex Goddesses of the Silent Screen*, pg. 25]

"The horrors in this five-part melodrama are piled on so heavily … to swallow the new sensationalism and merely laughed." [Lynde Denig, 'Review of Destruction,' *Moving Picture World*, Jan. 8, 1916, Vol. 27, #2 pp. 255-256, 261]

"Some critics pronounced Theda Bara a vampire and nothing else.… they had seen her in *A Fool There Was*." [L.E. Eubanks, 'Review of *East Lynne*,' *Motion Picture Classic Magazine*, July 8, 1916, pg. 266]

"And the interviews … I had a special dress made that I never wore at other times." [Agnes Smith, 'Confessions of Theda Bara,' *Photoplay*, pg. 58]

"I can tell you of at least four times that I have been on earth … concealed about my clothing when I am acting." [Archie Bell, 'Theda Bara the Vampire Woman,' *The Theatre*, Vol. 22, Nov. 1915, pg. 253]

"… an emerald ring given to me by a blind sheik … but it would take too long to tell all of them." [Theda Bara, 'Famous Superstitions of Theda Bara: Strange Talismans Influence Her Life,' *The Day Book*, April 18, 1916, pp. 13-14]

"Theda Bara aint nothin' but a Cincinnati kike!" [Miss Curtis Pierce, letter to the editor, *Motion Picture Magazine*, Aug. 1917, pg. 164]

"Were you born in Cincinnati, Miss Bara … Egypt.…" [Golden, pg. 68]

"What does it matter who I am or whence I came … but what's in a name?" [*The Des Moines Register*, May 7, 1916, pg. 32]

"You ask me why men feel as they do about the vampire … That is why she makes fools of men." [Nixola Greeley-Smith, 'Woman Must Choose Whether She Will Love or Be Loved—Can't do Both,' *The Day Book*, Feb. 19, 1915, pg. 14]

"But believe me, for every woman vampire … perhaps, but the heart of a *feministe*." [Nixola Greeley-Smith, 'Fat Women Can't Become Vampires, Asserts Theda,' The Seattle Star Vol. 17 #305, February 19, 1915, pg. 1]

"My own idea of a vampire is the thoroughly human woman ... vividly as they have appealed to me." [Genini, pg. 58]

"I am not as black as I am painted.... I sincerely hope no other girl shall be preyed upon in this fashion." [Golden, pg. 86]

"I wish to believe.... I see no reason for disbelieving what it most pleases me to believe." [Wallace Franklin, 'Purgatory's Ivory Angel,' *Photoplay*, pg. 69]

"No, it is impossible. Theda Bara must have been born on Saturn, Mars ... or perhaps on Venus." [Archie Bell, 'Theda Bara the Vampire Woman,' *The Theatre*, Vol. 22, Nov. 1915, pg. 253]

"Here comes the latest thing in Vampire Ladies! ... Pearl White in the Pathé serial, *Pearl of the Army*." [P.A. Parsons, 'Here comes the latest thing in Vampire Ladies! 'Ware Theda!' *Motion Picture Classic*, Vol. III, Feb. 1917, pg. 39]

"Usually, vampires are pictured as brunettes ... but welcome." [John T. Soister, Henry Nicolella and Steve Joyce, *American Silent Horror, Science Fiction and Fantasy Feature Films*, 1913–1929, McFarland, 2012, pg. 125]

"She doesn't steal the show. She *is* the show." [Walsh, p. 31]

"'If you rearrange the letters in her name, ... I saw myself oblivious to every- thing but the nectar of her lips ...'" [S. J. Perelman, 'Cloudland Revisited: The Wickedest Woman in Larchmont,' *The New Yorker*, Vol. 28, Part 3, Oct. 18, 1952, pg. 36]

"There was Theda Bara, ... longed in their secret hearts to resemble." [Olga Petrova, *Butter with my Bread*, The Bobb-Merrill Company, 1942, p. 315]

"... few are either daring enough or desirous ... they can do her deeds and live her life." [Zierold, *Sex Goddesses of the Silent Screen*, pg. 27]

"Some directors are wonderful....'Oh, just keep the audience guessing,' he said. [Agnes Smith, 'Confessions of Theda Bara,' *Photoplay*, June 1920, pg. 110]

"My cameraman is my artistic speedometer.... but I always do a re-take." [Wallace Franklin, 'Purgatory's Ivory Angel', *Photoplay*, pg. 71]

"As directed by J. Gordon Edwards ... not to be a dull moment in the throbbing and thrilling ." ['Review of *The Song of Hate*,' *Motography*, Vol. XIV #10, Oct. 2, 1915, pg. 712]

"... bull dog insistency and systematic operations ..." [Letter of William Fox to Sol Wurtzel, May 14th, 1920, Sol Wurtzel Papers, special collections, AMPAS

"The studio became a factory ... one after another." [Golden, pg. 47]

"... reproachfully asked me why I had never written a story for her.... and have fun myself." [Rex Ingram, *Long way to Tipperary*, pg. 273]

"It is true I have no heart, but then I am more comfortable without one." [Golden, pg. 101]

"It was just like getting home again ... where I spent my childhood or my earlier years." ['THEDA BARA WAS BORN IN THE SAHARA' *Albany Daily Democrat*, October 3, 1916, pg. 4]

"One of my earliest recollections ... the wild, unruly life of the desert children. [Ibid.]

"Juliet lived in a period of passionate abandon.... for a Sunday school girl." [Theda Bara, 'Curse on a Moving Picture Actress,' *The Forum*, Vol. 62, pg. 92]

"... usual intensity ... Chief Treasure of the House of Capulet." [Ball, p. 240]

"... riot of action and a bounty of beauty... Mlle Theda Bara, the famous Parisian actress...." [Ibid., pp. 240-241]

"I have been a vampire of fiction, not fact..." [Theda Bara, 'Curse on a Moving Picture Actress,' *The Forum*, Vol. 62, pg. 85]

"I cannot conceive how my appearance in pictures ... an audience larger than was ever had by any man or woman in the world's history."[Genini, pg. 62]

"Why should anyone declaim against the so-called sex drama ... Most people give the word sex a false meaning." [*The Daily Free Press*, Kinston, North Carolina, Aug. 1, 1916, pg. 2]

"After Theda Bara appeared in *A Fool There Was*...carmine-lipped woman of subtlety and mystery."[Mary Pickford, 'To Be Or Not To Be a Vampire', *The Day*, New London, CT, May 16, 1916, pg. 11]

"It is your type of woman that brings terror to the heart of a good woman...

I assure you, is very, very hard work." ['Behold in me, the Devil's Maid-servant' *Motion Picture Classic*, Vol. 2 #2, April 1916, pg. 26]

"Why do people hate me so...I am detested." [Zierold, *Sex Goddesses of the Silent Screen*, pg. 26]

"Save him! Save him! The vampire has my child!" [Genini, pg. 63]

"Please don't come in ... stand any more of these riots." [Ibid., pg. 89]

"I was walking near my home in Manhattan. ... sobbed like the littlest of them." [Wallace Franklin, 'Purgatory's Ivory Angel' *Photoplay*, pg. 72]

["Theda, the Misunderstood Vampire," *Motion Picture Classic*, Vol. 3 #2, Oct. 1916, pp. 25-27]

"... the flaming comet in the cinema firmament..." ['SOME 500,000 SPECTATORS FOLLOW HER EVERY DAY,' *The New York Times*, Feb. 20, 1916, pg. 8:2]

"The coming of Theda Bara... to give the name of the woman he was prophesying." [*Oakland Tribune*, Nov. 1, 1916, pg. 7]

CHAPTER FOUR: 'SHAKESPEARE- MODIFIED SLIGHTLY'

"For the next year Mr. Fox ... will maintain the Fox standard." ['William Fox's 1917 Program,' *Motography*, Jan. 6, 1917, pg. 21]

"Her beauty was not in itself incomparable ... but to converse with her had an irresistible charm." [Joyce Tyldesley, *Cleopatra: Last Queen of Egypt*, Basic Books, 2010, pg. 63]

"She captivated the two greatest Romans of her day, and because of the third, she destroyed herself." [Ibid., pg. 211]

"A plague on both your houses."[John T. Soister, et al, *American Silent Horror, Science Fiction and Fantasy Feature Films*, 1913–1929, pg. 127]

"*Civilization*, like *Intolerance*, was produced at enormous cost ... profits that is accorded the average picture."[Lee Royal, *The Romance of Motion Picture Production*, Royal Publishing Company, 1920, pg. 51]

"*Cabiria* was a huge success ... but fell just a little short of the intimate, human touch." [Randolph Bartlett, 'The Shadow Stage,' *Photoplay*, Jan. 1918, pp. 65-66]

"What *Uncle Tom's Cabin* did for the negro slaves ... ill-nourished, hard-working little factory slaves..." ['Review of "The Price of Silence,"' *Motography*, Jan. 22, 1917, pg. 206]

"William Fox has a private barber shop in his office . . . the audience in the theatre when portrayed." ["Jack Lait Tells How Fox Picks Scenarios," *Motion Picture News*, Sept. 1, 1917, pg. 1437]

"Here was a big book they could get for nothing . . . which they considered changing to *In the Sewers of Paris*." [Allvine, pg. 58]

". . . would be valuable as a very costly spectacle . . . would compensate for the cost." [Ann Maxwell, Synopsis of Haggard's *Cleopatra*. 20th Century Fox papers, UCLA, Special Collections Library]

". . . the loves and treachery of CLEOPATRA . . . would make a corking CLEOPATRA." [Ibid.]

"'It meant the realization of one of my supreme dreams. With emotions I could not describe I was told of a momentous decision. " [Theda Bara, manuscript, pg. 21]

"Screen's Supreme Artiste Portrays Role of History's Greatest Sorceress . . . has presented some of the greatest scenic effects ever shown." ['Screen's Supreme Artiste Portrays Role of History's Greatest Sorceress,' *Motion Picture News*, vol. 15, number 19, May 12, 1917, pg. 2921]

"Cleopatra, Miss Bara found. . . when she devised her make-up for the character." ['Cleo Blonde Siren? No, Declares History,' *The Buffalo Enquirer*, Nov. 16, 1917, pg. 11]

"The opinions of the producer . . . the job will unquestionably fall to a man." [Royal, pg. 17]

"Hats off to Mary Murillo . . . for Fox Film Corporation." ['Hats off to Mary Murillo,' *Motography*, June 16, 1917, pg. 1262]

". . . dead serious about writing for your studio . . . but writers— the poor schlemiels!'" [Marion Francis, *Off With Their Heads*, pp. 28-31]

"Excluding acting, considering . . . and producers." [Anthony Slide, *The New Historical Dictionary of the American Film Industry*, Scarecrow, 1998, pg. 233]

"There is one man in the motion-picture business that I should like very much to meet . . . and produce it he does." [Peter Milne, 'The Screen in Review' *Picture-Play Magazine*, Jan. 1919, pp. 122-123]

"The character of the voluptuous but crafty Queen of Egypt . . . fitted with the situation of climax of the modern school." [*Argument of the Play Cleopatra* by Victorien Sardou, F. Pullman, New York, NY 1891]

". . . fine history ruined by a music-hall writer." [Ronald Bowers, review of 'Cleopatra' *Magill's Survey of Cinema: The Silent Film*, Press Englewood Cliffs, NJ : Salem, 1982, pg. 324]

"How unlike—how so unlike—the home life of our own dear queen . . . everything the Western bourgeoisie affected to abhor." [Margaret M. Miles, *Cleopatra: A Sphinx Revisited*, California Press, 2011, pg. 200]

". . . probably the most stupendous and beautiful picture ever produced. . . wonderful production." [Ball, pg. 148]

". . . a complicated story of various loves and honours . . . indeed a sorry mish-mash." [Ibid., pg. 149]

"Go back a few years and recall . . . the death knell of Miss Gardner was sounded." ['Where are the Stars of Yesterday?' *Picture Play Magazine*, Sept. 1916, pp. 39-46]

"Anything we read on this subject will do us all good, I figure." [Johnson, pg. 24]

"... most accurate and concise historical record I have read on this subject ... authenticity stamped upon it unmistakably." [Ibid.]

"... considered one of the greatest authorities of the period ... protecting her throne for her family." [Theda Bara, unpublished manuscript, pg. 25]

"... the conception built up through the ages ... in his dry as dust nature, pictured her." [Ibid.]

"... dry-as dust bookworm who in following the ... deciphering hieroglyphics in a library." [Ibid., pg. 26]

"'"Caesar had strong Republican ideals.... the greatest moment in the life of the Queen." [Ibid. pg. 30]

"... that it is her fascinating, alluring, ambitious influence ... " [Ibid.]

"... which was activated by his love for Cleopatra." [Ibid.]

"... the 'friends, Romans, countrymen' stuff ... footage to photograph ACTION. ADVISE!!!" [Ibid., pp. 41-42]

"... might seem cruel but it is a good ...show a flash of all sides of her character— Advise!!" [Ibid., pg. 56]

"Mr. Edwards did not like—... without the magic effects specified by Rider Haggard. Please Advise!!" [Ibid., pg. 57]

"To me, it seemed that Haggard missed the whole ... not a 'drugged cup.'" [Ibid., pg. 73]

" ... if she came out flat and told him ... it would show her imperious nature and also show that she in finished with him ..." [Ibid., pg. 109]

"It appears, from his work, that Cleopatra never had or made a decision for herself..." [Ibid.]

"Cleopatra captivating the conqueror ... is fraught with drama." [Ibid., pg. 116]

"Bacchanalian and risqué ... Antony and Cleopatra in view of the diners." [Ibid., pg. 127]

... food is always disillusioning- " [Ibid., 128]

"... an intimate love scene with a strong dash of Orientalism." [Ibid., pg. 144]

" These love scenes should be as strong... slang is sometimes not pardonable but always expressive." [Ibid., pg. 145]

"... because there big dramatic scenes are sometimes difficult to do in exteriors, as Mr. Edwards once told me ..." [Ibid., pg. 167]

"... savage and terrible scene of oriental political violence—" [Ibid., pg. 79]

"... away from the dramatic nature of her Death scene and gives the audience the shivers generally ..." [Ibid., pg. 206]

"... it strikes me to have all the characters ... added dignity to the story." [Johnson., pg. 69]

"Some of the subtitles were from Shakespeare.... and there's an end on't." [Ball, pg. 253]

"Who art thou?...I could weep— I could kill ..." [Beulah Selig, 'Cleopatra,' *Motion Picture Classic*, Dec. 1917, pg. 24]

"Death, where is thy sting? Victory, where is thy grave?" [Ibid., pg. 26]

"Historically the picture is incorrect almost without a single exception," [Randolph Bartlett, review of *Cleopatra, Photoplay,* Jan., 1918, pg. 66]

"Historically *Cleopatra* is correct in practically every detail . . . and that is, as a consequence, unusually entertaining." [Peter Milne, review of Cleopatra, Motion Picture News, Nov. 3, 1917, pg. 3134]

"The scope of the story embraces many of the historical facts . . . the Egyptian queen's overmastering passion for Mark Antony." [Edward Weitzel, review of *Cleopatra, The Moving Picture World,* Nov. 3, 1917, pg. 708]

"The picture is a brave attempt to limn the outstanding features of Cleopatra's reign . . . it is a pity that part of this stupendous sum was not expended for a better scenario . . . [Review of *Cleopatra, The Dramatic Mirror,* Oct. 27, 1917]

"To essay such a role required practical preparations and study . . . or cheapness must mar the resurrection of that immortal tragedy." [Theda Bara, manuscript, pg. 24]

" . . . the Egyptologist who literally eats, drinks and sleeps with the Egypt of antiquity . . . every possible assistance." [Ibid.]

"Indeed, Mr. Lithgow has come to bear a certain resemblance of feature to the Egyptian type . . . These later guided the making of the film and were faithfully followed." [Ibid.]

"Mr. Smith, as always, proved he never fails in anything he is asked to do." [Ibid., pg. 32]

"In the picture there were a few minor anachronisms . . . Egypt must have been as the time of the celebrated queen. [Ibid., pg. 24]

"That the star actress in such a film herself . . . follow the instructions of the director." [Ibid., pp. 24-25]

"I believe that Cleopatra was little different . . . little to distinguish it from the cases of a thousand girls of our own day." [Zierold, *Sex Goddesses of the Silent Screen,* pg. 35]

"The deeper I delve into the personal history of Cleopatra . . . that preserved in them any honest or decent feeling whatever." [Movie Margerie, 'The Siren Of The Nile,' *Pictures and The Picturegoer,* June 1, 1918, pg. 545]

"Altogether, I believe Cleopatra was more sinned against . . . I think she turned out remarkably well." [Ibid.,]

"Although Cleopatra's part in history is already well established . . . not alone for herself but for her people." ['Theda Bara Works Secretly in "Cleopatra,"' *Motion Picture News,* May 5, 1917, pg. 2833]

CHAPTER FIVE: INTO A NEW WORLD

"Environment certainly affects creative workers . . . Southern California is the most ideal city for producing films." [Peter James Holliday, *American Arcadia: California and the Classical Tradition,* Oxford University Press, 2016, pg. 54]

"In 1919, Hollywood was still a village. . . . Lasky studio with its front lined by a row of lovely pepper trees." [John Kobal, *Hollywood, the Years of Innocence,* Abbeville Press, 1985, p. 50]

"Cahuenga Boulevard, leading out from the little town . . . they stayed right there until the car reached the top of the grade." [Fred J. Balshofer, and Arthur C. Miller, *One Reel a Week,* University of California Press, 1967, p. 90]

"After nine o'clock at night . . . and never hit anybody." [Kevin Brownlow and John Kobal, *Hollywood: The Pioneers,* Knopf, 1979, p. 108]

"When you talk about wild parties, they took place in the 30s. . . . but not too much in the 1910s." [Kobal, pg. 108]

'Laugh with Lehrman, the Wizard of Wit.' [Anthony Balducci, *Lloyd Hamilton: Poor Boy Comedian of Silent Cinema*, McFarland, 2009, pg. 57]

"Comedies have become a necessary part of every motion picture exhibitors' program . . . or we will stop trying altogether." ['Fox to Release Comedies *Motography*, Vol. XVI #21, December 9, 1916, pg. 1287]

"The monkey incident in this two-reel comedy . . . The first three Sunshine comedies are certainly laugh producers." [E. R. Mock, "What The Picture Did For Me," *Motography*, Jan. 9, 1918, pg. 249]

"Easy. The minute you get out there, fire everybody. . . . Then they'll know who's boss." [Zierold, *The Moguls*, pp. 225-226]

"Mr. Fox employs in his various departments several thousand men…who spent several years in the Canadian Mounted Police." ['Fox Forces to Aid Nation,' *Motography*, Vol. XVII, #16, April 21, 1917, pg. 780]

"There was a tremendous flurry of excitement . . . I was offered almost anything I wanted." [Krefft, pg. 270]

""Clothed in grey, with a grey veil floating yards behind me, I boarded the train feeling I was going forth into a new world." [Theda Bara, manuscript, pg. 26]

"The attempts of Miss Surratt to act . . . it would be impossible to tell any one emotion that she had registered." [McCord, pg. 61]

" . . . escaped the turmoil on an ammunition ship . . . " [Ibid.]

"William Fox captures the 1917 prize for effrontery without a close competitor. . . . too prevalent viewpoint maintained by a few producers." [Cal York, "Plays and Players," *Photoplay*, Feb. 1918, Vol. XIII #3, pg. 90]

"My interviews with reporters were staged with all the props and settings expected of a movie vampire." [Theda Bara, manuscript, pg. 27]

"The room in which I was received was draped with Oriental tapestries . . . banked with roses." [Ibid.]

". . . head and shoulders above all vamps of prewar No. 1 was Theda Bara. . . . or rather to the act put on by Theda—and the old Fox company." [Louella Parsons, *The Gay Illiterate*, pg. 33]

"The charmer from the land of the Sphinx . . . " [Ibid.]

" . . . apparently has never outgrown the 'Oh, girls' style of writing . . . as it ranks fifth of the industries of the nation." ['Latest News of Chicago,' *Motography* vol. XIX #7, Feb 16, 1918, pg. 238]

"Daring the ire of those who always abuse me . . . Theda Bara staggering naively about in her first high heeled slippers, I miss my guess."[Mae Tinee, 'Review of *Her Greatest Love*,' *Chicago Tribune*, April 5, 1917]

"The day was hotter than the proverbial hinges of the proverbial hot spot. . . .

It is very, very hot, and she is cold!'" [Parsons, pg. 33]

"I reclined on a Madam de Maintenon couch as I talked to the reporters . . . to carry away a full impression of that extraordinary freak, the vampire." [Theda Bara, manuscript, pp. 27-28]

"It was an interview to go down in the annals . . . She looked as ineffably bored as we felt." [Parsons, pg. 33]

"I was perforce compelled to preserve a very worldly-wise ... but having the role to play I hope I played it perfectly." [Theda Bara, manuscript, pp. 27-28]

"Finally, and probably because she couldn't stand the furs any longer ... and chance to howl our lungs out." [Parsons, pg. 34]

"Give me air!" [Ramsaye, *A Million and One Nights*, pg. 703]

"Dick Little, our dramatic critic, picked up the Bara catch phrase ... 'You know how it is in Africa.'" [Parsons, pg. 34]

"You've always been very decent to me, ... our first meeting was on the set in Fort Lee when I was making *Carmen*." [Genini, pg. 17]

"... made her hearers forget the vampire of the screen during her dissertation ... I am not satisfied that I have achieved good results." [Golden, pg. 127]

"I'm glad to hear it ... So bring on your husbands and sweethearts and I'll be conservative as possible." ['Many Organization at Convention,' *Motography*, Vol. 17 #4, June 23, 1917, pg. 1305]

"I replied that no honest-to-goodness vampire would be up and about at eight in the morning ... breakfasting with relish on French snails." [Theda Bara, manuscript, pg. 29]

"Naturally, I held out my hand, but he refused to shake hands with me ... 'That reporter thought I was going to kiss him.'" [Agnes Smith, 'Confessions of Theda Bara,' Photoplay, Vol. XVIII #1, June 1920 pg. 58]

"... found a reward surpassing my wildest dreams ... fragrance of the wreaths and roses which then they freely gave." [Theda Bara manuscript pp. 26-27]

"Bringing with her seventeen trunks of clothes ... who enthusiastically welcomed her with cheers, flowers and fruit." [Grace Kingsley, 'Champ Vamp Arrives,' *Los Angeles Times*, June 3, 1917]

"Facing a battery of cameras and a crowd of admirers ... looking like some demure Quaker maiden in her soft gray cloak and long gray veil." [G.F. Harleman, 'News of Los Angeles and Vicinity, Theda Bara Arrives in Los Angeles,' *Moving Picture World*, June 30, 1917, pg. 2107]

"This is Miss Bara's first trip West ... on account of the number of desert pictures in which she appeared." [Grace Kingsley, 'Champ Vamp Arrives,' *Los Angeles Times*, June 3, 1917]

"Pretending not to notice this I hastened my steps, seeking such a distance from that hot water bottle as if it had been the plague." [Theda Bara, manuscript, pg. 30]

"... is spending her few days of leisure prior to beginning work on her most ambitious picture ... in long and joyous motor trips through Southern California." [Grace Kingsley, 'Will Have Peace,' *Los Angeles Times*, June 10, 1917]

"I am going to have a house ... many more of them would succeed in their chosen fields." [Ibid.]

"The Fox star lives on West Adams street ... which aids peculiarly in her visualizing of a role." [Grace Kinsgley, 'Frivols; Cleopatra at Home,' *Los Angeles Times*, Aug. 16, 1917]

"Theda Bara, the world-famous William Fox screen artiste ... fits in with my mood while I am portraying the role of Cleopatra." ['Moon Has Strange Fascination for Noted Vampire,' *Los Angeles Herald*, Vol. XLII, Number 221, July 17, 1917, pg. 18]

CHAPTER SIX: 'IN SUPPORT OF THE DIVINE THEDA'

"Theda Bara, premiere vampire of the screen ... by the Fox Film Corporation on June 4." ['Theda Bara Works Secretly in "Cleopatra,"' *Motion Picture News*, May 5, 1917, pg. 2833]

"The picture is complete . . . so those who have seen parts of the production, say." [Ibid.]

"We hardly expected success . . . the woman was on hand." [Theda Bara, manuscript, pg. 32]

' . . . when she was still wearing her hair in a braid.' [Jay Jorgensen and Donald L. Scoggins, *Creating the Illusion: A fashionable History of Hollywood Costume Designers*, Running Press Adult, 2015, pp. 18-22]

"West, who had developed a penchant for sketching gowns . . . she was given the opportunity to costume *The Birth of a Nation*." [Ibid., pg. 18]

"Though a meticulous researcher . . . and tailoring that appealed to a modern audience." [Adrienne L. McLean (editor) Drake Stutesman, [et al] *Costume, Makeup, and Hair*, Rutgers University Press, 2016, pg. 29]

" . . . confraternal processions in the streets of Europe . . . " [Alison Kinney, 'How the Klan Got Its Hood,' *The New Republic*, Jan. 8, 2016]

"Madame Clare West . . . is now head of the Fine Arts costume department." ['Sifted from the Studios,' *Motography*, Vol. 15, March 11, 1916, pg. 600]

"Other than the fact that West had indeed been . . . nor had she ever left the country." [Jorgensen, pg. 18]

"She designed the gowns Dorothy Gish wears in The Pennsylvanian Dutch Girl . . . " ['Sifted from the Studios,' *Motography*, Vol. 15, March 11, 1916, pg. 600]

"West's *Intolerance* designed concepts . . . entitled 'Back to Babylon for New Fashions.'" [McLean, pg. 29]

". . . representing an immense and magnificent peacock tail outspread, undulated twenty-five feet back of me as I walked." [Theda Bara, manuscript pg. 32]

"I make a sketch first . . . drape fabric on it—and cut!" [Lisle Foote, *Buster Keaton's Crew: The Team Behind His Silent Films*, McFarland, 2014, pg. 219]

" . . . in impeccable Prince Albert dress. . . The retinue of five did not receive the order." [Theda Bara, manuscript, pg. 32]

". . . specifies priceless rings upon her and UPON HER TOES— This is a little outre, is it not?" [Johnson, pg. 128]

"I have said certain fairies come to my . . . he was inspired to a poetic fervor." [Theda Bara manuscript, pg. 32]

". . . been compelled to wear some tawdry modern sham jewelry . . . through the whole play would have run my sense of a conscious flaw." [Ibid., pg. 34]

"The whole costume echoes the sinuous . . . oozed sensuality." [Penny Proddow, Debra Healy, & Marion Fasel, *Hollywood Jewels: Movies Jewelry Stars*, Abradale/Abrams; Reprint, 1996, pg. 18]

'in recognition and sincere appreciation of the exquisite artistic and authentic jewelry' [Mark Shoemaker, "Cleopatra's Jewels," *Art Deco Society of Los Angeles*, Vol. 13, July 2002 : http://www.adsla.org/vol_13/vol_13_july02/vol_13_july02.htm

"The sparkle of diamonds fascinates me. . . . I do not care for diamonds as a personal decoration." [Theda Bara, 'Window Shopping' Favorite Pastime of the "Vampire,"' *The Day*, May 22, 1916, pg. 13]

"In the 1910s one of the most important fashion influences . . . stereotype for a host of exotic screen ladies yet to come." [Edward Maeder, Alicia Annas, Satch Lavalley, Elois Jenssen,

Earl A. Powell, *Hollywood and History: Costume Design in Film* organized by Edward Maeder, Thames and Hudson, text based on contributions by, LA County Museum of Art, 1987, pg. 46]

"Bara's makeup, typical of the silent era . . . used in costumes for films depicting ancient times." [Ibid.]

"Each of the Cleopatras has a hairstyle typical . . . So much for history!" [Ibid.]

". . .thousands of people, the making of plans . . . Hundreds of sketches are made only to be discarded." [Theda Bara manuscript, pg. 31]

". . . often, after a set was finished, Mr. Edwards and I found some detail that was incorrect," [Ibid.]

"Tropical gardens grew up out of the barren sands . . . Vast choruses were instructed in Egyptian dances." [Ibid., pg. 32]

"I also joined the Denishawn Dancing School . . . mirrors and practice bars . . . " [Lillian Gish, *The Movies, Mr. Griffith and Me*, Prentis-Hall, 1960, pg. 100]

"Fritz Leiber as Caesar possesses the . . . His acting is exceedingly good. . ." [Peter Milne, 'Review of *Cleopatra*', *Motion Picture News*, Nov. 3, 1917]

" . . . silent films were simply a summer job, an easy way to make money." [Virginia Leiber, *The Great Fritz*, unpublished manuscript, courtesy of Justin Leiber]

"Fritz was very impressed with Bara's vampish quality. . . . There was nothing on under those beads." [Ibid.]

"I had often been backstage with my parents . . . From Theda Bara." [Fritz Leiber Jr. letter, courtesy of F. Gwynplaine MacIntyre]

"When I played Marc Antony . . . I thought everyone had forgotten it." [Josie P. Lederer, 'Mark Antony Orates,' *Pictures and The Picturegoer*, March 1, 1923, pg. 10]

"I had been in a play with Irene Bordoni . . . and made up my mind to have another shot of it later." [Ibid.]

"Didn't see the beauteous Theda . . . her publicity people made her keep up the mystery business always." [Ibid.]

"He had her in his arms crying for air . . . sat on the running board of a Ford and lighted his pipe." [Golden, pg. 135]

"It was a great experience . . . which are required in motion pictures." [George A. Katchmer, *Eighty Silent Movie Stars: Biographies and Filmographies of the Obscure to the Well Known*, (filmographies by Richard E. Braff), McFarland, 1991, pp. 833-834]

"We took the exteriors in the morning . . . Can't you imagine what a terrible picture it must have been?" [Ibid., pg. 834]

"With no exception that I can remember . . . I not absolutely obliged to by historic precedent." [Theda Bara, 'What I Think of the Men on Screen,' *Cinema Chat*, Number 55, June 7 1920, p. 16]

"Monroe Salisbury has been engaged in a leading role in support of the divine Theda." [Grace Kingsley, 'Champ Vamp Arrives,' *Los Angeles Times*, June 3, 1917]

" . . . got in a big picture with Theda Bara and went down to Florida . . . but I think they were." [Grange B. McKinney, *Art Acord and the Movies*, Western Classics, 2000, pg.15]

"The funniest thing about that *Cleopatra* . . . even for the Serpent of the Nile." ['Tea With The Ladies,' *The Billboard*, Oct. 27, 1917, pg. 27]

"The story demands that he be played that war-grizzled veteran— dog-like in his devotion to Antony." [Johnson, pg. 70]

"A gratifying feature appertaining to the male members . . . Art Accord are useful members of the cast. . ." ['Review of *Cleopatra*,' *The Moving Picture World*, Vol. 34 #5, Nov. 3, 1917, pg. 708]

"Another point of interest to the people . . . that the balance of the cast seemed disturbed." [Theodore A. Liebler, 'the Legitimate Stage,' *The Billboard*, Oct 27, 1917, pg. 21]

CHAPTER SEVEN: A DAY IN THE LIFE OF CLEOPATRA

". . . an exalted and intoxicating dramatic carousal, . . . to create the stellar role is such a picture as *Cleopatra*. [Theda Bara manuscript pg. 37]

"There is joy, the truest joy any artist can know . . . which is unique and apart from the ordinary feelings of every day life." [Ibid., pg. 38]

". . . physical suffering and mental strain, wearisome rehearsals, hours and hours of work overtime and into the night. . ." [Ibid.]

" of ease, of joy rides . . . labor as is required. [Ibid., pp. 38-39]

"For two hours and more at a time . . . Every detail had to be perfect." [Ibid., pg. 39]

"Theda Bara, who, we are sure, . . . What did you expect?" [Longacre, 'Just for Fun,' *Motion Picture News*, Aug. 4, 1917, pg. 859]

"There was a costume which was deservedly called . . . over my forehead." [Theda Bara manuscript, pg. 39]

"For three hours I went through a . . . across my forehead." [Ibid., pg. 40]

". . . the heat beat into the studio with a torrid intensity . . . I'd go through the sensations of freezing to death." [Ibid., pg. 39]

"One can easily imagine that resources of energy and enthusiasm were required to carry one through the final filming. . . ." [Ibid. pg. 39]

". . . successor to Herbert Brenon . . . he's told her how to do it so often." ['Theda Bara Boss 'Round the Lot,' *Photoplay*, April 1918, pg. 27]

"J. Gordon Edwards was the nicest director I ever had . . . He was kind and considerate." [Agnes Smith, 'Confessions of Theda Bara,' *Photoplay*, pg. 110]

"In all of my experience, I have never met . . . posterity as the greatest actress of her time." [Krefft, 193]

"I rate Mr. Edwards one of the finest gentlemen . . . he put into these wonderful pictures." [Kevin Brownlow, *Parade's Gone By*, Knopf, 1968, pg. 378]

"We worked side by side for six months on Sheba . . . and all on of your knowledge of screen etiquette . . ." [Ibid.]

"The wonderful thing about Mr. Edwards was this: no matter how dramatic it was, it was never hammed." [Ibid., pg. 382]

"I believe that the less directing a director does . . . the thing that makes pictures as well as drama." [Golden, pg. 75]

"Before starting a scene Director. . . They are: 'Quiet.' 'Music.' 'Camera.'" ['Man of Few Words,' *Los Angeles Herald*, Vol. XLIV #129, April 1, 1919, pg. 24]

"While (Thomas) Ince was always to insist upon ... the first thing he would do was tear it up." [Paul O'Dell and Anthony Slide, *Griffith and the Rise of Hollywood*, A. S. Barnes, 1971, pg. 98]

"The man with the scenario brain ... recognize one if he saw it." ['R.A. Walsh Directs Without Script', *Motography*, XIX #10 March 19, 1918, pg. 496]

"I read the scenario once ... something static and dead." [Golden, pg. 75]

"I have always prepared myself for a new character ... but very much to my advantage as an actress." [Theda Bara, 'Curse on a Moving Picture Actress,' *The Forum*, Vol. 62, pg. 89]

"One realized at a glance her success ... realistic a picture of Miss Bara taken from the sidelines." [Ethel Rosemon, 'Our Classic Extra Girl Plays at the Fox Studio,' *Motion Picture Classic*, Aug. 1917, pp. 40-41]

"You can't put anything... Why should she?" answered another. [Ibid. pg. 42]

" ... handsome youths wearing ... by the thing." [Golden, pp. 168-170]

"The staging and methods of the moving-picture people ... to go on with the thing in such surroundings." [Bernard Weinraub, 'Movie History Emerges From a Basement,' *The New York Times*, Sept. 17, 1996]

"Wal, I'll be hornswoggled if it ain't my old pal MacDuff!... We'll slaughter the lousy buzzards!" [Marion, pg. 14]

"I had never seen a movie being made before ... I could tell she hadn't taken elocution lessons." [Fritz Leiber Jr. letter, courtesy of F. Gwynplaine MacIntyre]

"Lacking words, the picture people adopted ... you know that trouble is brewing." [Dorothy Donnell, 'Psychology and the Screen,' *Motion Picture Classic*, Vol. III #4, Dec. 1916, pg. 38]

"That she is an uncommonly good actress will be admitted by anyone who has seen her ..." [McCord, pg. 236]

"Miss Bara has a way of making the most of her parts. ... hold the attention of her audience." [Ibid. pg. 242]

"Miss Bara does most of her real acting through ... There is an intelligent foreign element about this actress that savors of the real thing. ..." [Zierold, *Sex Goddesses of the Silent Screen*, pg. 22]

"The 'Vampire' required an actress of the scope and ability ... splendid tribute to her genius." [*Motion Picture Classic*, Vol. 4 #2, April, 1917, pg. 38]

"Mlle. Bara's facial expression is wonderfully brutal and fiendish, but every physical movement shows grace and charm."[McCord, pg. 232]

"She gives the spectators their money's worth ... She has none of the three." [*Brooklyn Daily Eagle*, May 13, 1917, pg. 14]

"Miss Bara is not to be blamed for the picture's ... is what the Fox Company wants." [Lynde Denig, review of *Destruction*, *The Moving Picture World*, Vol. 22 #2, Jan. 8, 1916, pp. 255-256]

'bloodless cheek of chaste renunciation' [Theda Bara, 'How I became a Film Vampire,' *The Forum*, Vol. 61, pg. 717]

"It is impossible to act without feeling. ... Then I felt like myself again and studied and read." [Archie Bell, 'Theda Bara, the Vampire Woman,' *The Theatre*, Nov. 1915, pp. 245, 253]

"She throws herself into a part ... with so much force." Roberta Courtlandt, ' A Modern Jekyll-Hyde,' *Motion Picture Classic*, Vol. IV #5 July 1917, pg. 24]

"What a terrible woman ... " [Golden, pg. 69]

"...when I was supposed to beat the messenger ... I had in my zeal whipped him much harder than I realized." [Grace Kingsley, 'Frivols: Cleopatra at Home,' *Los Angeles Times*, Aug. 16, 1917]

"It was the emotional expression of Cleopatra's rage ..." [Theda Bara, *The Forum*, Vol. 62, pg. 91]

"We were all blind as bats.... and I really mean groped." [Bodeen, pg. 24]

"It was a scene which called for a consummate portrayal ... not so facile or painless as the putting on." [Theda Bara, manuscript, pp. 40-41]

"At the time of my first studio experience ... and stuck it in front of the painted walls." [William J. Mann, *Behind The Screen How Gays and Lesbians Shaped Hollywood*, 1910-1969, Viking, 2001, pg. 27]

"What kind of place was *this* for someone like me?" [Ibid., pg. 28]

"... the set inside the tent was supposed to be Cleopatra's throne room... entwined around not very impressive breasts." [Ibid., pg. 31]

"Remarkably self possessed and not at all glamorous. ... The liking was to become mutual for many years." [Ibid.]

"Aside from the painters and ... in which we all indulged upon occasion." [Ibid., pg. 32]

"J. Gordon Edwards, the producer of this big film ... rugs, divans, tapestries, hangings and what not. " [Randolph Bartlett, 'Review of *Cleopatra*,' *Photoplay* Jan., 1918, pg. 66]

"Miss Bara is very easy to design for ... for sirens are burning fountains of passion." [Celia Brynn, 'The Story of a Designing Man,' *Picture-Play Magazine*, Oct. 1919, pg. 61]

"Cameramen felt some strange reason that color ... This is a black-and-white film." [Mann, pg. 28]

"... left little mark on me beyond a most unpleasant memory of getting up at five every morning and making my face bright yellow." [Sheridan Morley, *Noël Coward*, Haus, 2005, pg. 12]

"For some roles I have had to literally be painted white.... Two or three baths were sometimes needed to take off this color." [Mary B. Mullet, 'Theda Bara, Queen of the Vampires,' *The American Magazine*, Vol. 90, September 1920, pg. 98]

"... can apply make-up so skillfully as to obtain excellent results, something quite rare in filmdom." [Golden, pg. 90]

"... which often melted one's make-up, blistered one's skin... were the major or minor attacks of klieg eyes." [Petrova, *Butter with my Bread*, pg. 266]

"The next day you would have no 'eyes' at all.... It was a dreadful thing." [Kobal, pp. 66-67]

"I had been in bed that night for some hours ... the pain and weeping continued." [Petrova, *Butter with my Bread*, pp. 266-267]

"What I was after was naturalism ... to make shadows where shadows would appear in nature." [Cecilia de Mille Presley & Mark A. Vieira, *Cecil B. DeMille: The Art of the Hollywood Epic*, Running Press, 2014, pp. 46-47]

"Even Bill Hart likes to have a violin about ... entitled 'Til the Clouds Roll By.'" [Alfred A Cohn, 'What Makes Them Cry', *Photoplay*, April, 1918 pg. 55]

"...does not hesitate to invoke the aid of Orpheus ... In rehearsals Griffith has used a phonograph many times to get unity of action by music cues." [Ibid., pg. 54]

"He never talked during a shot; . . . 'Ask Miss Blythe if she wants a change.'" [Brownlow, *Parade's Gone By*, pg. 382]

"I first discovered the inspiration given by music . . . he turned about and directed the music." [Theda Bara, manuscript, pg. 42]

"There were times when music made continuance in work almost impossible. . . . jazz picture on an adjacent stage to mine." [Ibid.]

"Music became the vogue at Fox's western studio when . . . ticket, as it were." [Alfred A Cohn, 'What Makes Them Cry', *Photoplay*, April 1918, pg. 56]

"...a string orchestra to play airs from *Aida*. . . music for the emotional scenes in Theda Bara's *Cleopatra*." [Ibid., pg. 53]

"While the redoubtable Theda vamped Marc Antony . . . or carried down through the ages by Cleopatra's posterity, if she had any." [Ibid., pg. 54]

"Imagine Marc and Octavius being vamped to a golden wedding anniversary song," [Ibid., pg. 67]

"In keeping with my conception of Cleopatra . . . it is the magic music to conjure a mystic mood." [Theda Bara, manuscript, pp. 42-43]

"Miss Bara vamps to the soft music of a harp— . . . play something spirited!'" ['Miss Cleopatra Bara is Summering in California,' *Los Angeles Times*, July 29, 1917]

"The perfume Theda Bara uses in aiding her . . . The fragrance is so strong that it would not be strange if it were detected on the screen." [*Motion Picture News* Vol. 15 #23 June 9, 1917, pg. 3514]

". . . the woman with the most wonderful nose in the world." Jessica Murphy, 'Ann Haviland, Forgotten Mastermind of the Signature Scent,' *Atlas Obscura*, Dec. 19, 2017

"My Cleopatra perfume may be likened to the music of a harp . . . 'What is this wonderful smell?'" [Theda Bara, manuscript, pg. 43]

"A woman, a most womanly woman . . . bare the secrets of her heart through the vehicle of a modern art." [Ibid., pg. 44]

". . . possessed a dead-on knack for capturing the public's eye with his vibrant, elegant portrait photographs." [Mary Mallory, 'Hollywood Heights: Albert Witzel, Early Glamour Photography Pioneer' *The Daily Mirror*, Aug. 12, 2003

"Motion picture companies periodically approached him . . . bare-navel vamp sexuality of Theda Bara proved irresistible." [David S. Shields, *Still: American Silent Motion Picture Photography*, The University of Chicago Press, 2013, pg. 82]

" . . . crawled over the faux Egyptian sets . . . had a major actress been made to seem so exotically vulgar." [Ibid.]

". . . express- ing various attitudes, and emotions in the scene . . . 'Go ahead, take as many as you want.'" [Theda Bara, manuscript., pg. 41]

"12,000 to 18,000 feet . . . all the labor of the day before had to be gone through again on the morrow." [Ibid., pp. 41-42]

"After all this, too tired to undress . . . or my head compressed in a red-hot iron crown." [Ibid., pg. 42]

CHAPTER EIGHT: 'WE CAN GET AWAY WITH MURDER HERE'

"You know from past experience ... as long as he can get away from the studio." [Letter of William Fox to Sol Wurtzel, December 28th, 1917, Sol Wurtzel Papers, AMPAS]

"I am, invariably more rattled than a stage struck girl ... perhaps none of us will live to see the splendor of its noon." [John Sheridan, 'Acting on the sidewalk', *Photoplay*, April 1915, pp. 87-88]

" ... with his face covered with lather ... He was rewarded by being shot at." [Leonard Pitt and Dale Pitt, *Los Angeles, A to Z*, University of California Press. 1997, pp. 193-94]

"... one of the most beautiful of the new residential show ... an Italian villa and five acres of sunken gardens ... " ['Home of Pioneer Is Show Place,' *Los Angeles Times*, Dec. 22, 1912, pg. VI-1]

"Two special trains and a dozen automobiles ... several hundred animals, including camels, burros and Arabian horses." [J.C. Jessen, 'In and Out of the Studios,' *Motion Picture News*, Vol. 16 #4, July 28, 1917, pg. 622]

"On the sands of Oxnard ... foot soldiers fell in line and followed their queen until the entire body disappeared over the sandhills."['Pomp of Egypt Revisited,' *Motography*, Vol. XVIII #11, Sept. 15, 1917, pg. 563]

" ... crowding the Bara car to the edge of the mountain highway...served to prevent the car from going over the cliff." [J.C. Jessen, 'In and Out of the Studios,' Motion Picture News, Vol. 16 #4, July 28, 1917, pg. 622]

'Chief Gimme' [*Cinema News*, Vol. 1 #8, April 1, 1917, pg. 2]

"He was a character of the world ... he could do it very well." [Brownlow, *The Parade's Gone By*, pg. 384]

"The banks of the almost stagnant body of water are ideal for. . . away the footage." ['Notes of Studio and Screen,' *The New York Times*, Aug. 26, 1917]

"The buildings erected are from ancient drawings ... and one of the most costly ever erected on the West Coast ..." [*Motion Picture News*, Vol. 16 #5, Aug. 4, 1917, pg. 862]

"Cleopatra Bara's palace ... one frequented by Caesar, Antony, and the other boys." ['Notes of Studio and Screen,' *The New York Times*, Aug. 26, 1917]

"Here, Marie, take them to my tent and give them so milk!" [Grace Kingsley, 'Studio,' Los Angeles Times, July 15, 1917]

" ... the sun was at its hottest, ... Get in the picture, dear, get in the picture!" [Ibid.]

"It was quite noticeable that Albert Roscoe ... Cleopatra's riding thru the streets. . ." ['Review of *Cleopatra,*' *Wid's Daily*, Oct. 18, 1917, pp. 663-664]

"The remarkable feature of the extra business ... Other nationalities and races were adapted with astonishing ease to the needs of the feature." ['EGYPT'S QUEEN LIVES AND LOVES AGAIN IN FILMLAND,' *Los Angeles Times*, July 29, 1917]

"There was a Negro man in the scene ... people often weren't so nice to colored people in those days." [Fritz Lieber Jr.]

"Preparations are now being made for the staging ... approximately fifty miles down the coast from Los Angeles." [J.C. Jessen, 'In and Out of the Studios,' *Motion Picture News*, Vol. 16 #4, July 28, 1917, pg. 622]

" ... reproductions of the oared galleys antiquity." [Jim Sleeper, *Great Movies shot in Orange County*, California Classics, 1980, pg. 82]

"Two hundred fifty thousand feet of lumber was used ... to reproduce this according to the best reports in history." ['Filming of "Cleopatra" Ends With Battle Scene,' *Motion Picture News*, Vol. 16#9, Sept. 1, 1917 pg. 1454]

"The making of these scenes was a gigantic undertaking ... Gordon Edwards and his staff." [Ibid.]

"... more sybaritical splendor and fury than any other beauty of the flickering films." [Sleeper, pg. 84]

'jewels and costumes worth $1,000'. [Ibid., pg. 82]

"I enjoyed Balboa immensely. ... I should have been entirely cut off from land." [Grace Kingsley, 'Frivols; Cleopatra at Home,' *Los Angeles Times*, Aug. 16, 1917]

"PLEASE ADVISE! AS TO MOTIVE AND NECESSITY!" [Johnson, pg. 135]

"A thrilling chariot race ... he guided the sliding horses back to the roadway." [*The Atlanta Constitution*, Oct. 7, 1917 pg. 4]

"Some were short and some were tall. ... looked like he might have been borrowed from a museum. ..." [Sleeper, pg. 83]

"The scenes made at this point show ... together with thousands of tents." ['Filming of "Cleopatra" Ends With Battle Scene,' *Motion Picture News*, Sept. 1, 1917, pg. 1454]

"The filming took weeks on end. ... we rode around the bluffs for a few dazzling moments." [Sleeper, pg. 83]

"The battle of Actium scenes required eight ... required for the men from the railroad station to the filming location." ['Filming of "Cleopatra" Ends With Battle Scene,' *Motion Picture News*, Sept. 1, 1917, pg. 1454]

"... really pretty much of a mudhole. ... could only be moved at high tide since it actually sat on mud at low tide." [Warren F. Morgan, *This Was Mission Country: Reflections in Orange of Merle and Mabel Ramsey*, Mission Printing Co., 1973. pg. 189]

"At the sound of a trumpet ... or being thrown into the bay." [Sleeper, pg. 83]

" ... refused to posture with a megaphone as Brenon had, instead gesturing with his arms to communicate instructions at a distance." [Krefft, pg. 193]

"Thousands of people daily drove ... where an advantageous view could be had." ['Filming of "Cleopatra" Ends With Battle Scene,' *Motion Picture News*, Sept. 1, 1917 pg. 1454]

"To make the battle as realistic as possible ... The result was a very real fight picture." [Morgan, pg. 189]

"I have thought it best to stage this fight at ... we can get away with murder here." [Johnson, pg. 178]

"The boats were equipped with catapults ... Some spectacular water night scenes were filmed." ['Filming of "Cleopatra" Ends With Battle Scene,' *Motion Picture News*, Sept. 1, 1917 pg. 1454]

"The climax to weeks of filming came one fine night. ... slaves screaming and jumping into the water." [Sleeper, pg. 83]

" ... the most magnificent and spectacular scene ever taken on water," [Ibid.]

"The payroll on the last day required $35,000 ... the amount of film exposed exceeding 100,000 feet." ['Filming of "Cleopatra" Ends With Battle Scene,' *Motion Picture News*, Sept. 1, 1917, pg. 1454]

"J. Gordon Edwards has furnished the picture ... The photography by Rail Schellinger and John W. Boyle needs no criticism...." [Peter Milne, 'Review of *Cleopatra,*' *Motion Picture News*, Nov. 3, 1917, pg. 3134]

"His preparation and oversight paid off.... he had to supervise ten to eighteen cameramen instead of six." [Krefft, pg. 193]

"... there was a lot of production value for the money spent on the screen." [Robert S. Birchard, interview with the author]

"Mr. Edwards does not spend a single penny more than he has to, for he, as you know, has my explicit faith and confidence." [Letter of William Fox to Sol Wurtzel, June 23, 1919 AMPAS]

CHAPTER NINE: 'DRESS YOUR USHERS IN ROMAN TOGAS'

'I am quite pleased with the picture ... having gone away on a short vacation trip." [Grace Kingsley, 'Frivols; Cleopatra at Home,' *Los Angeles Times*, Aug 16, 1917]

"I take all the parts of the film which the film editors ... spice to hold the public, I let it go." [Ruth-Dorothy Block, 'A Movie Stepmother,' *Filmplay Journal*, May 1922, pp. 18-19]

"Theda Bara, the incomparable William Fox artiste ... an antique of extraordinary value. " [*Motion Picture News*, Vol. 15 #21. May 26, 1917, pg. 3239]

"... just to satisfy her natural curiosity ... her valuable bauble was the gold setting." [*Motion Picture News*, Vol. 15 #20, May 19, 1917 pg. 3072]

"Homage to the beautiful lady Theda Bara ... her body against all things evil." [Zierold, *Sex Goddesses of the Silent Screen*, pg. 35]

"I felt the blood of the Ptolemys coursing through my veins ... I am Cleopatra!" [*Los Angeles Herald*, Vol. XLIII #256, Aug. 27, 1918, pg. 22]

"I was thirteen when I first went to the movies to watch elves and fairies flickering on the moon, to the accompaniment of a tinkling piano." [Edward L. Bernays, *Biography of an Idea: The Founding Principles of Public Relations*, Simon and Schuster, 1965, pg. 147]

"... a seedy-looking building ... looked like a saloon keeper." [Ibid., pp. 147-148]

"'Young man ... It was a disappointing beginning." [Ibid., pg.148]

"To be considered for such an assignment was as exciting ... more allure than a love goddess today can equal " [Ibid.]

"... repeated with gusto how colossal *Cleopatra* was." [Ibid.]

"...rapidly increasing the number of his storefront movie houses... relatively new Leavitt Building, at 130 West Forty-Sixth Street." [Krefft, pg. 198]

"Having always known privilege ... employer with contemptuous sangfroid." [Ibid, pg. 198]

"Looking back, I am surprised at the glowing report I wrote ... or instance, students of Egyptian and Roman history.'" [Bernays, pp. 148-149]

"I raised questions the public might discuss.... voluptuousness and sensuousness?'" [Ibid., pg. 149]

"'I looked for social values in *Cleopatra*.... Cleopatra's couch in art throughout history, another to reveal how armored men make love!" [Ibid.]

"—a silhouette in profile of Cleopatra reclining in her native costume.... one-inch advertisements stimulated public interest." [Ibid.]

"*The New York Times* turned down my advertisement . . . It was in Dec.." [Arnold Koch, Looking Back: 'Dancing with a legend: Edward Bernays, the 'father of public relations' *WickedLocal*.com, June 11, 2010]

"It was photographed in California. . . . battle and desert scenes." [Display Ad, *Fort Wayne Journal Gazette*, Aug. 11, 1918, pg. 16]

". . . contained stories and illustrations. . . they expressed the accepted attitudes of the movie editors of the times." [Bernays, pg. 149]

"Egypt! Alexandria! Rome! The immensity of the Desert! . . . the Ancients.'" [*Cleopatra* pressbook, Margaret Herrick Library, Academy of Motion Pictures Arts and Science]

"This play affords every Triangle exhibitor . . . hit in the lobby." [Ronald L. Davis, *William S. Hart: Projecting the American West* University of Oklahoma Press, 2003, p. 85]

"Fox carried out the program I suggested . . . the picture ran as a great box-office success." [Bernays, pg. 149]

". . . had advanced to the very top of artistic achievement . . . better than I had ever seen anybody make before." ['How Fox, the Exhibitor, Decided Upon "Standard Pictures,"' *Motion Picture News*, August 4, 1917, pg. 819]

"I'm afraid I paid very little attention to historical detail . . . capture the spirit of that time, the luxurious abandon." [Mann, pg. 32]

"In the little book which I compiled before I entered pictures . . . to save them from desecration." [Theda Bara, manuscript, pg. 36]

". . .an independent woman, a divorcee. . . happen if your morals were too loose." [Peter Edwards, 'Condemned spy Mata Hari glib during final interrogation: MI5 files,' *The Toronto Star*, April 24, 2014

". . . the plot of *The Soul of Buddha* . . . who becomes an outcast through her love of a man." [Theda Bara, manuscript, pg. 36]

"I have a trade to make with you . . . That is splendid!" [Ibid.]

"Somebody mentioned seeing Theda Bara . . . one in one scene and one in another." [Letter of Herbert E. Winlock to A. M. Lythgoe, Feb 10, 1918, Lythgoe papers, Metropolitan Museum of Art, NY]

"Is Theda Bara a Reincarnation of Cleopatra . . . fits Cleopatra as easily as Miss Bara." [Edward Wagenknecht, *The Movies in the Age of Innocence*, pg. 200]

" . . . stretching out illimitably, with the Sphinx in the distance. . . . raises one brow in the manner familiar to film fans. . ." [Genini, pg. 39]

"What will be your verdict after you see Theda Bara's portrayal of the passions and pageants of Egypt's vampire queen?" [Fox Company advertisement, *The Evening World*, Oct. 15, 1917, pg. 13]

" . . . completely overwhelmed . . . we do not blame Antony for renouncing Rome." ['New York Newspapers Laud Cleopatra,' *Motography*, Vol. XVIII #18, Nov. 3, 1917, pg. 930]

"The scenes are so gorgeous that they brought continued applause. . . . Needles to say, the photography and other technical points are above criticism." [Ibid.]

"Proud, defiant, willful, emotional, sinuous by turns, Miss Bara makes a representation the most auspiciously successful in her career." [Genini, Pg. 40]

"*Cleopatra* should have been a magnificent spectacle.... *Cleopatra* would have been a thing of joy." [Randolph Bartlett, 'Review of *Cleopatra*,' *Photoplay*, Vol. 13 #2, Jan. 1918, pg. 65]

"Cleopatra of Egypt was among the earliest of the vampires of history ... little comment ..." ['Theda Bara as Cleopatra,' *The New York Times*, Oct. 15, 1917, pg. 26]

"Those who like to see Theda Bara should not fail ... absence of a good interesting story." ['Review of *Cleopatra*,' *The Dramatic Mirror*, Oct. 27, 1917]

"It is a stupendous offering with many magnificent scenes and gorgeous costumes ... and it will be a good picture from the box-office viewpoint." [Helen Rockwell, 'Review of *Cleopatra*,' *Motography*, Nov. 1, 1917, pg. 940]

"*Cleopatra* is a magnificent picture as a spectacle ... before the forces of Octavius that presents the greater range of appeal." [Peter Milne, 'Review of Cleopatra,' *Motion Picture News*, Nov. 3, 1917, pg. 3134]

"There have been many mimic Cleopatras since the birth of the drama ... for the variety and beauty of garments employed." [Edward Weitzel, "Review of *Cleopatra*," *The Moving Picture World*, Nov. 3, 1917, pg. 708]

"Wore many marvelous creations which left her much undressed ... and that gives a touch of artificiality to what should have a very big dramatic climax." ['Review of *Cleopatra*,' *Wid's Daily*, Oct. 18, 1917, pp. 663-664]

"Caesar and Cleopatra are posturing and ... before the camera of a village photographer." [Golden, pg. 142]

"She makes a burlesque of the Serpent of the Nile ... When she is not repulsive, she is funny." ['Review of *Cleopatra*,' *The Brooklyn Daily Eagle*, Dec. 18, 1917, pg. 13]

" ... a low-cut gown for any attempt at clever acting ... 'Feeda Bara.' [Genini, pg. 40]

"*Cleopatra*, a nine-reel Fox feature ... what is up to the present time the prize smut film."['Review of *Cleopatra*,' *The Billboard*, Oct 27, 1917, pg. 66]

"Talking of prima donna directors in pictures another has been added ... And in a picture like this there is no second consideration." [Theodore A. Liebler, 'the Legitimate Stage' *The Billboard*, Oct 27, 1917, pg. 21]

"The Serpent of the Nile is spending a resplendent fortnight ... Just plain, frank nudity would have been easier to stomach." ['Tea With The Ladies' *The Billboard* Oct 27, 1917, pg. 27]

"... rolls her eyes and her hips in that manner which the circus side-show has taught us is thoroughly Egyptian" [Golden, pg. 142]

"... the brilliant work of Theda Bara, who grasped the subtleties of the character in a most wonderful way ..." [Ibid.]

"Theda Bara is excellent and does some of the best work of her career." [Ibid., pg. 141]

"If Cleopatra didn't look like Theda ... failed to take advantage of a warm and pleasant climate." [Ibid., pg. 143]

"How does she compare with other Cleopatras? ... She outstrips 'em all." [Edward P. O'Day, 'THEDA BARA IN CLEOPATRA,' *Madera Mercury*, Vol. XXXII #40, March 1, 1918, pg. 4]

"... the effect is unpleasant switchback kind ... significant in its allusiveness and musical." ['Review of *Cleopatra*,' *Manchester Guardian*, Oct 29, 1918]

"Poor lady, resting in her queenly tomb. . . . preserved in the moving pictures by filmland's chief vampire." [Genini, pg. 40]

CHAPTER TEN: "IT'LL NEVER SHOW IN PENNSYLVANIA!"

'Probably for the first time the history of films. . . . act together on the screen," [*Motography*, Vol. XX #1 July 6, 1918 pg. 19]

". . . has met with such success at the Lyric Theatre . . . and both days were sell-outs." [*Motion Picture News*, Jan. 5, 1918, pg. 102]

"Do not let cruel fortune cheat you . . . and stunned the imaginations of all beholders," [*The New York Times*, Nov. 25, 1917, pg. 101]

"Facts refute press agent publicity . . . Sphinx opened one eye for a peek, then closed it quickly in disgust." [*The Billboard*, Apr 20, 1918; pg. 57]

"Theda Bara appeared last night at Clune's Auditorium . . . we shall never forget what we have seen." [Antony Anderson, 'Bara as Cleopatra,' *Los Angeles Times*, Jan. 29, 1918]

"The pleasure of playing *Cleopatra* the third week . . . we are now subtracting from profits of the first two weeks . . ." [Letter of William Fox to Sol Wurtzel, March 8, 1918 AMPAS

"It was the aim of exhibitor to eradicate silence from silent pictures . . . could provide an extra dimension to the magic of the movies." [Brownlow, *The Parade's Gone By*, pg. 338]

"Unfortunately, the local moving picture managers think it necessary to have orchestras. . . . the old mother prays for her lost boy.". [Vachel Lindsay, *The Art of the Motion Picture*, Macmillan Company, 1915, pp. 191-192]

". . . the perfect photoplay gathering place would have no . . . and the people coming in." [Vachel Lindsay, pp. 192-193]

"Next to good films, the most important feature of a picture theater . . . But do not carry this idea so far as to burlesque a dramatic picture." [Mildred Maginn Fitz Patrick, 'Playing in the Picture; Helpful Ideas for Musicians and Exhibitors,' *Motography*, Vol. XVII #2, Jan. 13, 1917, pg. 71]

". . . one of the finest men in the world I have ever known . . . And I went down and wrote the music for William Farnum's *The Bondman*." [Bernard Rosenberg, Harry Silverstein, *The Real Tinsel*, Macmillan, 1970, pg. 389]

"Few wonders of the movie palace brought more shivery pleasure to audiences . . . gee, Dad, it was a Wurlitzer!" [Hall, Ben M. *The Best Remaining Seats ; the story of the golden age of the movie palace*, New York, C. N. Potter, 1961, pg. 93.]

"Each of these was marked by a spot of color . . . it was up to the organist to supply the melody." [Ibid., pg. 183.]

". . . some bathing suits that showed what a girl looked like . . . done the right thing." [Sennett, Mack, *The King of Comedy*, Doubleday, 1954, pp. 167-168)

"Women didn't even have bosoms in those days . . . and wear waistlines halfway down to their knees." [Kobal, pg. 86]

"Mayor Curley of Boston handed down a decision . . . if the producers would drape the naked figure of Truth in the film." ['The Players From Ocean to Ocean,' *Photoplay*, July 1915, pg. 146]

"While all this is done in rather an artistic manner working logically . . . chief appeal because of the display of the nude." [*Wid's Daily*, July 13, 1916, pg. 714]

"There are long passages where... It is positively abandoned." ['Review of *Daughter of the Gods*,' The New York Times, Oct 18, 1916, pg. 9.1]

"... if a boy was arrested for stealing, ... because he was a regular patron of a motion picture theatre." [Kennedy, pp. 301-302]

"Remedy does not lie in attack upon films ... They know such efforts would be short-lived." ['The Public Board of Censors,' *Photoplay*, July, 1915, pg. 93]

"I am not interested in the comment Franklin makes ... You are to blame for it being necessary for me to write this note." [Letter of William Fox to Sol Wurtzel, March 12, 1918 Sol Wurtzel Papers, Special Collections, AMPAS

'... the whorehouse film company.' [Charles Tarbox, *Lost Films* 1895-1917, pg. 219]

"Reel 1, eliminate two murder scenes; shorten one... shorten drinking scene of guardian to a flash." [Pratt, George C., *Spellbound in Darkness: A History of the Silent Film*, New York Graphic Society Ltd. 1973, pp. 236-237]

"I admit it, Dearest Elsie, I intend to keep you here for myself ... Marry you— marry you." [Pratt, pg. 237]

"It'll never show in Pennsylvania! ... That's how we worked." [Genini, 65]

"If it is so fixed that it *will* pass the censors ... open and all" (Ruth-Dorothy Block, 'A Movie Stepmother,' *Filmplay Journal*, May 1922, pp. 18-19]

"I have been put here ... pose in such pictures." [W. Stephen Bush, 'The First American Censors,' *Moving Picture World*, Vol. 19 #1, Jan. 3, 1914, pg. 27]

"Oh, I'm not opposed to good pictures ... Such things I would, of course, eliminate from a modern feature." [Ibid.]

"... exhibitor showing an unapproved picture in Ohio might easily ... if he runs a continuous show from 10 a.m. to 11 p.m." [Ibid., pg. 26]

"The rest of the population of Ohio might think ... Here is the real monstrosity of censorship." [W. Stephen Bush, 'The Tyranny of Censorship,' *Moving Picture World*, Vol. 1 #5, Jan. 10, 1914, pg. 153]

"*Othello* was turned down completely on the ground ... suggestive to impressionable youth and savors of violence..." [Tarbox, pp. 242-243]

"Major Funkhouser, we makers of moving pictures ... You have made Chicago a laughing stock." [Carl Laemmle, *Chicago Tribune*, Feb. 15, 1914]

"HOW LONG ARE YOU INTELLIGENT ALDERMEN GOING TO STAND FOR THIS STUPENDOUS NONSENSE?" [Carl Laemmle, *Chicago Tribune*, Feb. 18, 1914]

"They would have had much a harder time in proving that Balaam's ass never had any direct descendants." ['Close-ups,' *Photoplay*, Sept. 1915, pg. 92]

"The spectacular drama, Mr. Fox states, ... settings of desert, palace and sea. ['Starts "Cleopatra" On Road,' *Motion Picture News*, Jan. 5, 1918, pg. 102]

"Eliminate: suggestive advances of Cleopatra on Caesar ... where Cleopatra's body is exposed." [*Complete List of Motion Picture Films Presented to the Kansas State Board of Review for action October 1, 1918 to December 20, 1918*, Kansas State Printing Plant, 1919, pg. 4]

"I have always opposed censorship of any kind that would deprive the screen, meaning the public, of the worthwhile, artistic photoplay." [McCord, pg. 77]

"That is a company matter . . . heroine was one of the foremost women of ancient history." [Golden, pg. 139]

"Cleopatra trotted out all her wares . . . as one alderman said." ['Aldermen Take Look at Cleo and call for More,' *Chicago Tribune,* Dec. 8, 1917]

"Theda Bara is in town on her way . . . with tea and open arms." [Mae Tinee, 'Theda Bara's in Our Midst, but so Exclusively!' *Chicago Tribune,* Feb. 5, 1918]

"Reel 1, three scenes of the Queen . . . in costume exposing body." ['Official Cut-Outs by the Chicago Board of Censors,' *Exhibitors Herald,* March 16, 1918, pg. 26]

"After a careful review of the film Cleopatra . . . brought to the censor office." ['Starts "Cleopatra" On Road,' *Motion Picture News,* Jan. 5, 1918]

". . . wicked, suggestive performance. . . . interfere with church attendance, bring movies into the church." [Zierold, *Sex Goddesses of the Silent Screen,* pp. 3-4]

"Women of Omaha, Neb., have . . . This echoes the public sentiment and offers the best argument for clean pictures." [*The Billboard,* April 20, 1918, pg. 57]

"If the women condemn a picture, they are right . . . They are beautiful—and they are right." [Zierold, *Sex Goddesses of the Silent Screen,* pp. 4-5]

"It is with a great deal of reluctance that I make this statement . . . then to myself as a woman and heart and soul so with the public." ['Theda Bara Resents Omaha Attacks,' *Motography,* Vol. XIX #18, May 4, 1918, pg. 853]

"I wanted to go see Theda Bara in *Cleopatra* at the Washington Theatre . . . The picture was fine and had some grand scenes." ['Diary of John F. D. Carrico,' http://www.kevincarrico.com/jfc1918.htm]

"A few weeks later, the glossy still arrived in the mail with an actual signature scrawled across the bottom. I was enchanted." [John Franceschina, *Hermes Pan: The Man Who Danced with Fred Astaire,* Oxford University Press, 2012, pg. 16]

"I left instructions here in California that we must do all things . . . They came to forget there was a war, which we never allowed them to do." [Sinclair, pg. 61]

"There has been no more effective ammunition aimed . . . the devastation of France and the evil designs against America." [Louella Parsons, 'Propaganda!' *Photoplay,* Sept. 1918, pg. 43]

" . . . to try to stop the atrocity pictures because they made the job of securing a just peace yet more hazardous." [Frank Manchel, *Film Study: An Analytical Bibliography,* Fairleigh Dickinson University Press, 1990, pg. 213]

"KEEP YOUR HANDS OFF OF WAR PICTURES . . . See to it that it is and remains above suspicion." [Nasaw, pg. 218]

" . . . it would offend the Germans here, who did not start this war." ['Der Major Woof Madline in a Chicago daily paper,' *Variety,* July 20 1917]

"Let us hope that the Major will rub the . . . question is not only anti-German but is pro-American." [Mae Tinee, *Chicago Tribune,* July 3 1917 pg. 14]

"Mr. Fox . . . would not consent to the elimination . . . for use by the Imperial German Government." ['Fox Sues Mayor of Chicago,' *Motography,* Sept. 29, 1917, XVIII #13 pg. 668]

"Mr. Fox established the point that Funkhouser's power to condemn . . . The Spy was obviously not within that classification." ['Wins Right to Show "The Spy",' *Motography,* Vol. XVIII #13, Sept. 29, 1917, pg. 683]

"Reel 2 two scenes of a young man holding a bomb . . . and the lighting of the fuse." ['Official Cut-Outs by the Chicago Board of Censors,' *Exhibitors Herald*, Dec. 15, 1917, pg. 31]

" . . . provided the film industry with the opportunity . . . win the goodwill of those in positions of power in the government."[Leslie M. DeBauche, *Reel Patriotism: the Movies and World War I*. University of Wisconsin Press, 1997. pg.158]

"I really credit Hollywood on World War One." [Andrew Kelly, *Cinema and the Great War* (Cinema and Society), Routledge 1997, pg. 27]

"Eliminate close-up of Salome in opening bathing scene. . . . stretched on floor with head on platter." [Pratt, pg. 237]

"Hypocrisy is to blame for the present-day point . . . the latter is only an incident." [Zierold, *Sex Goddesses of the Silent Screen*, pg 41]

"But as to the matter of seduction appeal, I state that none such was intended in the production, and it is visible only to those who go seeking it." [Parish, pg. 27]

"Miss Bara is in her element as the arch vampire . . . was artistically handled, making it the most fascinating and devoid of vulgarity." ['Review of *Salome*,' *Variety*, Oct. 11, 1918]

" . . . without doubt the greatest Biblical spectacle so far made . . . characterization of Theda Bara." [Grace Kingsley,'FLASHES,' *The Los Angeles Times*, Sept. 20, 1918]

"There's no romance in whiskers." ['DEFEND "SALOME'S" LACK OF CLOTHING,' *The Moving Picture World*, February 22, 1919, pg. 1059]

" . . . colossal assault on common sense . . . Herod killed Salome after her dance." [Julian Johnson, 'Review of *Salome*,' *Photoplay*, Jan., 1919, pg. 69]

" . . . a fleshy conception and not the mental lady . . . thoughtfully pressed to my forehead?" [Frederick James Smith, 'Keeping an appointment with Theda Bara,' *Motion Picture Classic*, Vol. 7 #6, Feb. 1919, pg. 78]

" . . . he didn't champion *Salome* the way he had *Cleopatra*. . . . His heart wasn't in the movie and it showed." [Krefft, pp. 209-210]

CHAPTER ELEVEN: 'TIE A CAN ON HER'

"So the lunatics have taken charge of the asylum." [Ronald Bergan, *The United Artists Story*, Crown Publishers, 1986, pg. 1]

" . . . catch a glimpse of this man-eating tigress. . . let the public know that she is intelligent and unpretentious.'" [Marion, pg. 36]

"She was so bored, bored, bored . . . and the company turned out to be me." [Mann, pg. 28]

"Writing scenarios comes as easy to George . . . a story to them." [Celia Brynn, 'The Story of a Designing Man,' *Picture-Play Magazine*, Oct. 1919, pg. 60]

" . . . deals chiefly with the tremendous sacrifices of American mothers . . . will arise during the period of reconstruction." [McCord, pg. 65]

"It has always been my one ambition that as long as you are under my direction to add to your fame," [Parish, pg. 26]

"Mr. Fox seldom came to the studio . . . I only saw him a few times a year." [Agnes Smith, 'The Confessions of Theda Bara,' *Photoplay*, pg. 110]

"As in all Bara pictures, the picture is all Bara… and everything else. " ['Review of *The Soul Of Buddha*,' *The Wichita Daily Eagle*, May 31, 1918, pg. 4]

"Our patrons were little disappointed as they want Theda Bara as a vampire." [Gus Meyers on *Her Greatest Love*, 'What the Picture Did For Me,' *Motography*, Oct. 6, 1917, XVIII #14 pp. 700-701]

"Excellent vampire picture but such stories are losing favor." [S. H. Kinsey on *The Tiger Woman*, 'What the Picture Did For Me,' *Motography*, XVIII #14, Oct. 6, 1917 pg. 700]

"Counteracting Theda Bara's vampire reputation . . . the result is about convincing as if Charlie Chaplin should essay a Wm. S. Hart role." ['Review of "Heart and Soul,"' *The Billboard*, June 9, 1917, pg. 64]

"Folks either want to see Miss Bara on the screen . . . superior tone to bother with her pictures." [McCord, pg. 80]

"No actress, not even Bernhardt . . . could have saved some of the vehicles handed Miss Bara." [Bodeen, pg. 25]

"Tell me. . . . It's not as if we aren't trying . . ." [Krefft, pg. 311]

"The stories and the characters in the stories I had played . . . the sweet and ringleted ingénues." [Petrova, *Butter With My Bread*, pg. 267]

"Any young woman who can increase her weekly salary . . . even a vamp." [Semenov, Lillian Wurtzel and Carla Winter (ed.) *William Fox, Sol M. Wurtzel and the Early Fox Film Corporation: Letters, 1917-1923*, McFarland, 2001, pg. 41]

"Most insulting innuendo I ever read." [Telegram of Theda Bara to Winfield Sheehan, March 15, 1918, Sol Wurtzel Papers, Special Collections, AMPAS]

"My health was bad and I needed a rest . . . tales on men who need their day's wages." [Agnes Smith, 'Confessions of Theda Bara, *Photoplay*, June 1920, pg. 110]

"She came back, and from that time on never failed to appear on time at the studio." [Sinclair, pp. 57-58]

"I note what you say about Miss Brockwell . . . the lowest possible price any available stars can be hired for." [Letter of William Fox to Sol Wurtzel, December 28th, 1917 AMPAS

"Producer William Fox certainly branded her . . . limited the star's work in the 1920s." [Anthony Slide, *Silent Players*, University Press of Kentucky, 2002, pg. 51]

". . . before that he was working for the interest of the company . . . [Letter of Sol Wurtzel to William Fox, May 23, 1918, AMPAS

"'I would be very sorry to see disagreement between Lloyd . . . if he did anything to disturb the condition of the Fox Film Corporation." [Letter of William Fox to Sol Wurtzel, June 7, 1918, Sol Wurtzel Papers, Special Collections, AMPAS]

"Of course, I paid no attention to them as it is a very common occurrence for such stories to get around in all Los Angeles studios." [Letter of Sol Wurtzel to William Fox, July 13, 1918 AMPAS]

". . . an unprincipled, immoral and unmoral creature . . . "[Ibid., pg. 61]

"Winnie's girls are a pain in the ass. . . . or blow their nose, for Christ's sake." [Cooper, pg. 142]

"Sheehan loved to play God . . . great power does not?" [Allvine, pg. 82]

"On his jaunts to California . . . Wurtzel take the rap for his own ruthlessness." [*King Cowboy*, Robert Birchard, pg. 119.]

". . . "personality will often triumph over. . . I believe the Theda Bara star is on the wane." [James R. Quick 'Star Dust,' *Photoplay Magazine*, June 1918, pg. 19]

"Theda Bara has been felicitously styled . . . that the exhibitor who books her take no chance." [McCord, pg. 80]

"This is the best role I ever had . . . There isn't the slightest trace of the Vampire in Kathleen." [Golden, pg. 188]

". . . truly one of the greatest pictures Theda Bara ever made . . ." [*The Shelby Beacon*, Jan. 6, 1920]

"It is a picture of the regular Theda Bara style . . . with no cross to mark its grave." [McCord, pg. 80]

"Five practically uninterrupted years of vamping . . . There were not enough laughs in my life, and I do so love to laugh. . ." [Jute Dixon, 'Wrecker of Million Screen Souls Now Transformed: Bara on Strike Against Continuous Vampire Roles, *The Atlanta Constitution* October 5, 1919, pg.10]

"I can't afford to pay you what you are worth . . . I think he just got tired of seeing me around." [Cari Beauchamp, *Without Lying Down: Frances Marion and the Powerful Women of Early Hollywood*, pg. 174]

"Theda Bara is not dead. . . entitled *La Belle Russe*." ['Theda Bara's Last Picture,' *Arizona Republican*, June 09, 1921, pg. 9]

"I am the victim of overzealous press agents . . . I hardly know what is the truth anymore . . ." [Zierold, *Sex Goddesses of the Silent Screen*, pg. 53]

"It was an original idea, the designing of exotic fables . . . and the mystery which we had created aroused ridicule." [Ibid.]

"I will not slink and writhe and wriggle my eyes day in and out. . . . love for love's sake. I want to be— well, natural." [Golden, pg. 190]

"Why did you leave Fox? . . . and when I put words into her mouth they emerged honey-coated." [Petrova, *Shadowland*, March-April 1920, pp. 43-44]

"Vampires, poor things, are not cinematic vogue just now . . . They will come back— perhaps!" [*Motion Picture Magazine*, Sept. 1920, pg. 97]

"During my career as a screen star I have felt . . . present me in the spoken drama." [Parish, pg. 35]

"I chose it because it gave me an opportunity to play the sort of part the public wants to see me play . . ." [Agnes Smith, 'Confessions of Theda Bara, *Photoplay*, pg. 57]

"She is pretty bad . . . lost control of itself and shook with laughter." [Alexander Woolcott, 'Review of *The Blue Flame*,' *The New York Times*, March 16, 1920 pg. 18]

"It shows what very slight attainments are needed . . . anyone can become queen of the screens." [Agnes Smith, 'Confessions of Theda Bara,' *Photoplay*, pg. 57]

"Perhaps *The Blue Flame* is not a perfect title for Miss Bara's play . . . Why not: Tenting on the Old Vamp Ground?" [Ibid.]

"I really don't know what the critics said about me. . . . who go to theaters or the movies to be entertained, not to compete." [Zierold, *Sex Goddesses of the Silent Screen*, pg. 47]

"I shall go back to the stage after a few pictures . . . but not in the same sort of horrid role I had in *The Blue Flame*."[Ibid, pg. 48]

"Not all of my screen work was bad. . . . inside of me that rings when I hit my mark." [Agnes Smith, 'Confessions of Theda Bara, *Photoplay*, pg. 110]

"My most interesting character, to my mind, has been Cleopatra . . . in spite of the opinion of movie fans." [Theda Bara, 'How I Became a Film Vampire,' *The Forum*, Vol. 61, p. 71]

"I didn't want to get married. . . . It still fascinates me to sit and watch him approach me." [Golden, pg. 191]

"Neither of us had ever been on time in our lives . . . and sneezed throughout the ceremony." [Ibid., pg. 211]

"I would tell every girl . . . but I did, you know." [Zierold, *Sex Goddesses of the Silent Screen*, pg. 48]

"J. Gordon Edwards intends to make a special . . . more successful than they were with the stars." [Letter of William Fox to Sol Wurtzel, February 13, 1920, Sol Wurtzel Papers, Special Collections, AMPAS]

"Mr. Edwards made an immediate impression on me. . . . been great lovers of the arts to have lived in that style.'" [Brownlow, *Parade's Gone By*, pp. 379-380]

"Well, we've got to find Sheba now . . . I had been a student of the arts . . . [Ibid., pg. 380]

"Oh, she's terrible . . . opposed to having me." [Ibid., pp. 380-381]

"The actor who played Solomon was there . . . important between players." [Ibid., 381]

". . . showed me a real cute little lamp-shade with a few beads on it . . . put 'em all on at once I couldn't keep warm!" [St. Johns, Adela Rogers, 'When the Queen of Sheba Was a Kid,' *Photoplay Magazine*, Jan. 1921, pg. 50]

"No motion picture audience would stand for Sheba falling for a set of whiskers." [Ramsaye, *A Million and One Nights*, pg. 707]

"I was to have gone right on as Theda Bara had done . . . with one great production after the other." [Brownlow, pg. 384]

"We were to go over to Italy to make *Pelleas* . . . He ruined his career and he ruined mine." [Ibid.]

"Anyone who tries to make pictures in Italy must console themselves to their methods. . . . It takes three Italians to do what one American can do." [Krefft, 318]

"I had some very fine talks with Mr. Fox. . . . *Shepard King* will knock 'em dead." [Letter of Sol Wurtzel to J. Gordon Edwards, January 9, 1922 AMPAS]

"Mr. Edwards returned to this country . . . except that the blame lay with Fox." [Brownlow, *Parade's Gone By*, pg. 384]

'broken heart.' [Ibid.]

"A prince among men; one of the finest who ever entered into this business of motion pictures." [Krefft, pp. 362]

CHAPTER TWELVE: THE GRAND ILLUSION

"Will you all wish me to play the Vampire . . . have played in the past." [Golden, pg. 210]

"Come home— all is forgiven, . . . and soon you'll be seeing her again." ['Come Home—All is Forgiven,' *Photoplay*, Feb. 1923, pg. 44]

"When I realized that this was Theda Bara's comeback picture, and not just one of her old releases, I could hardly believe my eyes." [Golden, pg. 218]

"Vamping requires no artistry whatever. . . . For me, henceforth, high comedy!" [*Bakersfield Californian*, Nov. 19, 1925, pg. 9]

"Do you think ditch-diggers like digging ditches?" [Petrova, 'Mme. Petrova Interviews Theda Bara,' *Shadowland*, March-April 1920, pg. 74]

"Say, I haven't always been a villain. . . . My only fault is a tendency to grow unromantically solid." [Josie P. Lederer, 'Mark Antony Orates,' *Pictures and The Picturegoer*, Mar 1, 1923, pg. 10]

". . . who wrote almost all of Theda Bara's scripts. . . European productions." ['Scenario Expert is Engaged by Universal,' *Los Angeles Times*, April 14, 1923]

"Gloria was wearing the most . . . seem entirely logical." [Foote, pp. 218-219]

"The American motion picture has become virtually the . . . are months ahead of those of Paris and London." [Dorothy Calhoun, 'Styles Are Dictated in Hollywood and Paris Designers Follow Them,' *Motion Picture*, March 29, 1925, pp. 116-117]

"Clare West was the head of wardrobe at the Lasky . . . and I sweated the whole thing out myself." [Jorgensen, pg. 49]

"They've got me all dolled up like a Christmas Tree." [Foote, pp. 218-219]

"I was intrigued by the abrupt end in 1926 . . . wreaked havoc in both her professional and personal lives." [Jorgensen, pp. 22-23]

". . . had a professional encounter with Samuel Goldwyn. . . . I have continued to enjoy the movies occasionally as a spectator only." [Bernays, pp. 150]

". . . in the motion picture field since I handled Theda Bara in *Cleopatra*. . ." [Matthew Bernstein, *Walter Wanger: Hollywood Independent*, University of California Press, 1994, pg. 380]

"I don't think the attitude of the motion . . . have changed." [Bernays, pp. 149]

"From comfortable quarters in old Griffith Park . . . and eventful career."[Cara Giaimo, 'The Most Interesting Camel in the World' *Atlas Obscura*, April 4, 2017]

"For more than thirty years . . . being exhibited in some theatre in some part of the world." [Sinclair, pg. 5]

"The only way I could ever be with my husband . . . whatever hour we returned." [Altman, pg. 17]

"William Fox . . . He was the one no one liked."[Ibid., pg. 38]

"Fox doesn't have a friend in the world . . . I don't know how I am going to stand it.'" [Genini, pg. 10.]

". . . one of those hundred-dollar-plate dinners . . . when I am sitting on my money bags?" [Allvine, pp. 69-70]

"I think I can say that if nobody else grieves my passing I can at least depend upon the president of every large insurance company in the world." [Ibid. pg. 175]

"William Fox was dour and pugnacious . . . Forgotten were his pioneering contributions to the film industry." [Zierold, *The Moguls*, pg. 233]

"Don't let anybody push you around."[Angela Fox Dunn, interview with the author.]

". . . a steady flow of unpretentious, sentimental and folksy pictures . . ." [Allvine, pg. 35].

"The business of making pictures is unlike anything else. . . every idea that will make for better pictures." [Kennedy, pg. 315]

"The new medium will put a stadium . . . in front of the television screen." [Altman, pg. 233]

"To the cinema world there came the announcement . . . stage as Little Red Riding Hood…" ['Colossal Enterprise,' *Time*, Vol. 151, April 8, 1929, pg. 113]

"A daughter of mine go to college? . . . Become an *intellectual*?" [Phillip French, *The Movie Moguls*, Henry Regency Company, 1969, pg. 47-48]

"It was my job to make him my friend if I could." [Altman, pg. 175]

"You must have known that I have moved . . . difficult task. . ." [Ibid., pp. 175-178]

"In July, 1931, the use of the text . . . to eliminate William Fox in all copy." [Allvine, pg. 137]

"I do not know whether foxes ever run in packs . . . that the other wolves fall upon him and 'merge' him." [Sinclair, pg. 101]

"Now I've got the sonsabitches by the balls, and don't think I won't twist them." [Allvine, pg. 24]

"It was a lopsided . . . practically its only assets weighed in at about 300 pounds on four feet." [Ibid., pg. 153]

"The whole studio was shuddering behind drawn . . . Now he's going to fire everybody!'" [Leonard Mosley, *Zanuck: The Rise and Fall of Hollywood's Last Tycoon*, Little, Brown & Company, 1984, pp. 154-155]

". . . a far cry from the regal surroundings in which he . . . anticipated no difficulty either from within or without the industry." [Thomas M. Pryor, 'William Fox Plans Comeback As Film Producer,' *The New York Times*, April 9, 1944, pg. X3]

"Mr. Fox, former theatrical man, is alive." ['William Fox Alive,' *The New York Times*, Feb. 3, 1949, pg. 26]

". . . a frail, diabetic and stroke victim, semi paralyzed for the last year of his life, still grieving over the loss of his dream." [McCord, pg. 220]

"Don't ever marry a gentile. Someday he will turn on you and call you a 'dirty Jew.'" [Scott Eyman, *The Speed of Sound: Hollywood and the Talkie Revolution 1926-1930*, Simon and Schuster, 1997, pg. 355]

"His daring, initiative, and courage abled him . . . the present status of the screen as a medium of popular entertainment." [Michael Troyan, Jeffrey Paul Thompson, Stephen X. Sylvester, *Twentieth Century Fox: A Century of Entertainment* pg. 53]

"There is something in click of the camera as it registers . . . It is because the movie-actress is a bit of machine-made, not hand-made, art . . ." [Theda Bara, *The Forum*, Vol. 62, pg. 89]

"What is any movie studio but a chamber . . . I kept the better half." [Ibid., pg. 86]

". . . heard Mr. Brabin call the remote and dignified Theda . . . Cleopatra 'Cleo' for short . . .'" [Grace Kingsley, 'STEEPLECHASE,' *Los Angeles Times*, April 28, 1929]

"I don't plan to do anything. . . . we try to find happiness when we can." [Charles Lockwood, 'Priestess of Sin' *Horizon*, Jan. 1981]

"She lives in Beverly Hills and doesn't do anything . . . You know how they are?" [*The Pittsburgh Press*, July 6, 1933 pg. 28]

"The real reason why I left pictures. . . Need I say more?" [*The New Movie Magazine*, March 1933, pg. 76]

"Ah, potluck at Theda Bara's!" [St. Johns, *Love, Laughter and Tears: My Hollywood Story*, pp. 21-22]

"If you were invited to her home . . . celebrities in every field who are her close friends." [Ibid. pg. 21]

"Zis is for earlobes pulsing vit ze blood of love. . . . Seething passion." [Genini, pg. 128]

". . . visited a Hollywood friend of mine for cocktails. . . . the town car followed that taxi to her home in Beverly Hills." [Bodeen, pg. 25]

"Let's see if we can find your grandpa here . . . Your grandpa may be one of them!" [Joan Craig with Beverly F. Stout, *Theda Bara, My Mentor: Under the Wing of Hollywood's First Femme Fatale*, McFarland, pg. 24-25]

'. . . born in the shadow of the Sphinx . . . weaned on serpent's blood. . .' [Craig, pg. 40]

"What goes on behind those eyes, so unusual . . . some of them transients, others life residents." [Pauline Bara, 'My Theda Bara,' *Motion Picture Classic*, Vol. 11 #5, Jan. 1921, pg. 79]

'To my darling Mouchey-Mou— from your Wiffle Tree.' [Bodeen, pg. 24]

"To understand those grand days. . . . Now they know it's all just make believe." [St. Johns, *Love, Laughter and Tears: My Hollywood Story*, pg. 22]

"She had a world public. She filled a marvelous niche in our business, in her style. The world took it— and demanded her." [Brownlow, *Parade*, pg. 379]

"Mae West. . . Ah, there's a real vamp." [*The Indiana Gazette*, Feb. 19, 1934, pg. 2]

CHAPTER THIRTEEN: THE END

". . . ribs and plates for a Victory ship. . . " [*Hollywood Reporter*, June 4, 1943]

". . . who shall say that Theda Bara's 1917 *Cleopatra* . . . These Cleopatra troubles came after the death of the nineteenth century Fox." [Allvine, pg. 38]

". . . caused Siegmund Lubin many a heart ache which even this stoical business man could not well conceal." [*Motography*, Vol. XII #2, July 11, 1914, pg. 64]

". . . all of them rare and many extremely important as landmarks in the development of motion pictures." [Museum of Modern Art Press release, Dec. 3, 1935, Margaret Herrick Library, Academy of Motion Pictures Arts and Science]

"Theda described to us the filming of *Cleopatra* . . . loss of her films for the rest of her life." [Craig, pp. 45-46]

"*Flaming Youth* proved that Colleen Moore is an actress of talent. . . . *So Big* confirms the fact." ['Review of *So Big*,' *Bronxville Press*, June 19, 1925]

"Fox Film, an Old Hollywood firm run by mogul . . . A successful studio: not an important one." [Ethan Mordden, *The Hollywood Studios, House Style in the Golden Age of the Movies*, Alfred Knopf, 1988, pg. 263]

"The majority of surviving pre-merger Fox films . . . is rarely exhibited in any format and is seldom re-evaluated." [Aubrey Solomon, *The Fox Film Corporation, 1915–1935: A History and Filmography*, pg. 3]

"Though *East Lynne* received good reviews at the time . . . and the lack of badly needed intertitles to explain what was going on at times . . ." [McCord, pg. 254]

"Now I just carry in my heart the love of this beautiful thing— *The Queen Of Sheba*." [Brownlow, *Parade's Gone By*, pg. 384]

"At personal expense, he commissioned prominent Philadelphia . . . it would have ensured the preservation of early American movies . . ." [Krefft, pp. 190-191]

BIBLIOGRAPHY

BOOKS

Adams, Katherine H., Michael L. Keene, and Jennifer C. Koella, *Seeing the American Woman, 1880-1920: The Social Impact of the Visual Media Explosion,* Jefferson, NC : McFarland, 2011

Allvine, Glendon, *The Greatest Fox of Them All,* New York, NY : Lyle Stuart, Inc. 1969

Altman, Diana, *Hollywood East: Louis B. Mayer and the Origins of the Studio System,* New York, NY : Birch Lane Press, Carol Publishing Group, 1992

Ashby, LeRoy, *With Amusement for All: A History of American Popular Culture Since 1830,* Lexington, KY : University Press of Kentucky, 2006

Balducci, Anthony, *Lloyd Hamilton: Poor Boy Comedian of Silent Cinema* Jefferson, NC : McFarland, 2009

Ball, Robert Hamilton, *Shakespeare on Silent Film,* New York, NY : Theatre Arts Books, 1968

Balshofer, Fred J. and Arthur C. Miller, *One Reel a Week,* Berkeley & Los Angeles, CA : University of California Press, 1967

Bartok, Dennis, and Jeff Joseph *A Thousand Cuts, The Bizarre Underground World of Collectors and Dealers Who Saved the Movies,* Jackson, MS :University Press of Mississippi, 2016

Barton, Ruth, *Rex Ingram : visionary director of the silent screen,* Lexington, KY : University Press of Kentucky : 2014

Beauchamp, Cari, *Without Lying Down: Frances Marion and the Powerful Women of Early Hollywood,* New York, NY : Scribner 1997

Bergan, Ronald, *The United Artists Story,* New York, NY : Crown Publishers, 1986

Bernays, Edward L., *Biography of an Idea: The Founding Principles of Public Relations,* New York, NY : Simon and Schuster, 1965

Bernstein, Matthew, *Walter Wanger: Hollywood Independent,* Berkeley & Los Angeles, CA : University of California Press, 1994

Billman, Larry, *Film Choreographers and Dance Directors: An Illustrated Biographical Encyclopedia with a History and Filmographies, 1893 Through 1995* Jefferson, N.C. : McFarland, 1997

Birchard, Robert S., *King Cowboy : Tom Mix and the movies,* Burbank, CA. : Riverwood Press, 1993

Bowers, Q. David, *Nickelodeon Theatres and Their Music,* New York, NY : The Vestal Press, Ltd., 1986

Bowers, Ronald, "Cleopatra," *Magill's Survey of Cinema, Silent Films, Vol. II* Englewood Cliffs, NJ : Salem Press, 1982

Brown, Shane, (ed.) *Silent Voices, Vintage interviews with Silent Film Personalities,* CreateSpace Independent Publishing Platform, 2017

Brownlow, Kevin, *The Parade's Gone By,* New York, NY : Alfred A. Knopf, 1968

Brownlow, Kevin & John Kobol, *Hollywood: The Pioneers,* New York, NY : Alfred A. Knopf, Inc. 1979

Brownlow, Kevin, *The War, The West and The Wilderness,* New York, NY : Knopf, 1979

Brownlow, Kevin, *Behind the Mask of Innocence,* Berkeley, CA : University of California Press, 1990

Bodeen, Dewitt, *From Hollywood: The Careers of 15 Great American Stars,* South Brunswick, NJ : A. S. Barnes, 1976

Bowers, Ronald, review of 'Cleopatra' *Magill's Survey of Cinema: The Silent Film,* Englewood Cliffs, NJ : Salem Press 1982

Campbell, Craig W., *Reel America and World War I: A Comprehensive Filmography and History of Motion Pictures in the United States, 1914-1920,* Jefferson, NC : McFarland, 1985

Carey, Gary, *Lost Films,* New York, NY : Museum of Modern Art, Eastern Press, 1970.

Coniam, Matthew, *Egyptomania Goes to the Movies: From Archaeology to Popular Craze to Hollywood Fantasy,* Jefferson, NC : McFarland, 2017

Cooper, Miriam, and Bonnie Herndon: *Dark Lady of the Silents: My Life in Early Hollywood,* Indianapolis, IN : The Bobb-Merrill Company, 1973

Craig, Joan, and Beverly F. Stout, *Theda Bara, My Mentor: Under the Wing of Hollywood's First Femme Fatale,* Jefferson, NC : McFarland, 2016

Crawford, Mary Caroline. *Romantic Days In The Early Republic,* Boston, MA : Grosset and Dunlap, Inc., 1912

Custen, George F., *Twentieth Century's Fox Darryl F. Zanuck and the Culture of Hollywood,* New York, NY : Basic Books, 1997

Da, Lottie, and Jan Alexander, *Bad Girls of the Silver Screen,* New York, NY : Carrol & Graf, 1989

Davis, Ronald L., *William S. Hart: Projecting the American West,* Norman, OK : University of Oklahoma Press, 2003

DeBauche, Leslie M., *Reel Patriotism: the Movies and World War I.* Madison, WI : University of Wisconsin Press, 1997

Dent, Alan, *Mrs. Patrick Campbell,* London, UK : Museum Press, 1961

Desti, Mary, *Isadora Duncan's end,* V. Gollancz, 1929

Everson, William K., *American Silent Film,* New York, NY : Oxford University Press, 1978

Eyman, Scott, *The Speed of Sound: Hollywood and the Talkie Revolution 1926-1930,* New York, NY : Simon and Schuster, 1997

Felton, James P., *Newport Beach 75: 1906-1981,* A Diamond Jubilee History, Newport Beach, CA : City of Newport Beach and Sultana Press, 1981

Foote, Lisle, *Buster Keaton's Crew: The Team Behind His Silent Films,* Jefferson, NC : McFarland, 2014

Fox, Susan and Donald G. Rosellini, *William Fox: A Story of Early Hollywood 1915-1930,* Baltimore, MD : Midnight Marquee Press, 2006

Franceschina, John, *Hermes Pan: The Man Who Danced with Fred Astaire,* New York, NY : Oxford University Press, 2012

French, Philip, *The Movie Moguls an informal history of the Hollywood tycoons.,* London, UK : Weidenfeld & Nicolson, 1969

Fussell, Betty Harper, *Mabel,* New Haven, CT : Ticknor & Fields, 1982

Gabler, Neal: *An Empire of Their Own: How the Jews Invented Hollywood,* New York, NY : Crown Publishers, Inc. 1988

Genini, Ronald, *Theda Bara: A Biography of the Silent Screen Vamp, with a Filmography,* Jefferson, NC : McFarland, 1996

Lillian Gish, *The Movies, Mr. Griffith and Me,* New jersey : Prentis-Hall, 1960

Golden, Eve, *Vamp: The Rise and Fall of Theda Bara,* New York : Emprise Publishing, Inc. Vestal, 1996

Grant, Micheal, *Cleopatra,* London : Phoenix Press 2000

Gundle, Stephen, *Glamour : a History,* New York, NY : Oxford University Press, 2008.

Haggard, H. Rider, *Cleopatra,* London, UK : Longmans, Green, and Co., 1914.

Hall, Ben M., *The Best Remaining Seats: The Story of the Golden Age of the Movie Palace*, New York, NY : Clarkson N. Potter, 1961

Higashi, Sumiko, *Virgins, Vamps, and Flappers : The American silent movie heroine*, St. Albans, VT : Eden Press Women's Publications, 1978

Hollard, Larry Lee, Review of 'Daughter of the Gods' *Magill's Survey of Cinema, Silent Films, Vol. II*, Englewood Cliffs, NJ : Salem Press, 1982

Hollard, Larry Lee 'The Queen of Sheba' *Magill's Survey of Cinema, Silent Films, Vol. II*, Englewood Cliffs, NJ : Salem Press, 1982

Holliday, Peter James, *American Arcadia: California and the Classical Tradition* New York, NY : Oxford University Press, 2016

Hopper, Hedda, *From Under My Hat*, New York, NY : Doubleday & Co. Inc. 1952

Hutchinson, Tom: *Screen Goddesses*, New York, NY : Exeter Books, 1984

Jorgensen, Jay and Donald L. Scoggins, *Creating the Illusion: A fashionable History of Hollywood Costume Designers*, Philadelphia, PA : Running Press, *2015*

Katchmer, George A., *Eighty Silent Movie Stars: Biographies and Filmographies of the Obscure to the Well Known*, Jefferson, NC : McFarland, 1991

Katz, Ephraim, *The Film Encyclopedia*, New York, NY : Harper-Perennial 1994

Andrew Kelly, *Cinema and the Great War*, London & New York : Routledge, 1997

Kennedy, Edgar J. *The Story of the Films*, Chicago & New York: A.W. Shaw, 1927

Kerr, Walter, *The Silent Clowns*, New York : Alfred A. Knopf, 1975

Koszarski, Richard, *The Rivals of D. W. Griffiith: Alternate Auteurs 1913-1919*, Minneapolis MN : Walker Art Center, 1976

Kobal, John, *Hollywood: The Years of Innocence*, New York, NY : Abbeville Press, 1985

Koszarski, Diane Kaiser, *The Complete Films of William S. Hart: A Pictorial Record*, New York, NY : Dover Publications, Inc., 1980

Krefft, Vanda, *The Man Who Made the Movies: The Meteoric Rise and Tragic Fall of William Fox*, New York, NY : Harper Collins, 2017

Larue, Kalton C., *Ladies in Distress*, Cranbury, NJ : A. S. Barnes and Co. Inc. 1971

Liebman, Roy, *Silent Film Performers: An Annotated Bibliography of Published, Unpublished and Archival Sources for Over 350 Actors and Actresses*, Jefferson, NC : McFarland, 1996

Lindsay, Vachel, *The Art of the Motion Picture*, New York, NY : Macmillan Company, 1922

Lockwood, Charles, *Dream Palaces: Hollywood at Home*, New York, NY : Viking Press, 1981

Maeder, Edward … [et al.] *Hollywood and History: Costume Design in Film*, Los Angeles, CA : Los Angeles County Museum of Art, 1987

Maddox, Robert James, *American History: Reconstruction through the Present*, Boston, MA : Dushkin Pub. Group, 1997

MacCann, Richard Dyer, *The Stars Appear*, Metuchen, NJ : Scarecrow Press, 1992

Manchel, Frank, *Film Study: An Analytical Bibliography*, London, UK : Fairleigh Dickinson University Press, 1990

Mann, William J., *Behind The Screen How Gays and Lesbians Shaped Hollywood, 1910-1969*, New York, NY : Viking, 2001.

Marion, Francis, *Off With Their Heads!: A Serio-Comic Tale of Hollywood*, New York, NY : The Macmillan Company, 1972

Malone, Aubrey, *Censoring Hollywood: Sex and Violence in Film and on the Cutting Room Floor*, Jefferson NC : McFarland 2011

McCord, Merrill T., *William Fox and the Fox Film Corporation*, Bethesda, MD : Alhambra Publishers, 2016

McKinney, Grange B. *Art Acord and the Movies*, Raleigh NC : Western Classics, 2000

McLean, Adrienne L. (ed.), *Costume, Makeup, and Hair*, New Brunswick, NJ : Rutgers University Press, 2016

Mordden, Ethan, *The Hollywood Studios, House Style in the Golden Age of the Movies*, New York, NY : Alfred Knopf, 1988

Morley, Sheridan, *Noël Coward*, London, UK : Haus, 2005

Morgan, Warren F., *This Was Mission Country: Reflections in Orange of Merle and Mabel Ramsey*, Laguna Beach, CA : Mission Printing Co., 1973

Miles, Margaret M., *Cleopatra: A Sphinx Revisited*, Oakland, CA : University of California Press, 2011

Morley, Sheridan *Noël Coward*, London, UK : Haus Publishing, 2005

Mosley, Leonard, *Zanuck: The Rise and Fall of Hollywod's Last Tycoon*, Boston : Little, Brown and Company, 1971

Nasaw, David, *Going Out: The Rise and Fall of Public Amusements*, New York, NY : Basic Books, 1993

O'Dell, Paul, *Griffith and Rise of Hollywood*, New York, NY : International Film Guide Series, A.S. Barnes & Co. 1970

O'Leary, Liam, *Rex Ingram, Master of the Silent Cinema*, New York, NY : Barnes & Noble Books, 1980

Proddow, Penny, Debra Healy and Marion Fasel, *Hollywood Jewels: Movies Jewelry Stars*, New York, NY : H.N. Abrams, 1992

Parish, James Robert, *The Fox Girls*, New Rochelle, NY : Arlington House 1971

Parsons, Louella O., *The Gay Illiterate*, Garden City, NY : Doubleday, Doran and Co. Inc., 1944

Petrova, Olga, *Butter with My Bread*, Indianapolis & New York : The Bobb-Merrill Company, 1942

Pitt, Leonard, and Dale Pitt, *Los Angeles, A to Z*, Oakland, CA : University of California Press, 1997

Pratt, George C., *Spellbound in Darkness: A History of the Silent Film*, Greenwich, CT : New York Graphic Society Ltd. 1973

Presley, Cecilia de Mille and Mark A. Vieira, *Cecil B. DeMille: The Art of the Hollywood Epic*, Philadelphia, PA : Running Press, 2014

Quinlan, David, *The Illustrated Encyclopedia of Character Actors*, New York, NY : Harmony Books, 1985

Ramsaye, Terry, *Million and One Nights: A History of the Motion Picture*, New York, NY : Simon & Schuster, 1986

Riley, Phillip J. *A Blind Bargain*, Los Angeles, CA : Magic Image Filmbooks, Ackerman Archives Series, 1988

Rosen, Marjorie, *Popcorn Venus: Women, Movies and the American Dream*, New York, NY : Coward, McCann & Geoghegan, 1973

Lee Royal, *The Romance of Motion Picture Production*, Los Angeles, CA : Royal Publishing Company, 1920.

Sardou, Victorien, *Argument of the Play Cleopatra*, New York, CA : F. Pullman, 1891

Schickel, Richard: *The Men Who Made the Movies*, New York, NY : Atheneum, 1975

Semenov, Lillian Wurtzel and Carl Winter (ed.) *William Fox, Sol M. Wurtzel and the Early Fox Film Corporation: Letters, 1917-1923*, Jefferson, NC : McFarland, 2001

Sennett, Mack, *The King of Comedy*, Garden City, NY : Doubleday, 1954

Shields, David S., *Still: American Silent Motion Picture Photography*, Chicago : The University of Chicago Press, 2013.

Shipman, David: *The Great Movie Stars: The Golden Years*, New York, NY : Crown, 1970

Silverman, Stephen M., *The Fox That Got Away*, Secaucus, NJ : Lyle Stuart, 1988.

Sinclair, Upton, *The Autobiography of Upton Sinclair*, New York, NY : Harcourt, Brace & World, Inc. 1962

Sinclair, Upton, *Upton Sinclair Presents William Fox*, Los Angeles, CA : Published by the author, 1933

Sleeper, Jim, *Great Movies Shot in Orange County*, Trabuco Canyon, CA, California Classics, 1980

Slide, Anthony, *Early American Cinema*, New York, NY : International Film Guide Series, A.S. Barnes & Co., 1970

Slide, Anthony, *The New Historical Dictionary of the American Film*, Lanham, MD, The Scarecrow Press, 1998

Slide, Anthony, *Silent Players : a biographical and autobiographical study of 100 silent film actors and actresses*, Jefferson, KY : University Press of Kentucky, 2002.

Slide, Anthony, *American Racist : the life and films of Thomas Dixon*, Jefferson, KY: University Press of Kentucky, 2004

Soister, John T., Henry Nicolella, Steve Joyce, Harry H Long, and Bill Chase, *American Silent Horror, Science Fiction and Fantasy Feature Films, 1913–1929* Jefferson, NC : McFarland, 2012

Solomon, Aubrey, *The Fox Film Corporation, 1915-1935: A History and Filmography*, Jefferson, NC : McFarland, 2011

Spears, Jack, *Hollywood: The Golden Era*, South Brunswick, NJ : A. S. Barnes, 1971.

St. Johns, Adela Rogers, *Love, Laughter and Tears: My Hollywood Story*, Garden City, NY : Doubleday and Co., 1978

Sturges, Preston, *Preston Sturges by Preston Sturges: His Life in His Words* New York, NY : Touchstone, 1991

Tarbox, Charles H., *Lost Films 1895-1917*, Los Angeles, CA : Film Classic Exchange, 1983

Thompson, Frank, *Lost Films: Important Movies That Disappeared*, New York, NY : Citadel Press, 1996

Troyan, Michael, Jeffrey Paul Thompson and Stephen X. Sylvester, *Twentieth Century Fox: A Century of Entertainment*, Guilford, CT : Lyons Press, 2017

Tyldesley, Joyce, *Cleopatra: Last Queen of Egypt*, New York, NY : Basic Books, 2008

Wagenknecht, Edward, *Movies in the Age of Innocence*, Norman, OK : University of Oklahoma Press, 1962

Walsh, Raoul, *Each Man in His Time*, New York, NY : Farrar, Straus and Giroux, 1974

Zierold, Norman J., *Sex Goddesses of the Silent Screen*; Chicago, IL : Henry Regnery Company, 1973

Zierold, Norman J., *The Moguls*, New York, NY : Coward-McCann, 1969

PERIODICALS

Articles that are only quoted once or twice are listed in the notes. The following are articles that are quoted repeatedly or not quoted at all are listed here.

Bara, Pauline, "My Theda Bara," *Motion Picture Classic*, Vol. 11, no. 5, January, 1921, pp. 19-20, 79

Bara, Theda, "How I became a Film Vampire," *The Forum*, Volume 61, June 1919, pp. 715-727

Bara, Theda, "Curse on a Moving Picture Actress," *The Forum*, Volume 62, July 1919, pp. pp. 88-93

Bara, Theda, "The Ex-Vampire: Turning to the Right in the Moving Pictures," *Vanity Fair*, October, 1919

Bell, Archie, "Theda Bara the Vampire Woman," *The Theatre*, Volume 22, November 1915, pp. 246, 253-254

Cohn, Alfred A. "What Makes Them Cry," *Photoplay*, April 1918, pp. 50-56, 120

Courtlandt, Roberta, "Theda, Misunderstood Vampire," *Motion Picture Classic*, October 1916, pp. 25-28

Courtlandt, Roberta, "The Divine Theda," *Motion Picture*, April 1917, pp. 59-62.

Evans, Delight, "Does Theda Bara Believe Her Own Press Agent?" *Photoplay*, May 1918, pp. 62-63, 107.

Dunn, Angela Fox, "William Fox, Cinema Czar," *Westways*, November 1981

Franklin, Wallace, "Purgatory's Ivory Angel" *Photoplay*, Vol. VIII No. 4, September 1915, pp. 69-72

Gebhart, Myrtle, "The New Theda Bara," *Picture-Play*, September 1925, pp. 16-17

Hall, Gladys and Adele Whitely Fletcher, "We Interview Theda Bara," *Motion Picture*, November 1922, pp. 20-22, 116.

McKelvie, Martha Groves, "O-o-o-h Theda!" *Motion Picture Classic*, September 1918, pp. 24-25, 68.

Mullett, Mary B. "Theda Bara, Queen of the Vampires." *American Magazine*, September 1920, pp. 34-35

Petrova, Olga, "Mme. Petrova Interviews Theda Bara." *Shadowland*, March-April 1920, pp. 43-44, 74

Slide, Anthony, "George Walsh in an interview with Anthony Slide," *The Silent Picture*, Autumn 1972, Issue 16, pg. 14]

Agnes Smith, "The Confessions of Theda Bara," *Photoplay*, Vol. 17, #1, June 1920, pg. 57-58, 110-111.

LIBRARIES AND ARCHIVES

Margaret Herrick Library, Academy of Motion Pictures Arts and Science

Museum of Modern Art Press release, December 3, 1935

William Fox, Theda Bara, J. Gordon Edwards and Raoul Walsh files

Cleopatra pressbook

Sol Wurtzel papers

UCLA Special Collections Library

Ann Maxwell, Synopsis of Haggard's *Cleopatra*, 20th Century Fox papers

Adrian Johnson, scenario for *Cleopatra*, 20th Century Fox papers

University of Southern California, Research Library, Special Collections

Edwards, J. Gordon, scenario for *The Queen of Sheba*

Johnson, Adrian, scenario for *Cleopatra*

Johnson, Adrian, scenario for *Salome*

University of Cincinnati, Cincinnati, Ohio

Bara, Theda, Unprocessed manuscript

Trinity College, Dublin, Ireland

Ingram, Rex, *Long way to Tipperary*, unpublished manuscript

Metropolitan Museum of Art, New York, NY

Letter of Herbert E. Winlock to A. M. Lythgoe, Feb 10, 1918, Lythgoe papers

Leiber, Virginia, *The Great Fritz*, unpublished manuscript, courtesy of Justin Leiber

Fritz Leiber Jr. letter to F. Gwynplaine MacIntyre, courtesy of F. Gwynplaine MacIntyre

WEBSITES

Bara, Theda, "The Ex-Vampire Turning to the Right in the Moving Pictures, Rebels; She Tired of Playing The Vamp," *Vanity Fair Magazine*, 1919, *Old Magazine Articles*,

http://www.oldmagazinearticles.com/Silent_Movie_Actress_Theda_Bara_The_Vamp-pdf?fbclid=IwAR3FV4x4_ac3p_qbKWjtWsqPaLb9X_jDRCPK-4dQW77SMj6AB1B3VbRojwrw

Benzkofer, Stephan, "When a Chicago police censor ruled over films with an iron fist," *Chicago Tribune*, February 20, 2015, https://www.chicagotribune.com/news/history/ct-oscars-movie-censorship-chicago-funkhouser-0222-20150220-story.html

Carrico, John Francis DeSales, *Diary of J.F.D. Carrico*, February 3, 1918, http://www.kevincarrico.com/jfc1918.htm

Edwards, Peter, "Condemned spy Mata Hari glib during final interrogation: MI5 files," *The Toronto Star*, April 24, 2014, https://www.thestar.com/news/world/2014/04/24/condemned_spy_mata_hari_glib_during_final_interrogation_mi5_files.html]

Giaimo, Cara, "The Most Interesting Camel in the World," *Atlas Obscura*, April 4, 2017, https://www.atlasobscura.com/articles/old-topsy-camel-corps-griffith-park-zoo

Greene, R.H. "'Birth Of A Race': The Obscure Demise Of A Would-Be Rebuttal To Racism," *National Public Radio*, October 25, 2015, https://www.npr.org/2015/10/25/451717690/birth-of-a-race-the-obscure-demise-of-a-would-be-rebuttal-to-racism

Internet Movie DataBase "Plot summary of 'The Vampire,' from synopsis in *Moving Picture World*, November 26, 1910, https://www.imdb.com/title/tt0001441/plotsummary

King, Susan, 'Classic Hollywood: For generations, Kevin Brownlow has been the voice for silent films,' *Los Angeles Times*, April 26, 2019, https://www.latimes.com/entertainment/movies/la-et-mn-classic-hollywood-kevin-brownlow-20190424-story.html

Kinney, Alison, "How the Klan Got Its Hood," *The New Republic*, January 8, 2016, https://newrepublic.com/article/127242/klan-got-hood

Koch, Arnold, "Looking Back: Dancing with a legend: Edward Bernays, the 'father of public relations'" *WickedLocal.com*, June 11, 2010

http://www.wickedlocal.com/article/20100611/News/306119732?start=2

Lawson, Valerie, "Review of *Isadora: The Sensational Life of Isadora Duncan* by Peter Kurth," *The Sidney Morning Herald*, 27 April 2002, https://www.smh.com.au/articles/2002/04/26/1019441296375.html

Mallory, Mary, "Hollywood Heights: Albert Witzel, Early Glamour Photography Pioneer," *The Daily Mirror*, August 12, 2003, https://ladailymirror.com/2013/08/12/mary-mallory-hollywood-heights-albert-witzel-early-glamour-photography-pioneer/]

Meares, Hadley, "Building a beach town on Hollywood's favorite desert set," *Curbed Los Angeles*, January 5, 2017, https://la.curbed.com/2017/1/5/14167146/hollywood-beach-ventura-history

Murphy, Jessica, "Ann Haviland, Forgotten Mastermind of the Signature Scent," *Atlas Obscura*, December 19, 2017, https://www.atlasobscura.com/articles/ann-haviland-fragrances-new-york

Petersen, Anne Helen, "Scandals of Classic Hollywood: The Most Wicked Face of Theda Bara," *The Hairpin*, January 8, 2013, https://www.thehairpin.com/2013/01/scandals-of-classic-hollywood-the-most-wicked-face-of-theda-bara/

Shoemaker, Mark "Cleopatra's Jewels," *Art Deco Society of Los Angeles*, Vol. 13, July 2002 : http://www.adsla.org/vol_13/vol_13_july02/vol_13_july02.htm

Complete List of Motion Picture Films Presented to the Kansas State Board of Review for action October 1, 1918 to December 20, 1918, Kansas State Printing Plant 1919 https://archive.org/stream/completelistofmo233kans/completelistofmo233kans_djvu.txt

Dramatic Compositions Copyrighted in the United States, 1870 to 1916, United States Library of Congress, https://archive.org/details/dramaticcomposit01libr/page/n4

INDEX

18 to 45 AKA *Every Mother's Son* (Fox, 1919) 330
45 Minutes from Hollywood (Hal Roach, 1926) 362
Abbott, Jacob 121
Acord, Art *185*, 186, 187, 188, 239, *366*, 367, *418*
Actress, The (MGM, 1928) 402
Affairs of Anatol, The (Paramount, 1921) 367
All This and Heaven Too (Warner Brothers, 1940) 363
Alliance Studios 367
Allvine, Glendon 25, 28, 68, 110, 338, 372, 373, 378, 379, 393
Alma-Tadema, Sir Lawrence *105*, 271
Amanirenas 102
American Biograph (Biograph) 11, 19, 21, 32, 35, 49, 106, 145, 411
American Film Company 186
American Film Institute (AFI) 412, 413
American Tobacco Company 370
Anderson, 'Bronco Billy' AKA 'Broncho Billy' 120, 408
Anderson, Anthony 286
Andrews, Florence AKA Florence O'Denishawn 179
Angel on my Shoulder (United Artists, 1946) 363
Anna Christie (First National, 1923) 413
Anna Karenina (Fox, 1915) 29
Anthony Adverse (Warner Brothers, 1936) 363
Antony and Cleopatra (Biograph, 1908) 106
Antony and Cleopatra (play) 104, 106, 109, 121, 130, 135
Antony, Marc (historical) 103, 105, 123, 132, 138
Apfel, Oscar C. 141
April Folly (Paramount, 1920) 367
Arbuckle, Roscoe 'Fatty' 24, 147, 392
Arlen, Richard 411
Art of the Motion Picture, The (book) 288
Arvidson, Linda 120
Aryan, The (Triangle, 1916) 86, 189

Ashes of Vengeance (First National, 1923) 368
Astaire, Fred 315
AT&T 379
Auen, Signe AKA Seena Owen 86
Austin, Laurence 3
Avery, Tex 402
Avondale 37
Back to God's Country (Canadian Photoplays, 1919) 294
Backstage (1919) 177
Baggot, King 120, 408
Baker, Hettie Gray 107, 110, 147, 248, 301
Bakst, Léon 173
Balboa Amusement Producing Company 23, 284, 404
Balboa Bay (Newport Bay, California) iv, 236, 237, 238, 239, 240, *241*, 242, 243, 244, 265, 391
Balboa Beach 236
Ball, Robert Hamilton 8, 119, 133
Ballets Russes 173, 253
Ballin, Mabel 411
Balshofer, Fred J. 142
Baltimore Sun 370
Bara, Lori (AKA Esther Goodman) 38, 46, 100, 283, 343, *344*, 384
Bara, Theda iv, *1*, 2, 3, *4*, 6, 7, 8, 9, *34*, 35, (As Theodosia Goodman) 36, 37, 38, 39, 40, 47 (As Theodosia de Coppet) 41, 42, 43, 44, 45, 46, 47, 48, *49*, (As Theda Bara) 50, 51, 52, 53, 54, 55, 56, 57, 58, 59, 60, 61, 62, 63, 64, 65, 67, 68, 69, 70, 71, 72, 73, 74, 75, 76, 77, 78, 79, 80, 81, 82, 83, 84, 85, 86, 88, 89, 90, 91, 92, 93, 94, 95, 96, *97*, 98, 99, 100, 101, 106, 107, 110, 111, 112, 115, 116, 120, 121, 123, *124*, 131, 132, 133, 134, 135, 136, 137, 138, 144, 145, 148, 149, 150, 152, 153, 154, 155, 157, 158, 159, 160, 161, 162, 163, 164, 165, 166, 168, 169, 170, 171, 172, 173, 174, 175, 176, 178, 179, 180, 181, 182, 184, 185, 187, 189, *190*, 191, 192, 193, 194, 195, 196, 197, 198, 200, 201, 202, 204, 205, 206, 207, 208, 209, 210, 214, 215, 216, 217, 218, 219, 220, 221, *222*, 224, *225*, *226*, 229, 230,

231, 232, 233, 234, 237, 238, 239, 240, 247,
248, 252, 253, 254, 255, 256, 257, 261, 262,
263, 264, 265, 266, *267*, 268, 269, 270, 271,
272, 273, 275, 276, 277, 278, 279, 280, 281,
282, 283, 285, 286, 287, 297, 299, 300, 303,
305, 306, 307, 308, 309, 310, 311, 312, 313,
314, 315, 317, 321, 323, 324, 325, 326, 327,
328, 329, 330, 331, 332, 333, 334, 336, 339,
340, 341, 342, 343, 344, 345, 346, 347, 348,
349, 350, 351, 352, 353, 356, 358, 359, 360,
361, 362, 365, 367, 369, 370, 373, 374, 381,
382, 383, 384, 385, 386, 387, 388, 389, 390,
392, 393, 394, 398, 399, 403, 405, 406, 408,
414, 415, *418*, 419
Barbier, George 173
Bardot, Brigitte 254
Barker, Reginald 24, 188, 410
Barnum, P.T. 49, 155
Barrymore, Ethel 70, 402
Barrymore, John 413
Barthelmess, Richard 347
Bartlett, Randolph 108, 135, 207, 271
Basic Instinct (TriStar, 1992) 388
Bathory, Elizabeth 64
Battle Hymn of the Republic, The (Vitagraph, 1911) 289
Battle of Gettysburg, The (Mutual, 1913) 106, 188
Battle of Life, The (Fox, 1916) 187
Baudelaire, Charles 70
Baum, L. Frank 250
Bayne, Beverly 35, 47, 94, 96, 184
Beach, Rex 29
Beaton, Kenneth 182
Bedford, Barbara 365, 366
Beery, Wallace 184, 365, 366, 411
Beggars of Life (Paramount, 1928) 411
Behlmer, Henry 23
Belasco, David 179
Bell, Archie 81, 86, 202
Ben Hur (Kalem, 1907) 415
Ben-Hur (MGM, 1925) 210, 294
Ben-Hur (play) 182
Ben-Hur: A Tale of the Christ (novel) 77, 121, 239
Benchley, Robert 399
Bennett, Constance 177
Bennett, Joan 177
Benson, Sally 359

Berenice of Egypt 138
Bernays, Edward L. 1, 253, 254, 255, 256, 257, 258, 262, 369, 370
Bernhardt, Sarah 22, 33, 40, 41, 55, 116, 117, 118, 202, 331, 340
Bertini, Francesca 367
Best Remaining Seats, The (book) 291
Best Remaining Seats, The (book) 291
Better Films Committee of the Women's Club of Omaha 312, 313
Beyond the Rocks (Paramount, 1922) 415
Big City, The (MGM, 1928) 402
Big Trail, The (Fox, 1930) 375
Billboard, The 188, 189, 280, 281, 286, 312, 331
Biograph (American Biograph) 11, 19, 21, 32, 35, 49, 106, 145, 411
Birchard, Robert S. iv, 9, *69*, *91*,*159*, *160*, *191*, *192*, *193*, *196*, *206*, *216*, *225*, *226*, *230*, *232*, 246, *247*, 338, *344*, *383*, *385*
Birth of a Nation, The (Epoch, 1915) 5, 12, 24, 53, 106, 109, 167, 168, 235, 301, 302, 316, 327
Bison Film Company 186
Black Orchids (Universal, 1917) 92, 93
Black Pirate, The (United Artists, 1926) 210
Blackstone Hotel 152
Blackton, J. Stuart 14, 15
Blind Bargain, A (Goldwyn, 1922) 402
Blindness of Devotion, The (Fox, 1915) 92
Blinn, Genevieve *181*, 189, 365
Bliss (Pathé, 1917) 414
Blood and Sand (Paramount, 1922) 86, 368
Blotto (MGM, 1930) 403
Blue Angel, The (Paramount, 1930) 54, 388
Blue Flame, The (play) 347, 348, 349, 358
Blum, Daniel 3
Blythe, Betty 195, 214, 231, 351, 352, 353, 354, 356, 358, 365, 370, 388, 406
Bodeen, DeWitt 385
Bondman, The (Fox, 1916) 290
Bordoni, Irène 182
Borgia, Lucrezia 64
Borzage, Frank 374
Boston Post 208
Boston Sunday Post 347
Bosworth, Hobart 396
Boudicca 102
Bound in Morocco (Fairbanks, 1918) 177

Bow, Clara 187, 383, 408
Box Office Attraction Film Rental Company AKA Box Office Attraction Company of America 22, 23, 25, 50
Boyle, John W. 210, 219, 246
Brabin, Charles 350, 351, 358, 383, 384, 385, 386, 387, 388, 399, 400, 401
Bracken, Bertram 90
Braddon, Mary Elizabeth 58
Brenon, Herbert 3, *27*, 55, 56, 57, 59, 90, 106, 107, 108, 110, 194, 214, 243, 246, 332, 335, 342, 356, 358, 396, 401, *406*
Bride of Fear, The (Fox, 1918) 299
Britain-Gaumont 375
British Film Institute 412
Brockwell, Gladys 72, 144, 334, 335, 336, 342, 358, 404
Broken Oath, The (IMP, 1910) 49
Bronx Zoo 57, 253
Brooklyn Daily Eagle, The 42, 199, 202, 279
Brooks, Louise 179, 411
Brown, Alice 269
Browne, Porter Emerson 31
Brownlow, Kevin iv, *143*, 195, *231*, 248, 288, 351, 406, 412
Brynn, Celia 329
Bubble, The (play) 46
Burne-Jones, Sir Philip 30, 31, 53, 395
Burr, Aaron 36
Burr, Theodosia 36
Burton, Richard 393
Bush, W. Stephen 22, 302
Bushman, Francis X. 24, 35, 94, 96, 184
Business Woman, The 114
Cabiria (Italy, 1914) 106, 109
Caesar and Cleopatra (play) 121, 123
Caesar, Julius 103, 104, 135, 384
Caillaux, Joseph 115, 116
Caius Julius Caesar (Italy, 1914) 106
Calafia 139
Califerne 139
California 2, 4, 29, 72, 101, 139, 140, 141, 142, 143, 145, 147, 148, 149, 156, 161, 165, 166, 168, 169, 178, 185, 186, 194, 205, 206, 207, 211, 223, 224, 228, 229, 231, 234, 235, 239, 257, 284, 285, 286, 308, 318, 338, 352, 364, 369, 390, 391
Camille (First National, 1927) 412

Camille (Fox, 1917) 76, 94, 115, 184, 197, 303
Camille (France, 1912) 22
Camille (play) 40, 41
Campbell, Bartley 79
Campbell, Mrs. Patrick 31
Capra, Frank 413
Caprice, June *71*, 72, 144, 294, 341, 342, 404
Captive God, The (Triangle, 1916) 261
Card, James 414
Carlos, Abraham 147, 161, 225, 332, 333
Carmen (Fox, 1915) 74, 75, 76, 77, 78, 156, 164, 204, 297, 330, 406
Carmen (Paramount, 1915) 74, 78, 106, 164, 297
Carmen AKA *Burlesque on Carmen* (Essanay, 1916) 78
Carmen, Jewel (AKA Evelyn Quick) 144, 299, 336, 337, 338
Carson, Johnny 135
Caruso, Enrico 253
Case of the Sgt. Grischa, The (RKO, 1930) 401
Casselton, Harold 'Rusty' 414
Cassius, Dio 103
Catherine II of Russia 138
Caught in the Act (memoir) 369
Cavalcade (Fox, 1930) 336, 379, 399
Cavell, Edith 267
Celebrated Scandal, The (Fox, 1915) 29
Cellini, Benvenuto 170
Chadwick Pictures, 359, 405
Chaney, Lon 402, 408, *411*, 412, 413
Chaplin, Charles 'Charlie' 4, 5, 24, 35, 78, 90, 98, 100, 102, 113, 145, 153, 247, 284, 317, 327, 331, 339, 407, 413
Chatterton, Ruth 177
Cheat, The (Lasky, 1915) 315
Chevalier, Maurice 24
Chicago Board of Censors 18, 275, 292, 303, 304, 307, 308, 310, 320
Chicago Daily News 153, 156
Chicago Evening Post 67
Chicago Record Herald 152, 282
Chicago Tribune 153, 156, 304, 308, 320
Chicago, Illinois 1, 8, 12, 18, 40, 141, 142, 146, 152, 156, 157, 179, 184, 200, 275, 289, 292, 303, 304, 305, 307, 308, 321
Chronochrome 210
Church, Fred 119

Cincinnati, Ohio v, 6, 36, 37, 38, 39, 40, 69, 81, 82, 86, 94, 96, 300, 345, 388
Cinema Chat 185
Cinema News 231
Cinémathèque Française 413, 414
Citizen Kane (RKO, 1941) 401
City Lights (United Artists, 1931) 413
Civilization (Triangle, 1916) 106, 108, 188
Claire, Ina 177
Clark, Marguerite 72, 182, 407
Clemenceau Case, The (Fox, 1915) 56, 57, 76
Cleopatra (20th Century-Fox, 1963) 172, 174, 315, 370, 393
Cleopatra (Fox, 1917) 1, 2, 3, 4, 5, 6, 7, 8, 9, 76, 102, 103, 109, 110, 111, 115, 116, 120, 123, *124*, 129, 131, 132, 135, 136, 137, 139, *143*, 144, 148, 149, 164, 165, 166, 168, 169, 170, 171, 172, *173*, 174, 178, 179, 181, 182, 184, 185, 186, 187, 188, 189, *190*, 191, 192, 194, 200, 202, 204, 205, 207, 209, 210, 212, 214, 215, 219, 220, 222, 224, 225, 227, 229, 231, 234, 239, 240, *241*, 245, 246, 247, 248, 249, 250, 251, 252, 253, 254, 255, 256, 257, 258, 259, 260, 261, 262, 263, 265, 268, 269, 271, 272, 273, 274, 275, 280, 281, 285, 286, 287, 288, 292, 305, 306, 307, 308, 309, 311, 312, 313, 314, 315, 317, 324, 325, 326, 327, 341, 351, 352, 356, 362, 364, 365, 366, 369, 370, 373, 388, 390, 391, 393, 397, 398, 399, 412, 414, 415, 419
Cleopatra (Helen Gardener, 1912) 118, 119, 120, 133, 134, 164, 174, 393
Cleopatra (novel) 109, 110, 115, 116, 120, 121, 125, 127, 131, 132, 133, 134, 196
Cleopatra (Paramount, 1934) 108, 172, 174, 393
Cleopatra VII of Egypt 7, 8, 41, 102, 103, 104, 105, 106, 111, 112, 115, 116, 118, 121, 123, 132, 134, 137, 138, 161, 163, 196, 217, 253, 267, 270, 278, 282, 350, 384
Cleopatra: A Sphinx Revisited (book) 118
Cléopatre / Cleopatra (play) 117, 118, 119, 120, 121, 128, 129, 130, 131, 132, 133, 134, 135, 196
Cleveland Leader, The 279
Cleveland News 332
Cleveland Plain Dealer 67
Cleveland Press, The 279
Clifford, William 119
Cloud, Margaret 367
Clune Film Company 186
Clune's Auditorium 286
Cobra (Paramount, 1925) 365
Coffee, Lenore 142
Cohan, George M. 382
Cohn, Alfred A. 214, 215
Colbert, Claudette 172, 174
Columbia Pictures 387
Committee on Public Information (CPI) 316, 319, 321, 369
Conklin, Henie 147
Connecticut Yankee in King Arthur's Court, A (Fox, 1921) 413
Connelly, Edward 406
Conscience (Fox, 1917) 177
Coogan, Jackie 413
Cooper, Gary 403
Cooper, Miriam 75, 76, 78, 204, 338, 341, 342, 392
Costello, Maurice 120
Costume Designers Guild Hall of Fame 369
Costume, Makeup, and Hair (book) 167
Courtship of Miles Standish, The (Charles Ray, 1923) 409
Covered Wagon, The (Paramount, 1923) 108
Coward, Noël 208
Crafts, Reverend Wilbur 17
Craig, Joan iv, 39, 163, 324, 386, 399
Craig, Nell 184
Creating the Illusion: A Fashionable History of Hollywood Costume Designers (book) 166, 168
Creel, George 316, 319, 322, 369
Criminal Code, The (Balboa, 1914) 23
Cruze, James 108
Crystallizing Public Opinion (book) 370
Cunard, Grace 113
Cuneo, Lester 184
D'Annunzio, Gabriele 57, 58, 79
Daddy Long Legs (play) 253
Damon And Pythias (Universal, 1914) 106
Dana, Viola 143
Darling of Paris, The (Fox, 1917) 95, 110
Daughter of the Gods, A (Fox, 1916) 106, 107, 108, 109, 110, 223, 246, 296, 297, 298, 306, 326, 398
Davidson Theater 40
Davies, Marion 367, 410

Davis, Jefferson 227
Davis, Judge J. Warren 380
Davis, Will S. 90
de Coppet, Pauline Louise Françoise Bara (see Goodman, Pauline)
de Coppet, Theodosia (see Theda Bara)
De Vries, Henri *181*, 189, 365
De Wolfe, Elsie 205
Dearborn Independent 373
Death Takes A Holiday (Paramount, 1934) 365
DeBauche, Leslie M. iv, 322
DeFoe, Louis 349
Delilah 64
Delsarte, François 200
DeLuxe Laboratories 397
DeMille, Cecil B. 3, 24, 47, 74, 78, 79, 106, 108, 141, 148, 177, 186, 212, 320, 347, 356, 360, 365, 367, 368, 393, 406
Democracy Film Company 235
Dempster, Carol 179
Denig, Lynde 80, 202
Denishawn School 177, 178, 179
Desti, Mary 42, 43, 44,
Destruction (Fox, 1915) 76, 79, 80, 201, 202, 415
Detroit Free Press 59
deux orphelines, Les (play) 59
Devil, The (play) 41
Devil's Daughter, The (Fox, 1915) 57, 58, 202, 304
Devil's Wheel, The (Fox, 1918) 404
Diaghilev AKA Diaghileff 253, 254
Dick Stanley's Wild West Show 186
Dietrich, Marlene 54, 187, 388
Dinehart, Alan *348*
Divine Lady (Warner Brothers, 1929) 336
Divine Woman, The (MGM, 1928) 402, 412
Divorcee, The (Metro, 1919) 402
Dixon, Thomas Jr. 143, 290, 301
Don Juan (Warner Brothers, 1926) 374
Donatelli, Nicola 288
Donnell, Dorothy 200
Dorothy Vernon of Haddon Hall (United Artists, 1924) 394
Dr. Jekyll and Mr. Hyde (Paramount, 1920) 87, 347
Dracula (novel) 411
Dracula (Universal, 1931) 389

Drag Harlan (Fox, 1920) 365, 405
Drake, Dorothy *188*, 189, 365
Dramatic Mirror (*see New York Dramatic Mirror, The*)
DuBois, W.E.B. 414
Dumas, Alexandre 94
Duncan, Dell *188*, 189, 365
Duncan, Isadora 42, 43, 44, 53, 265
Duncan, Raymond 44
Dunkelmyer and De Coppet 36
Dunn, Angela Fox 373, 381
Duse, Eleonora 57, 202
East Lynne (Fox, 1916) 80, 81, 405
Eastman Kodak 11, 21
Ebony Pictures 235
Edison Manufacturing Company 10, 11, 14, 77, 140, 284, 322, 350, 396, 398, 412, 415
Edison, Thomas Alva 10, 11, 12, 66
Edwards, Blake 406
Edwards, J. Gordon 2, 3, 23, 27, 29, 90, 91, 92, 93, 110, 111, 115, 123, 125, 126, 127, 130, 131, 132, 137, 148, 161, 164, 165, 174, 182, 184, 187, *192*, *193*, 194, 195, 196, 197, 198, 205, 207, 212, 214, 220, 224, 225, 228, 229, 231, 232, 233, 236, 237, 239, 243, 245, 246, 248, 249, 252, 264, 273, 276, 277, 280, 285, 313, 325, 326, 327, 340, 351, 352, 353, 354, 355, 356, 357, 362, 365, 403, 404, 405, 406
Egg and I, The (Universal, 1947) 365
El Paso Herald 67
Elis, Alice 31
Elizabeth I of England 138
Emmons, Edith 178
Essanay Film Manufacturing Company 11, 35, 66, 78, 184, 350, 407
Eternal Sapho, The (Fox, 1916) 93
Eubanks, L.E. 80
Execution of Mary, Queen of Scots, The (Edison, 1895) 398
Experience (Paramount, 1921) 347
Fairbanks, Douglas 247, 327, 337
Fall of a Nation, The (Dixon, 1916) 143, 290
Fall of the Romanoffs, The (First National, 1917) *406*
Famous Players Film Company 12, 90, 396
Famous Players-Lasky 72, 90, 376, 396
Farnum, Dustin 144, 187, 321, 342, *357*

Farnum, William 29, 50, 67, 70, 92, 109, 144, 234, 261, 290, 335, 337, 339, 342, 356, 357, 364, 404, 405
Farrar, Geraldine 78, 106, 213, 297, 342, 343
Fédora (play) 116
Feil, Adolph iv, 170, 171, 172, 205
Fielding, Romaine 119
Fields, W.C. 6, 410, 411
Film Daily 357
Film Trust *see* Motion Pictures Patents Company
Fine Arts Studio 72, 168
First Auto, The (Warner Brothers, 1927) 250
First National Exhibitors' Circuit, Inc. 102
First National Pictures 102, 368, 396, 401
First World War 5, 24, 34, 35, 63, 90, 102, 108, 142, 147, 148, 162, 235, 240, 253, 279, 284, 315, 316, 317, 318, 319, 320, 321, 322, 323, 327, 330, 366
Fischer, Budd 284
Fischer, Margarita 31, 100, 294, 318
FitzPatrick, Mildred Maginn 289
Flaming Youth (First National, 1923) 401
Fleming, Victor 186
Flirting with Love (First National, 1924) 368
Flynn, Errol 135
Fool There Was, A (Box Office Attraction, 1915) 32, 48, 49, 50, *51*, 52, 53, 54, 55, 57, 61, 70, 76, 80, 86, 98, 120, 156, 222, 223, 299, 332, 345, 360, 382, 398, 405
Fool There Was, A (Fox, 1922) 373
Fool There Was, A (play) 31, 32, 340
Forbidden Path, The (Fox, 1918) 285, *328*
Ford, Francis 113
Ford, Henry 90, 373
Ford, John 374, 399, 415
Forman, Ada 179
Fort Lee, New Jersey 29, 30, 73, 81, 90, 140, 148, 156, 197, 223, 285
Four Devils, The (Fox, 1929) 411
Fox Film Company iv, 2, 3, 5, 8, 21, 25, 26, 27, 29, 32, 49, 50, 54, 55, 57, 59, 64, 68, 70, 72, 73, 77, 78, 79, 80, 86, 94, 96, 100, 102, 106, 107, 108, 109, 110, 111, 112, 113, 114, 115, 120, 123, 134, 144, 145, 146, 147, 148, 149, 151, 152, 153, 159, 160, 163, 164, 165, 172, 175, 180, 182, 184, 187, 189, 194, 195, 202, 206, 207, 218, 224, 227, 229, 230, 232, 235, 236, 237, 240, 246, 252, 253, 254, 256, 257, 261, 262, 270, 280, 281, 284, 285, 294, 299, 304, 307, 308, 315, 317, 320, 323, 324, 326, 327, 330, 331, 333, 335, 336, 337, 338, 339, 340, 341, 342, 343, 344, 346, 347, 350, 351, 354, 356, 357, 358, 360, 365, 367, 370, 373, 374, 375, 376, 378, 379, 380, 381, 386, 391, 392, 393, 397, 403, 404, 405, 406, 415
Fox publicity department 3, 6, 8, 9, 25, 28, 48, 49, 50, 52, 53, 57, 58, 59, 60, 61, 62, 64, 65, 78, 80, 81, 84, 94, 96, 100, 102, 108, 112, 134, 145, 146, 151, 152, 162, 163, 164, 165, 172, 182, 195, 197, 215, 225, 228, 230, 237, 239, 240, 252, 253, 254, 256, 257, 262, 270, 282, 285, 288, 315, 329, 340, 341, 343, 344, 345, 350, 358, 378
Fox studios 29, 86, 90, 92, 113, 143, 144, 145, 147, 148, 165, 174, 176, 187, 194, 196, 206, 207, 211, 214, 223, 225, 227, 281, 285, 315, 328, 330, 333, 334, 337, 340, 357, 359, 370, 371, 373, 374, 375, 379, 380, 386, 391
Fox Woman, The (Majestic, 1915) 86
Fox, Aaron 25
Fox, Anna Fried 13
Fox, Eva Leo 14, 23, 30, 110, 353, 371, 376, 380
Fox, Maurice 25
Fox, Michael (Fuchs) 13, 14, 25, 26
Fox, William iv, 2, 3, 7, 8, 9, *10*, 13, 14, 15, 16, 17, 18, 19, 20, 21, 22, 23, 24, 25, 26, 27, 28, 29, 30, 32, 33, 36, 37, 48, 52, 54, 55, 56, 57, 59, 65, 67, 68, 69, 70, 71, 72, 73, 74, 76, 78, 80, 81, 90, 91, 92, 93, 94, 95, 96, 102, 107, 108, 109, 110, 111, 112, 113, 114, 115, 116, 123, 133, 134, 143, 145, 146, 147, 148, 149, 150, 151, 152, 163, 164, 165, 166, 194, 196, 216, 222, 223, 229, 234, 246, 248, 252, 253, 254, 255, 261, 262, 263, 264, 265, 268, 269, 274, 275, 285, 286, 288, 290, 298, 299, 305, 307, 308, 311, 313, *317*, 318, 321, 326, 329, 330, 331, 332, 333, 334, 335, 337, 338, 339, 340, 341, 342, 343, 344, 345, 347, 351, 352, 353, 354, 356, 358, 259, 371, 372, 373, 374, 375, 376, 377, 278, 379, 380, 381, 382, 389, 393, 403, 404, 416, 417, 418, 419
Fractured Flickers (television show) 394
Frank A. Keeney Corporation 338
Frankenstein (Edison, 1910) 77, 412, 415
Frankenstein, or the Modern Prometheus (novel) 77, 347

Franklin, Sid 299
Franklin, Wallace 63, 86
Freckles (RKO, 1935) 401
Frederick Douglass Film Company 235
Frederick, Pauline 72, 213
Freeburg, Victor 89
French, Bert 31
Freulich, Jacob 'Jack' 60
Fried, Anna (See Fox, Anna) 13
Frohman, Charles 205
From the Manger to the Cross (Kalem, 1912) 113
Fuchs, Michael (see Fox, Michael) 13
Fuller, Mary 19
Funkhouser, Major Metellus Lucullus Cicero 1, 303, 304, 307, 308, 311, 320, 321, 322
Galley Slave, The (Fox, 1915) 79, 91
Gance, Abel 24, 412
Garbo, Greta 153, 402, 412
Gardner, Helen 118, 119, 120, 133, 134, 164, 174, 196, 393, 411
Gaskill, Charles L. 118
Gaumont Film Company 210
Gauntier, Gene 19, 113, 120
Gaustark (Essanay, 1915) 184
Gautier, Théophile 120
Gay Illiterate, The (book) 8, 153
Gaynor, Janet 374
Gebhart, Myrtle 114
General Film Company 19, 20, 22,
Genini, Ronald iv, 68
George Eastman House iv, 414
Gérôme, Jean-Léon 122, 124
Gertie AKA *Gertie the Dinosaur* (Fox, 1914) 29, 285
Gibson, Hoot 186
Gilbert, John 372, 385
Gioconda, La (play) 57, 58, 197
Girl with the Hungry Eyes, The (short story) 181
Gish, Dorothy 35, 47, 168, 177, 408
Gish, Lillian 35, 47, 64, 177, 342, 343
Glass, Murray 415, 419
Glaum, Louise 86, *87*, 88, 177, 178, 347
Glorious Adventure, The (Goldwyn, 1918) 402
Gold and the Woman (Fox, 1916) *79*, 98, 299, 300,
Golden Bed, The (Paramount, 1925) 368

Golden, Eve iv, 55, 57, 69, 76, 84, 96, 163, 384, 386
Goldfish, The (First National, 1924) 368
Goldfrap, John Henry 'Johnny' 50, 62, 65, 81, 82, 84, 100, 345, 347
Goldman, Emma 90
Goldstein, Robert 167, 316
Goldwyn Pictures 13, 90, 213, 402
Goldwyn, Frances 403
Goldwyn, Samuel (AKA Samuel Goldfish) 90, 342, 343, 369, 403
Goodman, Bernard 36, 40, 47, 283, 345
Goodman, Esther (AKA Lori Bara) 38, 46, 100, 283, 343, *344*, 384
Goodman, Marque 37, 100, 283
Goodman, Pauline 36, 37, 38, 39, 40, 46, 50, 60, 81, 100, 283, 386
Goodman, Theodosia (see Bara, Theda)
Gordon, Cliff 14
Gosfilmofond 412
Grand Guignol (Le Théâtre du Grand-Guignol) 36, 62
Graybill, Joseph 120
Great Train Robbery, The (Edison, 1903) 14
Greater New York Rental Company 17, 20
Greed AKA *McTeague* (MGM, 1925) 412
Greenstreet, Sidney 179
Greenwich Village 45, 329
Griffith and the Rise of Hollywood (book) 195
Griffith Park 227, 370
Griffith, D.W. 3, 4, 5, 21, 24, 32, 35, 53, 54, 59, 72, 75, 76, 106, 111, 132, 167, 168, 177, 179, 195, 196, 208, 214, 235, 271, 294, 301, 322, 327, 331, 342, 343, 356, 404, 406, 411
Guazzoni, Enrico 106, 164
Gulf Between, The (Technicolor, 1917) 210
Gundie, Stephen 40, 41
Guy-Blaché, Alice 113
Hading, Jane 62
Hadji Ali (AKA 'Hi Jolly') 227, 370
Haggard, H. Rider 109, 110, 116, 120, 121, 125, 127, 131, 132, 133, 134, 170, 187, 196
Hall, Ben M. 291
Hall, Thurston *129*, *181*, 182, 185, 189, *192*, 196, *364*, 365
Hamilton, Lloyd 147
Harbeson, John Frederick 416
Harding, Muriel (see Olga Petrova)
Hardy, Oliver 362, 396, 402, 413

Hart, William S. 5, 24, 86, 87, 114, 188, 189, 214, 247, 261, 303, 331
Hartman, Gretchen (AKA Sonia Marakova) 151, 152
Hartsook, Fred 219
Haver, Phyllis 294
Haviland, Anne 1, 216, 217
Hawley, Wanda 86
Hayakawa, Sessue 24, 179, 236, 317
Hazard, Henry T. 181, 224, 391
Hearst, William Randolph 29, 315
Heart and Soul (Fox, 1917) 187, 222, 331
Hearts of the World (Paramount, 1917) 208, 322,
Held, Anna 159
Hell's Hinges (Triangle, 1916) 86
Hello, Dolly! (20th Century-Fox1969) 369
Her Double Life (Fox, 1916) 93
Her First Kiss (Fox, 1919) 415
Her Greatest Love (Fox, 1917) 93, 153, 331
Herbert, Victor 290
Hi Jolly (AKA Hadji Ali) 227, 370
Hickman, Alfred 406
Hidden Pearls (Paramount, 1918) 177
Hilliard, Harry 95
Hilliard, Robert 31, 32, 340
Hirschfeld, Al 389
His Greatest Sacrifice (Fox, 1921) 405
History of Cleopatra, Queen of Egypt (book) 121
Hit the Deck (RKO, 1930) 401
Hitler, Adolf 380
Hoff, Vanda 178
Hollander, William 153, 156
Hollister, Alice 31, 86
Hollywood (Paramount, 1923) 368
Hollywood and History: Costume Design in Film (book) 172, 173
Hollywood Jewels: Movies, Jewelry, Stars (book) 172
Hollywood Studios, The (book) 404
Holmes, Helen 113
Holmes, Stuart 23, 202
Honeymoon, The (Paramount, 1930) 415
Honor System, The (Fox, 1917) 109, 406
Hoover, Herbert 377
Hopkins, George James iv, 205, 206, 207, 264, 323, 329, 369
Hopkins, Una 205

Hopper, DeWolf 45
Hopper, Hedda 45, 156
Hotel Alexandria 161, 170, 391
Howe, James Wong 210
Hugo, Victor 95, 110
Humoresque (Warner Brothers, 1946) 363
Hunchback of Notre Dame, The (novel) 95
Hunchback of Notre Dame, The (RKO, 1939) 363
Hungry Lions in a Hospital (Fox, 1918) 147
Hutton, Betty 387
Hyland, Peggy 342
Hypocrites (Paramount, 1915) 294, 295, 302
If I Were King (Fox, 1920) 405
Impossible Catherine (Pathé, 1919) 404
In Old Arizona (Fox, 1929) 375
In the Sage Brush Country (Kay-Bee, 1914) 189
Ince, Thomas 24, 35, 86, 106, 114, 188, 195, 211, 356, 406
Independent Motion Picture Company (IMP) 49
Independența României / The Independence of Romania (Romania 1912) 407
Ingram, Rex (actor) 234
Ingram, Rex (screenwriter-director) 70, 92, 93
Inspiration (Thanhouser, 1915) 297
Intolerance (Triangle, 1916) 5, 106, 108, 109, 111, 166, 168, 176, 177, 214, 234, 294, 301, 316, 337
Iron Horse, The (Fox, 1924) 374, 399
Isadora Duncan's End (book) 42
Italian, The (Paramount, 1915) 410
Jail Birds of Paradise (MGM, 1934) 403
Janice Meredith (Metro-Goldwyn, 1924) 410
Jannings, Emil 54, 409, *410*
Japanese Photoplayers' Club of Los Angeles 235
Japanese-American Film Company 235
Jazz Singer, The (Warner Brothers, 1927) 374
Jeffries-Johnson Fight 292
Jess (novel) 187
Jesse L. Lasky's Feature Play Company 90, 141, 142, 184, 212, 315, 368
Jewels of the Madonna, The (play) 79
Joan of Plattsburg (Goldwyn, 1918) 318
Joan the Woman (Paramount, 1917) 106, 109, 177

Joanna Enlists (Paramount, 1918) 318
Johnson, Adrian 2, 3, 115, 116, 121, 123, 124, 125, 126, 127, 128, 129, 130, 131, 132, 133, 134, 135, 137, 165, 170, 188, 196, 200, 232, 233, 236, 237, 239, 245, 249, 250, 327, 340, 367, 393
Johnson, Julian 325
Johnson, Noble 234
Jones, Buck 186
Jorgensen, Jay 369
José, Edward 32, 33, 48, 51, *53*, 54
Joy, Leatrice 385
Julius Caesar (play) 109, 121, 123, 135, 260
Just Like John (play) 45
Kaelred, Katharine 31
Kaiser, Norman AKA Norman Kerry 318
Kaiser: The Beast of Berlin, The (Universal, 1918) 319, 412
Kalem 11, 19, 31, 77, 102, 113, 147, 407, 415
Kalich, Bertha 111
Kansas State Board of Censors 292, 299, 300, 301, 307, 324
Kathleen Mavourneen (Fox, 1919) 341, 350
Keaton, Buster 368, 404
Kellermann, Annette 50, 106, 107, 296, 297, 318
Keno Bates, Liar (Ince, 1915) 189
Kent, Sidney 380
Keystone Studios 24, 35, 113, 145, 146, 147, 218, 236, 293, 294, 304, 336
King Kong (RKO, 1933) 401
King Lear (Thanhauser, 1916) 199
King of Kings (Pathé, 1927) 365
King Solomon's Mines (novel) 110
Kingsley, Grace 160, 161, 163, 185, 204, 238, 247, 248, 325, 384
Kipling, Rudyard 31, 53, 109, 395
Klansman, The (novel) 301
Kleine, George 11, 164
klieg lights 211, 285
Kliegl brothers 211
Klu Klux Klan 167, 235, 327
Knickerbocker Cloth Examining and Shrinking Company 14
Knight, Arthur 4
Knox, Judge John C. 378
Krefft, Vanda iv, 27, 48, 68, 69, 71, 78, 79, 195, 243, 246, 254, 317, 326, 343, 416
Kreutzer Sonata, The (Fox, 1915) 55, 56, 76

L'assassinat Du Duc De Guise (France, 1908) 290
La Belle Russe (Fox, 1919) 341, 344, 350
La Grande Station 160, 390, 391
La Marr, Barbara 114, 347, 368
LaBadie, Florence 47, 407
Ladies of The Mob (Paramount, 1928) 408
Lady Audley's Secret (Fox, 1915) 58
Laemmle, Carl 12, 21, 25, 28, 49, 113, 304, 308, 343, 403
Lang, Fritz 24, 412
Langlois, Henri 414
Lasky Home Guard 148
Lasky lighting 212
Lasky Studio 142, 368
Lasky, Jesse L. 90, 108, 141
Last Command, The (Paramount, 1928) 409
Last Days of Pompeii, The / Ultimi giorni di Pompei (Italy, 1913) 106
Last of The Mohicans, The (Maurice Tourneur, 1920) 365
Laurel, Stan 362, 402, 413
Lawrence, Florence 19, 49, 106, 120, 343
Lawson, Valerie 44
Leathernecking (RKO, 1930) 401
Lee, Ellen K. 243
Legion of Death, The (Metro, 1917) 177
Lehrman, Henry 'Pathé' 145, 146, 147, 336, 342
Leiber, Fritz iv, 179, 180, 185, 189, 200, 318, 352, 353, 362, 363
Leiber, Fritz Jr. 180, 181, 182, 200, 234, 363, 364
Leiber, Justin iv
Leiber, Virginia 'Bronnie' Bronson *179*, 180
Leo, Eva (see Fox, Eva Leo)
Leo, Jack 25
Leo, Joe 25
Leslie, Lillie 86
Liebler, Theodore A. 189, 280
Life and Times of Cleopatra, Queen of Egypt, The (book) 121
Life's Shop Window (Box Office Attraction, 1914) 23, 29
Light, The (Fox, 1919) 330
Lily and the Rose, The (Triangle, 1915) 177
Lincoln Motion Picture Company 235
Lindbergh, Charles 374, 375
Linden, Einar 78

Linder, Max 24
Lindsay, Vachel 288, 289
Little American, The (Artcraft, 1917) 320
Little Ferry, New Jersey 397, 399, 403, 405, 411
Little Meena's Romance (Fine Arts, 1916) 168
Little Princess, A (Artcraft, 1917) 177
Little Red Riding Hood (Disney, 1922) 412
Little, Dick 155
Lloyd, Frank 335, 336, 337, 342, 404,
Lloyd, Harold 401, 414
Loew, Marcus 12, 376, 377
London After Midnight (MGM, 1927) 402, 411, 412, 414
London, Jack 396
Look Your Best (Goldwyn, 1923) 177
Loomis, Margaret 179
Loos, Anita 113, 323
Lorraine, Louise 367
Los Angeles 3, 26, 140, 141, 142, 144, 147, 148, 160, 161, 162, 166, 167, 170, 171, 172, 177, 181, 184, 212, 218, 219, 223, 224, 225, 227, 230, 231, 235, 236, 240, 242, 243, 245, 247, 248, 286, 288, 314, 317, 335, 336, 337, 353, 367, 368, 369, 370, 373, 380, 386, 390, 391
Los Angeles Chamber of Commerce 141, 224
Los Angeles Herald-Examiner 155
Los Angeles Times 155, 160, 203, 215, 232, 234, 241, 286, 336, 367, 392
Louis B. Mayer Productions 402
Louisville Times 66
Love, Bessie 47
Loy, Myrna 177
Lubin Manufacturing Company 11, 86, 102, 182, 396, 407
Lubin, Siegmund 396
Lubitsch, Ernst 409
Lugosi, Bela 187, 389, 405
Lure of Ambition, The (Fox, 1919) 341, 342
Lusitania, RMS 63
Lyric Theatre 269, 271, 274, 275, 280, 281, 285, 288
Lythgoe, Albert M. iv, 136, 137, 269
MacBeth 199, 303, 304
MacIntyre, F. Gwynplaine iv, 182
Macon Telegraph 66
MacPherson, Jeanie 113

Madame Du Barry (Fox, 117) 76, 115, 164, 194, 214, 215, 264, 303, 365
Madame Mystery (Hal Roach, 1926) 361, 362
Madison, Cleo 93, 113
Malatesta, Mary 120
Male and Female (Paramount, 1919) 108, 367
Mallory, Mary 218
Mammy Chloe, or, The Pendletons of Virginia (play) 46
Manchester Guardian 282
Mandarin Film Company 235
Mann, Hank 147
Manslaughter (Paramount, 1922) 108, 368
Mantell, Robert 92
Marc Antonio E Cleopatra / Marc Antony and Cleopatra (Italy, 1913) 106, 164
Marion, Frances 113, 114, 328, 329
Mark of Zorro, The (20th Century-Fox, 1940) 365
Markey, Enid 143, 211
Markova, Sonia (AKA Gretchen Hartman) 151, 152
Marsh, Mae 167, 177, 402
Mary, Queen of Scots 138
Mata Hari (AKA Margaretha Zelle) 265, 267, 268, 362
Matinee Idol, The (Columbia, 1928) 413
Maverick (television series) 365
Maxwell, Ann 110, 111, 116
Mayall, Herschel *181*, 188, 189, *193*, 365
Mayer, Arthur 258
Mayer, Louis B. (Lazar) 12, 114, 376, 377, 381
McCay, Windsor 29
McCord, Merrill T. iv, 14, 28, 246, 317, 405, 418
McDermott, Edward 248
McDowall, Roddy 415
McEdwards, Jack 406
McGuire, Kathryn 368
McLean, Adrienne L. 168
McLeod, Tex 187
McTeague AKA *Greed* (MGM, 1925) 412
Méliès, Georges 398, 407
Méliès's Star Film Paris 11
Melville, Herman 77
Merry Widow, The (MGM, 1934) 365
Metro Pictures Corporation 13, 35, 72, 87, 94, 115, 180, 327, 332, 346, 402, 410

Metro-Goldwyn-Mayer (MGM) 13, 294, 373, 376, 377, 381, 394, 402, 403, 408, 412
Metropolis (Germany, 1927) 412
Metropolitan Museum of Art iv, 136, 174, 265
Meyer, Laura Augusta 168
Micheaux Film Corporation 235
Micheaux, Oscar 235
Miggins, Mike 231
Miles, Margaret M. 118
Milk Fed Vamp, A (Fox, 1917) 146
Miller, Henry 253, 254
Miller, Maude Murray 302, 303, 311
Miller, Walter 120
Milne, Peter 115, 135, 180, 245, 273
Milwaukee, WI 40
Miner, Randolph Huntington 162
Miner, Tulita Zoila Wilcox 162
Minter, Mary Miles 35, 72, 210, 312
Miracle Man, The (Paramount, 1919) 408
Misérables, Les (Fox, 1917) 335, 404
Misérables, Les (novel) 110
Mitchell Cameras 376
Mix, Tom 145, 148, 186, 187, 239, 340, 356, 373, 399, 401, 404
Moby Dick (novel) 77
Molly O (First National, 1921) 412
Molnár, Ferenc 41
Monkey's Paw, The (RKO, 1933) 401
Monroe, Marilyn 345, 383, 388
Monsieur Verdoux (United Artists, 1947) 363
Monzon, Chula 179
Moore, Colleen 177, 368, 401
Mordden, Ethan 404
Moreau, Émile 117
Morgan, Warren F. 244
Morosco, Oliver 199, 205
Morris, Gouverneur 372
Morris, William 182
Motion Picture Classic 80, 86, 133, 134, 201
Motion Picture Exhibitors' League 157
Motion Picture Magazine 82, 281
Motion Picture News, The 27, 109, 111, 135, 138, 164, 180, 216, 228, 232, 236, 240, 243, 245, 262, 273, 285, 305, 391
Motion Pictures Patents Company 7, 11, 12, 17, 18, 19, 20, 21, 22, 28, 140, 377
Motography 26, 50, 86, 91, 109, 112, 146, 147, 152, 153, 158, 168, 196, 229, 273, 285, 289, 321, 331, 396
Mount Vernon, NY 254
Mountain Eagle, The AKA *Fear O'God* (UK, 1925) 408
Movietone 374, 375
Movietone News 374, 399
Moving Picture World, The 22, 31, 73, 80, 135, 161, 186, 200, 275, 302
Mowat, Jean 167
Mulhall, Jack 144
Munson, Audrey 295, 297, 303
Murillo, Mary 112
Murnau, F.W. 374, 411
Museum of Modern Art (MOMA) v, 397, 398, 399, 401, 419
Mussolini, Benito 399
Mutt and Jeff Meet the Vampire AKA *Meeting Theda Bara* (Fox, 1918) 284, 285
Mutual Film 90, 294, 407
Mutual v. Ohio 292
My Fair Lady (Warner Brothers, 1964) 369
My Four Years in Germany (Warner Brothers, 1918) 284, 322
Myers, Carmel 177
Myers, Harry 119, 413
Naldi, Nita 86, 87, 88, 204, 347, 368, 408, 409
Nansen, Betty 28, 29, 91, 404
Napoleon (France, 1927) 412
Nation, Carrie 16
National Board of Censorship 57, 91, 292
National Board of Review of Motion Pictures 292, 305
National Independent Motion Picture Board of Trade 23
Nazimova, Alla 108, 264, 396
Neely, Hugh Munro iv, 44
Negri, Pola 347
Neptune's Daughter (Universal, 1914) 107
Nero (Fox, 1922) 354, 356
Nesbit, Evelyn 28, 342, 404
New Jersey 73, 198, 235, 298, 396, 397
New Orleans 26
New York Academy of Music 18, 23, 280, 285
New York City 12, 13, 16, 17, 18, 20, 23, 26, 29, 37, 41, 42, 43, 45, 46, 51, 60, 63, 72, 81,

88, 99, 101, 115, 118, 134, 140, 142, 144, 146, 152, 168, 170, 182, 184, 186, 205, 206, 216, 236, 263, 265, 268, 269, 285, 300, 326, 325, 338, 343, 349, 353, 380, 396, 397, 403, 417
New York Daily Tribune, The 12, 270
New York Dramatic Mirror, The 54, 57, 66, 135, 177, 272
New York Evening Journal 201
New York Evening Mail 35, 80,
New York Morning Telegraph 54, 201, 270
New York Public Library v, 115, 136, 317
New York Review 271
New York State 102, 292
New York Stock Exchange 414
New York Times, The 22, 70, 100, 231, 232, 255, 256, 257, 258, 259, 260, 271, 325, 349, 380, 381, 417
New Yorker, The 89
New Zealand 365
New Zealand Film Archive 415
Newport Bay, California 236, 391
Newport Beach Library v
Newport News 240
Nicholas II of Russia 102
Nigger, The AKA *The New Governor* (Fox, 1915) 234
Nigh, William 148
Niles, Claire 179
Norah's Chance (play) 46
Normand, Mabel 17, 24, 47, 113, 177, 213, 312, 318, 341, 402, 412
North, Sir Thomas 196
Norton, Loys 46
Nosferatu (Germany, 1922) 411
nuit de Cléopâtre, Une (short story) 120
O'Dell, Paul 195
O'Neil, Nance 50, *55*, 404, *406*
O'Day, Edward P. 282
O'Denishawn, Florence AKA Florence Andrews 179
Occoquan Workhouse 102
Ochs, Weil and Goodman 36
Octavia 103
Octavius 103, 105, 196
Ohio Board of Censors 292, 302, 304, 305, 311
Oland, Warner *60*
Oliver Twist (First National, 1922) 413

Omaha Daily Bee 313
Omaha, Nebraska 312
On the Night Stage (New York, 1915) 189
Orange County Register 238
Ordynski, Ryszard 'Richard' 206, 264, 329
Orphans of the Storm (United Artists, 1921) 59, 294, 301
Ouida 93, 94
Outwitting Dad (Lubin, 1914) 396
Over the Hill to the Poorhouse (Fox, 1920) 374
Oxnard, California 225, 227, 228, 229, 230, 391
Pan (Panagiotopoulos), Hermes 314, 315
Panzer, Paul 119
Parade's Gone By, The (book) 195, 288, 351
Paramount Pictures 12, 54, 86, 90, 102, 108, 318, 347, 373, 376, 393, 394, 403, 407, 408, 409, 415
Paris, France 41, 42, 44, 50, 53, 58, 59, 60, 61, 62, 81, 95, 116, 140, 167, 168, 173, 200, 216, 268, 330, 368, 373, 374
Parsons, Louella 8, 152, 153, 155, 156, 282, 319
Patents War 11, 12, 17, 18, 19, 20, 21, 22, 28, 140, 141
Pathé (American Pathe film Company) 11, 24, 32, 48, 86, 404, 405, 408, 414
Pathé Frères 145, 250, 407
Pathecolor 250
Patria (Pathé, 1917) 315
Patriot, The (Paramount, 1928) 409, *410*
Peacocke, Captain Leslie T. 235
Pearl of Paradise, The (Mutual, 1916) 294
Pearl of the Army (Pathé, 1916) 86
Pearson, Virginia 32, 85, 86, 110, 151, 341, 342, 404
Peck, Frances (see 'Mae Tinee')
Percy, Eileen 247
Perelman, S.J. 89
Perils of Pauline (Pathé, 1914) 24
Perrin, Adelaide 242, 245
Pershing, General John 116
Petersen, Anne Helen 64
Petrova, Olga 35, 87, 89, 211, 332, 346, 362, 402
Pettigrew's Girl (Paramount, 1919) 177
Phantom of the Opera, The (Universal, 1925) 210, 412

Phantom of the Opera, The (Universal, 1943) 363
Photoplay 30, 63, 66, 86, 108, 135, 152, 156, 168, 207, 214, 223, 271, 295, 298, 305, 325, 339, 359
Pickford, Mary 5, 19, 24, 35, 47, 60, 64, 71, 72, 90, 98, 100, 102, 113, 114, 303, 313, 316, 318, 320, 327, 337, 339, 341, 345, 394, 407, 413
Picture-Play Magazine 115
Pictures and The Picturegoer 182
Pierce, Curtis 82
Plutarch 103, 130, 134, 135, 196
Plutarch's Lives (book) 103, 121, 130, 134, 135, 196
Poe, Edgar Allan 70
Poiret, Paul 173
Polasek, Albin 303
Polly of the Circus (Goldwyn, 1917) 414
Popescu, Leon 407
Porter, Edwin S. 14
Pound for a Pound, A (Essanay, 1915) 184
Powell, Frank 27, 32, 33, 48, 50, 54, 70, 90
Powell, Paul 177
Power, Tyrone 223, 224
Price of Silence, The (Fox, 1917) 109
Primitive Call, The (Fox, 1917) 180
Prussian Cur, The (Fox, 1918) 319, 406
Pryor, Thomas M. 381
Ptolemaic dynasty 102, 120, 138, 174, 253
Ptolemy XI of Egypt 138
Purity (American, 1916) 297, 306
Quaker Girl, The (play) 45
Québec, Canada 59
Queen Elizabeth (France, 1912) 22
Queen of Sheba, The (Fox, 1921) 195, 214, 231, 239, 288, 340, 351, 352, 353, 354, 356, 362, 365, 370, 373, 405, 406
Quick, James R. 339
Quigley Jr., Martin 372
Quirk, Billy 120
Quo Vadis? (Italy, 1913) 106, 302
Rae, Isabel 120
Ragged Princess, The (Fox, 1916) 294
Ramona (Clune, 1916) 186
Rappe, Virginia 147, 392
Ray, Adele 120
Realart Studios 206
Regeneration (Fox, 1915) 73, 406

Reid, Wallace 72
Resurrections (story) 335
Revalles, Flore 253
Rhames 100, 101, 269
Richard III (Film d'Art, 1912) 199
Riders of the Purple Sage (Fox, 1918) 335, 399
Ridgely, Cleo 86
Ringling Brothers Circus 227
Ripley, Arthur 248
Rise and Fall of Free Speech in America, The (pamphlet) 301
Road to Yesterday, The (PDC, 1925) 368
Roaring Lions and Wedding Bells (Fox, 1917) 147
Roaring Lions on the Midnight Express (Fox, 1918) 147
Rockwell, Helen 273
Rodríguez de Montalvo, Garci 139
Rogers, Will 379
Rogue Song, The (MGM, 1930) 402, 412
Roland, Ruth 19, 400
Romance of Motion Picture Production, The (pamphlet) 112
Romeo and Juliet (Fox, 1916) 8, 94, 95, 100, 101, 110, 115, 164
Romeo and Juliet (Metro, 1916) 94, 180
Roosevelt, Theodore 22
Roscoe, Albert *125*, 183, 184, 185, 189, 234, 365, 366
Rose of Blood, The (Fox, 1918) 264, 321, 329, 365
Rose, Norman 46
Rosemon, Ethel 197
Rosen, Marjorie 64
Rosenthal, Herman 20
Rowland, Richard A. 327
Royal, Lee 108, 112
Rubinstein, George 288
Runaround, The (RKO, 1931) 401
Russell, Lillian 182
Russian Tragedy, A (play) 46
Sacramento Union 66
Sacramento, California 140
Sadie Thompson (United Artists, 1928) 413
Safety Last! (Hal Roach, 1923)
Sainted Devil, The (Paramount, 1924) 408, *409*
Salisbury, Monroe 185, 186

Salome (Fox, 1918) 3, 76, 116, 134, 178, 185, 198, 234, 264, 286, 323, 324, 325, 326, 327, 332, 333, 351, 353, 356, 365, 370, 399, 414
Salomé (Nazimova, 1923) 264
Samson (Fox, 1915) 404
Samson and Delilah (Paramount, 1949) 363
San Antonio Light 66
San Francisco, California 140, 171, 288, 341
Sandra (First National, 1924) 120
Sandy, Reformer (American Film Company, 1916) 186
Sanger, Margaret 90
Sardou, Victorien 91, 116, 117, 118, 119, 120, 121, 128, 129, 130, 131, 132, 133, 134, 135, 196
Sarno, Hector V. *188*, 189, 204, 365
Saved from the Vampire (Biograph, 1915) 32
Scardon, Paul 353
Scarlet Woman, The (Metro, 1916) 87
Schellinger, Rial 210, 246
Schenck, Joe 28, 379, 380, 392
Schenck, Nicholas 372, 376, 377
Schlitz Hotel 40
Schmaltz Brothers 14
Schoedsack, Ernest B. 401
Scoggins, Donald L. 166, 369
Scuttlers, The (Fox, 1920) 365
Sea Beast, The (Warner Brothers, 1926) 77
Sea Hawk, The (Warner Brothers, 1940) 363
Sea Wolf, The (Lubin, 1913) 396
Seattle Star, The 62
Seattle, Washington 62, 218, 326
Second World War 315
Secrets (First National, 1923) 368
Seely, Walter Frederick 218, 219, 220
Selig Polyscope 11, 29, 31, 141, 143, 145, 206, 284, 407
Selig Studio Zoo 225, 284
Selig, Al 50, 53, 62, 65, 81, 82, 100, 152, 158, 159, 347
Selig, William N. 140, 141
Selwyn, Edgar 90
Selznick, David O. 358, 359
Sennett, Mack 24, 35, 145, 293, 294, 336, 338, 367, 412
Sergas de Esplandián, Las (novel) 139
Serpent, The (Fox, 1915) 73, *74*, 96, 406, 415
Seventh Heaven (Fox, 1927) 374
Sex (Pathé, 1920) 177, 347

Sex Life of the Polyp, The (Fox, 1928) 399
Seyffertitz, Gustav von 318
Shakespeare on Silent Film (book) 133
Shakespeare, William 42, 94, 103, 104, 106, 109, 116, 117, 120, 121, 122, 123, 124, 130, 131, 132, 133, 134, 135, 196, 217, 260, 304
Shaw, George Bernard 121, 123, 399
Shawn, Ted 177, 178
Shay, William E. 56
She (Fox, 1916) 110
She (Fox, 1917) 110, 398
She (novel) 110
She-Devil, The (Fox, 1918) 329
Shearer, Norma 402
Sheehan, Winfield 20, 21, 51, 56, 68, 72, 262, 312, 332, 338, 353, 374, 378, 380
Sheik, The (Paramount, 1921) 391
Shelley, Mary 77
Shepherd King, The (Fox, 1923) 355, 356
Sherlock Jr. (MGM, 1924) 368
Shipman, Nell 294
Shoemaker, Mark iv, 171
Should a Mother Tell? (Fox, 1915) 29
Sign of the Cross, The (Paramount, 1932) 108
Silent Command, The (Fox, 1923) 405
Silents Please (television show) 394
Silks and Satins (Paramount, 1916) 407
Sills, Milton 328
Sin (Fox, 1915) 59, 60, 79, 299
Sinclair, Upton 27, 30, 145, 318, 333, 358, 359, 378, 379
Singin' in the Rain (MGM, 1952) 394
Sinnard, Yvonne 179
Siren of Hell AKA *Siren of Seville* 73
Siren's Song, The (Fox, 1919) 330
Sister to Carmen, A (Helen Gardener Picture Players, 1913) 119
Skouras, Spyros 393
Sky High (Fox, 1921) 399
Slide, Anthony iv, 335, 404, 414
Slim Princess, The (Goldwyn, 1920) 402
Smith, Agnes 156
Smith, Al 137, 165, 166, 168, 232, 236
Snow White (Paramount, 1916) 407
So Big (First National, 1924) 401
So this is Marriage? (MGM, 1924) 402
Solomon, Aubrey iv, 404
Song of Hate, The (Fox, 1915) 29, 91, 92
Song of Love (First National, 1923) 368

Song of Roland, The (poem) 139
Soul of Buddha, The (Fox, 1918) 179, *267*, 268, 285, 331
Sower, The (statue) 303
Spanish influenza pandemic 284, 288, 340
Spanish Main, The (RKO, 1945) 363
Sperling, Milton 380
Spirit of '76, The (Continental, 1917) 316, 320
Spoilers, The (Selig, 1914) 29
Spy, The (Fox, 1917) 321
Squaw Man, The (Jesse L. Lasky, 1914) 24, 141, 186
St. Augustine, Florida 51
St. Denis, Ruth 1, 176, 177, 178, 265
St. Elmo (Balboa, 1914) 23
St. John, Adela Rogers 343, 384
St. Paul Daily News 67
Stagecoach (United Artists, 1939) 375
Stain, The (Pathé, 1914) 32, 48, 404, 405
Stanfill, Dennis 403
Stanschi, Tom 119
Steiner, Max 290
Sterling, Ford 24, 147
Stewart, Anita 100
Stoker, Bram 70, 411
Stone, Sharon 388
Stonehouse, Ruth 113
Story of Louis Pasteur, The (Warner Brothers, 1936) 363
Streetcar Named Desire, A (Warner Brothers, 1951) 369
Stroheim, Erich von 412, 415
Studlar, Gaylyn 41
Sturges, Preston 42, 43, 386
Sullivan, C. Gardner 24, 114
Summerville, Slim 147
Sunday, Billy 358
Sunrise (Fox, 1927) 374, 375, 399, 404
Sunset Boulevard (Paramount, 1950) 394
Suratt, Valeska 32, 86, 110, 150, 281, 333, 334, 336, *398*, 404
Swanson, Gloria 108, 113, 347, 367, 413, 415
Sweet, Blanche 24, 47, 86, 408, 413
Sweeter Than Revenge (Lubin, 1915) 182
Taft, William Howard 22
Tale of Two Cities, A (Fox, 1917) 335, 404
Tale of Two Cities, A (MGM, 1935) 363
Talmadge, Constance 47, 368
Talmadge, Norma 47, 72, 368, 392, 408, 412

Tammany Hall 15, 20, 380
Taylor, Elizabeth 172, 174, 393
Taylor, Estelle 373
Taylor, William Desmond 312
Technicolor 210, 401, 402
Temple, Shirley 379
Ten Commandments, The (Paramount, 1922) 108, 210, 347, 368
Teutonic, RMS (ship) 45
Thanhouser Film Corporation 199, 297, 407
That Royle Girl (Paramount, 1926) 411, 412
Thaw, Harry 28
Théâtre Antoine 50, 58, 62, 81
Théâtre du Gymnase 62, 81
Theda Bara, My Mentor (book) 39
Thomas Ince Studio 86, 114, 211, 293, 410
Thompson, Margaret 293
Thor: Ragnarok (Walt Disney, 2017) 389
Thorndike, Sybil 179
Three Bad Men (Fox, 1926) 399
Three Stooges 291, 403
Tichenor, Edna *411*
Tiger Woman, The (Fox, 1917) 76, 93, 115, 303, 331
Tillie's Punctured Romance (Keystone, 1914) 304, 394, 411
Tillie's Punctured Romance (Paramount, 1928) 411
Time Magazine 376
Timeline Films iv, 8, 414
Tinee, Mae AKA Frances Peck or Mrs. Zack Elton 153, 156, 308, 309, 320
To Hell with The Kaiser (Metro, 1918) 319
Todd, Thelma 338
Toledo Blade 67
Toll of the Sea, The (Technicolor, Metro, 1922) 210
Tolstoy, Leo 55, 335
Tom and Jerry (cartoon series) 402
Topper (television series) 365
Topsy (camel) 2, 227, 228, 242, 370, 371
Tosca, La (play) 91, 116
Tourneur, Maurice 410
Traffic in Souls (Universal, 1913) 30, 408
Travail (novel) 79
Traverse, Madlaine 86, 151, 342, 404
Triangle Productions 35, 86, 261, 337
Tucker, George Loane 408
Turner, Florence 19

Tutankhamun 137
Twentieth Century Productions 379
Twentieth Century-Fox iv, 370, 380, 382, 393, 397, 398, 399, 403, 404
Two Orphans, The (Fox, 1915) 59, 106, 110
Typhoon, The (Paramount, 1914) 188
Ulric, Lenore 177
Unbeliever, The (Edison, 1918) 322
Unchastened Woman, The (Chadwick, 1925) 359, *360*, 405
Uncle Tom's Cabin (Lubin, 1903) 396
Uncle Tom's Cabin (novel) 109
Under the Yoke (Fox, 1918) 286
Under Two Flags (Fox, 1916) 93, 94, 222
Universal Pictures 12, 21, 30, 55, 93, 106, 107, 113, 142, 145, 146, 186, 261, 304, 366, 367, 396, 403, 408, 412
Upstream (Fox, 1927) 415
Upton Sinclair Presents William Fox (book) 145, 333, 358, 378
Valentino, Rudolph 86, 204, 347, 365, 368, 391, 408, 415
Vampire, The (Kalem, 1913) 31, 86
Vampire, The (painting) 31, 53, 395
Vampire, The (poem) 31, 53, 395
Vampire, The (Selig, 1910) 31
Vampire, The (Solax, 1915) 87
Van Der Decken (play) 179
Vanity Fair (Goldwyn, 1923) 411
Vanity Fair (Vitagraph, 1911) 118, 411
Variety 325, 367, 368, 374, 382
Victoria Cross, The (Paramount, 1916) 177
Victoria, Queen of Great Britain 117
Vidor, Florence 177
Vidor, King 384
Villa, Pancho 90
Vincent, James 90
Vitagraph 11, 14, 19, 23, 102, 118, 289, 350, 351, 352, 407
Viva Villa! (MGM, 1934) 365
Vixen, The (Fox, 1916) 93, 415
Waldo, Rhinelander 20
Waldorf-Astoria Hotel 372
Walker, Charlotte 182
Wallace, Lew 77, 121, 239
Walnut Hills High School 38
Walsh, George 28, 88, 144, 189, 342, 404

Walsh, Raoul 8, 17, 72, 73, 74, 75, 76, 78, 90, 109, 195, 204, 300, 319, 338, 342, 374, 392, 406, 413
Walthall, Henry 72
Wanger, Walter 393
War Bride's Secret, The (Fox, 1917) 108
War Brides (Selznick, 1916) 108, 316, 320, 396
Warde, Frederick 199
Warner Brothers 12, 20, 77, 250, 284, 322, 372, 374, 376, 378, 396, 407, 413
Warner, Ben 12
Warrens of Virginia, The (Paramount, 1915) 212
Washington Square 41
Washington Theatre 314
Washington, DC 99, 285, 321, 349, 417
Waters, Percival L. 20
Way Down East (United Artists, 1920) 343, 404
Way of All Flesh, The (Paramount, 1927) 409
Wayne, John 187, 375
Wayne, Marie 86
Weber, Lois 113, 294, 302
Wedding March, The (Paramount, 1928) 415
Weigall, Arthur 121, 137
Weitzel, Edward 135, 189, 275
Wellman, William 411
West of the Pecos (RKO, 1934) 401
West, Clare *165*, 166, 167, 168, 169, 173, 177, 205, 207, 367, 368, 369
West, Mae 388
West, Roland 338
What Price Beauty? (Pathé, 1928) 408
What Price Glory? (Fox, 1926) 374
Wheeler, Margaret 352
Wheelwright, Julie 266
When A Man Loves (Warner Brothers, 1927) 412, 413
When A Woman Sins (Fox, 1918) 327, 365, 415
When False Tongues Speak (Fox, 1918) 404
When Men Desire (Fox, 1919) *154*, 300, 330
When We Were Twenty-One (play) 182
White Moth, The (First National, 1924) 368
White Raven, The (Metro, 1917) 70
White Shoulders (RKO, 1931) 401
White, Pearl 24, 86, 151, 342, 400, 404
White, Stanford 28

Whiteman, Paul 179
Whitney, Claire 23
Whitney, Clare Frances (see Clare West)
Who's Afraid of Virginia Woolf? (Warner Brothers, 1966) 369
Why America Will Win (Fox, 1918) 116
Why Change Your Wife? (Paramount, 1920) 108, 360, 367
Wickoff, Alvin 212
Wid's Daily 26, 150, 276, 297, 331
Wild Youth (Paramount, 1918) 177
Wilde, Oscar 134
Wildfire (play) 182
Will o' the Wisp (Balboa, 1914) 23
Will of Destiny, The (American Wild West Company, 1912) 336
Williams, Clara *293*
Wilson, Margery 113
Wilson, Woodrow 22, 90, 147, 315, 316, 317, 319, 320, 321, 322
Wings of the Morning (Fox, 1919) 365
Winning of Barbara Worth, The (1926) 403
Wishing Ring, The (World, 1914) 410
Witzel, Albert 218, 219, 220
Wolf-Ferrari, Ermanno 79
Woman God Forgot, The (Paramount, 1917) 106
Woman There Was, A (Fox, 1919) 329
Woman with the Hungry Eyes, The (Timeline, 2006) 414
Woman's Resurrection, A (Fox, 1915) 29
Women's suffrage movement 5, 84, 102
Wong, Anna May 210
Wood, George Cabot 417
Woods, A.H. 347, 349
Woods, Frank 72
Woollcott, Alexander 349
World Pictures 114
Wrath of the Gods, The (Mutual, 1914) 188
Wurtzel, Sol M. 147, 223, 246, 287, 288, 299, 333, 335, 337, 338, 339, 351, 356
Young Rajah, The (Paramount, 1922) 408
Young, Brigham 141
Young, Clara Kimball 24, 72
Youx, Dominique 36
Zanuck, Darryl F. 379, 380, 393, 404
Zelle, Margaretha AKA Mata Hari 265, 266, 268, 269
Zenobia 102

Ziegfeld, Florenz 159, 179, 205
Zierold, Norman J. 25, 372
Zola, Émile 79
Zukor, Adolph 12, 90, 372, 376, 377

www.ingramcontent.com/pod-product-compliance
Lightning Source LLC
Chambersburg PA
CBHW061923220426
43662CB00012B/1788